Yesterday's Faces

Yesterday's Faces
Volume 4
The Solvers

Robert Sampson

Bowling Green State University Popular Press
Bowling Green, Ohio 43403

Acknowledgements

Covers reprinted by permission from the following sources:
Blazing Publications, Inc., proprietor and conservator of the respective copyrights and successor-in-interest to Popular Publications, Inc., The Frank A. Munsey Company, Red Star News Company, Butterick Publishing Company and Pro-Distributors Publishing Company, Inc., for *Adventure* (Copyright © 1929 by Butterick Publishing Company and Renewed copyright © 1957 by Popular Publications, Inc.), *All-Story Cavalier Weekly* (Copyright) 1915 by The Frank A. Munsey Company and Renewed copyright © 1943 by Popular Publications, Inc.), *Argosy*, (Copyright © 1933, by The Frank A. Munsey Company and Renewed © 1961, copyright © 1962 by Popular Publications,Inc.), *Argosy All-Story Weekly* (Copyright © 1922, copyright © 1923 by The Frank A. Munsey Company and Renewed copyright © 1950, copyright © 1951 by Popular Publications, Inc.), *The Black Mask* and *Black Mask* (Copyright © 1930, copyright © 1934 by Pro-Distributors Publishing Company, Inc. and Renewed copyright © 1958, copyright © 1962 by Popular Publications, Inc.), *Flynn's* and *Detective Fiction Weekly* (Copyright © 1925, copyright © 1929 by Red Star News Company and Renewed copyright © 1953, copyright © 1957 by Popular Publications, Inc.) All Rights Reserved. For *Blue Book* (Copyright © 1912 Story-Press Corporation Inc., and Renewed Copyright © 1940, by the McCall Co.); *Real Detective Tales & Mystery Stories* (Copyright © 1927 by Real Detective Tales, Inc.).

Certain of the character discussions in this volume have appeared, in somewhat different form, as follows:
"The Solving Sixth" in *The Mystery Fancier*, Vol. 5, #5 (9/10 1981).
"Life as a Series of Abstract Analyses" in *Clues, A Journal of Detection*, 2:2 (Fall/Winter 1981).
"The Professionals" in *The Mystery Fancier*, Vol. 6, No. 1 (1/2 1982).
"Bring Them In Dead" in *Echoes*, Vol. 1, No. 1 (August 1982)
Half Nick Carter and Half Sherlock Holmes" in the *Dime Novel Roundup*, Vol. 50, No. 6, Whole Number 552 (December 1981).
"Amazing Grace" in *The Mystery Fancier*, Vol. 6, No. 4 (7/8 1982).
"Doctor Wonderful" in *The Mystery Fancier*, Vol. 5, No. 6 (11/12 1981).
"A Practical Psychologist Specializing in the Feminine" in *The Armchair Detective*. Vol. 16, No. 4 (Winter 1983)
"The Fattest Man In the Medical Profession" in *The Mystery Fancier*, Vol. 7, No. 3 (May/June 1983).
"A Few Kind Words for Ashton-Kirk" in *The Mystery Fancier*, Vol. 7, No. 6 (November/December 1983).

For Will Murray, partner in crime.

Acknowledgements

Even a grazing glance at the early pulp magazines requires more knowledge and resources than a single individual can command, given only one life and limited shelf space. I have been fortunate enough to receive substantial assistance from a number of thoroughly informed people. These have turned out their memories, their libraries, and their information files to ease my fugitive requests, and to them, and to the following individuals and organizations, my warmest appreciation and thanks.

To Robert Weinberg, for years of help, and to Blazing Publications Inc. for permission to reproduce covers and quote from copyright material, as identified elsewhere.

To Hilda Boehm, Special Collections, University of California; Carolyn Davis, the George Arents Research Library, Syracuse University; and the staff of the Rare Book Room of the Main Library, Ohio State University, Columbus, Ohio: for their patience, indispensable help, and unruffled professionalism.

To Ed Hagemann, whose high editorial polish on Poggioli and the *Black Mask* chapter brightened all these other pages as well, serendipity at its most agreeable.

To Walker Martin and his treasure house where all the answers are stacked and waiting for the question.

To Editors Tom Johnson (*Echoes*), Guy Townsend (*The Mystery Fancier*), and Penelope Wallace (*The Edgar Wallace Newsletter*) for help/advice, direction/assistance and a great deal of warm encouragement.

To Winston Dawson, Diggs LaTouche, Steve Miller, Leonard Robbins, and Fred Siehl for their invaluable assistance and support over these many years.

To Will Murray for all those pages of commentary, suggestions, and good sense.

To John A. Hogan and Christopher Lowder for their authoritative work in clarifying the publication history of Edgar Wallace's short stories.

To John F. Suter, whose comments on Dr. Poggioli explained so much.

And to J. Randolph Cox, the Godfather of these pages.

CONTENTS

To the Curious Reader

A substantial fraction of mystery fiction remains unexamined. It exists unread, largely unknown, in masses of newspapers, magazines, paperbacks that were published from (say) 1870 through 1950. You find it unexpectedly heaped in iced New England attics and in crowded Minnesota basements where mice construct ethereal palaces from 1918 *All-Story* magazines. You discover it in tight bundles stacked along lanes, odorous with old paper, beneath the Library of Congress. Or it lurks in a box in a dusty barn room behind a gray Alabama farmhouse, or in a cardboard carton in a Fort Worth used-book store. Some part of it waits for formal review at Syracuse University or the University of California. And, at even greater distance, mysteries by the thousand, unrecorded, unconsidered, fill Canadian and English and Continental storerooms.

Mystery fiction waits for its great archeologist. Its lines of evolution are not exactly what we think.

The conventional history of detective fiction weaves a cloth of familiar names:

Dupin lucidly discovering strange pets and stolen letters.

Sgt. Cuff and the enigma of the vanished moonstone.

Then Holmes, gaunt giant, deducting through a London so distant in time that it seems less probable than Oz.

After Holmes, a rush of names: Dr. Thorndyke and Mr. Fortune. Inspector French. Wimsey, Poirot, Campion. Miss Marple knitting in St. Mary Mead. Maigret. Ellery Queen, lean and silver-eyed. Beaming Dr. Fell. Philo Vance and Superintendent Alleyn.

Well, it was like that and it was not. History is deceptive, its gilded cloth riddled with gaps. So much is omitted. What is out of print is out of mind. The richness of the past, the thousands of books, the millions of magazines, reduces at last to a few current titles and a modest selection kept bright by reprinting. Behind these sprawl libraries of forgotten fiction. Each month adds its burden of additional titles, unsung, unreprinted, eventually unrecalled.

We struggle with this mass, weighed down by competing reputations and narrative styles and critical recommendations. Fortunately there are certain guidelines to this chaos. Among these are such critical classics as Dorothy Sayer's *The Omnibus of Crime* (1928), Howard Haycraft's *Murder for Pleasure* (1941), and Ellery Queen's *101 Years' Entertainment (1941)*. These basic volumes have been followed by other authorities, other criticism, flowing through the years like a literary Mississippi.   All are supplemented by such specialized journals as *The Mystery Reader's Newsletter, The Armchair Detective, Xenophile, The Mystery Fancier, The Poisoned Pen, Clues*. Some of these remain; others have already become footnotes. But each year the historical information grows, until what seemed a simple progression, Poe to Doyle to the Golden Age and the Hardboiled Age and our own supreme Age of Excellence, blurs with complication. New titles are discovered, forgotten faces recalled, pieces of a shining mosaic, each piece demanding its proper place.

There is the puzzle. The history of detective fiction is linear, laid out along the inflexible ladder of years. The development of character types within that history shows no such regularity. To the contrary. Development of such a clear type as the amateur detective is crooked as a rabbit track. That character influenced by Dupin merges with that character influenced by Holmes. And on that star-crossed union further influences bear, be they Nick Carter or occult detectives.

Part of the difficulty is that much commentary on the detective story is based on books. Books have their own permanence. Some were always books. Others, less formal, appeared first, whole or sliced bite size, in magazines and newspapers. In that form, they are rightly termed "ephemeral." If no publisher converted them to cloth covers, or rather transient paperback editions, they tended to vanish like last week's resolutions.

And if a character or series did not transfer from the magazines to books, extinction was almost certain. But what survives and what does not calls for luck, as well as excellence.

Conventional histories of the detective story are confined largely to discussing stories preserved between the covers of books. All too often, the detective fiction from magazines is overlooked except to indicate that a story had an appearance prior to book publication. Readers of books, in a sense, are thought of as reading one type of story, while readers of magazines are in a separate class. Over the years, for every serial which became a book, there may have been a hundred which didn't. Locked away in the files of once popular magazines may be found the works of prolific writers whose names are missing from or under-represented in the standard bibliographies. Yet these too were read by people wanting entertainment, by writers looking for a formula on which to create a variation, or by would-be writers waiting to say, "I can do better than that." Nothing is created in a vacuum and the popular magazines are sources for a whole matrix of trends often ignored by those who are interested in the shape of popular taste in crime fiction.[1]

Dig deeply enough into the stacks of old magazines and there you find the pages bursting with faces forgotten for generations. Their eyes blink in the light. Who are you? Why are you waking us after so long?

Faces innumerable, hundred of faces. To ferret out even major figures requires effort beyond a single person's strength.[2] A national effort, a literary Manhattan Project, might not be enough. Of all these it is possible to select only a few. That will necessarily be a biased selection, skewed by chance, by opportunity, by what is accessible to the inquirer. We stand in a wilderness of trees and collect a few leaves. But what remarkable leaves they are, how beautiful, how strange.

In this, the fourth volume of *Yesterday's Faces*, we turn again to the old pulp magazines, selecting a few of their series characters so long at rest. Not many. Our business is evolution, not resurrection. We are interested in the mystery solvers of the past, what major lines of development they represent, and how they changed across the decades in a society where change was the only constant.

These investigators are the antithesis of those criminal geniuses met in Volume 3 of this series. For it is only right that the genius of crime be tumbled by an equally powerful genius on the side of social order. Some of these geniuses are professional policemen. Others are employed by public offices and businesses. Still others work on their own in small agencies.

Many are amateurs, their professions remote from police matters. But no matter. Crime problems are their hobby and mysteries quicken their blood. Some few are doctors, deriving from Conan Doyle and R. A. Freeman, although they do not often share Dr. Thorndyke's passion for the over-determined proof. Others are psychologists or criminologists, magical terms meaning omniscience in matters of human motive.

Amateur or professional, these investigators shine in silver splendor. Their minds glitter. They are impelled to explain puzzles. Wrongs inflame them. Before complex trickeries, they stand resolute and unconfused, as is proper when genius flares in the blood.

Characteristically, they are drawn broadly, great primary splashes of red and green, like painting of the Non-Representational School. A very few, more subdued, have the subtlety of a Turner nocturne. There are not many of these, but they are wonderful when discovered.

Most are forgotten now, their gifts hidden in unread pages. It is unfortunate. The history of the detective story is richer than we know.

Robert Sampson
Huntsville, Al
1987

Chapter I—The Geniuses

1-

...I am no detective nor do I pretend the smallest gift of foresight above my fellow man. Whenever I have busied myself about some trouble it has been from a personal motive which drove me on, or in hope of serving some one who henceforth should serve me. And never have I brought to my aid other weapon (*sic*) than a certain measure of common sense. ("The Ripening Rubies")

That voice of dispassionate pragmatism belongs to Bernard Sutton, jewel dealer in 189— London. Over the generations, many reasons will be advanced to explain the motives of the amateur detective. None will be so forthrightly commercial. Or so businesslike.

Sutton is a businessman. The art of detection concerns him not at all. Yet such is the nature of the 189— jewel business, that precarious trade, he constantly bumps against dark passions, dark motives, darker actions.

The more curious events he has written up in first person. He keeps a notebook detailing these experiences. His opinions are candid. They ring with cool malice, particularly on the subject of his clients' foibles. He remarks on these like a man hammering cold iron.

Ten stories from Sutton's notebook were published in 1894 under the title, *Jewel Mysteries I Have Known: From A Dealer's Notebook*. Each mystery dealt with a different jewel. In the United States, the book was titled, more succinctly, *Jewel Mysteries (1904)*. An undetermined number of these stories were later reprinted in the 1907 *Short Stories* magazine.

At this particular time, *Short Stories* had begun Volume LXV and was, by no stretch of the imagination, a pulp magazine. It was printed on quality book paper, the front cover chastely decorated, with no interior illustrations to disturb the rich impassivity of its pages.

The magazine had first appeared in 1890, offering stories by Kipling, Zola, Bret Harte, Turgenev, and Anna Katharine Green.

After two years, it began reprinting older short fiction, mainly from Europe, although salted by a few new American stories. It advertised "Twenty-Five Stories for twenty-five cents," quality being priced as high then as now.

In 1904 the magazine changed hands and, in 1910, Doubleday, Page and Co. took over management. *Short Stories* was converted to a quality pulp, edited by Harry E. Maule, who would remain until 1936. No longer did reprints rule. It was original fiction now, fresh and new and active.

Standards of craftsmanship remained high. For *Short Stories*, like *Adventure* and *Blue Book* to follow, rose above the expedient prose of rival magazines like ivory towers thrusting up from swampland.[1]

The 1907 *Short Stories* had not yet converted from reprints or turned to pulp paper. Its fiction was stiff with formal English, sound, substantial prose by people who changed their socks before they began to write: William Le Queux, Florence Guertin Tuttle, Ambrose Pratt, Erckmann Chatrian, and Max Pemberton among them.

Max Pemberton was the real face behind the fiction of Mr. Sutton. Sir Max Pemberton, he later became. Born in England, 1863, a Cambridge graduate, he was editor of *Cassell's Magazine* (1894 to 1906) and later directed the destinies of a newspaper chain. During an active literary life, he turned out plays and novels, historical romance, and much mystery fiction. He died in 1950.

The stories of *Jewel Mysteries* reflect a less agitated time than our own. The book was published in England during the same year that saw *The Memoirs of Sherlock Holmes* and Arthur Morrison's *Martin Hewitt, Investigator*. Pemberton's approach to mystery fiction was considerably more phlegmatic than either of these lively volumes.

Jewel Mysteries was partial to elaborately scrolled opening scenes, heavy as brocade, a methodical introduction of characters, and a solemn slow story movement which developed gradually, like rosy-fingered dawn rising among the nouns.

"The Ripening Rubies" (May 1907, *Short Stories*) begins in leisure at a society ball, languidly stirs to motion. Then, in a sudden fever, hurls recklessly to its ending.

The scene is London, 1893. Sutton's business has seriously slumped because of a series of jewel thefts at social balls. Since the situation is exceedingly annoying, he has taken to attending these affairs, observing them at first hand, his eyes careful.

That very night, brash Mrs. Kavanaugh's ball gown is accidentally torn. Sutton notes that she wears jewelry pinned to her chemise or whatever you call that garment. Immediately dispatching his servant for the police, Sutton trails Mrs. Kavanaugh home and enters her residence by a ruse.

Surprise. Upstairs, four rogues and Mrs. Kavanaugh hunch over the evening's stealings. Sutton fires a pistol. In pour thousands of police.

Once the brocade is stripped away, there is not much content to this story. The ending reflects the delicacy about shedding blood and hitting people on the head that caused so much "good" literature to pull its final punches. In the dime novels, similar endings bounded, shouted, leaped. But then Frederic Van Rensselaer Dey never got knighted for Nick Carter.

"The Comedy of the Jeweled Links" (June 1907, *Short Stories*) contains no detection and barely a sneeze of mystery. Miserly Lord Harningham falls in love with the glorious cuff links he gave his nephew as a wedding present. So he steals them back. Or tries to. Too late he discovers that he has stolen the wrong gift. Sutton quickly finds him out, and, with the help of the nephew, manages to conceal the crime—after exacting some gentle blackmail: The nephew is granted a small annual allowance, which should have been his to begin with; Sutton receives payment of an overdue bill.

These adventures were restrained even by 1894 standards. To 1907 readers they must have seemed as bland as boiled rice. It was, after all, twenty years since publication of "A Study in Scarlet." A great deal of change had occurred in the mystery story during that time. Holmes, himself had died and returned. He was a fascinating, sharply realized, and virulently influential figure. Like a huge sun, Holmes warmed generations of imitators. If he were far from being the only detective in town, he was by all odds the most popular. But here were enough others for any taste.

There were diplomatic agents, professional police, and private investigators, male and female. The scientific detective, personified by Dr. Thorndyke, had only just appeared. The medical mystery story, if not the doctor detective, had been created. And the amateur detective scrambled about, already exhibiting notable eccentricities.

Both the amateur detective and Sherlock Holmes looked back to that penniless aristocrat, Monsieur C. Auguste Dupin, the night-enamoured man, whose capacity for intellectual analysis was revealed in 1841 by E. A. Poe. The Chevalier Dupin's mind, swift as light, bounded from the observed fact to the deduced conclusion. Fond of books, classical quotations, and given to the occasional theatrical touch, he preferred anonymity to acclaim. So the Paris police got the credit; the first-person narrator of the cases got three stories to publish; and Dupin had the pleasure of resolving problems. Although his services did earn him 50,000 francs in the affair of the Purloined Letter.

If Dupin glows luminously behind Sherlock Holmes, he positively glares from the figure of Prince Zaleski. The Prince was introduced by M. P. Shiel in 1895. He figured in only four stories, which were collected after considerable delay in the 1977 *Prince Zaleski and Cummings King Monk*. Zaleski was "victim of a too importunate, too unfortunate love, which the fulgor of the throne itself could not abash; exile perforce from his native land, and voluntary exile from the rest of men."[2] To nurse his ravaged heart, the Prince takes up residence in England in a ruined Monmouthshire abbey. There, in a green-lit tower stuffed with treasure, he sprawls among the fumes of *cannabis sativa*, occasionally rousing to play the organ, attended only by his servant Ham. In spite of this depressing life style, there is nothing whatever inexact in the function of the Prince's intelligence.

Mental precision, eccentricity, and remoteness from common life characterized other detectives of the early 1900s. *The Man In the Corner* (1902) and the *Thinking Machine* (1905) represent the intellect honed to a thin white point. They thrive on facts, arranging them in orderly chains. For two and two always make four—not*some* times but *all* the time. And thought is more potent than muscle. Dupin would have agreed.

These many specialized detectives jostled for public favor through the books and magazines of 1907. Their strivings were paralleled, at a less grand level, by a second fictional world, also brimming with detectives, accomplished criminals, and crimes spectacular. This world lay in plain sight and was invisible. That is not quite a paradox. The world of popular story papers and dime novels was successful, pervasive, and a scandal. Respectable literature hastened by these tatterdemalions, twitching its skirts, eyes averted, not seeing and not caring to see.

Story papers and dime novels enjoyed no social status. They were accorded the same iced smile reserved for the antics of the disreputable uncle at the family reunion. In consequence, few appreciated that these amiable publications had been at the mystery business for years. They had been successful for years and had a modest lesson to teach respectable literature.

Simplifications are odious, and so to simplify: As a class, story papers and dime novels substituted violent melodrama for reality's slower processes. Customarily, characters were less complex than paper dolls. Deficiencies, certainly. However the publications also displayed an extraordinary grasp of action narrative, contemporary scene, and vividly colloquial dialogue. And they certainly provided a fascinating selection of investigators, including such notable series figures as Old Sleuth (1872), Old King Brady (1885), Nick Carter (1886), and, in England, Sexton Blake (1893).

These admirable gentlemen solved crimes after intense physical effort and danger. Their adventures were written in lighting. It was this narrative vigor, like an underground river quietly nourishing a valley, that flowed silently into certain early pulp magazines. Particularly those published by the Street & Smith Corporation.

The Popular Magazine, first issued by Street & Smith in 1903, featured a variety of characters whose dime novel origins were evident. Among them was Felix Boyd, a private detective and a raffish blend of Sherlock Holmes and Nick Carter. (Boyd will be discussed in a later chapter.) In 1908 appeared that distinguished amateur investigator, Sidney Garth. It seems hardly possible that Garth and Sutton were featured in series within a year of each other. They are as different as ragtime and the minuet. But there they stand, each an amateur detective, each representative of a different story type.

Sutton finds mysteries of interest only when they impact his income. Garth seeks out crimes to solve—but not for payment or glory. Revenge is what he wants. He appeared in a series of five stories that carried the overall title, "A Master of Mysteries." *Popular Magazine* published them from February through June 1908. They were written by that respectable literary man, Scott Campbell, pseudonym for Frederick W. Davis.

Sidney Garth is perhaps the most bad-tempered detective in fiction. Solid ice, self-contained, remote, he is described as being "Firm as a rock and hard as nails." He stands six feet tall, is muscled massively and built like a tackle. He thinks nothing of taking on four villains at a time:

(Garth)...dealt Linneham a blow that turned him lax and limp from head to foot, then hurled him bodily upon Jason, and sent both crashing to the floor with a violence that shook the house.[3]

Mr. Campbell remarks that Garth "combined leonine strength with the sinuous grace of a leopard." So it appears. But at first glance, you might believe him to be a minister. His face is deadly pale, his hair dark, wavy, dramatically shot with gray, his eyes frigid blue. He is in his middle thirties and enjoys a large, independent income.

He spent three years in Sing Sing for a crime that is never explained. Hints at the end of the first story suggest that he was framed—but the suggestion is not developed. When the series terminates in mid-stride, the mystery of Garth's imprisonment is unresolved.

While he was away breaking rocks, both parents died. He cancelled his engagement to the lovely girl, resigned from all clubs. By the time he got out, disgrace had permanently ruined his disposition and he had become that universal favorite, the Driven Man.

He returned to New York City. Once there, he refuses to accept friendship from anyone under any circumstances. His closest associate is his assistant, red-headed Michael Macklin, a 25-year old Irishman. Mike is cheerful, bright, and inept. His function in the series is to make mistakes—because Garth certainly isn't going to make any.

Other ex-cons walk in fear of the police. Not Garth. He detests police. His only joy is showing them up as fools and scorching their ears as they blunder about the scene of the crime.

Garth: "Your theories are absurd. They haven't feet to stand on. Rubbish... You can't make black out of white."

This to the investigating officer of the first story, the remarks delivered in a sharp, metallic voice, aggressive and insulting.

He has a ferocious tongue. You and I couldn't get away with savaging the police. However, Garth is "a genius in the art of solving abstruse problems in crime, and a veritable demon in his eager search and pursuit of criminals." He can get away with abusing the police; success protects him.

For all practical purposes, Garth is a private investigator, having an office, an assistant, and a public reputation. He does not accept payment for his services and, by that delicate distinction, may be classified an amateur investigator, not a professional. In most other ways he resembles Nick Carter and Felix Boyd, series to which Frederick W. Davis contributed. The primary variation is that Garth gets along with no one really well. It makes him a distinctive character. It also limited his reader appeal and this may account for the briefness of his series.

The Garth stories follow the general patterns laid down in the Felix Boyd stories: The problem—the police astray—the detective who grasps the situation at a glance. After further investigation, frequently in disguise, he confronts the criminals, often overpowering them single-handed. The adventure concludes with a column or two of explanation.

The first story, "The Right of Way" (February 1908) is typical. An unidentified man, bloody, battered, unconscious, is found in the fancy hotel rooms reserved for Lord Carrington. Scattered strips of flannel are the only clues.

Detective Hoffman of the Central Office thinks that crooks met to rob Lord Carrington and fought among themselves.

Garth reduces Hoffman and his theory to cinders, learns that the Lord was buying a valuable jewel, questions everyone in sight, then strides grimly off stage.

This activity has carried us to the halfway point, where most of the stories pause. A few hours or days lapse and then we move hotly to an action conclusion and the final explaining. In this adventure, Garth has reasoned that the unconscious man (conveniently without identification) is from the jewelers. Therefore, the gang has impersonated Lord Carrington and carried off the jewel. Therefore, a member of Lord Carrington's party is an inside man.

Garth shadows the suspect, confronts the crooks, and takes them after a violent fight. He then dazzles Mike Macklin by spelling out his reasoning.

The story is the usual small entertainment from the Scott Campbell detective-adventure machine. It is crisp, vigorous, implausible stuff, relying on assorted improbabilities to work in Garth's favor. If only the jewelry store had called, asking what could have happened to its messenger...

"The Girl and the Crime" (April 1908) tells how the rich man's niece rises in the middle of the night and vanishes, leaving behind a few blobs of candle wax and a looted safe. The rich man thinks she did it. So does his glib son. Garth investigates and comes to other conclusions.

"The Mantle of Moissan (June 1908): a friend is accused of murderously assaulting an unidentified man. Detective Hoffman thinks that he has a case—until Garth discovers the damp shaving brush, the ink-caked pen, the missing suit, and constructs from these trifles an entirely different case. A quick shadow from the post office to an old house in Harlem (followed by a brisk gun fight) reveals the truth. It's all over a formula for making diamonds, that fine old standby of the popular action story.

Garth and Sutton represent two popular, if contrasting, forms of the amateur detective. Garth is action action, the stated problem ending in a fight and final statement. Characters are sketched in a few vivid lines, a wash of flaming color. No more. The lead character is magnified—his physical and mental abilities, his tragedy, his emotions. The air trembles around him, like the air above a heated sidewalk. The melodrama swoops and darts against real backgrounds, crisp with exact detail. The criminals are street thugs; the police can get nothing right; and, with some help from the author, Garth observes at the scene of the crime, reasons, and departs for war.

Sutton is hardly so spectacular. Unlike Garth, a dishonored genius, or Zaleski, an alienated intellectual, Sutton is a pragmatic man of business. Essentially the ordinary man, he is prudent, not exceptionally foresighted, acute but not gifted by a hyperactive analytical sense. His self interest and impulses toward adventure coincide. But he is far from the heroic stature that delights in visiting violence on the rascals. Instead he calls the police, for they possess the technical authority that he lacks. However intense the amateur's intellectual superiority, he can rarely do more than deduce, detect, discover. He plays no role in that elaborate punishment cycle which begins with arrest.

2-

By the 'Teens, amateur detectives spread through the popular magazines like a head cold through the second grade. Every writer bristled with ideas for amateur geniuses. Every magazine featured some—once, twice. Then that face vanished in the turbulence, as others appeared, each brilliant, and eccentric, and odd.

The odder the better. A story could survive improbability, edematous description, flimsy dialogue. But without an unusual detective, editors scowled while readers, blushing, turned away.

Most amateur detectives faded quicker than a drug store rose. They exerted negligible influence on other characters being, themselves, imitations of Nick or Thorndyke or Sherlock. Particularly Sherlock.

The influence of Sherlock Holmes, like a powerful wind, quested through the paragraphs of popular detective fiction, rattling nouns and shaking verbs, hurling before it leafy cascades of Watsons and Lestrades and hawk-faced detectives, wonderfully astute. The manner of Holmes, rather than his substance, was most frequently borrowed, a surface correspondence being easier to attain than a living character. Personal eccentricities and deductive ability are not enough to hold a character together. For this reason, many of the amateur detectives patterned after Holmes ring hollow as an empty can.

There was, for example, Hodges, the Wonder Sleuth (*Blue Book*, 1912, series by Guy C. Baker). Hodges blathers brightly in the clever young man mode, replete with effete Easternisms. When in the grip of thought, he smokes quantities of black cigars, does it all night long. By daybreak:

...there was a light of confident conviction in his face—a light such as invariably betokened a definite conclusion born of thoughtful analysis.[4]

Hodges is equipped with the usual steel physique. He can easily slug down a leering foeman or bravely brush aside a gun muzzle. His wonders seem fairly obvious. Most of the supporting story characters seem hardly better than dim wits.

The admirable Ashton-Kirk represents a more satisfactory Holmes variation. He does Sherlock with a flair:

Ashton Kirk: "Crimes are growing no fewer; and if we must have crime I should personally prefer those perpetrators to have some little artistry."

Or you may favor this pleasing exchange:

Friend: "Have you done anything in your line for the Treasury Department lately?"
Ashton-Kirk: "Oh, a small matter of some duplicate plates. It had some interest, but there nothing extraordinary about it."

Or this may strike the original Baker Street note:

Young Lady: "I am very sorry that I deceived you yesterday morning."
Ashton-Kirk: "I was not deceived; so there was no harm done."

The adventures of this young Holmes reflection were collected into four novels: *Ashton-Kirk Investigator* (1910), *Ashton-Kirk Secret Agent* (1912), *Ashton-Kirk Special Detective* (1914), and *Ashton-Kirk Criminologist* (1918). Magazine appearances have only been partially traced. "The Singular Experience of Ashton-Kirk" appeared as a three-part serial in *The Popular Magazine* (July 15, August 1 and 15, 1910). It was published that same year as a book titled *Ashton-Kirk Investigator*. Six years later, for unexplained reasons, "The Singular Experience" again resurfaced—this time as a two-part serial in *Detective Story Magazine* (July 5 and 20, 1916).

Ashton Kirk's adventures were written by John Thomas McIntyre (1871-1951), who early built a reputation for himself with stage comedies and boys' books. In the'Teens, he made a transition to the writing of magazine articles and novels of detective and historical fiction. In 1936, he was the United States winner in the All-Nations Prize Novel Competition, the book being *Steps Going Down*, the prize being $4,000. In 1939, McIntyre created the series detective, Jerry Mooney, who appeared in four novels, all signed by the pseudonym Kerry O'Neil. McIntyre continued publishing books until 1943. He died May 21, 1951, in Philadelphia, age 79.

McIntrye's Ashton-Kirk is a very bright young man, indeed. Keen eyes shine in a keen, dark face. He is of impeccable lineage, tracing his family back through the centuries. From their interminable excellence, he has inherited that distinction of mind and physique necessary to qualify as a popular series hero.

He is immensely wealthy. And never less than perfectly dressed in unostentatious clothing—unless adventure has coaxed him off in some rough disguise. At least once a novel, he gets himself up as a street tough, a sick man, an Italian laborer with a comic strip accent. His characterizations are as deft as those of Nick Carter—or Sherlock Holmes, for that matter. And, like Holmes, he relishes the instant when the disguise is stripped away, confounding friend and reader alike. Heaven knows, they both should have been prepared for such wonders.

Other Holmes borrowings float, like bright sparks, through the stories. Ashton-Kirk, for instance, has a commonplace book—a set of canvas-covered reference books filled with "carefully spaced entries in a copper-plate hand." When he is not studying these references, or playing in his chemical laboratory, or smoking his Coblentz pipe, he is out aiding the poor sluggish authorities.

His investigations are in the classical mode. He flings himself down on the carpet. He bends close to the ground. Out with the strong lens, out with bits of paper in which he tenderly encloses little dust samples, his eyes flickering brightly. All the while, he is deducing. From a partly drawn blind, a candle stump, a discharged revolver, a red fragment from a punched railroad ticket. After which, the dazzle:

Ashton-Kirk: "What would you say if I told you that I draw from these (clues) that the gentleman (involved in the crime) was short, well-dressed, and knew something of the modern German dramatists?"[5]

During these frequent excursions into ratiocination, Kirk is usually accompanied by a friend, all agog in the manner of Dr. Watson:

Friend:"Now I suppose I'm all kinds of an idiot for not understanding how you know all those things about a man you never saw. But I confess candidly; I *don't* understand."
Ashton-Kirk:"It all belongs to my method of work. It's simple enough when you go about it in the right way."[6]

Every series detective benefits from a distinctive home base. Ashton-Kirk has one. He lives in a distinguished row house, faced with alternating black and white brick, set squarely in a boiling New York City slum. Within this wilderness, Ashton-Kirk dwells as serene as a jewel in a toad's head. All floors of the house are filled with that polished perfection found mainly in magazines. In one respect, this house differs from other glassy set-pieces of cultivated living—it is entirely abrim with books. Books, pamphlets, folios, rare, desirable, unobtainable. Mr. Ashton-Kirk is an unrestrained bibliophile, long before Lord Peter Wimsey took up the hobby. He is passionate concerning American first editions, books on crime, special editions of almost anything.

His conversation reflects these interests. As the smoke of fine cigars coils up, Ashton-Kirk natters brightly of literary matters, of writers and books and special press runs.

As he revels in his hobby, a fairly substantial household buzzes around him. There seem to be no female servants. But there is a grave-faced German butler and a French cook. And somewhere below stairs you may find the American chauffeur, who threads Ashton-Kirk's big French automobile among the push carts in the street outside.

The remaining staff is less conventional. It includes a dapper young man named Fuller, brisk, boyish, and infallible, who acts as a combination secretary and chief investigator. Whenever Ashton-Kirk feels the need for data, Fuller materializes, his hands filled with typewritten sheets.

Since every mystery requires endless probing, Fuller does all the legwork, all the boring research, all the drab labor. He is aided by a nest of others—Burgess, Neill, Purvis, and associates who float anonymously, waiting the call to action.

Apparently Ashton-Kirk employs all these people, every one, as his investigative arm, a cadre of full-time investigators to support his casual dips into amateur detection. There he lounges in his slum, his long, supple fingers controlling hordes of expensive specialists. Who they are, where they come from, what they do outside the novels—these matters are delicately left unresolved. Amazing. It is like a piece of fiction.

As is Ashton-Kirk's relationship with the police. Down at police headquarters, he is the golden boy. He's done them favors and they beam on him. Oh, certainly, it might please them to see him fall on his nose once in awhile. Not that he ever does. When he succeeds, they get the credit;

he gets the fun. It is a perfect symbiosis. The beat cops know him. So do the detectives and the higher-ups in administration. Let him ask that a man be held, or a man released, and lo, it is done. He wanders about crime scenes, picking up clues and putting them down. He confers with the officer in charge—no secrets between them. And when he needs a strong force of the boys in blue, they come racing to his call, eager as pups.

It's the same nice relationship that Nick Carter had with the police. Since then, if we are to believe Ed McBain, things have changed. But back then...

When compared to the richness of Sherlock Holmes, Ashton-Kirk seems rather transparent and precious. His adventures are minor amusements, hollow as a glass ball. For all their brightness, they only reflect. They show nothing new—deft, nimble, unoriginal as a mirror, shallow as a reflection, guileless.

Defects, certainly. Defects that have been accorded history's usual punishment of oblivion. No doubt this is not altogether just, for Ashton-Kirk is a thoroughly charming young man, rather modest and essentially nice. A book collector can hardly be all bad. Within the rigor of the Holmes formula, he is a cheerful figure, vivacious and agreeably competent. Sassy humor sparks in his adventures. The dialogue often prances. The lost world of the early 1900s often rises around us, rattling with life.

These are minor virtues to be sure. But Ashton-Kirk's adventures are charming, even in their fragile obsolescence. They are still worth reading on those dark and stormy nights when modern complexities have rasped you gravely and what your spirit craves is a few hours with a young man, unruffled by difficulty, who manages, against all experience, to be forever and entirely correct.

A less conventional figure is Cuthbert Clay (*Detective Story Magazine,* "Marked By the Dead," August 20, 1917, by J. Allan Dunn).

Clay does not seem to be a series character and, properly, should be omitted from these pages. He is, however, the quintessence of the amateur detective out of Holmes, as seen by the early pulps. For this alone, he deserves recognition. In addition, his story illustrates how the mystery story that concentrated on motive, character, and atmosphere had merged with the dime novel action line.

The Clay adventure is interesting in another way. In this fictional world, as in ours, limitations are the rule and must be accepted. It was a radical idea. Much mystery fiction of the period (and for a decade after) professed the real world and wallowed in fantasy. Its heroes possessed supreme strength and intelligence, manly beauty, luck beyond that of mortal man. At their feet, the grateful police groveled, eager for a kick.

That benign environment is denied Clay:

Clay: "Inspector, admitted that I am an amateur, my amusement is a harmless one as long as I do not interfere with your work."[7]

Clay is in that reasonable position of being able neither to dominate the police nor to dispense with them. As was Sutton. He is free to pursue lines of inquiry outside official consideration, but as soon as these inquiries show promise, the police must be informed. They carry the official burden—Clay does not.

Between Clay and Inspector of the Police Ross grows a mutual respect.

Ross: "You may not be an operative, but you are out of the amateur class... You ought to be on the force."[8]

So highly does Ross hold Clay that he endangers his official position by allowing the amateur rather too much freedom to participate in the case. The problem concerns evidence. The difference between amateur and professional is the difference in their regard for evidence. to the police and the District Attorney's office, evidence is hard, verifiable data, subject to confirmation, linked to crime and the criminal by carefully preserved steps. Evidence must be traceable between the scene of the crime and the ultimate courtroom. The chain of evidence—the history of the evidence after its collection—must be scrupulously preserved and unimpeachable.[9] Though on this point alone, the bulk of early mystery fiction may be discarded as fantasy.

The amateur detective—in fiction, at any rate—is uninterested in these rigors. To him, the case is closed once the guilty party is demonstrated. For this purpose, solutions based on reasoning serve admirably. They reveal. They do not, however, provide that hard evidence needed to convict.

(This identical problem nipped at the heels of no less a figure than Ellery Queen during his early novels. His logic was impeccable. But, as one of the villains remarks, the Queen method is deficient in solid evidence. The courtroom requires more specific matter.)

Reality's unsympathetic demands, when reproduced in fiction, burden the narrative with details and slow the action. (In 1917 the competition of other titles had not forced the mystery magazines—there were two at the time—into stripping their prose to the action bones. That time was fifteen years off.) Neither *Detective Story Magazine* nor *Mystery Magazine* were bastions of realism. Much of their fiction seems incredibly sedate now, and it was most certainly not loaded with realistic detail. Which is all the more reason to admire the emphasis on hard evidence in Cuthbert Clay's adventure, as well as a consideration of the amateur detective *vis a vis* the professional detective. Few magazines, then or later, would bother with these details. As mentioned, they slowed up the narrative.

Mr. Cuthbert Clay, the amateur detective occasioning these abstract thoughts, has been nicknamed "Eagle" since college. From his over-solemn face juts a fiercely aquiline nose. He is so nearsighted as to be almost blind and wears shell-rimmed glasses that magnify his eyes. His forehead is unusually high; his hair unusually fine.

He is stocky, hard muscled by deliberate exercise. He is also nervous, inclined to jitter. Since he has the good judgment to be independently wealthy, he does not work. Studies, instead. Studies human nature, specializing in "psychology and physiology... Aside from his strange gift of inviting confidences, he possessed—and educated—the rare ability of being able to place himself in the mental condition of others."

It is a useful gift. Clay is afflicted with that itch which comes upon peculiar looking, wealthy young men—he has made a hobby of the "unveiling of mysteries." Providing that the mysteries interest him. That is another difference between the amateur and the professional.

"Marked By the Dead" (August 20, 1917) nicely demonstrates these characteristics and differences. A business man is found dead in a room spotted by the bloody fingerprints of a criminal who has been dead for two years. In spite of these fingerprints, the crime seems to have been committed by an English-looking fellow who has vanished from this earth. Clay hangs around the crime scene after the police are gone and nearly gets himself shot by two mysterious figures.

Reasoning then leads him on a twisting trail. All manner of clues appear: empty cans of California tamales, an un-British spelling of "dishonoured," a frightened secretary, chemical crystals in a discarded paper. Guided by these, and aided by his handyman Haynes, Clay tracks down the principals of the plot.

It is almost fatal. Barely in time do the police arrive, saving Clay from being shot to pieces by a killer with a rifle. They capture the murderer. But there is not a scrap of proof that he is the murderer—not until Clay reasons out the whereabouts of the craftsman who prepared the rubber stamp with which the fingerprints were made.

If Dr. Thorndyke had been on the scene, he could have saved everyone a world of trouble.

The pulps took the Holmes image and set it glowing in their windows, a pleasure and a delight to Baker Street addicts. These images were never pure copies—not even Ashton-Kirk was that. While the pulps responded sensitively to such popular enthusiasms as Holmes, they also blended and modified these enthusiasms. It was not intentional. They used everything that was available and in the indiscriminate mixing, something different occasionally appeared. Something that became ever more different as the months slipped smoothly by.

In the Cuthbert Clay adventure, you can see the story of action, violence, and personal danger being merged with elements of the Holmes story. What resulted was neither melodrama nor deductive adventure nor realistic narrative, but an interesting puree of these. It influenced stories of private investigators and stories of amateur detectives.

As this happened, the amateur investigator was changing in other ways.

3-

And there you sit in your green-lighted room, your amanuensis tense over his tablet, waiting for your least word; your mind weaving clear cold deductions from inconsiderable scraps of fact. You speak twelve languages, play the Krummhorn brilliantly, have written one hundred and sixteen monographs and two poems, are an internationally recognized authority on the omphalos, and have collected three manuscripts of Emily Dickinson's lesser known fiction.

You are brilliantly equipped to be an amateur detective. There remains only the question of how you find cases.

The fact is that the amateur and the crime must somehow come together. It is simpler when you are a professional and the office door opens and Brigid O'Shaughnessy saunters in. An amateur has no office door and, to some extent, the crime must seek him out. It is one of the more honored conventions of detective fiction.

The initial pulp magazines were not much bothered by this problem. They featured professional detectives and the stories came with the clients. Through about 1911, the professional detective or police officers outnumbered the amateur by more than two to one. Between 1912 and 1917 came a sudden burst of amateurs and, for a brief period, the professional slumped almost out of sight. It was only a temporary fading. By the mid-1920s, the professional was again in favor, five or six times as many being introduced as amateur detectives. It was telling testimony to the popularity of the private detective and the sudden rush of magazines— *Black Mask, Real Detective Tales, Flynn's,* and *Clues*—publishing that story type.

The series amateur detective, however, whatever his degree of excellence, was always faced by the problem of credibility: How did he manage to encounter so much crime so continuously? As previously mentioned, various techniques were used to rationalize this. One of the most useful was to allow the amateur to stumble across crime while working at his interesting profession. From this simple idea evolved long chains of stories.

The most favored professions were those permitting a lot of mobility, throwing up new faces, new scenes, new professional challenges. And because of that the amateur's incessant discovery of murder, theft, blackmail, and mayhem seemed almost natural.

Few of these professions involved sitting at a desk and reviewing statistical tables. Most had a wonderful sound—newspaper photographer, deep sea diver, fireman, taxi driver, rare book dealer, magician. And even, man of religion.

G.K. Chesterton firmly established, as amateur detective, the man of religion whose contest with worldly evil was aided by his abilities at detection. Chesterton's first dozen Father Brown stories appeared in *The Storyteller* (September 1910 through February 1911) and *Cassell's Magazine* (February through July 1911). All were immediately collected into the 1911 *The Innocence of Father Brown*.[10] Father Brown proceeded intuitively, having little contact with secular authorities and a great deal of contact with that spiritual authority which guided him through the high Andes of moral dilemma. At the core of each Father Brown adventure lies not only a violent deed but a moral position, and these give a pleasing heft and weight to the fiction.

Father Brown initiated a highly regarded, if thinly populated, branch of detective fiction. Not many religious figures have practiced detection (in that narrow sense of solving crimes). Those that did so have usually been excellent, and we regard with affection the steady lights of Sister Ursula, Rabbi Small, and Brother Cadfael.

Others have been less successful. Among these we must regretfully include Reverend Bryson Brace, Congregational minister and highly intermittent figure in the *Detective Story Magazine*, 1917-1918.

Brace appeared in a thin scattering of stories written by Ellis Parker Butler. As a character, Rev. Brace never wholly develops. He is almost consistent, almost distinct, almost alive. But not quite. It is the fault of Mr. Butler's story making. For each story is built around a central device and that device is the sole reason for the story. That device twists the fiction, twists the characters, twists the very sentences. Within the distorting field of the device, nothing natural can grow, and Rev. Brace has no real chance to join detection's elite.

Brace is a small-town minister, married, with an admiring congregation. Tall, brown-haired, about forty years old, he is "Quick and nervous in actions, somewhat careless in dress, and tremendously energetic. To see him hurrying along the street on week days, one would have said he was a second-rate real estate agent... He had a hearty, boyish laugh and his sermons sparkled with imagination."[11]

His private library is split equally between theological works and detective fiction. "I will say," he remarks, "that if I had not been chosen to be a minister, I would have chosen to be a detective."

Which sounds wonderfully promising. Unfortunately, device-oriented stories prevent Rev. Brace from rising to classical heights. Or to any height. "Bread Upon The Waters" (September 25, 1917) tells how a good deed repaid itself. Several years earlier, rich broker Graydon sent Rev. Brace to Paris to recover from nervous exhaustion. If you are nervous, one place is like another. Brace recovered nicely, thank you, and returned to his ministry. And now, years later, Graydon, in precarious financial shape, lies threshing fitfully on his sick bed.

At this time, a rich lady gives Brace a wad of negotiable bonds. He is to sell them and the church keeps everything over $5,000. Immediately he takes the bonds to Graydon and immediately they are stolen from under Graydon's pillow. He was too ill to put them in the safe, poor chap.

His story is that he woke to find the bedroom reeking with gas, the bonds gone, the bedroom door slowly closing. Receding through the doorway is an arm in a gray sleeve. Graydon promptly whips out his gun, fires, sees a hole leap into the gray cuff. It was—he is certain—the cuff of his servant, Henri.

Next day, Graydon calls Brace. Together they examine Henri's gray coat cuff, find no bullet hole.

It is instantly apparent that Graydon's story is tosh, simple tosh.

The Rev. Brace does not think so. A memory from Paris tickles his mind. He learns that Henri was out of the house all morning, makes a single telephone call, and behold—learns that Henri has just had a hole through his cuff rewoven.

Thou art the man. And the man confesses in a thick French accent.

Around that device, invisible reweaving, the entire story circles. The alibi must be based on reweaving; there a hole must be shot in the cuff, and Rev. Brace must remember the Paris reweaving shops along the Seine, and Henri must be French.

Reason totters. A sick man awakes in a gas-filled room (Henri was trying to kill him with gas, it is explained). He discovers the bonds gone and by the unsteady gleam of the nightlight, he sees an arm in gray hovering by the door. He draws his pistol and fires and, in that light, under those conditions, sees a hole leap into the fabric.

The word tosh was mentioned before. That seems a restrained assessment.

"Chicken Bait" (April 2, 1918) is another story that exists entirely for the device. The situation is this: A negro has stolen three prize chickens and eaten them. Since we are wallowing in racial stereotypes here, you might assume that watermelons would be even more amusing, but you do not allow for Mr. Ellis P. Butler's dark ingenuity: the story would not work with watermelons; it must have chickens.

At any rate, the thief has been arrested, confessed, and lightly sentenced. The only interesting feature of the case, as Brace points out, "is one that is as old as detective fiction; it is a problem that was, perhaps, the oldest problem of all those proposed by writers of detective fiction—the locked room that cannot be entered but is entered."[12]

The chicken house, you see, was locked and the lock greased to show fingerprints, a precaution always taken when locking the chicken house. Moreover, the fence around the chicken yard is locked, and this high, impervious enclosure is under observation from the house. So how was the theft accomplished? By dislodging the top ventilator with a pole, then fishing for chickens through the hole, using a hook baited with bread. A projecting tree limb helped the criminal sit and fish.

Brace doesn't really reason this out. You think he has done so, and he spins the problem out to incredible length, mystifying all those good old boys down at the lunch room. But actually, the miscreant's wife explained it all to Brace before the story opened. This you learn in the last few lines. It is one of those snappy twists designed to leave you chuckling. The end effect, in this case, is to leave you heartily sick of Rev. Brace and all his works, deductive and otherwise.

A considerably more satisfactory example of the man of the cloth as detective appeared in *The Popular Magazine*, February 7, 1920. The story, titled, "The Tower of Treason," by G. K. Chesterton, was about Father Stephen. The Father appeared in only one story for the excellent reason that he was shot dead at the end of it. Like the Father Brown stories, "The Tower of Treason" is so engulfed in an atmosphere of determined paradox that you hardly realize how slender the basic story is.

Once upon a time, Father Stephen was somebody in the naughty world:

In the world of what has come to be called secret diplomacy, he was something more than a secret diplomatist. He is one from whom no diplomacy could be kept secret...he not only saw small things, but he saw them as large things, and largely. It was he who had anticipated the suicide of a cosmopolitan millionaire, judging from an atmosphere and the fact that he did not wind up his watch. It was also he who had frustrated a great German conspiracy in America, detecting the Teutonic spy by his unembarrassed posture in a chair when a Boston lady was handing him tea.[13]

Civilization and its spiritual ills eventually drove Stephen to shave his red hair to a tonsure and retire to live in a cliff. The location seems to have been in the Balkans. The cliff, of symbolic white stone, was pierced by a small black opening, coffin-sized. At the side of the opening was painted a colored ikon of the Holy Family.

Unlike Father Brown, Father Stephen is tall, bony, erect, looking as if he were stimulated by "a secret sun or fountain of life... or drew nourishment from the roots of the mountains."

In his elaborate style of calling white black and both neither, Chesterton saturates the story with situations that make no sense—until later:

—A young man walking backward through a forest.
—A tremendous wooden crucifix towering up in the wilderness.
—A man, inexplicably dead, hovered over by a giant fellow with a sword.
—An impervious, impregnable stone tower jutting up in the wilds, manned by zealots who guard a steel casket containing 100 perfect diamonds. Or 99. Or 98. They are vanishing, one by one.

A young man is suspected of the crime. He appeals to Father Stephen, who has the matter solved even before he sees the curious pock marks at the base of the crucifix. Before he can explain those, or what that sin is which hovers over the forest, he is struck dead. Which makes this a remarkably brief career, even for a magazine detective. To ease the reader's pain, the mystery is cleared up in the final paragraphs, based on Stephen's final remarks, and the glittering object that the doctor removes from his stilled heart.

4-

Neither sweet reason, nor sweet paradox, nor sweet plot devices trouble the stories about Charlie Fenwick, the telephone detective. Charlie was one of the many amateur detectives whose fascinating profession led him to interminable confrontations with crime.

From the Editor's Page, *All-Story Weekly*, August 30, 1919:

Something new! That's what the whole amusement-seeking world is always looking for. And readers, too, are ever on the lookout for novelty—for a new kind of story. That is one reason why the telephone-detective stories of George J. Brenn have been so cordially received by *All-Story Weekly* readers. They are along an entirely new line.[14]

The detective adventures of Charlie Fenwick, Wire Chief of the Springfield Central Office, began in *All-Story Weekly* about mid-1919. The first story noted, "No Publicity" (June 7, 1919) introduced a long series of short stories and serials that continued into 1925.

How such a mass of material could have been wrung from telephone equipment is as amazing to the modern reader as the telephone was amazing to the 1919 reader. Seldom do you find such a clear example of fiction exploiting technology.

Charlie Fenwick is a "phonic criminologist"—popular magazine jargon for an amateur who solves crimes by using telephone—related equipment. If the solution does not require wire bundles, volts, technical coils, insulation, and similar items of giddy technical elan, Charlie is uninterested. He will not play.

He is totally committed to telephone science. It gives him personal focus. He would gladly spend his days climbing up poles or peering down carbon diaphragms. A monomanic in his way. But such a nice boy. A red-headed, blue-eyed boy, quite young, slender, and a most facile talker. He needs to be. His adventures require vast lumps of talk to conceal the absence of story content. In a Charlie Fenwick adventure, you get constant movement, lots of hardware talk, and demonstration of a cascade of technical marvels now as obsolete as the horse-drawn street car.

All this matter covers the fact that the story does not amount to much. It is merely the vehicle for demonstrating a new wrinkle in telephone equipment.

As in the story, "Making A Martyr" (May 7, 1921), designed to show how Charlie set up a telephone remote to a political meeting. All story events circle about this magnificent achievement. The logic of the dramatization is forced and rings false from the beginning—although, admittedly, the story has its moments.

Political rivals plan to kidnap Mayor Fielding just before the big rally. Fenwick accidentally learns of the plot while trouble-shooting a line.

Instead of turning the matter over to the police—who apparently wear chin whiskers and push against doors marked "Pull"—Charlie and his friends work out a dramatic reversal of the plot. They will rescue the Mayor *after* the kidnapping, then allow him to address the people by telephone link to outdoor loud-speakers at the public reception area.

Alas for advanced planning. No sooner is the Mayor rescued, than along comes this terrible storm—flood—wind damage—wires and poles down—Fenwick and company marooned by walls of wild water...

Even as you despair, Fenwick repairs the crucial circuits, risking his life, applying his technological expertise, *etc.* The Mayor then speaks his imperishable words, unfortunately not quoted.

"We Have With Us Tonight—" (April 28, 1923), features a telephone operator who has memorized the entire New York City telephone book, a less ample document than now. Fenwick is helping his good buddy, Corson, Chief of Detectives, New York City. A brokerage house is tipping off the crooks, and doing it by telephone! At a banquet, Charlie arranges an elaborate charade, introducing the talented telephone operator as a "thaumaturgic" marvel, able to read phone numbers in the mind. Just give someone's name and address and think... The charade so unnerves the tip-off man (claiming that he is thinking of the robber's telephone number) that his heart beats fast and he gives himself away.

"Voices" was a 5-part serial (November 25 through December 23, 1923). Charlie is asked to investigate a case of harassment by anonymous telephone voices—Chinese voices, Irish voices, Jewish voices, voices of old men and young women. All these harangue and threaten the victim with exposure.

The story, vastly padded, tells how Charlie runs down the voices and corrects the essential wrong. In this work he is mightily helped by his old reliable assistant, Seth Boyden—a comic rube. Seth has memorized every passage in the Bible that may be remotely applied to the telephone art. Thus:

James 19: Let every man be swift to hear, but slow to speak...
Galatians, 1:13: Ye have heard my conversation in times past.

or thus:

Boyden:"I guess we'd better be leavin', sir. We ought to be doin' what the fellers did in the fourth chapter of Acts, twenty-third verse... 'They went to their own company and reported'."

"Babble," another 4-part serial (December 13, 1924 through January 3, 1925) concerns murder in a sealed house. No one could have done it. It's impossible. And it takes a transatlantic telephone call to Scotland Yard before the final puzzle piece is secured.

"You Can't Get Away From It" (February 14, 1925) employs a device for transmitting a photograph by telephone line. (The equipment is far more sophisticated than that used by Craig Kennedy only a few years before.) Fenwick is visiting Corson again and appears in only two of the six chapters, spending much of his time making long distance calls in an attempt to frustrate an attempted stock swindle.

Poor Old Charlie Fenwick is obsolete now—at least until Charlie Fenwick, Electronics Data Chip Criminologist, arises. The figure of Balbane, the Conjurer Detective, who appeared at about the same time, is still alive and well.

Balbane stands near the beginning of that long and brilliant line, the magician-detective. It is a particularly distinguished branch of the amateur detective, including such splendid fellows as George Chance (The Ghost Detective), The Great Merlini, Don Diavolo, and Norgil.

In no way is Balbane inferior to these gifted men. He appeared in *Detective Story Magazine* during 1921-1922, eleven stories written by Lewen Hewitt. Six of these were later reprinted in the 1930-1931 *Best Detective Stories*.

Since it is the nature of magic to be eternal, Balbane's adventures remain fresh as morning air. The first sentences of the first story, "Balbane, Conjurer Detective" (January 22, 1921), set the mood:

"He opened his hand. The cards had disappeared."

Balbane, Man of Mystery, is a professional magician. To the public he is a world-famous conjurer; to himself, a "trickster."

Balbane: "I'm not a detective; I'm simply a performer, a sleight-of-hand expert with no claim to mysterious powers."[15]

His appearance is curiously vague. You read that his face is long and smooth-shaven and that his eyelashes are long and black. More definitive information is lacking. His long fingers constantly manipulate coins, cards, that finger ring glittering with green and red jewels.

In relaxed moments, he seems a "great, healthy, self-confident boy." In more formal moments:

Like one who covers himself with a cloak, he had donned his stage presence; calm and superior, gifted with unfathomable depths of knowledge. It was the presence which had brought the conjurer to the peak of his profession.[16]

Balbane finds that his professional skills lap over into civil life. He does not sniff out crime for amusement; crimes intrude themselves upon him. Whatever happens, he handles himself with that exquisite self-possession of the stage performer:

Balbane: ". . .ever since I reached the age of fifteen I've been averaging at least one magical performance a day the year round. And during each performance I've had to meet some emergency that wasn't foreseen, that couldn't be foreseen. But I've never been stumped yet."[17]

He is fortunate to enjoy that professional background. For the variety of troubles dropped on him would daunt a man of lesser skills.

"Balbane, Conjurer Detective" (January 22, 1921) concerns a relatively minor problem—he is asked to detect the card cheat in a group of six. But take care. The story, itself, is as much a miracle of misdirection as a hand sleight. All stories, in fact, contain carefully calculated twists.

"The Twisted Bullet" (February 12, 1921) confronts Balbane with murder at the seance. The victim dies right there at the table, cut down by vengeful spirits, the only possible explanation—until Balbane gaffs the revolver to point out the murderer.

"Beneath the Brand" (September 3, 1921) introduces a society of black magicians, who seem to have loosened an elemental. Or that's what the rich girl tells Balbane. The elemental has torn her father to shreds and swept away her young man in a blast of white flame. It is most provoking.

Balbane has no belief in elementals and black magicians. He does know what ignited flash paper looks like and he can smell conspiracy and kidnapping, no matter how they are packaged.

Through all these excitements, Balbane is aided by young Frank Clark, Confidential Assistant and Secretary-in-Chief. Clark works on the stage and attempts to keep Balbane's slovenly financial affairs in order. Dark, exuberant, and tough, Clark is almost as fast on the update as his boss. He throws solid punches when required and calls the police, at story's end, to collect the guilty. He also fills that invaluable literary role as the series Listener.

It is the duty of the Listener to sit quite still at the end of each story, his face blank with wonder, while Balbane explains the fine points of the adventure and the detection. The reader is expected to eavesdrop shamelessly. At the end of each story, before Balbane and Clark yawn off to their beds, both sit over black coffee an black cigars and Clark listens and Balbane explains. It is one of the detective story conventions: the mystery must be explained or the reader becomes very cross. Over the generations, an inordinate effort has been spent on the technical problem of presenting the explanation without, at the same time, allowing the story to sag away in anti-climax. The final monologue, as the detective explains his wonderful methods, is not particularly dramatic, unless the name of the guilty is withheld until the final sentence. But whether the story ends in dramatic revelation or sags limply over the final period, like a stalk of boiled broccoli, the Listener is imperative. Someone has to sit there so that the reader can eavesdrop.

"The Very Curious Canvas" (April 1, 1922) leaps from Tangier to Paris to the Sahara Desert and back to Paris. All this movement because a legendary painting, thoroughly cursed, has been stolen. In its place is a copy whose paint literally fades away in sunlight.

Balbane goes after the original painting. Secures it, too, after he has charmed back to life a dying son of a desert chief. But all to no avail. Experts say that the recovered picture is also a fake.

Not so. With a simple gesture, Balbane....

During "The Crooked Roulette Wheel" (May 20, 1922), Balbane demonstrates a fine new way to beat dishonest play in a French gambling hell. You merely make the wheel operator think that he is being hypnotized. It helps if you have a commanding presence.

The final story in the Balbane series, "Balbane Meets the Real Thing" (May 27, 1922), is a distinctly dangerous adventure in Morocco. Balbane has been sent by the French government to show up some fake magic workers who are thumping up a native insurrection. He is also on a private mission of his own—somewhere in the city is an innocent man who is accused of stealing $22,000 from a Boston construction company. Balbane wishes to warn the fellow that a detective is close behind. William Naylor, the falsely accused man, has recently lost his wife, and must somehow take care of Jessie, his little girl.

She is an extraordinary little girl possessing a number of talents. These include light mind-reading, prediction of the near future, and observation of events occurring in places where she isn't. She brings news that the Berbers—the Blue Men from the hills—are about to attack town. And so they are.

They may be withstood if the natives remain loyal, if an influential charm doctor is exposed before his followers, if the French troops arrive in time.

With young Clark's help, and the aid of Balbane's other stage assistant, Desiree Lenoir, the Conjurer Magician plunges into a battle of magic. He spurts flame from his mouth, catches bullets in his teeth, predicts the arrival of the French troops.

And is staggered when the charm doctor reveals the head of the French general in a box. It would appear that all their heads will soon grace boxes. At this dramatic point, Jessie applies her second sight to expose the charm doctor's machination. And since he was careless enough to carry written evidence of his crimes, his associates bind him tightly and carry him off to doom.

Which leaves the problem of the detective snuffling direly after Mr. William Naylor. Well, matters couldn't work out better—and fortunately so, for there is only a page and a half remaining. The detective has not come to arrest Naylor. The was only a suspense device. Instead, he wants to tell Naylor that the real embezzler has been caught and father and daughter may safely return to the States.

Didn't it all work out splendidly, just like a story. In the final paragraphs, as emotion, warm as the scent of Christmas, ravages our hearts, Balbane confesses his love for Desiree. They'll likely get married after page 129. It is, perhaps, a technical fault that Desiree has had nothing to do in the series until this final story. Still love leaps all obstacles, as they say, and it should have no trouble flying over this minor difficulty.

Cool rationality gleams within the Balbane series like neon lights illuminating a white room. Reason, discipline, training, those unsentimental essentials, enable Balbane's miracles. Even that startling flare of wild talents during the final story only accentuates the pragmatism of the rest of the series. No magic; no miracles. Nothing but cleverly devised deceits by a technician of extraordinary skill and understanding.

For all their reputation as repositories of giddy romanticism, the pulp magazines reflected the national passion for a reality which could be organized, manipulated, and exploited. Nothing is impossible if you catch the right handle, understand the essential fact.

That assumption of rational order underlies all pulp fiction. Its fantasies have iron bones and optimism, like a bright thread, winds through its pages. Any problem may be solved. You have but to find the proper handle, and if you are trained, skilled, vigorous, alert, you grasp that handle for the world's betterment.

If you are flexible enough, you could even establish a detective agency with a ghost as your chief sleuth.

It seems an unlikely premise, but that is the central idea in the brief series, "The Ghost Detective," three connected stories which appeared in *Detective Story Magazine* during 1922.

"The Ghost Detective" owes something to the Houseboat on the Styx series, a group of humorous fantasies by John Kendrick Bangs in which the shades of departed great, from Cleopatra to Sherlock Holmes, amuse themselves by boating about the River Styx.[18] It owes even more to Conan Doyle's lectures on spiritualism, delivered while touring the United States in 1922.[19]

The difference between spiritualism as expounded by Doyle and as popularized in public print is the difference between a living rabbit and one starring in a comic book. To its advocates and devotees, spiritualism was a religion emphasizing development of the soul through this, and subsequent worlds, to that highest sphere where Godhead dwelt. Among its several assumptions was survival of the personality and under certain conditions, communication with the dead. That latter point, communication, got the bulk of public attention to the almost total exclusion of everything else. Yells of derision greeted Doyle's message—or what was believed to be his message. Magazine fiction, that mirror of popular enthusiasms, promptly reflected the uproar. For more than twenty years, the pulps would revel in the tackier aspects of spiritualism—the ouija boards and seances, materialized entities, trances, spirit controls, and fraudulent mediums swindling fools. Amid these dizzy thunders, Doyles' actual beliefs got shuffled into the lumber room. Few noticed their absence.

"The Ghost Detective" is of those turbulent times.

There is always a certain amount of discussion and debate going on about spiritualism....Sir Arthur Conan Doyle's recent visit has aroused public interest to an unusual degree.

Quite naturally Willis Parker Butler wished to lend his agile brain and facile pen to the subject... Mr. Butler's efforts may not convert you to spiritualism, but we will guarantee that they will entertain you.[20]

This is the same Ellis Parker Butler who gave us the Reverend Bryson Brace and his concocted exploits. Such defects do not mar The Ghost Detective, which is bland farce.

As "The Haunted Policeman" (July 15, 1922) opens, New York City detective Arthur Bull has arrested Madame Fatima Caro, a trance medium. Quite unexpectedly she materializes the ghost of Diogenes—the original Diogenes, cynic philosopher of ancient Greece. The cynics were

...the lot that taught that pleasure was a crime, and that most of the good things of life were wicked... Diogenes was the crabbedest of them all. He go so grouchy that he did not believe there was a decent man or woman alive, and he went around with his lantern trying to find a honest man and could not find one. So when he died he gave that job up as time wasted, and now he was spending all his time hunting dishonest men—a much easier job as he looked at it. He has been hunting dishonest men for over two thousand years...and had become such an expert at it that he made all of the famous detectives look like thirty cents...[21]

As an amateur detective, Diogenes is nearly perfect. As a personality he is a sour, querulous, snarling, whining old sourball who makes Sidney Garth seem like a sunbeam.

In short order he helps Bull and his associate, Jack Horton, solve a bond theft and a murder. But their relations are difficult:

Diogenes: "I come when I please, and I go when I please. I say what I please, I do. They can't shut me up when I don't want to shut up. I speak my mind to man and woman—yes, and to kings, too. I tell them what is what, I do! What do you want?
Bull: "Do you know anything about the Hammidge case?"
Diogenes: "All about it! All about it!"
Bull: "Now that is fine. Now my idea is that Mrs. Hammidge killed her husband."
Diogenes: "You're a fool."
Bull: "And Jack, here thinks Bunce killed him."
Diogenes: "Jack? Jack? Jackass, you had better call him. Couple of idiots."
Bull: "All right, if you know so much, who did kill him?"
Diogenes: "His wife killed him."
Bull: "That's what I said, didn't I?"
Diogenes: "You did not. Nothing of the sort."
Bull: "Then Mrs. Hammidge was not his wife? He had a wife when he married her?"
Diogenes: "I said so. Anybody but a fool would know it..."[22]

At this point it develops that Madame Caro is the murderer. And, at this point, she drops dead, leaving Diogenes fully materialized and unable to return to ghostland.

Unfortunate. Air causes him to burn all over, as if he had been dipped in fire. In a rage, he swears that he will haunt Bull forever. No mean threat, since Diogenes glows in the dark like a "white hot stove." On this pleasing perplexity, the first story ends.

"The Second Mr. Rawdonbury" (July 22, 1922) tells how Bull and Horton manage to get Diogenes into the body of Elias P. Rawdonbury, a mild-manned millionaire who has committed suicide. The personality change is appalling, particularly to the unwitting widow and her daughter. They find it excessively odd that father, like a cynic philosopher, should sleep in a washing machine and eat dog biscuits.

Bull and Horton have, in the meantime, resigned from the police department and set up as private detectives, relying on Diogenes as the main investigator. "The advantage of having a ghost in a detective firm," Bull remarks, "is that a ghost can work fast."

As ghost communicates with ghost by means of the sixth or intuitive sense, little actual time was consumed. I have known Diogenes to leave..., interview the ghost of a dead man, and solve a mystery that would have taken the best mortal detective ten years to solve, and be back...in one eighth of a second. Possibly our ghost solved some mysteries in even less time, but we had no stop watch that registered less then one eighth a second, so I cannot positively claim that he did.

On the whole, I consider one eighth of a second fairly rapid work in mystery solving.[23]

Unfortunately for the detective agency, matters complicate at once. Mrs. Rawdonbury reacts to Diogenes' peculiar ways by having her husband's body carted off to the insane asylum. Once there, Diogenes is so uncomfortable that he abandons Rawdonbury's body and returns to grouse and carp around the detective agency.

"Who Killed Dikkory" (July 29, 1922) continues the adventures without varying their literary merit. Diogenes now takes over the body of "Cranky Sam" Haley, a cantankerous detective killed in the line of duty. The agency has just been retained by Miss Carol Golthorpe, beautiful show girl, to discover who killed her fiance Reginald Dikkory.

Diogenes investigates and, in one eight of a second, learns that "Cranky Sam" did the murder in a jealous rage.

Is it possible to conceal the culprit and so preserve "Cranky Sam's" comfortable body for Diogenes' use? Afraid not. Jack Horton has fallen violently in love with Miss Goldthorpe and wants her name cleared. He is determined that the body of "Cranky Sam" pay the extreme penalty.

At this, Diogenes flies into a temper tantrum, hurls himself out of the body, out of the offices, and out of the series, once and forever. Which concludes a charming set of stories. Even though Conan Doyle might have contested some of the views on spiritualism.

5-

The most distinguished of all figures in this shadowland of ghosts and magicians is probably not real, surely not human. Nor is he an amateur detective but a stimulator of that inclination toward amateur detection implicit in others. His name, if such an incorporal entity must be named is Harley Quin, one of Agatha Christie's notable character creations. Quin stands astride the twilight line between the fantasy and the detective story, blending them into dramas small but intense and filled with echoes as disturbing as a sigh heard in a deserted hallway.

Agatha Christie's reputation now soars close to the sun. Few readers remember that her reputation first blazed up in magazines; in the United States, they were pulp magazines.

It seems improbably to categorize her as a pulp magazine writer. Yet in the mid-1920s, her work slipped smoothly into the fictional stream, a wave among many waves. Verifiably *Blue Book* published Poirot short stories, and serialized "The Big Four" and "The Man in the Brown Suit"; *Flynn's* printed "The Murder of Roger Ackroyd"; *Detective Story* published many short stories, including the detections of Miss Marple. And the adventures of that strange pair, Harley Quin and Mr. Satterthwaite, appeared in publications as diverse as *Munsey's Magazine, Flynn's,* and *Black Mask.*

The Quin/Satterthwaite series comprises thirteen stories, twelve of them collected in *The Mysterious Mr. Quin* (1930)[24] These concern crimes, or near crimes, among English aristocracy—crimes which are comprehended, rather than solved. For Mr. Quin has a way of causing you to look at familiar things in a wholly different light.

Just when the human drama has built to the bursting point, Mr. Quin appears without warning. He vanishes even more abruptly. He is associated with no fixed address, yet somehow he does know everyone. He is a tall thin man, his complexion dark, his expression at once sad and mocking. He dresses soberly. yet how queerly light falls upon his clothing, splotching it with color. Across his face falls a bar of shadow, like a half mask. Not always. If there are shadows, he has a way of melting into them.

Of this figure, Christie remarked:

Mr. Quin was a figure who just entered into a story—a catalyst, no more—his mere presence affected human beings... Always he stood for the same things: he was a friend of lovers, and connected with death.[25]

Who is he, after all? Satterthwaite does not really know. He suspects. He knows that Quin's face possesses a certain curious fluidity, that he is easily overlooked, even in plain sight.

When Quin appears, Satterthwaite's old heart rises up. It is, he recognizes, a sign that drama impends. Something is at the verge of ripening. At the last possible moment, a player in the human drama will be snatched from Hell. For Quin appears only when the situation is desperate.[26]

In "Mr. Quin Passes By" (*Munsey's Magazine*, March 1925), he appears for the first time, knocking for admission at the door of a country house on New Year's day. Once welcomed in, he guides the guests into a discussion of a crime long in the past, that favorite Christie theme. Under his guidance, they discern the truth of an old death. Mr. Satterthwaite, filled with sudden understanding, explains an act that has, for years, warped certain human relationships, and a woman's suicide is averted.

Departing, Quin recommends to Satterthwaite's attention, the harlequinade—a traditional pantomime, featuring traditional characters in a series of dances. "Immortals," Quin remarks, magnificently ambiguous, "are always immortal, you know."

Other Quin stories were published in *Flynn's* during late 1926. "The Soul of the Croupier" (November 13) tells of a dazzling woman at the end of her luck, the young fool infatuated by her, the failed man who loves her. The theme is obsession. The story ends warmly, if not with happiness. It is queer fare for *Flynn's*.

"World's End" (November 20) is an exercise in Christie misdirection. The point is suicide, whatever you might think. Quin appears from nowhere on a cliff overlooking the sea, and matters improve at once. "The Voice In the Dark" (December 4) whispers deadly things at night to a terror-strickened heiress. Mr. Satterthwaite, inspired by Quin, rises to an understanding of an identity substitution and meets, too late, a young friend grown old.

"The Face of Helen" was reprinted in the July 1951 issue of *Black Mask*, the final issue of that noble magazine. In this story, a woman of intolerable beauty makes her choice between two young men. The result is a clever murder trap, employing that old favorite, a lethal, untraceable gas. Satterthwaite barely frustrates the murder but fails to prevent a suicide.

Satterthwaite is in the Christie tradition of aged amateur detectives. Sixty-two years old at the beginning of the series, he is a bent little dried-up gentleman, a wealthy bachelor, whose curiosity about people is overpowering. Like Poirot and Miss Marple, his intelligence has been honed by time to a silken edge. He is old-maidish, observing and "beneath his gallant manner he had a shrewd and critical mind."

Frankly he is a snob. He has chosen to stand outside of life—safely back from the intense emotions—observing, not participating. His attention is fixed on the activities of that social set engendered by English society to expend their lives in well-bred excursions to the continent; in well-bred rounds of entertainment; in visits, one to the other, that are as ritualized as the positions of classic ballet.

Through these sculptured formalities glides Mr. Satterthwaite. Discreet, immensely sensitive to nuance, he is the ideal confidant. He knows everyone and everything within the limits of that slender social slice he adorns. He senses drama from afar. And because the human drama fascinates him, he comes to observe. Because of Quin's presence, Satterthwaite remains to understand.

"I see things," he says in "Harlequin's Lane." "I may have been only a looker on at Life—but I see things that other people do not."

God help the man. It is the best he can say for himself.

6-

Harlequin: From the ancient French mystery plays, a devil-faced jester, first named Harlequin, wearing a jacket patched with multi-colored triangles and carrying a lath—otherwise known as a slapstick. The character entered the improvised Italian comedies as Arlecchino in the 1550s. This character wore a black half mask, dressed in sprightly rags, played the ribald, jesting, prancing servant, who loves the flirt, Columbine. From Harlequin budded the white-faced Pierrot and Mr. Punch. The original French concept presented Harlequin as a spirit of the air, invisible when he wished, an acrobatic and fantastic dancer. These attributes reappeared in the harlequinades of the mid-1700s. The 1920s again revived these heavily symbolic dances and pantomimes. Harlequin, a mocking nature spirit, affirms the spirit of love and life and the celebration of joy, while wearing a costume of black and red diamonds.

The Harlequinade features no character named Satterthwaite or Christie.

7-

Through the films and magazines of the 1930s swarm newspaper reporters, newspaper photographers. Each is an amateur investigator of repute, hot on the scent of crime. Blasting machine guns do not deter them, or blue-chinned muscle men from the mob, or unsympathetic cops, or diamond-hard action adventures.

Nor are they affected by being beaten senseless once or twice a month. Or by smoking nine packs of cigarettes a day, washed down with quarts of the reddest rye.

They are tough men, aware and canny, and if they swarmed in the 1930s, they were rather rare in 1920s fiction. City-room folklore celebrated the red-hot reporter who stamped on the Ten Commandments to get his story. But that energetic figure did not become public property until production of the 1928 play, *The Front Page*, by Ben Hecht and Charles Mac Arthur.

During most of the 1920s, the hardboiled news hawk rarely won his own magazine series. Newsmen were secondary characters, not leads. When they did appear in series, they were not very hardboiled. Cute, yes. As, for example, Ruddy—Robert Ruddy.

Ruddy appeared briefly in the 1923-24 *Short Stories*, the series written by Albert Edward Ullman. At this early date, Mr. Ruddy is what we now call an investigative reporter on *The World*. That is, he pokes his nose into everything, in the tradition of the amateur detective. He seeks News, the Big Story.

It is hardly his fault that his cases are littered with borrowings from silent movie comedy.

"Help Wanted" (December 25, 1923) tells how Ruddy investigates a crooked employment agency whose charges, by 1923 standards, are staggering. (What was a crime then is usual now.) He saves an idiot girl and her equally idiotic boy friend from the tolls of excessive placement fees. With no trouble, he proves that the crooked Personnel Manager is in cahoots with the crooked employment agency. After which the wicked are punished by exposure and being hit in the face with a pie, a jolly retribution.

Mr. Ruddy possesses two distinguishing characteristics: He has gray eyes and rolls his own cigarettes. He is otherwise as faceless as a fistful of air. As if to compensate for this ill-defined character, the prose in which he is embedded closely resembles a baroque ceiling:

> Even as (the criminal) floundered to the floor, Ruddy was astride the balustrade and traveling at a lightning-like pace toward the lower level. He had a flashing picture of the crook as the latter attempted to scramble to his feet, of a cake of soap and mess of water that impeded the other's progress, and then his body catapulted into some object and was left breathless. As he recovered his breath and opened his eyes it was to find himself in the bear-like embrace of some big man with whom he was rolling over and over on the floor.[27]

This is the action climax of a story titled "Quick Change" (January 10, 1924), concerning a missing Wall Street messenger and a half million dollar bond theft. Hot on the story, Ruddy darts off to the broker's home, is refused admission by the police. Enters disguised as a laundryman. Finds the broker's safe forced and $50,000 gone. Promptly goes to the roof, when he finds footprints.

Next, disguised as an Italian window cleaner, Ruddy goes to the office of the man who owned the bonds. He finds footprints there matching those on the roof. Instantly working out the solution, he corners the crook. Gets shot at. Knocks the fellow down with a scrubwoman's bucket. Plunges into hand-to-hand battle and, with the aid of the police, captures the wicked wretch. A masterful triumph, very very cute.

These energetic caperings are omitted from the rather more placid world of Matthew Sallowby, a used book dealer who encountered a series of trifling mysteries in the 1925 *Flynn's*.

Booksellers as lead fictional characters are unusual, and booksellers who dabble in detection are scarce as good sense in the state legislature. The most notable bookseller of the Teens was Roger Mifflin, proprietor of The Parnassus on Wheels and Parnassus At Home. While steeped to the beard in literature, Mifflin is no detective—although, in *The Haunted Bookshop* (1919), he does solve a simple code and helps capture a fierce German spy.[28]

Matthew Sallowby does more during his comparatively short career. He derives not from Mifflin but from Sax Rohmer's Moris Klaw in a misty and indistinct way, with all the color, audacious imagination, and occult splendor of The Dream Detective filtered out.

Sallowby is a tall, broad-shouldered old man, with thick eyebrows on a large white face. In common with other sellers of second-hand merchandise, his expression is grim and impassive. He is constantly dressed in an old black suit, wears a black bow tie, and methodically smokes his way through a succession of black cigars. He deals in used books from a shabby little shop on Lower Grimes Street, apparently in London.

His niece, Joan, is as fresh and bright as Sallowby is forbidding and dark. She is a slim young beautiful thing, wearing her golden hair bobbed. Her vitality brightens the grim premises at Lower Grimes Street. Sallowby certainly doesn't. He is busy saving bits of string, his face set, the cigar reeking in his locked teeth. The bookstore smells of darkness and dust, old paper, thrifty habits, old cigar smoke. A dour place to bring up a young girl.

"What Was In Lot 109?" (Flynn's, January 10, 1925), written by John Harris-Burland, presents Sallowby with a puzzle he cannot solve. He has purchased a thoroughly conventional bundle of books at a county auction for $280. Immediately a crazy little man appears at Lower Grimes Street, begging to buy the book of sermons included in the bundle. It was, he explains, his mother's book and sentiment demands that he recover it. Sallowby has grave suspicions concerning sentiment. But they are most ordinary books and so he sells them for cost.

Only later does he learn that the sermons were bound with two missing pages of a rare old Bible, the pages being worth 5,000 dollars.

"The Book With a Curse" (January 17, 1925): To Sallowby's shop comes a black-bearded stranger, asking for the rarest book in the world—a Tyndale 1525 New Testament printed in Cologne by Peter Quental. No sooner has Black Beard left than Sallowby opens a package of books and discovers this identical volume. It has apparently been mailed to him for appraisal or sale. But there is no letter. As he examines it, he notices that it seems to radiate fear and malice, a glow of dark emotion.

Two days later, in the middle of the night, an Albert Toxteth wakes Sallowby, claims to be the owner of the book. Or is he. As Sallowby tries to strike a bargain for the book, they are interrupted by the black-bearded man. In a blind panic, Toxteth kills himself. Black Beard explains that his brother had been killed by Toxteth and the Bible stolen.

And now, does Black Beard want the Bible back? Heaven's, no. "It is soaked in blood. If it were all I had in the world I would destroy it."

Which he proceeds to do, page by page.

So far, Sallowby hasn't done three cents worth of detection. He gets around to this in "What The Parrot Knew" (January 31, 1925), when he buys a parrot from a sailor. It is a morbid parrot which chatters in Latin, calls out for water, chants "All dead—all dead." Soon afterward, the sailor is found knifed and stark in an alley. Then the parrot escapes from the shop.

The story has now reached a dead end. Since Sallowby has no intention of going out to investigate the mystery, the mystery must come to the bookshop. Sallowby has advertised for the return of the parrot and its corpse is brought back by another sailor. By noticing discrepancies in the sailor's speech, and observing his hands caressing the binding of a rare old book, Sallowby hazards a guess that he is the murderer. And so he is, since the story is almost over. He tells a story of shipwreck, thirst, and betrayal, then flees into the street where he is killed by a bus.

One or two more Sallowby stories were published before the series was terminated. You wonder how it survived so long. Even for the 1925 *Flynn's*, the stories seem inert as a load of gravel. Sallowby encounters mysteries but he does little more than look at them with a dour expression. Accident and chance are the real detectives.

A slightly more effective amateur detective was the little fragile countryman inventor, Old Windmills, who shuffled cutely around *Detective Story Magazine* during 1925. Old Windmills—more formally, Mr. William Clayton—takes his nickname from the wooden windmills he carves to set over rural mailboxes. He lives in a tiny hamlet outside Boston and the crimes he encounters are usually small country crimes.

The stories are slow, simple, determinedly darling. Their uneventful pages rock gently along. Through them wanders Old Windmills wearing carpet slippers held together by bits of string. A black kitten peeps from his pocket. The kitten is named Robert E. Lee because that is cunning. It is all cute and cunning and adorable, as if hand-painted wooden figures had been sprinkled with the Powder of Life and were toddling about, conversing in little shrill voices.

Here is a cute little crime. Only Old Windmills sees what the real clue is. Hesitantly he inquires about it. Reluctantly he understands. But it grieves him so. A turgid gentleness grips him. He clears his throat modestly and offers forth a paragraph of synthetic wisdom:

Old Windmills: "Love, what is it? It's a safe harbor, ain't it, where ships that have been battered and tossed on life's sea can sorta be quiet and rest before they start out on a voyage again?"

He can flow out these woolly sentimentalities without effort:

"Say, what is wisdom? Wisdom's havin' sense enough to not show you got any, make folks think you're a fool."

"Truth—truth? What is it? A clear winda, and through it you can see things as they really are."

"Love? Love? What is it? It's like a well. Some folks look inta it and see a star shinin'. Other folks look in it and see just themselves reflected."

Since these jewels are written in dialect, they must have something to do with folk art.

The series was written by Ruth Aughiltree, who contributed busily to *Detective Story*. The first of the series, "Old Windmills," appeared in the February 7, 1925 issue. In this, Old Windmills foils a slick con man who puddy near gets this young farmer's money and jus' about compromises the virtue of his girl friend, too. It's ral folksey.

At this time, the magazine editor assumed that readers were enthralled by the adventures of convicts, ex-convicts, and those about to become convicts. Given this environment, it is not surprising to discover that Old Windmills was an ex-con, out of Raeburn for fifteen years.

While there, for crime unspecified, he was known as the "Tinker." He is a clever maker of gadgets and, outside those cold stone walls, supports himself by royalties from an ice-box device he has invented.

Old Windmills appeared irregularly through 1925. A final story, "Murder Rapids," was published long afterward in the August 9, 1930 issue. This deals with murder and drug smuggling at a logging camp. Since old Windmills is too fragile to handle much action, a heroic undercover narc is introduced. He is almost killed by the fiendish logger but he isn't. The evil are punished and the tale ends in a blaze of wise saws about love.

Old Windmills has little force as a character. He is a bundle of traits methodically selected to warm your girlish heart. When these are put to motion, he performs his single, simple little trick. The author gasps admiringly. The reader's reaction may be somewhat less positive.

8-

Notoriously, detective story writers strive for unique detectives. Which is to say that certain unscrupulous practitioners of this high calling often bolt together a bundle of traits from the literary erector set. Once manufactured, the unique thing may creak hesitantly about, a Ruddy or an Old Windmills. More often, it stands shedding commas and platitudes until public indifferences puts an end to the pitiful thing.

We have met a number of these golems, disguised as amateur detectives.

In spite of them, 1925 was a shining high-point in the history of mystery fiction. In 1925, T. S. Stribling introduced Dr. Henry Poggioli, S.B., M.A., Ph.D., docent, psychologist, criminologist, amateur detective. He would survive handsomely and long, while lesser figures dimmed away. If Poggioli could rise from 1925, then there is hope for us today. He is a giant. He transcends to literature.

For a magazine series character, Poggioli's career is not particularly complicated. It comprises thirty-six adventures (unless others remain undiscovered) spread over thirty-two years and perhaps seven magazines. It is a lengthy history, if not a densely documented one, and with more than usual neatness separates into three distinct groups of stories.

The first comprises five novelettes published during 1925 and 1926. During these, Poggioli is introduced, detects marvelously, and dies in a miscarriage of justice. (In 1929, these five stories were collected into a beautifully bound and decorated book titled *Clues of the Caribees*.)

During the second group, eight short stories, 1929-1934, Poggioli is resurrected and proceeds brilliantly, although his adventures are less challenging.

There follows a long pause, more than a decade. Then Ellery Queen, a Poggioli enthusiast, commissioned additional short stories. From these developed the final group—twenty-three stories, 1945 to 1957, which appeared in four different magazines.

This extended history was written by Thomas Sigismund Stribling— T.S. Stribling—who began in the pulps but whose literary reputation rested primarily on realistic novels of the South, past and present.

He is a facile, witty writer. In twenty words, he evokes a detailed landscape; in ten words, a national character. His pages flash with common sense, uncommonly applied. His language is tuned to those fragile delicacies of meaning that resonate beneath conversation.

All this illuminates stories of immediate dramatic weight, adventures in the richest sense; the mystery is really secondary. First of all these are studies of place and character.

They appeared in *Adventure*, a 25 cent, 192-page magazine printed on acceptable paper with a cloth-reinforced spine. *Adventure* published literate fiction of considerable originality, used evocative covers unmarred by violence, and addressed its readership as adults—unaccountable behavior for a pulp magazine.

Poggioli's initial adventures occur while he is on a year's sabbatical from Ohio State University. There he is a Professor of Psychology. (His title and profession will vary from story to story, so that inconsistency is the only consistency.) He spends his year traveling in the West Indies. Each adventure occurs on a different island, and each expresses a different mood.

For every story, a solid core situation exists. This never changes. But the characters' understanding of that situation constantly alters. It is this flowing evolution of understanding which gives the Poggioli novelettes their special fascination. They emphasize reality's slippery surface, a striking departure from conventional mystery fiction, which ruthlessly limits and simplifies itself. The conventional detective, confronted by a problem, proceeds like a farmer digging up a rock. But not in Stribling's work.

As a detective, Poggioli's psychological penetration is stunning. He deduces splendidly. Yet his deductions persistently capture the truth too late or are the least bit incomplete. The essential point, making the total situation comprehensible, somehow eludes him.

Irony is central to these stories. No situation is the way it appears. Obvious reality and understandable human behavior continually melt to expose aspects unsuspected until the final page. Stribling's fictions are full of ambiguities and grand strokes that never fall true.

If irony is the blood of this prose, wit is it breath.

American Tourist (just denied opportunity to see a murdered man): "It's a shame we can't go in and look at the body. I paid my three bucks a day here, and they told me it included everything."[29]

Each jet of humor reveals character:

Poggioli (in danger and considering his own behavior) The imbecility of his own approach amazed him, but in the same breath explained itself to him in the highly complimentary terms a man's own mind always explains itself.[30]

Or note this flowing little exchange:

American (to Poggioli): "I see you are a —a psychologist. That's a—er—a man who m-m—weighs the soul, isn't it? I saw a notice of it in a Sunday supplement. Picture of one coming out of a dead woman's mouth. They weigh about an ounce, don't them?"
Poggioli: "Something like that," not caring to split milligrams over so simple a matter.
American: "By George, science is a wonderful thing. No telling what we'll find out in the next ten years."[31]

Through scenes of ascending tension move characters of competence and complexity. Poggioli, himself, is an outright genius. This does not mean a superman. He is gifted but fallible. Consistently he is thrown against men whose competence is as extraordinary as his own.

In the first novelette, "The Refugees," (*Adventure*, October 10, 1925), a Curacao hotel keeper drinks poisoned wine while entertaining a deposed dictator and so dies.

Poggioli, "a smallish, dark-eyed gentleman of a certain academic appearance," is invited to observe the investigation. Soon it is learned that the dictator, Pompalone, and the hotel keeper have met in the past. The dictator, exercising the right of an August Person, had once commandeered the hotel owner's wife. It was a fringe benefit of power, long ago in Venezuela.

That offense is the motive for the crime although not the explanation. What happened was simple error, compounded by fate. To revenge himself, the hotel owner had long planned to poison the dictator. The poison was in a wine bottle, attractively coated with cobwebs and dust, proof of the wine's age. Unfortunately, the hotel owner's daughter wipes the bottle clean before serving it. Her father gets the poison, instead.

Daughters can be trying.

Before Poggioli quite works this out, the dictator escapes into the night, taking with him the daughter. Thus by an appalling irony, the ravager of the mother will ravage the daughter. The daughter has accidentally murdered her father. And the father's twenty-year plan for revenge has gone all wrong because he had disciplined his daughter to neatness.

In the face of all this, Poggioli remarks: "Sometimes it seems to me that men have a reverse theory of the gods... Suppose that men assumed that the gods were inimical or satiric toward them instead of friendly, how many of the perplexities of life that would explain."

Such grand inevitability rings through all the stories. Matters are always more tangled then they look. Nothing resolves finally. You stop at the last period, but the threads of the story continue on, losing themselves in the future.

"The Refugees," by the way, records the first of two meetings between Poggioli and Pompalone. The dictator had appeared by himself in at least one other piece of Stribling's fiction, the short novel titled "The Mating of Pompalone," *Everybody's*, February 1923.

The second Poggioli adventure, "The Governor of Cap Haitien" (November 10, 1925), is a novelette of great brilliance. On Haiti, Poggioli is drawn into an intricate political situation. A powerful voodoo group is challenging the governor's authority. The governor, an astounding genius, frankly manipulates Poggioli like a checker on a board. The finale is blood-soaked, shocking, ferocious.

How neatly Stribling works. The end is foreshadowed at the very beginning, in the second paragraph:

Mr. Poggioli...was interested perhaps too strictly in the racial psychology of the West Indian Island, and not sufficient in their politics...

Yet the whole story is about politics and political manipulation. Poggioli's academic indifference to politics is a small flaw. But the Governor exploits it vigorously.

By "Cricket" (December 10, 1925), the newspapers widely acclaim Poggioli's ability. Complex emotions fill him. Yes, he disparages fame. Yet he yearns for recognition. And now apprehension gnaws him: What if he fails? As these emotions sizzle in him, his inglorious role as the Governor's pawn blurs in his mind. He recalls that he was *instrumental* in breaking a voodoo ring. He pronounces didactically on crime investigation. He finds himself unexpectedly excellent.

This psychological foaming is so vividly drawn we assume that Poggioli is revealed complete. But, no. Most details of his inner world are not explored. Stribling's pyrotechnics do not attempt completeness. They illuminate quite a different target.

Stribling is using Poggioli to take satiric aim at mystery fiction's most beloved figure, the amateur investigator. Here now (Stribling says), this is what the brilliant amateur is really like. Here, his strengths. Here, less publicized, his follies and self-delusions.

In "Cricket," Poggioli reasons with penetration and force, and goes entirely astray. Reason leads him to precisely the wrong man who must then save Poggioli from violent bodily harm. Although Poggioli has done nothing but blunder, the adventure ends successfully. Again the newspapers cheer him. And, once again, that loud public adulation slowly ousts discomfiting reality from his memory.

"The Prints of Hantoun" (January 20, 1926) concerns the fingerprints found in the vault of a pillaged Martinque bank. Poggioli (now identified as a criminologist) tracks down the thief by an elusive clue—the melody the robber hummed. Poggioli is entirely successful. He does not realize this until it is too late to catch the thief

The fingerprints, as it happens, were forged. The method used involved stripping skin from a dead hand. A freight car would not hold all the 1920-30 pulp stories using this device. It persisted into the 1950s, always advanced as a new idea, although if the police use enough lab equipment, it doesn't work.

The final story of the first group, "Passage to Benares" (February 20, 1926), approaches perception of reality from another angle. And the deeps reel open, swallowing us whole.

In Trinidad, Poggioli's curiosity concerning the psychologic influence of architecture leads him to spend the night in a Hindu temple. The next morning, he finds himself in the fist of nightmare. A young Hindu bride has been murdered. Poggioli is inveigled into investigating. To his horror, he discovers himself the chief suspect. In a kind of formless gray numbness, he watches the evidence clamp him in. He is arrested. Jailed. To solve the crime, he must recall what he had dreamed in the temple.

He enters a trance. He becomes Krishna.

...alone in an endless, featureless space. No other thing existed because nothing had ever been created; there was only a creator. All the creatures and matter which had ever been or ever would be were wrapped up in him, Poggioli, or Buddha...
...at last after what seemed millenniums of effort, he formed the thought:
"I would rather lose my oneness with Krishna and become the vilest and poorest of creatures...than to be lost in this terrible trance of the universal."[32]

He wakes, finally understanding who killed the girl and why.

He calls the guard. Sees approaching him "the form of a man coming up the dark aisle with a lamp." The guard confirms the solution. Poggioli has correctly named the murderer and the police have already caught him. It gives Poggioli the creeps:

For what goes with this passionate, uneasy force in man when he dies? May not the dead struggle to reanimate themselves as he had done in his dream?...perhaps living things are the result of the struggles of the dead, and not the dead of the living?[33]

Why hadn't Poggioli been advised of the confession? It came too late, says the figure with the lamp; the confession was not made until a month and ten days after Poggioli had been hanged for the murder.[34]

We can only conclude that Stribling intended the series to end at this point, having disposed of his amateur investigator in a manner beyond recall.

But, as Conan Doyle discovered, death is not necessarily the end of a successful series character.

The June 1, 1929, issue of *Adventure* was advertised as the "Old-Timers' Annual All-Star Number." For this special issue, Stribling was apparently asked for another Poggioli story. Thus the second series begins. The June 1, 1929, "A Pearl at Pampatar," completely ignored the fatal adventure in Trinidad. No explanation was offered then or later. Ignore the matter and press forward audaciously. And possibly with a secret grin, for it may not entirely be coincidence that the next story, "Shadowed" (*Adventure*, October 15, 1930) strongly suggests the survival of personality after death.

"Shadowed" is high black comedy. It pummels sacred things, such as academic propriety, newspaper feature writing, intellectual smugness, and the solemnity of science. At the core of this free-for-all is an unfortunate man named Morday who is pursued by a vengeful magician.

That potent fellow conceals coded threats in Mr. Morday's pockets, poisons his cat, and permits fleeting glimpses of himself, convulsing Morday with terror. In attempting to help, Poggioli meets all manner of improbable situations a rational man is ill-equipped to understand. The adventure ends tainted with the supernatural.

Unwisely, Poggioli writes an account for a professional journal. He concludes that his adventure "strongly suggests the existence of an actual spiritual hell after death for those who die unforgiving and unforgiven." As his paper also treats as credible such matters as demoniac possession, mediumistic exteriorization, and life after death, Poggioli finds himself enmeshed in the intellectual's equivalent of the 1925 Scopes Trial in Dayton, Tennessee. Poggioli, however, is tried in Dayton, Ohio. He is dismissed from Ohio State University for committing scientific heresy. Appropriately enough, he later takes a teaching position in Tennessee.

From this point on, the stories change fundamentally.

They shorten to single intense points of narrative. Character drawing shallows. Poggioli's motives and psychological processes receive less attention, for Stribling is no longer holding his amateur investigator under the lens of irony, but is writing of an amateur detective's accomplishments— two different matters. Poggioli is presented as a quirky, bright fellow who can reason a galaxy from a grain of sand. The scene is the United States, primarily the deep South.

"The Resurrection of Chin Lee" (*Adventure*, April 15, 1932) concerns a Chinese seen dead on a Florida wharf, yet immediately found alive. Poggioli deduces in broad, dazzling style, hurling up possibilities and instantly discarding them. This habit leads one character to remark: "You are the hardest man to get to agree with anybody I ever saw. You won't even agree with yourself."

"Bullets" (*Adventure*, May 1, 1932) is also set in Florida. It concerns murder in a general store, a bullet hole in the wall, footprints in the sand, a rusty bullet, and massed small change. Poggioli reasons out the murderer within an hour. The atmosphere of a small Florida town is evoked with deadpan humor, and Poggioli succeeds although disadvantaged by being neat, citified, and speaking an academic language barely understood by the Good Old Boys.

"The Cablegram" (November 1, 1932) features a final meeting with ex-dictator Pompalone who deceives Poggioli once more. "The Pink Colonnade" (February 1, 1933) is a more routine where-did-the-body-go problem and the final story to appear in *Adventure*. A single story, "The

Private Jungle," was published in the August 1933 *Blue Book*. In 1934 (the exact date has not been confirmed), *Red Book* published "The Shadow," a galloping tour-de-force which was the final Poggioli story for eleven years.

"The Shadow" is told almost entirely in dialogue. Poggioli, now described as a psychiatrist, deduces wonderfully. His clues are a woman's smile, a photograph, and a newly furnished apartment; the deductions permit him to save an abducted woman and snare an embezzler. The cast contains only three people, one of them a walk-on. An extraordinary piece of work.

Now eleven years pass. Stribling writes novels and pieces for *The Saturday Evening Post*. Poggioli wanders unrecorded through the Southern states. And Ellery Queen methodically reprints every Poggioli adventure he can locate, then commissions Stribling to write more for *Ellery Queen's Mystery Magazine*.

The third group of stories begins in the July 1945 EQMM. These are crisp, tight little problems, like celery hearts, and are told by a first-person narrator. Presumably he is Stribling, himself, since he earns his living writing up Poggioli's cases for publication. He is a walking satire on the whole clan of Watsons.

The narrator lives with Poggioli in Tiamara, Florida, occupying a small house at 23 Acacia Street. Like most Watsons, the narrator lacks the gift of reasoning from observed detail to the concealed situation: "Poggioli's reasoning always seems simple and obvious, but it invariably makes me dizzy to follow it."

The narrator is in a constant sweat to have Poggioli involved in interesting cases which will write up strongly and sell well. The personality comes across as narrow, rather selfish, unpleasantly self-seeking. These faults are humorously and mercilessly exaggerated.

Nor is the narrator's portrait of Poggioli always sympathetic. Between the two lie certain abrasive emotions—envy, at least, and a trace of jealousy. Poggioli seems not to notice these, an unusual oversight, since he is pictured as being astonishingly sensitive to psychological minutiae, reasoning constantly from these. As the narrator remarks: "Poggioli's life is a series of abstract analyses."

Logically it would be. The formalities of the mystery story condition us to assume that the amateur detective exercises his skills only at the scene of a crime, when they suddenly flare as if a switch had been flipped. The reality, says Stribling, is different. The investigator functions constantly. The crime is merely another problem in a daily series of problems.

The first new story is "The Mystery of the Chief of Police." It features an honest, intelligent police chief whose department runs the numbers game for the public good, and had things more dire than trials and jails for criminals. Two things fascinate Poggioli: The town's traffic accident rate is 31% higher than normal; and, while the police solve all cases of theft, they are able to return only stolen cash. (Such inexplicable discrepancies irritate Poggioli, who prefers his data neatly ordered, as becomes a Professor of Psychology from Ohio State University.)

Neatly ordered does not mean conventionally interpreted. Poggioli's interpretations are highly personal, with brightly honed edges. Consider his comments on American democracy:

"Today America owes her liberty to the fact that she has been ruled in the main by crooks who have no moral standing and can be tossed out of office like so much trash... An honest brainy individual can't be handled like that. He really sees what is best for a country...[and] gathers about him a strong enough minority to force his measures. That creates a self-perpetuating dictatorship. No, I always thank God that America elects to public office numbskulls, clowns, and thieves. If we ever should put our finest brains in power, on that day we cease to be a democracy."[35]

"The Mystery of the Paper Wad" (July 1946) is a wildly complex tangle served up as an unassuming problem. The physical clue is a chewed wad of paper with an address written on it. It is a lovely little problem that ends, to Poggioli's surprise, in gunfire.

"Count Jalacki Goes Fishing" (September 1946) and "A Note to Count Jalacki" (October 1946) form a two-part story, each part complete in itself. The Count is a first-water intellect, cold as midnight on the moon, more competent than any character in the story. He is efficiently murdering his way to control of a substantial block of industrial stock. He fails only by being too intelligent and misinterpreting a blunder made by the narrator, which leads to murder and the Count's downfall. If you scorn hooded killer masterminds and their lethal hordes, you would enjoy Jalacki whose abilities are so refined that he is beyond reach of everything but chance.

The stories appearing in *Ellery Queen's Mystery Magazine* and, later, in *The Saint Mystery Magazine* are as highly wrought as Cellini goldwork. On the surface they are simple crime problems, but they are embedded in a complex of motives that requires a near-magician to sort out. The prose is stripped and polished. It glitters with witty malice. You would never believe that such a thick-headed narrator could write such prose.

In the early 1950's, three Poggioli stories appeared in the unlikely market of *Famous Detective Stories* (November 1952 and February 1953) and *Smashing Detective Stories* (March 1953). These pulp magazines, edited by Robert W. Lowndes, offered violent detective fiction whose quality suggests that it was unsaleable anywhere else.

These Poggioli stories contain such flaws as to make them unacceptable for more fastidious markets. "Death Deals Diamonds" (*Famous Detective*, November 1952) tells of diamond smuggling. Poggioli pursues his theory that newspapers publish all information needed to solve such crimes. He spends the story reading newspapers—successfully. The narrator, a hopeless ignoramus, wallows blindly. During the off-scene activities, a young woman is butchered and her stomach sliced open to retrieve a swallowed diamond. The device was garish enough to make *Famous Detective* the publisher of a story which might better have appeared in *Ellery Queen's Mystery Magazine,*

"Dead Wrong" (*Smashing Detective Stories*, March 1953) contains a number of very funny lines surrounding a situation of painful improbability. A famous artist had been killed in a traffic accident. His mutilated corpse is displayed at a local art gallery; the public is invited to view the corpse, the corpse's paintings, and to express an opinion about his death:

Examine his body; decide who, and what killed him. Was it a truck, a passenger car...was it a careless driver, a drunken driver... Dr. Henry Poggioli will judge your various analyses and the Matisse Galleries will award any paintings in the studio, as a prize.

This satirical view of advertising as a fine art is lightened by stabs of wit:

What interest could there be in a traffic death? It would be like reporting that hens of America had laid another egg.

Poggioli's mind works with customary penetration. He detects a particularly queer arrangement with the police and an ugly conspiracy spoiled by accident. But even Poggioli can't rise far above that corpse on public view in the gallery.

The final Poggioli, "The Man In the Shade" was published in the April 1957 *The Saint Mystery Magazine*. The slight story is fattened by sparkling exchanges between Poggioli and the narrator. Poggioli wins them all. The situation is that mysterious forces seek to frame the captain of the ship. These forces sneak on board $15,000 worth of marijuana. The captain is accused. Arrest impends. And arrest means that he will be unable to exercise the proxy votes he carries which will cause a sugar corporation to convert to tung-tree growing.

If you are abnormally attentive, you will need read the final explanation only three or four times to understand what it was all about. Poggioli seems to have known about the plot before the story started. It is, perhaps, an unfair advantage.

Thirty-six stories spread over thirty-two years.

Plenty of staying power in the old boy. Neither hanging nor public disgrace dimmed his fire. To this day, Ohio State University does not recognize him as a former faculty member. It is an ungraciousness surprising in an university addicted to the sentimental strains of *Carmen Ohio* whose harmonies make the strong weep.

Such neglect would interest Poggioli. Not in personal terms but as an abstract problem. Perhaps a correlative factor could be derived: Faculty obscurity as a function of newspaper articles about the football team (expressed in metric tons) times televised appearances of the OSU Marching Band.

Across the University, new expensive buildings cluster richly. Older structures have vanished. University Hall is long gone. For decades, Poggioli walked those creaking wooden floors. Down along the Olentangy River, new sweating heroes caper gravely with footballs. New excitements crowd out memories of aged professors. Other faculty members plan diet/ performance tests on white rats. Poggioli walks elsewhere.

Age has nothing to do with it. He was born in 1888, but that astringent intellect neither blunts nor ages. Elsewhere it glitters piercingly as ever, worming out the human content of the day's problems. Literature persists.

9-

Series featuring amateur investigators were rather less common in the early pulp magazines than single stories. There are even fewer single stories than you would expect. If you explore *All-Story, Cavalier,* and *People's* hoping to find swarms of clever fellows detecting after work and on the weekend, you may be dolefully cast down.

The amateurs are there. But so few, thinly scattered among swarms of adventurers and professional detectives. It is as if a field expected to produce corn had burst forth in a riot of cabbages and roses. Even in that bastion of detective and mystery fiction, *Detective Story Magazine,* few enough amateurs grace its pages, either in series or single adventure.

This astounding lacuna is, in part, because the story of adventure was so popular and consumed so much magazine space. The adventure story normally included some sort of mystery which was solved casually, amid frenzied activity, rather as a chef might pause in the preparation of a banquet to swat a fly. The mystery was not usually basic to the adventure story, merely one of its suspense elements.

The amateur detective faced other, and equally severe competition, from the highly popular crook story. In that form, the emphasis was on the criminal and his crimes, and, less frequently, on his detection and arrest. At the same time, the professional detective was vastly popular. His exploits derived from Sherlock Holmes, Nick Carter, and from highly romanticized accounts of the Pinkertons and Their Battle with Evil. The professional detective could be hired to investigate and have the crime solved while the amateur was still peering in the window, wondering how to introduce himself. And the professional detective possessed those contacts with police and official information sources which seemed reasonable in his case, and faintly improbable in the case of the amateur.

Propose a problem and some writer will invent a solution. One of the most effective solution for making the amateur detective probable was to make him a doctor. It was admirable. Doctors have quasi-official ties and are constantly consulted by all sorts of people. A doctor comes and goes and is in a splendid position to sniff out crime.

And so he did, even before the coming of Sherlock Holmes.

Chapter II—Detecting Doctors

1-

Before doctors discovered those great distractions, golf and investment planning, their amusements were less sophisticated: a glance through professional journals; a stroll through city streets or a walk to a nearby woods. Perhaps, late at night, a few notes scribbled on aspects of the daily practice.

Simple pleasures amid the gas light. Necessarily simple. Only famous medical reputations—practitioners with society figures filling their office like rare blooms—could afford more worldly joys. The more usual practitioner was not so favored. As pointed out by such authorities as Conan Doyle and R. A. Freeman, most doctors found their case load heavy, their income light. Since they lacked both time and funds, you wonder that so many doctors found the opportunity to adventure and to detect. And yet detect they did.

Fiction, that doubtless perfect mirror of reality, tells us that medical men were constantly involved in adventures of detection, adventures into mystery, and some first-class adventures with the super-natural. The bulk of this mixed feast initially appeared in English magazines and books. We may begin with "Stories from the Diary of a Doctor," a short story series published in *The Strand Magazine*, 1894, and written by L. T. Meade and Dr. Clifford Halifax.[1] (The name Halifax was used for the doctor who narrated the series.) Another group of medical adventures were published by Conan Doyle as *Round the Red Lamp* (also 1894), some having previously appeared in *The Idler*. The red lamp, Doyle pointed out, "is the usual sign of the general practitioner in England."

About ten years later, six stories were published in *Cassell's Magazine* under the series title of "From a Surgeon's Diary" (December 1904 through May 1905). These were signed by another pseudonym, Clifford Ashdown, standing for R. Austin Freeman and John J. Pitcarin.[2] The protagonist of the series, Dr. Wilkerson, serves as a substitute for doctors who must leave their practice for a time, a customary Freeman situation. As Dr. Wilkerson moves from practice to practice, he encounters all manner of skullduggery and curious events, and the stories, if obsolete in structure, are fascinating in content.

45

These series doctors were not so much amateur detectives as urban adventurers.They detect little but experience much. And they are often as startled by the resolution of the mystery as are the other cast members.

Giants now stirred. In 1907, with the publication of *The Red Thumb Mark*, John E. Thorndyke took up residence at 5A King's Bench Walk, brilliantly combining law, forensic science, and applied technology. As Thorndyke stepped on stage, an overwhelming figure even today, the detective story budded out in a fine new form—the tale of scientific detection.

The scientific detective employed the methods, equipment, and intellectual precision of science to resolve mysteries. It was his profession, and the cases marched in as gaily as if he were a consulting detective at Baker Street. The scientific detective story, however, was difficult to write because it required copious amounts of specific, accurate information knit into a plotted narrative. Although Dr. Thorndyke marched onward, apparently for eternity, the field veered from his intellectual rigor. It grew infatuated with scientific equipment, as in the Luther Trant series, and semi-scientific applications, as in the Craig Kennedy series. Equipment was not enough. Eventually the line wound down to the lowlands, with *The Scientific Detective Monthly*, and vanished as a viable literary force.[3]

Before that disconcerting end, magazine fiction had discovered that doctors could function as amateur detectives without the scientific trappings. From that illumination developed the more usual medical detective with whom this chapter is concerned.

These doctor detectives never quite lost their association with scientific detection. Laboratory retorts bubbled as merrily for Dr. Reginald Fortune in the Twenties, as for Dr. Coffee, generations later. The whiff of special information still seasoned the air. The difference was that scientific information and scientific apparatus no longer served as the central means for unraveling a mystery. They were, instead, used as supporting elements at a level with the detective's magnifying glass.

Several medical detectives from this transitional period were previously discussed in Volume 2 of the series. The most prominent early figure was Dr. Bentiron (1919-1929), a lean, rumpled, caustic psychiatrist who showed as many eccentricities as his patients. A less successful figure, Dr. Goodrich, began as a tedious scientific detective and ended as a Nick Carter clone, all within the 1921-1922 *Everybody's* magazine.

Dr. Goodrich had been preceded by another equally short, equally disastrous series published in *People's* magazine from February 1917 to about mid-year. Written by David Douglas, it presents that wonderful fellow, Doctor Reginald Blake, another footnote to Sherlock Holmes.

Blake is an exceedingly bright young man in his late twenties, a medical prodigy, and a firm believer in spiritualism. "His intuitions and his unerring instincts he claimed to be the fruit of his faith in the nearness of the spiritual to the natural world."[4]

He is positive that, in periods of intensive thought, he is advised "by our friends who have gone before..."

Blake and his brother Dick (two years younger, already married) share a wildly successful practice. To their main office uptown flock the fashionable. Down in the Tenderloin, they have a clinic for the poor. Over the door of this clinic shines a red light. This seems most unwise.

Behind the reception room is a small study. The reading table is illuminated by a human skull fixed up as a lamp, suggesting certain deficiencies in Dr. Reginald Blake's personal tastes.

But he is very young. He is a little fragile fellow about the size of a 14-year old boy. His head is large ("splendidly shaped") and he has yellow hair—which makes him a dead ringer for Professor Augustus S.F.X. Van Dusen, The Thinking Machine, although the author never mentions the resemblance.

The series is narrated by Blake's friend, Blunderstone, There is no cure for this form of humor.

Dr. Blake occupies a tiny cellar apartment in fiction's abyss. Dr. John Hudson occupies a slightly larger apartment, up where there is air and sunlight and a modest view. But then Hudson was an altogether more satisfactory detective than Blake, unless you deliberately favor mannered poseurs.

John Hudson appeared in *Blue Book* during late 1921 in a series of original and complexly plotted stories by William Almon Wolff. Hudson is a psychiatrist, psychologist, amateur detective, and is sharply drawn, his character agreeably knotted by enthusiasms, opinions, and some self interest.

His cases are narrated in first-person by his best friend, Joyce of the *Clarion*. If Hudson may be said to have a best friend. He is a very uncomfortable person. Joyce treats him gingerly, like a man attempting to kiss a porcupine.

The more human qualities of my friend John Hudson were, I am forced to admit, usually in eclipse... he had a forbidding manner and a habit of saying exactly what he thought; and he had fewer illusions about the human race than anyone else I have ever known.[5]

Elsewhere, Joyce remarks (sounding a trifle rushed, as if afraid of being overheard): "Hudson, who could be as brutal as any man I've ever known, had a sure instinct for real trouble, and an infinite tenderness for those afflicted by it."

Hudson has had his own share of troubles. He studied medicine, went to Europe to finish his training, specializing in psychiatry. He got to messing around in Vienna and pretty soon he was hanging out with that fast Freud crowd, talking s—x and whispering things that would have sent his Aged Mother to the grave, had she but known. After plumbing the deeps of Hell, presumably with those Imps of Satan, Jung and Adler, he returned to the United States.

His own profession would have nothing to do with him; his fellow doctors regarded him pretty much as a charlatan. He was, I suspect, an excellent physician, and might have been a good surgeon; his specialty, however, lay in the disorders of the mind. And he had strayed far from the regular paths of the psychiatrist, along the road pointed out by certain European pioneers like Freud.

Burton, my chief, the owner of the *Clarion*, really set Hudson on his feet after Hudson had interested him in his theory that the whole modern system of detecting crime was based upon a false foundation. Hudson's idea was that the conventional approach to the solution of a mystery, which consists in asking *how*, and devoting the principal effort to answering that question, is clumsy; the proper question, in his judgment is *why*. His contention was that once the true motive was isolated, the rest would be simple...

...no human action, however fantastic and illogical it might appear, was without a motive. He explained that the motive was often unknown by the person moved by it, and that lives were ruled, to an extent only just beginning to be understood, by the unconscious or subconscious mind[6]

Professionally equipped with a copy of *The Psychopathology of Everyday Life* (1904), Hudson breaks a few spectacular cases for the *Clarion* and, in return, Burton quietly backs the doctor and gives him an opportunity to establish his practice.

Nonetheless, as Joyce remarks, Hudson is "rather an uncomfortable companion; it was profoundly unwise, for example, to tell him about your dreams."

We have previously seen how Craig Kennedy applied certain of Dr. Freud's theories, as recorded in the *Cosmopolitan* short story, "The Dream Doctor" (August 1913). Now here is Hudson, eight years later, a student of the same teacher, investigating cases in which the psychological twist creates the story.

As in "For Better—For Worse" (*Blue Book*, August 1921), which is concerned not with a psychological twist but personality disassociation. This flares up within an action plot concerning stolen war loot, gangsters, gangster vengeance, and heartbreak. Seems that Joyce's friend, Ted Drury, loves Betty. One night Joyce sees her jazzing around a nightclub, insolent and gay, with that notorious underworld character Amory. Betty later tells Joyce that she is often taken over by another personality, a brazen baggage named Cally.

They trot off to consult with Hudson, who estimates that at least six months treatment is required. They break the news to poor old Ted. While he's recovering from the blow, Cally reappears. Off she prances to the nightclub where she announces that she is going to marry Amory right now, this very night. And *phfft* to that poor stick Betty.

She trips off with Amory. Hudson, Joyce, and Drury follow, having nothing better to do. They confront Amory in Central Park. he scoffs at their reasonable pleas and swaggers back to his car.

Just in time to be machine-gunned by a pack of gangsters. Betty/Cally is not harmed, since Amory saw the machine guns coming and hurled her from the car, just in time. He sincerely loved her, you see.

Still, he was an unrepentant criminal who had double-crossed his associates, stealing from them what they had jointly stolen.

Betty, it appears, will be cured by Hudson's advanced psychological treatment. Perhaps. This world, like ours, is rich with gray shadings.

In "The Play Doctor" (*Blue Book*, September 1921) gangsters are not used to resolve plot complications. Hudson and Joyce attend the rehearsal of a new play. The leading lady, Margaret North, seems unable to remember her lines. The play, itself, is brand new, and the author's identity, carefully concealed, is known only to his agent.

Curious about Margaret's memory lapses, Hudson gives her a word association test. Later he borrows the script, reads it, and makes certain alterations. The following day she breezes faultlessly through the revised part.

The unknown author, very irritated, watches this rehearsal. By this time, Hudson has discovered his identity, and gives a curt little exposition of the psychological meaning behind the scene that the author had originally provided.

That troublesome scene reflected an actual situation between Margaret and the author. (It is suggested that you read this rather slowly.) It was not the actual situation but the author's misinterpretation of the situation and his script showed a woman behaving as Margaret did not. Unconsciously she rebelled against the false position stated in the script and therefore forgot her lines.

(Yes, by all means, read it over again.)

Dr. John Hudson's cases are quite satisfactory examples of the amateur detecting doctor at work. Despite melodramatic action patches and considerable compression of the endings, the characters have sturdy and individual life. Hudson is drawn with shadow as well as light, and Joyce, careful, wary, and astute, reflects none of Dr. Watson's stolid simplicity.

The psychiatrist-psychologist—distinctly different professions outside of magazine fiction—enjoyed a position in the pulps that was rivaled by the criminologist. The very names roused vague, if God-like, echoes thundering in the reader's mind. How penetrating they were. How swiftly they saw into a soul. How astutely they manipulated others. What wonderful bills they submitted for payment. They were the new magicians, and the readers did them homage. And editors, as editors will, were delighted to oblige the readers' infatuation.

If the fad for psychological detection spread wildly in the United States, it flared as brightly in England, where the Golden Age of Detection Fiction was in in the process of opening like an enormous flower.

2-

Reginald Fortune is hardly a character associated with the pulps. He belongs to mainstream detective fiction and is one of those major characters who contributed to the shaping of the form. He was highly popular in England, first appearing in short stories during 1920. Thirteen collections of these stories were issued across the generations, and nine novels, the final one appearing in 1948.

This influential history was written by Henry Christopher Bailey (1878-1961), whose first book, a historical novel, was published when he was still an undergraduate at Oxford. From 1901 to 1946, he worked for the *London Daily Telegraph* in various capacities, including such romantic positions as drama critic and war correspondent.

His admirable detecting doctor, Mr. Fortune, occupies the best of all possible positions. He serves as Special Adviser to Scotland Yard on medical matters. Practically, this means that he can pick and choose those cases that he wishes to become deeply involved with. Scotland Yard calls upon him to examine an inexhaustible stream of corpses, most badly used. He performs the sacred rites of examination upon these, his knives glittering, his fingers deft, the equipment of science gleaming in the laboratory behind. For Mr. Fortune is touched by the rigor of the scientific detective, although in his case, the equipment aids without overwhelming.

At intervals in this constant flow of death, Mr. Fortune notes a unique irregularity, a fascinating discrepancy. At that point (which is not always triggered by the examination of a corpse), he ceases to be a Special Adviser (Medical) and becomes a Special Investigator (Amateur). Although amateur is hardly the word to describe a man whose successes fill twenty-two books.

When not aiding Scotland Yard, he is a doctor and surgeon in private practice. Some of the time. The rest he spends indolently, at rest, moving as little as possible, viewing nature with the open wonder of a child. He can afford to lounge, being well off and most obviously of the upper class.

In person, Reginald Fortune is middle-aged, tending to fat, with a round face, chubby-cheeked as a boy child. His hair is smooth, his palate tuned to fine wines and expensive foods. In 1923, he married the actress Joan

Amber. It was a good match, although she complained, in moments of exasperation, that it is difficult being married to a small boy.

Fortune goes to extreme lengths to maintain a facade of boredom and general listlessness. One of the conventions, back in those early years, was that the detective should trickle bonelessly about the crime scene, vacant-eyed and bored. Later it would turn out that he saw everything. Certainly more than Scotland Yard. In part, this was a mechanical inversion of Sherlock Holmes' exceptional energy; in part, a mannerism transcribed from the social oddities of the Twenties.

Whatever the source, Mr. Fortune is a triumph of boneless mannerisms. A cascade of boneless, mannered words describe his every movement: wandered, groaned, sadly, murmured, lounged, drifted, dreamily.

All suggest that Mr. Fortune is not quite with it. He works the facade for all it is worth. He moans and murmurs. He drops his "g's" in a most distressin' upper-class way.

This trifling matter aside, the Fortune cases are excellent. They flow smoothly on, intricate problems, full of quiet character insights, quick flashes of the countryside, glimpses of interiors that explain more about the characters than pages of description.

With the exception of "The Profiteers" (*Flynn's*, February 7, 1925), which has a supernatural explanation, the stories turn on personality and a few, carefully selected, clues. Fortune relies as much on intuition as reason, although he firmly states that he is interested only in facts. Give him facts. Give him concrete evidence. He believes only the evidence. He has, he loudly states, no imagination. None at all. Evidence only. Although his idea of evidence is most flexible.

As flexible as his idea of justice, which is flexible, indeed. He has no hesitation about protecting the guilty, particularly if their cause is good and the murder accidental. He is equally adept at baiting the wicked to self destruction. Privilege and lack of evidence may shield them. But that terrible Fortune mind, ruthless as a meat slicer behind his cherubic exterior, can detect the slightest crack in their protection. After which, destruction. Like so many popular heroes, Mr. Fortune rises above the limitations of the law. If, by doing so, he becomes an accessory or worse, he remains undisturbed. He serves abstract justice in his own way.

This complex and subtle man in his complex, subtle stories seems unlike any figure you would expect in a pulp paper magazine. But the pulps would try anything. Even quality. And so Mr. Fortune appeared in *Flynn's* in three groups of stories. The first of these, a six-story series, began January 24, 1925, with "The Young God" and continued, every other week, through the April 4, "The Long Barrow." A second group began with the September 18, 1926 ("The Missing Husband") and continued irregularly into early 1927.

A third series began late 1927, ended March 17, 1928, with "The Woman In the Wood."

Through these stories moves a cast of solidly realized characters: Sidney Lomas, the sharp-tongued, hard-minded Chief of the C.I.D.; Superintendent Bell, a highly competent and wary professional; and an extensive group of inspectors, officers, judges, coroners, and lawyers. They continue from story to novel and spill over into the twelve-novel Joshua Clunk series.

Each character is different and each is precisely calibrated by description, taste, and dialogue to a specific social level. Bailey's sensitivity to the exact nuance of social shading will escape most American readers and, perhaps, many English readers in these decadent times. The delicately adjusted society of the mid-1920s has taken many a cruel lick since then. Bailey's philologic precision has become a historical curio, as have his meticulously rendered paragraphs of spoken speech patterns, rhythms, and slang from the war years. Less able authors, presenting only a bare problem narrative, may be read more easily because they possess less content.

Mr. Fortune demonstrated, for all the world to see, how effectively the amateur detective, the detecting doctor, could perform when closely associated with the police. Bentiron or Hudson most usually investigate unofficially, on behalf of their patients. Thorndyke normally enters only when retained. Fortune is an official member of the investigation, although not constrained by the police organization. He has close personal friendships with the high authorities of Scotland Yard. He knows equally influential members of the political and social establishment. It gave his remarkable freedom, and other writers were quick to follow his pattern.

3-

Amid deafening self-applause, the February 7, 1925, issue of *Flynn's* announced a new short story series by Anthony Wynne. Featuring Dr. Eustace Hailey, the "Harley Street Giant," the series would be:

...a fund of pure, inductive reasoning of a type that seemed, unfortunately, to have been going out of style in detective literature. It is a cheering thing that the entrance of *Flynn's* into the field of detective literature has given rise to a new energy and a new spirit among creators of this types of story.[7]

Flynn's was then barely four months old (its first issue was dated September 20, 1924). At this early stage, the magazine bubbled with English authors and English detectives, and fiction that heaved massively onward through well-mannered crime among the wealthy. It was a peculiarly sedate beginning for one of the 1930s prime publications of slug and shoot 'em fiction. But in 1924, whenever a pulp paper magazine was able to feature a new English detective, they called out the drum and bugle corps.

In Dr. Hailey's case, such festivities might not have been entirely misdirected. He was one of the mainstream figures following Holmes and Thorndyke, about the third generation. Among the doctor detectives of the 1920s, he was a significant figure, although he has since fallen into obscurity.

A significant figure need not be one of the first rank. Dr. Hailey never quite reached the ultimate peak. He was always an almost celebrity, popular but not furiously so, sufficiently well known but not accorded spontaneous ovations. He was, however, quite popular enough to sell a novel a year (both British and American editions) for more than twenty years. Way back there in the 1920s, when the world brimmed with innocent light, Dr. Hailey stood massively on the detective novel scene.

He was "believed to be the fattest man in the medical profession... Somehow, Nature had compensated him for his great bulk by affording him the grace to wear it becomingly." He had "one of the kindest and most charming faces in the world."

And so he joins that distinguished list of famous fat men, including Mycroft Holmes, Dr. Fell, and Nero Wolfe. As a class, fat men are inclined to inactive contemplation. But not Hailey. Improbably enough, he is a man of action, forever swarming over walls, through hidden passages, up drain pipes.

It is not clear how a man of immense fatness can fly about so. It is easier to do in books than in size 68 trousers. Dr. Hailey is, by the way, excessively tall and possessed of a strength that would be exceptional in a professional strong man. Certainly the weight tells on him. He naps after dinner (Or perhaps it is the wine that lulls him away, for he has a sensitive palate.) Normally he moves at a gait best described as sluggish. "There was a slowness about the doctor's movements which suggested an ox browsing in rich pasturage."

This rather unflattering comparison also mentions that his eyes are ox-dull, listless and indifferent. But, like the eyes of Dr. Bentiron, they miss nothing.

His residence and professional chambers are at 22 Harley Street. They are presided over by the butler, Jenkins, nearly as fat as Hailey, himself. At this address, the doctor practices medicine, specializing in mental diseases, by appointment only. (Amateur detecting seriously interferes with regular office hours.) Hailey pursues his profession "in a desultory sort of fashion. He was a man of independent means, a bachelor..."

By these casual remarks, we free our hero from the chains of making a living and amusing a wife. He can devote himself utterly to crime detection, his devouring joy.

It is not that piddling crime which fills the blotter down at the police station. No, no. The Doctor's interests are restricted to the crime puzzle, the intricate winding of motive and desire common to fiction, if not reality— where the primary murder problem is who called whom a liar first.

Such rude crimes have their own appeal. But not to Doctor Hailey. He requires something to make the dull eye glint. Something complex and unobvious, requiring at least a pinch of snuff every ten minutes.

He carries a silver box of snuff and snorts that noxious medication shamelessly, in the antique way. No slovenly behind-the-lip addiction for him.

However amateur is Hailey's detection activity, Inspector Biles believes "that there was no detective at the Yard with greater powers of deduction and analysis than the doctor."

Inspector Biles is the official arm of the law for the series. Once Hailey treated him for a nervous breakdown and their friendship grew. Biles is

...a tall lean man whose eyes and mouth seemed to be very widely separated. This peculiarity...gave him a cold, rather inhuman appearance, yet he was...a good fellow, if a trifle severe in his point of view.[8]

"Severe" means that he has the tendency to fix tenaciously on the most likely suspect and the most obvious solution. This is not to suggest that Biles is completely the fool cop of fiction:

Bile's capacity as a detective was very great, perhaps supremely great...(although) he lacked...knowledge of the human mind in its nobler manifestations.[9]

Of course, his business is not generally with the nobler manifestations of the human mind. But we need not quibble.

In the United States, Dr. Hailey's adventures appeared from 1924 to 1950 in magazine serials and short stories, and in books—including a short story collection and twenty-nine novels. This mass of fiction was written by Anthony Wynne, pseudonym for Dr. Robert McNair Wilson (1882-1963). Born in Glasgow, Wilson spent a lifetime as a doctor and surgeon, and his record is studded with such gleaming titles as:

—House Surgeon, Glasgow Western Infirmary
—Editor, Oxford Medical Publications
—Consulting Physician of Ministry of Pensions

In parallel with these professional activities, he wrote forty or fifty books, including a long series of biographies, several on Napoleon and his circle, and other volumes on medical subjects. As a hobby, he also wrote mysteries. You wonder where he found the time.

The magazine appearances of Dr. Hailey, as far as they have been traced in the United States, were in *Flynn's* from 1924 to about 1927. The magazine title tended to vary, then and afterward. Beginning as *Flynn's* in 1924, it became *Flynn's Weekly* (1925-1927), *Flynn's Weekly Detective Fiction* (1927-1928), and finally *Detective Fiction Weekly* (1928-1942). After Popular Publications bought the magazine from Munsey at the end of 1941, the title was continued as *Flynn's Detective Fiction* (1943-1944) and *Detective Fiction* (1951).[10]

In its initial, 1924 form, *Flynn's* was a thick-bodied magazine with a posed, photographic cover. It offered a mixture of serials, novelettes, and short stories, and was seasoned by occasional crime articles in which the writer's imagination floated high above the fields of fact. The magazine's chief competitor, at this time, was Street & Smith's *Detective Story Magazine*, which was publishing as many crook stories as mysteries. To carve out a share of the market, Flynn's turned to such well-known English names and series as R. A. Freeman's Dr. Thorndyke, Edgar Wallace's J. G. Reeder, and H. C. Bailey's Mr. Fortune.

And, of course, Anthony Wynne's new detective, Dr. Hailey, who made his first appearance in *Flynn's* in a six-part serial, "The Sign of Evil," (November 29, 1924, through January 3, 1925).

The serial explores, in methodical detail, the can of worms exposed after the murder and mutilation of Sir William Armand. The body has vanished entirely away, but Dr. Hailey reasons out its location. When the poor fellow is discovered, they find he has been stabbed through both eyes. And on the tree at the murder scene is a charm against the evil eye.

Consternation.

Jack Derwick, fiance of Armand's daughter, Estelle, is arrested and tried for the murder. His situation, hopeless enough, is complicated by an embezzling lawyer, who has spent it all on a glittering actress. Later the lawyer confesses in court and flops over, full of poison.

Such revelations do not deter British justice. Derwick is found guilty, a decision leaving Dr. Hailey bewildered, confused, and annoyed. For all the evidence leads one way and all his instincts lead another.

As usual, instincts are correct. At the very final, last hour, Hailey goes flying down a new trail, dragging behind him a flutter of Scotland Yard men. Not only does he prove Derwick innocent, but uncovers an astounding series of previously unsuspected murders by a mass killer.

This gentleman is a frequently insane justice figure—a real true justice figure in the grand tradition. He undertakes to detect and punish when authority fails. In this instance, he is punishing cruel fathers who are guilty of frustrating their daughters' love affairs.

Considering the nature of young girls, it is hard to understand how so may fathers survived.

Thus well launched, Hailey next appeared in a series of short stories, the most sprightly and interesting of the Hailey series. The first *Flynn's* story, "The Moveable Hands" (February 7, 1925), concerns the murder of a lovely society girl, stabbed in an artist's apartment. On her throat is found A Significant Clue—a small green spot. It is the mark of a collar button.

From this evidence, Hailey penetrates an unusual masquerade. The girl was a two-faced criminal who had been stripping jewels from all the fine old houses.

But who killed her? And where are the jewels?

A lie gives Hailey the first answer; the hands of a clock reveal the second.

"The House of Death" (March 14, 1925) is an improbable adventure, very busy. The search is on for the head of England's cocaine traffic. Hailey gets too close and is attacked by a radio-controlled airplane. Undaunted, he ignites a forested hillside and destroys the hideout, the Master Fiend, the works.

"The Lonely Skipper" (March 28, 1925) is a religious fanatic who returns as his own ghost, preparing to hand grenade his own wife. At the last possible second, Dr. Hailey shoots him dead. It is surprising how many of these stories end violently. The sedate mystery abruptly turns crimson in its final pages, an action overwhelms the intellectual puzzle.

"The Death Moth" (April 25, 1925) is released by a blackmailer. His impeccable business instincts lead him to murder people whose wills are in favor of the blackmailer's victims. He dies accidentally at Hailey's hands.

"The Double Thirteen" (four-part serial, September 5 through 26, 1925) contains one of those tangles you get when mono-filament line backs up. It buzzes with Russian refugees intriguing bloodily, as Russian refugees do. Cipher messages float about, and hypnotism has its numbing way. Dr. Hailey finds himself plunged into endless trouble, and all because he has a certain susceptibility to blond girls with pink cheeks.

Through the heart of the novel, our massive hero, dressed in Falstaff costume, charges about night-time London. It is a diverting spectacle. In this rig, he shadows a young man to a drunken revel, where he, Hailey, gets clobbered with a poker alongside his head.[11]

In other conscious moments, he solves a complex cipher and clambers up a ruined castle wall in time to shoot down the sneering fiend.

All these stories blend the real world with melodrama, like failing marriages. They begin as traditional puzzles and end galloping across the hedgerows of Hell. Along the way, all sorts of wonderfully obsolete gimmicks are tossed in: death rays in "The Lost Ancestor" (October 24, 1925); secret panels and a concealed passageway to a mystic temple in "The Horseman of Death" (five-part serial, September 17 through October 15, 1925). (The serial is cram full of jealously, drug addiction, double murder, and a gaggle of infantile people struggling for a rich inheritance; all this, and it still manages to be dull.)

Other short stories are built about specific locations: a revolving stage in the October 10, 1925, "The Revolving Death"; a ski run in the October 31, 1925, "The Heel of Achilles." They are in the fine old tradition of seeing an interesting place for a murder, then thinking up a story to go with the scene.

"The Wizard's Race" (March 6, 1926) tells how The Wizard, the Derby favorite, is found trembling in his stall, victim of a horrific fright. Yet no one could possibly have entered the stall. A broken cobweb, a scrap of shawl, a lost monkey enable Dr. Hailey to spoil a marvelous horse race fix at the final second.

The action of the July 9, 1927, short story, "The Telephone Man," is as concentrated as an Army fruit bar. In true pulp style, it is a succession of crises. Within an hour, Dr. Hailey faces a revolver, hits a spy with a shoe, detects an attempt to set fire to an apartment by means of a lens concentrating sunlight, wrecks a fire engine, wrecks his car, and frustrates the theft of Naval plans.

During the grand finale, he plays a less than heroic role. He is stuck inside his wrecked automobile, puffing redly. The heroine must shoot the Head Spy, who is scampering away with the plans.

A few stories rise above this shallow trifling and touch the mainstream of the detective story. Such a story is "The Cyprian Bees" (published originally in *Hutchinson's Mystery Story Magazine*, 1924), which was anthologized by both Dorothy Sayers and Ellery Queen. It is one of Hailey's more business-like cases and assures him a modest pedestal in the hall of great detectives. But few of his adventures are so classical. Most are bright little romps, interesting but spoiled by irrelevant racing about. Still they are more beguiling than the novels.

Like Dr. Hailey, himself, the novels lumber massively along. They are dense with interesting matter that is introduced without celerity and presented in a monotone. They are the literary equivalent of valium. Their plots are brutally complex, requiring a huge cast of characters to dart feverishly about the scene of the crime, dropping clues and picking them up again. Each character conceals a secret. After the crime, usually tainted by supernatural overtones, each character dodges and evades and talks talks talks. As a result, each novel seems a thousand pages long, stuffed by endless conversations that are recorded to the ultimate subordinate clause. A gray droning suffuses the prose. Alibis are chewed and rechewed. Then, suddenly, action. A burst of movement for two pages or three. After which the narrative sags back into torpor, without color, without movement, a soporific hum.

The Hailey series falls into the classic period of the mainstream detective story, the scene being England, the detective being the brilliant amateur. The stories are complicated puzzles filled with easily remembered characters who move across stoutly English backgrounds, here and there flecked with stoutly English bloodstains.

It is the familiar 1920s detective story format, later polished by John Dickson Carr, Margery Allingham, Agatha Christie, and other eminences. But with this difference. The masters of the classic mystery concentrate on fairly realized people in clearly realized settings—or as realized as the writer's skill permits. Within these frames, murder is the great abnormality. The problem is almost always to determine who committed the crime and why. The solution depends on untangling skillfully tangled evidence that points to a single individual.

In other forms of mystery fiction—in the thriller or the mystery-adventure story—the emphasis is displaced from the problem to the struggle between opposing characters. While one or more mysteries are presented, they are not the central point of the narrative but merely the matches applied to the fuse. Concurrently there is increased emphasis on physical action, and on the use of gadgets and the tried machinery of melodrama—trap doors, secret rooms, and passages dramatically concealed.

As many variations of these forms exist as there are choruses to the *Tiger Rag*. Still, if you climb to a high enough peak, the two types are reasonably distinct. In his 1945 novel, *Enemy Unseen*, Freeman Wills Crofts makes the distinction with his usual clarity:

> . . . The detective story is the story of the elucidation of a problem. The solution is reached by inference and deduction from the given facts. In any story worthy of the name all the facts are given to enable the reader to find out the truth for himself. If he fails and continues reading, he can watch the detective succeed by the reasoning he should have employed himself.
>
> . . . the thriller is quite different. Here the object is thrills. Premise and deduction take a second place and conflict is in the forefront; the struggle of the criminal and the police, or of the evil gang and their righteous pursuers.[12]

The Dr. Hailey stories are a cross breeding of these two mystery forms. In all the Wynne serials and most of the short stories, a specific problem is to be fathomed. This is accomplished after many adventures and physical dangers. During the action, the innocent are always suspected and often arrested; Dr. Hailey is always hopelessly stumped; supernatural elements and impossible situations grin hatefully; semi-science-fictional devices buzz and hum. Unfortunately, so much time is spent manipulating situations and devices that there is no character development. The people are decals, named and pasted down. The story swirls up around them.

Although the stories are carved from wood, their central situations are fascinating. In *The Silver Scale Mystery* (1931), supernatural horror accompanies a tricky murder, and there is a killing device that couldn't quite work as it is said to do. *The Case of the Gold Coins* (1934) offers us a dead man on an unmarked beach. *The Toll House Murder* (1935) varies this idea by providing a corpse in an automobile on an unmarked snowfield. *The Red Lady* (1935) shows how a man may be stabbed to death while standing alone facing an audience. And *Death of a Golfer* (1937) demonstrates how you can be stabbed to death on a tee, although no one could possibly have done it.

To all these problems, Dr. Hailey eventually digs out the solutions. He is a stronger and more interesting character than his own series. He is not just an athletic fat man but functions, more seriously, as a modified justice figure. Although he works closely with the police, these official connections in no way impede his solitary adventures. He has the assurance that, at the end, the police will look blandly on his transgressions—which are many and violent.

No limit is placed on the number of corpses he can find. Scotland Yard never questions his right to do so. Nor does the Yard ever growl about all those men he kills. If he kills (almost always by accident), it is to preserve the English way of life. And with that justification, he moves ponderously through the series, a goblin on the side of virtue.

The 1925 world is sound and good. He does not quarrel with it. His thought is undarkened by those rude problems which occupied H. G. Wells and the Socialists. Hailey is a protector of society, willing to see it improved, but not deeply modified. If he were aware of social faults, he never said so. He sees progress. He delights in man's inventions that lead, on a rising spiral, to new, cool beauty.

Lounging in a speeding car, he reflects on the situation of man:

> . . . speed of this exquisite impulsive kind thrilled him. It was, he told himself, the reward of science, of man's infinite labor against over-whelming odds, against darkness and doubt and superstition and weakness. He reflected that only knowledge, accurate observation and meticulous application is certain. The art of the detective is the art of civilization.[13]

If only science were enough. If only civilization were less fragile. It was less than five years to economic collapse. It was less than fifteen years to The Battle of Britain.

4-

Where masters walk, disciples follow. Behind the disciples trample the converts, rejoicing that the way is marked, the forms established, the reaping easy.

After Holmes, came the towering figures of Thorndyke, Fortune, Hailey. After them, the converts. By 1925, the major variants of the detecting doctors had been developed. Already their attributes were passing from novelty to convention, from convention to conventional variations, as a jazz musician wrings ever changing choruses from a familiar melody.

The doctor detective experienced that familiar cycle of acclaim, popularity, and imitation which had elevated the scientific detective to an international fad, then exhausted it within fifteen years. Readers desired doctors pursuing crimes and the magazines obliged. What they provided was often tarnished by mediocrity. It made no difference. Where one series failed, another leaped up, and all the while, the established series ground on. From 1923 to 1926, the cases of Thorndyke, Hailey, Bentiron, Fortune, Carmichael, and Moran, and others competed in the magazines. They appeared in bursts of four to six stories, quick stutters of literary machine gun fire, first one doctor, then another, first *Argosy*, then *Detective Story*, and *Flynn's*.

Dr. Michael Carmichael appeared in *Flynn's*. It was a brief series written by John Laurence and was slipped nearly between the first and second series of Dr. Hailey adventures.

Michael Carmichael, M.D., F.R.S., Professor of Criminology at Central University, was "one of the most brilliant scientists and reasoners of his time." We expect no less.

Like the earth after creation, Dr. Carmichael was without form and void, and it may be said that darkness was on his face, since none of his physical characteristics are described. He is an expert tennis player. Not a sluggish fat man, then. And he is the Official Expert Adviser to Scotland Yard, a reasonably exalted position.

He is also a man who can glance at a crime scene and find two dozen clues the less able police have kicked into corners. These clues are rarely discussed with the reader. Not that the reader would gather much from them, for he is entirely bemused by the pace of the adventure, the peculiar characters, the lard-witted police, the glaring excellence of Dr. Carmichael as he bounds along, seeing everything and sharing nothing.

"The Mascots of Mah Jongg" (September 5, 1925) opens with the theft of 20,000 pounds stolen while being transferred from the bank to a branch. Only the manager and three cashiers knew of the transfer. Still worse, the driver is found murdered. Dr. Carmichael has been called in by Superintendent John Bradfield, Scotland Yard, no professional detectives being capable of handling such an outrage.

Dr. Carmichael notes that the dead man's blood is still fluid, proof that he has died of carbon monoxide poisoning. A clerk who rode in the transfer car is deathly ill. It is all a grave mystery. Not, however, to Dr. Carmichael, who begins detecting the moment he sees a row of Mah-jong figures on a girl's desk at the bank. One of the three cashiers has been giving her these figures. Only Carmichael sees that the letters on each figure have been arranged to spell out the Russian word for "Tomorrow." That the figures face a window. That across the street are the offices of a Russian who has been dealing with the bank . . .

And so the conspiracy is laid bare. The police sweep away that Russian and the gift-giving cashier, and the reader slumps gaping in his chair, his blood still fluid.

"Carmichael Up A Tree" (September 12, 1925) concerns the murder of Robert Helston, found shot through the head just after he had quarreled with his brother. And his brother's revolver lies by the body. The police clench their great red hands and stare significantly at the surviving Helston. But Carmichael views the body, sprawled in a meadow pool beneath a giant oak, then climbs the tree. Up among the branches, he obtains definitive clues. These are not shared with the reader or the police, but saved till the revelations at the end. Then we learn that the murdered man was a heartless womanizer and that the gamekeep had a fair daughter and you can work the rest out for yourself. The clue in the tree involved shreds of coarse tobacco dropped on a limb. That proved someone had climbed and lurked. Perhaps it was the kind of tobacco used only by gamekeepers. Hard to say.

In "Sailor's Knots" (October 10, 1925), Sir John's lovely daughter, Felicity, has vanished. Obviously the gypsies have got her. Dr. Carmichael investigates and collects some unlikely clues—a cheap blue bead necklace, a letter from a friend, a bit of knotted string, and a missing pair of walking shoes. To you this is all confusion. That's why you are not a Special Adviser to Scotland Yard. To Carmichael, it means that Felicity has eloped with her lover, the sailor.

The October 24, 1925, story, "The Sweet Tooth," achieves in every respect equally towering heights of triviality. Carmichael attends a moving picture with the enticing title of "The Scientific Detective's Second Case." A girl in the audience quarrels with her escort and he stamps out. She eats a chocolate from a box and tumbles straight over. Aided by a Dr. McPherson, also in the audience, Carmichael examines the girl, finds her dead. He also discovers that the bottom layer of chocolate are full of cocaine.

Scientific examination of the girl's body reveals that she died from an injection of muranin, a drug which destroys the red blood cells. Now further discoveries rain in—a needle mark on the girl's leg; a box of chocolates with a red, not blue, ribbon; and a dishonest chauffeur. It is the same man who quarreled with the girl. He must be guilty. The great red hands of the police clench significantly.

But he isn't. He was only blackmailing a doctor who was deep in the cocaine business, and that doctor killed the girl so that the chauffeur would be blamed. The name of that doctor is... No, not Carmichael, for heaven's sakes.

As you have likely noted, Dr. Carmichael is a doctor, a scientific detective, and a criminologist—this latter term being a buzz word of high popularity during the 1920s. Criminologist was a magnificent word which meant almost nothing and implied almost everything. To state that a character was a criminologist was to bring him on the page with the laurels already circling his head. The title was as impressive as that of psychiatrist and rather more satisfactory. For the psychiatrist could be expected to riddle off words difficult to spell and hard to explain. A criminologist need do nothing but investigate.

Writers rather favored the ambiguity of the criminologist. He appeared in stories less technically demanding than those of the scientific detective or the detecting doctor. Relatively few writers enjoyed the medical backgrounds and the easy familiarity with medical technicalities of either Conan Doyle or R. A. Freeman. Or, for that matter, Ernest M. Poate, a practicing physician who kept the pages of *Detective Story Magazine* filled from the late Teens to the mid-Thirties.

Back in 1919, Poate had created the scarecrow figure of Dr. T. Bentiron, psychiatrist and deductive genius. Bentiron is an eccentric in the grand tradition—a bearded, starvling, slouching figure, chain-smoking hand-rolled cigarettes and spilling sparks across his disreputable clothing. He affects extreme exhaustion. He sprawls listlessly in the bare white office at his clinic, snarling at the telephone, meeting no one's eyes—a rough-tongued wonder, full of sentiment under his crusty manner.[14]

For ten years, Poate supplied *Detective Story* with tales of Dr. Bentiron, intermixed with stories and serials of less formidable doctors who encountered crime and puzzled out solutions. None developed into series until the appearance of Aloysius Moran in 1926.

Dr. Moran, the Chief Medical Examiner of New York City, has performed at least 40,000 autopsies and seems afflicted in the head. He is a lion masquerading as a man. His hair is thick and tawny, his eyes yellow-brown, his voice a rumbling roaring bass. Except when one of his fits jerks the bass to a high, passionate tenor squeal. He was

...a man of sixty-odd, somewhat under middle height, but with a body as long and wide and thick as a barrel. His shoulders were abnormally wide, and perfectly square, and his huge head was set upon them without interposing any visible neck, so that it looked rather like a pumpkin set on top of a big dry-goods box. His arms are very long and thick, like a gorilla's, and his legs were short, and thick also, and much bowed out at the knees. He wore a sort of shepherd's plaid that fairly screamed, it was so loud, and seemed absurdly out of place with his ministerial-looking hat.[15]

A little trace of Professor Challenger, perhaps. But on the whole, the description methodically reverses that of Dr. Bentiron. Where Bentiron is tall and lean, Moran is short and stocky; where Bentiron is colorless and laconic, Moran is colorful and gabby.

If they differ physically, they are brothers under the crusty surface. And both have their adventures recorded by a nice, soft, tame, younger doctor: Dr. Blakely in Bentiron's case; Dr. Pelton in Moran's.

"The Tiger's Touch" (*Detective Story Magazine*, February 20, 1926) opens with four solid pages of exposition and padding. You despair of ever reaching the story. Which tells of Dr. Pelton's unsettling experiences at the mansion of reclusive millionaire, Parke Cunningham.

Cunningham is an invalid, confined to bed, tended by a male nurse, Pete Duffy. Pelton arrives at the mansion for a routine house call and discovers chaos. There sprawls Cunningham in bed, unconscious, a single shoe on his foot. By the bed lies a dead man, his neck broken. Over the corpse bends Duffy.

Since it's early in the story, you know instantly that Duffy isn't the killer. But who was? Who is the dead man? How was his neck broken? There are no apparent scratches or bruises. The problem being too intricate for the police, Pelton summons Dr. Moran, who arrives promptly, sounding like a tea-kettle at full steam:

"Well, Pelton? Well, well?" His deep, rumbling voice held a tone of strained calm; his expression was that of a man who remains patient under tremendous difficulties—and is rather proud of it. But there was a friendly twinkle deep in those yellow eyes.

"Well, well? Where's your murder. Get going; I've other things to attend to, you know. And mind, now! ...Mind now, Pelton, my son! You'd better show me something pretty; something...any other deputy examiner couldn't handle exactly as well as I—or it'll be the worse for you. You savvy?"[16]

Into the bedroom strides, Dr. Moran. He examines the dead man's neck. He examines the dark-red deposit under the fingernails of Cunningham's middle and forefinger. And he flies into a shrieking rage.

It is nothing. Don't think a thing about it. It's nothing but Dr. Moran exhibiting the mannerism of an amateur detective. His eyes bulge. The veins knot in his neck and forehead. His voice leaps a full octave to an exasperated, shrill, querulous squealing. His finger vibrates madly before Dr. Pelton's face.

In a moment the paroxysm passes.

His tawny eyes ceased to glare balefully; a pleasant smile replaced the look of fury on his leonine countenance. His falsetto shriek dropped to a low bass rumble.

"So that's how it is, you see, Pelton, my boy. Perfectly simple and obvious on the face of it. Quite so! You agree with me, don't you?"[17]

The case is simplicity, itself. Cunningham, that feeble sick helpless invalid, has killed the hefty stranger by The Tiger's Touch, a Jujutsu blow. A sudden kick (hence the shod foot), a jab to the eye; as the victim sprawls, a touch to his chin so that, in falling, he breaks his own neck. Elementary, my dear Pelton.

Since the crime must now be explained, Cunningham rouses from his death bed to explain that the dead man seduced Cunningham's sweetheart, long long ago. Then the fiend abandoned her. But now, at long last, she is revenged. Revenged.

"Murder On the Brain" (three-part serial, January 1 through 15, 1927) tells of serial death in the spooky Demarest house. Old Mrs. Demarest lies lifeless, a pillow over her face. But she was not smothered. Old Mr. Demarest stark in his bed, his dinner poisoned. But there is no poison in him. Murder? Natural death? The police can't tell. Even Dr. Moran, alternately ranting and beaming, can't tell.

Suspects clog the paragraphs. The grim old family physician. The mysterious Dr. Seaman, his coarse face sinister. The brazen young step-daughter, heiress to millions, her lips brightly painted, the ice-hearted vamp.

After sundry alarms and excursions, Dr. Moran proves that it's murder. A hat pin has been slipped into the victims' brains. Since there is no other evidence, Moran tricks the murderer into an interminable confession, four pages long, as the forces of justice listen tensely behind a curtain.

In "Satan's Wood" (three-part serial, June 14 through 28, 1930), Moran and Pelton go on vacation to Witch Wood. They have an interesting time, what with baby kidnapping, murder, a coven run amok, and celebration of the Witches' Sabbath out there in the horrible dark. The *Weird Tales* atmosphere is sustained throughout. Grotesque gigantic shapes gyrate about a flaming altar stone. The Queen of the coven speaks in the voice of a woman that Pelton knows died in prison. Both doctors are scratched by a pin tipped with curare. Pelton find himself totally paralyzed. Then, as the Black Mass howls to its climax, as the deadly Queen shrieks toward them, knife in hand, Dr. Moran...

But surely it's unethical to reveal an ending.

In 1930, the twelfth Dr. Thorndyke novel, *Mr. Pottermack's Oversight*, was published. In June of that year, the same month that "Satan's Wood" appeared, the Thorndyke short story, "The Blue Spangle," was reprinted in *Amazing Detective Tales*.

It hardly seems possible, but Thorndyke was contemporary with Dr. Moran. They do not seem to belong on the same planet. They are separated by an immense gulf of concept and taste. On one hand, the disciplined Thorndyke, master of his profession, meticulously applying the resources of science, medicine, and law to establish unassailable evidential chains. On the other, Dr. Moran, unstable and disconcerting, a bundle of mannerisms, ranting through pugnacious adventures in which excitement is paramount.

It is the difference between a portrait and a caricature.

It is not altogether Dr. Moran's fault. He is a mechanically contrived character, an inversion of Dr. Bentiron, set amid strong echoes of that earlier series. But Dr. Moran was a child of his time, and his faults are common faults of the period's pulp magazines, written in a smaller hand.

When *The Red Thumb Mark* was published in 1907, the pulps offered a general fiction mix suitable for all family members. Twenty-three years later, when "Satan's Wood" was published, the general fiction magazines lay in the twilight. Specialization had gripped the magazines. Each was now a vehicle for a specific story form—for love or war, fantasy or mystery or adventure. Each form threw off variants like sparks blown from burning log.

The style of magazine fiction had also changed. Stories shortened and accelerated, their opening clipped, their diction tightened. More action filled them, and a great deal more violence. There was more dialogue, fewer descriptions, shorter paragraphs. The silver-gray prose of 1907 had altered to scarlet and vivid green.

The detectives of the day reflected these changes, as they had reflected all the other fads of the past. They had reflected Holmes when he was fashionable. As they had reflected scientific detectives, as they reflected detecting doctors, and psychiatrists, and criminologists. When the reader yearned for action, rather than slivers of medical terminology, the doctors turned to action. The magazine fiction reacted to everything, assimilated everything, reworked revised recast everything. Tiny changes accumulated through all the weeks of two decades and, at the end, the magazine form, itself, was profoundly modified. It was evolution at its most graphic. A weak magazine, a weak series character, failed at once.

Among the survivors, consider that most interesting character type— the feminine detective.

Chapter III—The Clever Women

1-

We of the Female Department (of Scotland Yard) are dreadfully snubbed by the men, though don't tell me that women have not ten times as much intuition as the blundering and sterner sex; my firm belief is that we shouldn't have half so many undetected crimes if some of the so-called mysteries were put to the test of feminine investigation.[1]

Ida Jones swiftly slipped into the impenetrable disguise of an old flower woman. She swiftly hobbled to the corner of the thoroughfare.

Across the street she saw yawning the dark entrance to the grim old stable into which Nick Carter had stepped more than an hour before.

A grim smile touched Ida's disguised face and she lightly touched the little revolver concealed under her rags.

As she coolly hobbled closer to the stable, a tough looking man peered out...

"I don't care twopence-halfpenny whether (Loveday Brooke) is or is not a lady. I only know she is the most sensible and practical woman I have ever met. In the first place, she has the faculty—so rare among women—of carrying out orders to the very letter; in the second place, she has a clear, shrewd brain, unhampered by any hard-and-fast theories; thirdly, and most important item of all, she has so much common sense that it amounts to genius...."[2]

She was a small, slight woman whose naturally quaint appearance was accentuated by the extreme simplicity of her attire....no other personality could vie with hers in strangeness, or in the illusive quality of her ever-changing expression. She has vivacity incarnate and, to the ordinary observer, light as thistledown in fibre and in feeling. But not to all. To those who watched her long, there came moments...when the mouth so given over to laughter took on the curves of the rarest sensibility, and a woman's lofty soul shone through her odd, bewildering features.[3]

Dorcus (Dene) had had a hard and exciting week... She had just succeeded in rescuing a young lady of fortune from the toils of an unprincipled Russian adventurer, and stopping the marriage almost at the altar rails... Dorcas had only a short time previously undertaken...a delicate investigation, in which the son of one of the noblest houses of France was involved, and nipped in the bud a scandal which would have kept the Boulevards chattering for a month.[4]

The man started, and turned and saw (Dora Myrl) half a dozen yards off standing clear in the sunlight, with a mocking smile on her face...

The sunlight glinted on the barrel of a revolver, pointed straight at his head, with a steady hand.

"Up with your hands or I fire," and his hands went up over his head. The next instant (Dora's assistant) came crashing through the underwood...

"Steady!" came Dora's quiet voice; 'don't get in my line of fire. Round there to the left—that's the way. Take away his revolver. It is in his right-hand coat pocket. Now tie his hands."[5]

2-

It is not clear whether Mrs. Paschal, The Lady Detective, or the anonymous Female Detective, took priority as the first woman detective. Specialists, like little birds in their nests, disagree.

Both feminine detectives appeared a trifle over twenty years after Dupin's initial ratiocination. *The Female Detective* by Andrew Forrester Jr. was issued in 1864. Either three years before or six months afterward, depending upon which authority you embrace, the exploits of Mrs. Paschal were issued as *The Experiences of a Lady Detective* by Anonyma. As to which was first, it is a considerable mystery and not to be resolved in these pages.

At any rate, here stands the pair of them, fresh birthed in the dawn of a new fiction form. The future opens before them, an enormous room, richly clustered with lady detectives, female detectives, clever woman all, of repute and intellectual agility.

During the next fifty years, the female detective would develop in all her variety. Some became amateur detectives, that ever-popular class; they included women of special gifts and women possessing abnormally sensitive understanding of human relationships. Still other women became police detectives or private investigators. Many found that their careers led to marriage. Some discovered that marriage introduced a stimulating career in detection. A few women began as criminals, then reformed to become detectives; notable sinners have often become saints.[6]

Fifty years of feminine detectives. During the period were created most of the character types so well known today. Only one major category was omitted—that familiar contemporary heroine who mixes sexuality with violence. The times were not then ready for her exacting skills.

The times imposed other harsh limits on lady detectives. Few were permitted to experience severe personal danger or physical violence. Even fewer enjoyed an emotional life with human heat in it. To husbands and lovers, they were uniformly correct, uniformly restrained, uniformly tepid. Convention permitted them to sacrifice their lives for a man, but they could not hug him in public.

They could not hug. Nor could they chew loudly, flaunt, shout, smoke and take strong drink. Constantly they must cherish their modesty, that readily stained treasure. They were ladies and subject to a rigid code of manners. They must investigate in white kid gloves. They must never poke about those interesting stews and slums where their composure might be affronted by vulgarity. And even when their feet were wet, their stomachs empty (if ladies were permitted stomachs), their heads hot with ache, they must radiate sensitivity. The requirements were demanding.

The first female detectives give you the impression of physical plainness, energy, and solid common sense. Mrs. Paschal was a model for the form. If her cases now seem the obvious small change of crime detection, her common sense remains uncommonly sound. She was a widow of a good family, well educated. A lady, you might say, except for her profession. She was connected with the Detective Department of the London Metropolitan Police (about twenty years in advance of actual historic fact). At that time, employment with the police carried no prestige.

But only a few women worked with the police. Most were private investigators, which was hardly an improvement. For the most part, these women worked undercover, blithely ignoring the social odium of their craft. They entered where the police could not. Their identities were veiled, their purpose hidden. They entered a crime puzzle in the guise of servants or paid companions or friends of crime-racked families. Once in place, sitting quietly among the whispered confidences of other women, sensitive to the light breezes stirring the foliage of gossip, they detected swiftly and wonderfully.

Some of these lady detectives were married. Clarice Dyke (1883) was the wife of a professional detective, a good enough fellow, we may suppose, although dimmed by her luster. Dora Myrl (1900) was, at first, a private consultant, successful on her own. Later she met Paul Beck and married him, after competitive adventures. They promptly had a son who continued the family tradition by becoming a detective and appearing in his own book.[7] After the Becks, it was only a short distance to the felicities of the husband and wife detecting team.

For other women, the question of marriage, or of a private life, never seemed to come up. Ida Jones (1892) worked with the Nick Carter crowd for years, a valued member of the staff. She was tall, cool, self contained, ready with a disguise and a pistol whenever the action deepened to purple. Ida was the very essence of a lady detective, although she is unaccountably omitted from critical surveys of the field.

Loveday Brooke, also a private investigator, was the star of her agency. And of her own 1893 series in *The Ludgate Monthly*, "The Experiences of Loveday Brooke." Like most successful detectives, Loveday melted into the background, a masterpiece of anonymity. "She was not tall, she was not short, she was not dark, she was not fair; she was neither handsome nor ugly. Her features were altogether nondescript..."[8]

What was suitable in 1893 became less so a few years later. At about that time began the feminization of the lady detective. They abandoned their carefully cultivated professional plainness and edged cautiously toward cultivated feminine attributes: Curiosity, intuition, taste, social standing, beauty wondrous to behold.

Curiosity came first. It is a trait not restricted to women. Cats are curious, and squirrels, and people who read old magazines. But if we attend to the voice of convention, the trait is fully developed in spinsters—ladies of advanced age who listen and question and watch, and soak up information about their neighbors. These ladies are unofficial, unrecognized, expert amateur detectives. As Mrs. Amelia Butterworth demonstrated. She appeared in two novels by Anna Katharine Green, *The Affair Next Door* (1897) and *Lost Man's Lane* (1898). If Mrs. Butterworth's investigating technique was unpolished, her enthusiasm was intense and her character type traditional. After Mrs. Butterworth, the snoopy lady became an accredited variant of the amateur detective and so continued through eternity.

From their earliest appearance, most female detectives were dainty, were modest, were charming, were adept in society. But not necessarily all at once. By 1900 there was an obvious trend to concentrate these qualities in a single character. By 1910, the trend had gathered force and form and was as apparent as loud perfume in a small room.

In 1910, Baroness Orczy published *Lady Molly of Scotland Yard* and captured the femininized female detective in all her womanly, not to say ethereal, radiance. The world adored. At least that portion of the world adored which was contained between the covers of *Lady Molly*.

For Lady Molly is as far from Mrs. Paschal as an evening dress is from housedress. She is an exquisite jewel of a woman, done in a series of superlatives—of luminous brown eyes, graceful figure, delicate hands, immaculate clothing, the essence of wish fulfillment at its most wishful. In her vibrant and feminine way, she is given to abrupt transitions of mood, from thoughtful to somber to frivolously gay. That womanly trait might drive more phlegmatic men mad. Not, however, Mary Granard, who seems smitten with an incurable infatuation for "My dear lady" and her delicate fingers and her soulful eyes.

Mary Granard is Lady Molly's former maid, private secretary, friend, and narrator of the series. She adores Lady Molly and never lets us forget it. So does The Chief, Lady Molly's superior at Scotland Yard. In fact, the entire police force adores her; they defer to her, their voices thick with admiration, as they tug their forelocks and shuffle their huge feet.

Lady Molly is the head of the Female Department, a nebulous organization of vague responsibilities, floating dimly within the deeps of Scotland Yard. To her position of awesome responsibility, Lady Molly rose by merit. Joined the detective staff and worked swiftly upward, "analyzing and studying, exercising her powers of intuition and deduction until (she became) the greatest authority among them on criminal investigation."[9]

Whatever the Female Department does, it does with small guidance from Lady Molly. She spends little time administrating, a great deal of time bailing out Scotland Yard. Whenever the men have got a case hopelessly bogged down, she is called in and given " *carte blanche* from headquarters to do whatever she thought right in the investigation of the mysterious crime." You can hardly express confidence more concretely.

Off she trips to the scene of the crime. Mary follows close beside her, radiating adoration. Let someone else sign the timecards in the Female Department; Lady Molly is in the field, disguised to the hairline, her intuition pulsing, her voice crisp, her instructions unexpected.

In a matter of hours, the crime is penetrated. It is detection by "bold guess." Thereafter, the wicked are trapped, jam all over their mouths, and the case is dismissed with a page of explanation.

As if you could rationally explain the "extraordinary facility which she possesses of divining her fellow creatures motives and intentions."

But it is hardly necessary that Lady Molly concern herself overmuch with verifiable evidence. Her femininity excuses her from the rigor of consecutive thought. Intuition and coincidence, those powerful allies, work for her in wonderful harmony. Dr. Thorndyke must prove his case, but Lady Molly need only state her conclusions. Or so it was in that permissive time.

The Lady Molly series consists of twelve stories, loosely chronological. The final two stories are parts of a single adventure and reveal everything you wished to know about Lady Molly, her past, her problems, her future. And how her husband, falsely convicted of murder was vindicated at last.

It is hardly necessary to detail the supporting complications of this case, snared around as they are by family history, biography, character interactions, all splashed with snazzy names. Briefly, Lady Molly Robertson-Kirk, the daughter of the Earl of Flintshire, loved Captain Hubert de Mazareen. Hubert's grandfather hated Lady Molly's father, and threatened to deny the boy's inheritance if he dared marry Molly. But then the grandfather died, and his lawyer got murdered, and the new, mean will was stolen.

A British jury gave Captain Hubert de Mazareen life imprisonment for the murder.

It seems a poor enough wedding present. For the honorable Captain had just married Lady Molly in a secret ceremony. Thereafter, he went to jail and she went to work with the police. She rose brilliantly, constantly laboring to prove her husband innocent. Which she did during the twelfth story, having deftly tangled a pair of conspiring plotters in her womanly wiles.

However fragile its substance, Lady Molly's series certified at a blow that female detectives could perform brilliantly, given only femininity and intuition. It also established that woman could function in a masculine world on their own terms. That the female equivalent of Dr. Watson remained a useful literary device. And that wealth, beauty, social position, and the admiration of your fellows could somehow be endured—for these demonstrated your excellence, just as a store of gold bars illustrated your affluence.

Lady Molly was the visible summation of trends long developing in magazine fiction. Now fiction seized up the femininized female detective and rushed to publication a hundred variations on her perfection.

One variation appeared immediately in the 1912 *The Cavalier,* a thick pulp magazine strongly slanted toward women readers. On March 23 began a five-part serial titled "The Honeymoon Detectives" and the husband-wife detecting team stepped forth as popular fiction series characters.

3-

"The Honeymoon Detectives" suggests prose like syrup. It is not. It is prose as bland as unsweetened farina. Honeymoon may shine in the title, but intense love does not tumble the sentences. In this series there is no lodging for high passion, high fear, melodrama with flaming pistols and muscles knotted.

No, indeed. All is quiet here, like the voices of well-bred matrons at a society funeral. Orderly discipline rules.

The scene is 1912 Paris, changing later in the series to 1915 New York City. Through a gentle, affluent glow, a young couple moves—Richard and Grace Duvall. He is a private investigator, having offices on Union Square, New York City. So great are his gifts that, for more than six months (as the series opens), he has been attached to the personal staff of Monsieur Lefever, Perfect of Paris.

And Grace, that lovely girl, also has the questing mind. Sympathy rises quick in her. She is clever, impulsive, sensible, All things are possible, for she loves.

Together this attractive pair moves through a series of six simple mystery adventures. These were written by Frederic Arnold Kummer under the pseudonym Arnold Fredericks. Frederick Kummer (1873-1943) had a prodigious career. He married twice, had five children. Before 1900, he had been General Manager of a paving brick company, and Chief Engineer, later General Manager, of a wood preserving company. He published extensively in these technical fields prior to taking up a literary career in 1907. Immediately he began a torrent of plays, musical comedies (one each with Sigmund Romberg and Victor Herbert), motion picture films, and a grand opera. Between these efforts, he sandwiched thirty-three books: novels, histories, mysteries. He died in Baltimore, Maryland, still working.

The six "Honeymoon Detective" adventures were published between 1912 and 1917. The stories are sequential, each referring to incidents in past cases. Grace is the heroine. By all rights, she should be half the team, collecting half the dangers, half the clues, and slightly less than half the exposure. But she manages to run away with the whole thing.

It is better, for narrative unity, to have one lead character than two. The trouble with a two-part team is that, sooner or later, the wife plunges into peril and must be rescued, this being a formal convention. Since a lot of dramatic effects can be milked from her pitiful plight, the single point of view fractures here. Two action lines form. We encounter the end result often noticed in Edgar Wallace: the story has divided into such clear parts that it seems to have been written in sections and strapped together.

This structural problem occurs constantly during the "Honeymoon Detective" novels. There is his story and her story. At the end, after exhaustion has set in, it becomes Their story, a charming if inexact conclusion.

In keeping with the beliefs of 1912, Richard Duvall, the nominal lead of the series, is considered a rare genius. In the Introduction to "The Mysterious Goddess," we are told:

Duvall is unlike any other detective you have ever met in fiction; his methods are not those of *Sherlock Holmes,* or of the myriad sleuths of whom he is the prototype. They are absolutely unique.[10]

Compared to Grace, Richard is a dullard. He spends much time being made unconscious or writhing in the hands of the fiend or muttering, "I have been uncommonly slow in this case!"

He is correct. But it is not really his fault. He is a victim of a double standard, that reverse discrimination which requires the husband to be a dullard whenever his wife gets more than 3% of the action.

Customarily, Richard goes striding off along one branch of the investigation. (Call that branch "Reason.") Grace accidentally follows a separate line. (Call this line "Intuition.") Over about 300 pages, their paths gradually close and it turns out that each had a different end of the same rope.

Until the final pages, various improbabilities keep them from exchanging information. Finally they are united in a moment of high peril. At this point, Richard explains all those exceedingly strange circumstance that surround the crime. How did the child vanish in a wide open meadow? How do threatening letters materialize from the air? How did the snuff-box vanish during the Ambassador's shave when no one could possibly have approached him?

Richard tells all and is conceded to be a bright fellow and a credit to civilization. But if it weren't for Grace...

The series is too long to summarize all material. However, the continuing story of the Duvalls and a few interesting adventures may be sketched out.

Matters begin in "The Honeymoon Detectives" (*The Cavalier,* 5-part serial, March 23 through April 20, 1912; (For book publication the title was changed to *One Million Francs.*) Richard Duvall, the splendid young detective, has become assistant to the Paris Perfect of Police. While doing whatever assistants do, he meets Grace Ellicott, victim of an elaborate conspiracy. Her aunt has left her a fortune. Her step-uncle, Count d'Este, is determined to have this.

Things look dreary for poor Grace. Fortunately, she and Richard have had the good sense to fall in love immediately. And love, as it will, finds a way to foil the Count. After which, events round off in a lovely wedding and the blessings of the entire Paris Police is showered on "The Honeymoon Detectives."

Exactly one hour later, fictional time, "The Ivory Snuff-Box" begins: (*The Cavalier,* May 11, 1912, complete in that issue.) Before Richard can kiss his bride a second time, a sudden crisis. With deep regrets, Monsieur Lefever must send Richard flying to London. There, a tiny, pearl-ornamental snuff-box has been stolen from the French Ambassador.

No one will explain to Richard why the box is so intensely valuable. Only that its loss means that France may fall. Maybe so. What galls Richard is not the stuffy secrecy but that:

...in leaving his wife without even so much as a farewell word, he had given her good reason for doubting his love for her.[11]

Highly annoyed, he interviews the Ambassador, traces the snuff-box quickly, through various hands and across various corpses. By a series of deductions (just like Sherlock Holmes, that individual he does not resemble), he determines that the box is being smuggled back to France. All through these adventures, he is in a fearful sweat that Grace will never speak to him again, that she is weeping, etc. etc.

Grace has no time to weep. She is back in France, sitting in a private insane asylum, run by the silky plotter, Dr. Hartmann. Let us hasten to say that Grace is self-committed. It was Lefever's idea. Seems that Hartmann is to receive the snuff-box. (The Paris police know everything except how to get the treasure back.) Naturally Hartmann will not suspect the American lady who has asked treatment for her sleep-walking.

The first night, she slips right to the Doctor's private door and overhears him plotting. Such good luck wouldn't happen again in sixteen years.

Next, Richard learns that the man he is after is heading toward the sanitarium. Richard gets there first. By a fortunate series of events that wouldn't happen again in, uh, sixteen years, Grace happens by the door and lets Richard in.

Darling!

Darling!

Then Richard impersonates one of Hartmann's henchmen, gets the snuff-box.

But he cannot escape without Grace.

He is captured.

He has only enough time to conceal the snuff-box in the hollow crown of his silk hat.

Then Hartmann straps him to a table and tortures him for hours and hours by blazing a spotlight at his face.

Spying on this terrible scene, Grace's nerve fails. After the third torture session, she is wailing and crying for Richard to give up a the snuff-box. (Her nerve will never again fail like this.) Meanwhile, Richard has worked himself loose in the torture-room and is frantically examining the snuff-box to understand its secret.

(By an extraordinary stroke of fortune, that wouldn't happen again for many years, the hat and snuff-box have been in the torture chamber all the time. Hartmann never noticed them.)

At the last possible second, Richard solves the secret of the box: The pearls move around. There are twenty-six of them. They are keys to a complex code. Inside the box, a thin slip of paper holds the key numbers.

Enter Hartmann, cool, sneering. To me, the snuff-box geben sie hereingesein auch.

His spirit apparently shattered, Richard yields up the box and both Duvalls are released. The Paris police promptly arrest them as traitors to the French Republic.

This means that France is destroyed.

The box contained the key to the secret code in which all the secret papers were written that give vital information about French interests that is absolutely imperative the Boche shall not have information concerning although if they have the code they can decode the papers and then pouf France she is up the as you say creek hein!

Pouf! Think you, Richard, he of men all, would to the enemy yield up a single secret, *Mon Dieu!* He has left a false code in the box and walked out with the true code concealed deep in his pocket, that clever one.

All is elation.

Grace...with one cry of happiness...flung herself into her husband's arms.

She hasn't even kissed him since they were married; it has been a most peculiar sort of honeymoon.

Covered with glory, Richard and Grace now return to America. After a modest length of time, he retires from the detective business in New York, turning over operations to his assistant. They buy a run-down mansion in southern Maryland and go to work as gentlemen farmers. As usual, in such cases, Grace exacts Richard's promise that he will go no more adetecting.

But things keep coming up.

The next adventure is told in "The Changing Lights" (*The Cavalier*, 4-part serial, January 11 through February 1, 1913; for book publication, the title was changed to *The Blue Lights*.)

The son of an American millionaire is kidnapped in Paris. As usual, the French police boil helplessly. They appeal to Richard—but too late. He has just accepted the case at the request of the millionaire and is now headed to Paris by way of New Jersey. Grace believes that he has gone directly to France and hops a liner across. On the other side, she is enlisted by Monsieur Lefever as an investigator.

Lefever: "I have faith in woman's intuition. You will find this child for me, and give your husband the surprise of his life."[12]

This establishes the series' usual situation: Grace and Richard fly off to work independently, with Mr. Kummer performing the literary equivalent of the one step to keep them separated.

As usual, Grace has all the luck, aided by improbable coincidence and favorable stars. With remarkable dispatch, she wanders directly to the crooks' hide-out. The poor kidnapped child is there, shut up inside an enormous plaster statue.

After spending a day inside a closet, Grace is able to signal Richard. He arrives with a regiment of police and there is a fine rough and tumble. After quiet settles, Richard sums up the matter and explains all those circumstances Kummer used to expand a short story to a novel.

Back to the USA go the loving pair. So sweet, like a couple of newly weds.

To more problems.

First the pursuer on a transatlantic liner vanishes with $30,000 of someone else's jewels. It is told in "The Little Fortune: (*The Cavalier*, 4-part serial, August 9 through 30, 1913).

Then a bomb destroys the home of the Secretary of State in Washington. ("The Mysterious Goddess," *All-Story Cavalier*, 4-part serial, April 17 through May 8, 1915; this is the only novel of the series not to appear in book form.) A suffragette was observed near the scene of the bombing. Will women stop at nothing to obtain the vote? And she has vanished, leaving only a scrap of clothing and a 10-inch doll dressed in an American flag. What can it mean?

After this case, Grace firmly insists that Richard give up detection for good. They now have a son. The farm needs work, and so time flies among the ducks and daffodils.

But peace is not for series characters. Just in time for the next novel, Grace decides that Richard needs a little mental exertion. For no wife believes that her husband can survive without constant attention and correction. In placid times, wives grow especially tense and begin worrying about their husband's mental condition. They know only too well what he is capable of if not constantly patted back into shape, like a stray curl. A safe rule is, Get His Mind Off It.

What arrives to get Richard's mind off it is "The Film of Fear" (*All-Story Weekly*, 5-part serial, March 17 through April 14, 1917). Seems that the beautiful Ruth Morton, movie star from New York City, moving-picture capitol of the world (which it was, then), has received letters reading:

YOUR BEAUTY HAS MADE YOU RICH AND FAMOUS. WITHOUT IT YOU COULD DO NOTHING. WITHIN THIRTY DAYS IT SHALL BE DESTROYED AND YOU WILL BE HIDEOUS.

Sealed with a skull in wax

This message unsettles Ruth something wonderful.

Richard disguises himself, exactly like a real-true detective, and goes to Ruth's apartment. There he learns that threatening letters are appearing out of the air, dropped in a room where the only open window faces an empty courtyard. Near the window is a freshly painted fire escape and the paint shows *no marks at all!*

Replacing his disguise, Richard now goes to the movie set. No leads. Then a defaced photograph of Ruth is delivered. This gives her the fantabs. Richard traces the picture to the movie president's office and, once again, a dead end.

Now, at night, a fearful face floats frowning over Ruth's bed, staring down into her eyes.

She has seizures and palpitations.

To keep her from shaking free of her bones, Richard arranges that Ruth and her mother move to other rooms. Then he prepares a sly stratagem. He has a special strip of film prepared and inserted into Ruth's new film. And suddenly, at the gala prevue, there flashes upon the screen a large skull with the words:

WE KNOW THE WOMAN!

Causing a woman in the audience to rear back and faint. Since she later evades Richard's questions, he concludes that she is guilty. Her name is Marcia Ford and she works in the movie president's office.

MEANWHILE...

Grace has intercepted a threatening telephone call for Ruth. Attempting to tell Richard, she unwittingly reveals the secret lodgings of Ruth and mother. Immediately, Miss Ford appears to throw a pungent liquid into Ruth's face. Grace trails Ford to another apartment but is attacked and choked unconscious.

She wakes, all tied up, to hear Miss Ford and another woman talking. Here's what the conspiracy amounts to:

Miss Ford: "I've gotten my revenge on that baby-faced Morton girl. The stuck-up thing. I'll bet she won't act again in a hurry. What right does she have to be getting a thousand a week, when they wouldn't give me a chance at any price? I may not be as good looking as she is, but I'm a better actress. I hate her. I believe she told the director I wouldn't do—that's why I didn't get the job."[13]

As this harangue concludes, in bursts Richard. With a fierce sound a terrible figure leaps at him. Before he recognizes it as a monkey in a red silk suit, he shoots and kills it.

The secret is revealed. It was the monkey that delivered the letters. It was the monkey that did not mark the paint. It was the monkey that peered weirdly into faces. Explains a lot.

So now they have caught Marcia Ford with a dead monkey. But there's no proof she did anything. Until Richard deducts that the skull seal, used to sign the terror letters, must be concealed in her umbrella.

And so it is. She confesses. Since she is unbalanced, they agree to let her go—if she will return home to Rochester, New York, where, apparently, her affliction will not be noticed.

And so the series closes, its final story as insubstantial as a silken wisp. Ruth, by the way, got a faceful of ammonia but is not hurt at all.

Such routine excitements as "The Film of Fear" were common throughout the history of *The Cavalier* and *Argosy All-Story*. No higher virtue was required of a serial than that it temporarily amuse and seduce next week's dime from the reader. Thousands of similar stories fill the magazines. They deserve neither condemnation nor memory.

From our perspective, the stories are less important than the presentation of Grace Duvall. In turn of the century fiction, numbers of single women went adventuring—adventuring in the nice sense. After the marriage ceremony, they tamed down suddenly, content to wear sensible shoes and speak with authority to the Irish maid. Marriage was too serious to spend it, like small change, bustling about disguised, constantly menaced by ruffians smelling of cigars and wine. Marriage ended as much as it began.

In popular fiction, marriage was portrayed with rigid conservatism. If the magazines swallowed up the most trifling technological change and turned each of these into a series, they were excessively cautious about fiction depicting changes in social mores. Long after the ancient social cliches about women and marriage had begun to break up in practice, popular fiction remained glued to the images of the past.

Certain of these images remain familiar today: Since women are fragile and scented and dress oddly, they cannot be taken seriously. They are all emotion and whim, lacking orderly thought processes. They decorate themselves. It is true that they have an innate spirituality, permitting them to sense concealed truth. Don't even think about it: They just know. How cunning.

But even popular fiction, blushing red, must recognize change.

Eventually, brave editors published fiction telling of married women who did not huddle in their husbands' shadow. Not bold minxes, these, but modest, competent women, dipping into danger without soiling their purity.

Grace Duvall is an early step along this road. Marriage did not extinguish her. Her experiences dictated the story. Modesty Blaise might consider her prim, but how refreshing Grace was to the readers of 1912.

4-

If you were a mature lady in 1864, you could apply your solid common sense on a job with the local police. If you were an 1898 spinster, only slightly marred by age's scurrility, when crime touched your neighborhood, your mental dossiers were all prepared. If, in 1900, you were an attractive young woman, with or without a husband, you could become a consulting detective or a member of a larger agency. Either way, your intuition, as abrupt as electric light, revealed answers to problems armored against mere reason.

And if you continued as a private detective, as the years slipped away into the 'Teens, you became more delicately feminine, younger, more intuitive, ever more admired by your friends and applauded by your professional associates.

The girl of twenty-four, or twenty-two, or eighteen possess remarkable powers of insight. Surely you have noticed. Her blithe eye absorbs character in an instant. She has only to touch the deep life-tangles of her elders, and promptly they all unwind. Before her serene glance, the interwoven complexities of human experience grow as pellucid as melting sugar. How delightful, then, to be a detective. You need be only feminine, beautiful, young. Particularly young, a state of grace which, according to popular fiction, confers remarkable wisdom. Those with eighteen-year old daughters may be inclined to dispute the point. But those with eighteen-year old daughters are generally in a poor psychological state of repair and inclined to dispute all absolute statements.

Still it is indisputable that the young girl detectives of the mid-Teens, were usually gifted. Judith Lee, for instance. She is inimitably talented. Her mother was deaf and hardly able to speak; her father was a highly successful teacher of the deaf and dumb. Judith, herself, teaches lip-reading. So proficient has she become that she can read your lips as far away as she can see them. It's "a sort of sublimated eavesdropping," she remarks.

This useful ability tangles her in complicated lives and grisly dangers. Eternally she sees plots being spun, snares being readied. Each is a challenge to her. She is impelled to render little services. It is a hobby with her and Judith is one of our most distinguished amateur detectives, although her gift reduces the detection to a minimum. Unlike most teachers, Judith has sufficient time and funds to indulge her hobby. She doesn't seem to know fear—or much caution. For that reason, she enjoyed enough adventures to be collected as *Judith Lee, Some Pages From Her Life* (1912) and *The Adventures of Judith Lee* (1916). Four of these adventures, written by Richard Marsh, appeared in *All-Story Weekly*, during July and August 1915.

During her first American appearance, "The Clarke Case" (July 10, 1915), she is able to save the rich young idiot, Gilbert Clarke, at least twice. He dodges the drugged cigar but drinks the drugged champagne. Wakes three days later, tied tight in an abandoned house. From this Judith rescues him, for she has been able to read a secret whisper. She has also located one of the criminals who mistreated this fine young man. Does she wish pay or a fine dinner? No, no: Do not misunderstand. She was merely rendering a service. And she bows gracefully away. And the fine young man folds his fingers to fists and beats the criminal into homogenized paste.

"How strange," Judith reflects, "it must feel to be a young man."

Between the first and second stories published in *All-Story*, Judith makes herself a terrible bother to London's crooks. Says one, "She's the most dangerous thing in England... If she catches sight of your face at a distance of I don't know how many miles, and you happen to open your lips, you are done."

A murderer she has tracked down remarks, more colorfully: "You hellcat! The man who rids the earth of you will perform a service to humanity. You are everybody's enemy."

Judith narrates this scene in the second story, "The Finchley Puzzle" (July 24). She has got people so upset that they are sending her tiny bombs encased in chocolate, and vicious little vipers in bunches of roses.

The viper stimulates her interest. Off she goes on its trail. Uncovers a doctor who collects snakes and also a double murder, the weapon being a viper. After thoughtfully notifying Scotland Yard, she assumes the disguise of a house maid and enters the home of the master plotter. Gets discovered at once. He attempts to kill her with a cobra. The cobra kills him.

Inspector Ellis of Scotland Yard takes care of all the sticky details. He must have a warm feeling for Judith. She is certainly not the usual amateur detective. She does "not like to draw deductions; I prefer to deal with facts." Singular. Almost no intuition, either.

In subsequent stories, Judith observes a conversation in a Paris cafe. This leads "to astounding complications and the exposure of a gigantic plot against the world's monetary system." ("The Tango Tangle," August 7.) In "The Hand Invisible" (August 21), she saves "a woman threatened by a rare and terribly subtle poison and (saves) a man from mortal sin."

She is altogether an admirable young lady.

Her series kicked off a satisfactory row in the *All-Story Weekly* letter columns. The editor skillfully lined up Those Who Believe in Lip Reading and Those Who Will Never Believe, and so squeezed extra sales from the controversy.

The art of lip reading, once introduced to pulp fiction, remained permanently, like ink on a white coat. In the Judith Lee stories, lip reading served as a the initiating device, an unique skill that made possible her adventure. In later pulp fiction, lip reading became a device to speed up the story, to make available necessary information without the tiresome process of investigation. It was a most useful skill—and one of the reasons the narrative tempo of the 1930s single-character magazines never moved at less than *allegro vivace*.

Most amateur detectives enjoyed at least one unique skill. This served the dual purpose of fascinating the reader and simplifying the hard labor of detection.

Here, for example, is Constance Dunlap, up and doing in the scarlet morn of the scientific detective craze. Her fascinating skill is an ability to solve problems by looking at them through lenses of wonderful design, or measure them by meters and scopes, or to employ this hyperthiolating octograph to determine the calacofostic bivalence, and just in time, as you may well believe. Constance appeared soon after Craig Kennedy. If her adventures whiff lightly of his, it is because Arthur B. Reeve wrote both series. In retrospect, Constance uses fewer gadgets more mechanically than Craig. In both series, the science was half spurious then, and obsolete now, quaint as great-grandmother's boots. But it did tickle the Pre-War imagination.

Constance Dunlap's series appeared in *Pearson's Magazine*, twelve stories being published from September 1913 through August 1914. Later these were collected as *Constance Dunlap, Woman Detective* (1916).

She did not begin as a detective. When her career opened, she was busily forging checks to help her lackwit husband make good his embezzlements. He can't and doesn't. Instead he commits suicide, concealing Constance's connection with his naughty deeds. For the rest of the series, Constance struggles to put her life back together. This involves penitence, hard work, and good deeds. She helps others, inadvertently caught in criminality, as she once was, using all sorts of pseudo-scientific gadgets to help matters along. There is not much detection. In its place is a lot of hurrying around, while struggling to frustrate evil schemes. At every turn, she is pressed by Drummond, the corrupt detective from the Burr Detective Agency. It was one of the period's conventions that, if the lead character were a criminal trying to reform, the chief representative of the law would be knotted up with evil. Drummond is no good. His darkness makes Constance's rather crinkled integrity gleam like a neon tube. A pearl is so showy on black velvet.

Amateur detectives, such as Constance and Judith Lee, investigate rather haphazardly. They apply their unique talents as chance dictates, as they encounter crime. Then, as now, the amateur detective, moves through a world sloshing with crime. Crime everywhere. Crime behind the door and up the tree and out in the elderberry bush.

This incessant drizzle of crime would strain the credulity of all but readers of detective fiction; these are, however, notoriously adept at suspending their critical judgment for the duration of a story. Does the amateur detective stumble upon seven murders in seven separate issues? Why that is the way of amateur detectives. What do you suppose will happen in issue eight?

In this matter of contact with crime, the professional detective has a clear edge over the amateur. You expect a professional to spend his life immersed in investigation. Every day, a new crime. You can accept that fact; you can accept it even when the detective is young, gifted, delightful, a well-known social flower.

A Violet Strange, for instance. Even then.

"Why she uses her talents in this direction—why, with means enough to play the part natural to her as a successful debutante, she consents to occupy herself with social and other mysteries, you must ask her, not me."[14]

Thus an official in the Police Department concerning the enigma of the heroine of *The Golden Slipper and Other Problems for Violet Strange,* a 1915 collection of short stories written by Anna Katharine Green.

Violet poses as a social butterfly. She pretends a disinterest in crime and detection and must be coaxed into accepting cases—for she is a highly specialized detective, working best on cases involving other women and the higher reaches of society. Once committed to an investigation, she is subject to moral vapors. She feels that it is repugnant to play the spy on friends and associates of her class. Even for justice. Even for truth. Her position is, she feels, ambiguous, and is as disturbed by it as Nigel Strangeways would be disturbed, thirty years later.

In spite of her over-tender sensibility, Violet is an occasional professional detective. The police employ her to probe situations too delicate for them to touch. Something like that. She has accepted such emotionally wearing work to earn money. She is secretly paying for the musical education of a "dishonored and disinherited sister." It is the convention of the willing sacrifice, the valiant woman dedicating her life and talent to aiding a destitute sister. Or, for that matter, a blind or falsely convicted husband, or absent lover. Woman's life is hard.

Granted that Violet Strange was an improbable police agent and an atypical case. The pulp magazines much preferred improbable, atypical private detectives. These were less entwined in regulation than the police. And they radiated a quasi-authority that pleased the reader, however little that authority reflected reality.

During the early 1920s, a small fad developed within the Munsey pulps for series featuring feminine private detectives. Their femininity was, in fact, alarmingly accentuated, and their fictional worlds were frequently distorted by the obvious adoration of their authors.[15]

Consider this cute little girl. She is beautiful, even ethereal. Men look into her eyes and turn to sugar. And clever! Well, I say. She works in a rich gem of an office, daintily feminine, scented and lovely and exquisite. Outside the office is a big admiring world, closely resembling a chocolate marshmallow sundae. Out there, every person regards her with admiration and reverence, and all the men adore her, and all the girls think she's just the sweetest thing.

The perfect inhabitant of this perfect world is named Nan Russell. She appeared in a six-part series, "Nan Russell: Investigatrix," written by Raymond Lester and published in the 1920s *All-Story Weekly.*

Nan has reached success the hard way. As the series opens, she is a working chorus girl, now completing her fifth season on the stage. "Beneath the Make-Up" (March 13, 1920) tells us that she had learned "all the tricks of the spangled profession and not a few of the queer idiosyncrasies of the majority of her companion performers."

But she is more than an enameled beauty. She has been hired by the Paddington and Paxton Detective Agency for a special undercover assignment. It is the type of assignment that would have given Violet Strange the vapors.

Nan is to watch over Langton Whitely, a spoiled rich boy who has been hurrahing it up in Kern's society gambling hall. At this place, "under the mask of smug respectability, crooks, grafters, criminals and fools foregathered to gratify a common passion."

Boozing and gambling are meant.

Kern is a tough "des an' dose" roughneck. *He* has hired Nan to be the seductive tout at his tables. He pays her ten dollars a night for the 11:30 to 4 am shift. And he expects obedience: "You gotta can that highfalutin' manner with me. I'm boss here an' what I say goes. Get me?"

After which admonition, he sloshes out two glasses of liquor, just to show that he ain't really mad. The story doesn't mention that Nan spurns the drink, so we must assume that she threw it down without choking.

Now that we have established our heroine as a whisky drinking chorus girl touting for a gambler, we learn that, this very night, Langton Whitely has won $12,000 at the tables.

Much annoyed by this breech of etiquette, Kern drugs the boy and prepares to forge his name to a promissory note. At that same moment, Nan inserts a small pistol in his ear and calls the law. She escapes with the young simp, leaving Kern tied and livid.

Properly impressed, Whitely offers to marry her. She gently refuses. This will become a standard ending for each story.

Although Nan begins as hourly help at the P&P Detective Agency, she rapidly becomes so indispensable that she is given a separate office. This tasteful place is unprofessionally furnished with a mahogany bureau, a narcissus in a jade bowl, and books of poetry and contemporary short stories tucked into a small revolving book case.

In the office of Michael Paxton (the younger partner), Nan's portrait, done in oils, hangs ever before his desk. It is an honor that Pinkertons never accorded Dashiell Hammett.

No real description is given of Nan. She is apparently a slender young thing, innocent, appealing, whose large grey eyes drive men mad. All the men of the series love her, the author included. When Nan is on stage, his writing is fondly hysterical.

Under all the adoration, we dimly make out a sensible, energetic girl, who exudes an air of remote competence, rather like a Louis XIV computer.

By "None So Dumb" (March 27, 1920), Paxton is mad mad mad in love with her. Every sixth paragraph, he proposes, undaunted by constant refusals. As he slobbers in his rich office, she flies off to a new case on the Isle of Ooma in the St. Lawrence River.

Up there, some sneak is stealing a wealthy woman's coin collection, item by item. For a day, Nan glides about, smiling a beguiling small feminine smile. The following day, she goes to pick flowers on a near island and the mystery is solved. The reader is advised of nothing until an ending, mildly surprising, in the black of night. The story title, by the way, refers to the household god, helpless victim of a dark plot.

"The Better Way" (April 17 and the final story) concerns the outwitting of a debauched blackmailer. Not only does he hold the confession of Mrs. Wilmot's husband, but the leering brute (the blackmailer) offers our heroine a cocktail.

As you must know, the "colorful, scented little cocktail is often the most insidious weapon of the sybarite. . ." It's right up there alongside glasses of whisky.

Nan must cope with more than lusty blackmailers. Dan Kern (refer to the first story) has died, still mad. His will offers $5,000 to anyone who will bump Nan off.

She is not disturbed by a near miss at the elevator. However, the incident does touch off a final major proposal from Paxton. "Let me take care of you," he bubbles. And numb with love's folly, the author follows with a long passage about flushed cheeks and the worlds of meaning in a woman's eyes.

We seem building toward the engagement ring. But we aren't. Nan gives poor Paxton the decisive refusal. He drags heavily back to his office and slumps before her painting, languishing.

Meanwhile, dressed enchantingly, Nan has gone off for a visit to Sing Sing. There, she so impresses Two Round Dick, a tough con, that he reveals where he hid the papers he stole from the blackmailer's safe.

Things are looking up. Nan goes alone to the blackmailer's home. There he offers the insidious cocktail, only to have her dash it into his face. As she secures the papers (concealed in the davenport), Paxton comes crashing through the window in fair imitation of Batman.

Having upheld justice by shattering three or four laws, they depart, the case successfully concluded. As for Mr. Paxton's one-sided romance:

Nan (eyes glowing, her handshake energetic): "You are very much of a man, a white man, Mickey and you have made real friendship possible for us. Tell the chief not to expect me at the office to-morrow. I'm going to rest up."[16]

She rests up by packing her truck and leaving for Europe on the next boat. As explained to us, this is because she needed to throw off "a cloud of weariness that was settling upon her. During her experience a burden of knowledge had come to her of human nature; its crime and its noble deeds; its greeds, its charities."[17]

More likely, being proposed to by all the male characters has exhausted her. Away she goes to France, where they do things differently. We will never see her again.

Of clever women, however, we have only glimpsed the beginning.

5—

But Miss Russell did not long survive. Suggesting that, contrary to editorial expectations, feminine readers were not eternally fixated in adolescent day dreams. However, the concept of a highly feminine private investigator persisted, unmarred by Nan's failure. The character type reappeared in 1922, this time in a major series. This time as a polished, mature, competent, dryly ironic woman, a fascinating creation.

"I have yet to meet a man bold enough to face me down. How could I surrender myself to one whose soul was secretly afraid of mine? So here I sit. You know that the Madame I have hitched to name is just to save my face. No one would believe that a woman as beautiful as I could be still unmarried and respectable. But I am both, worse luck."[18]

That is the authentic voice of Madame Rosika Storey, celebrated psychologist and consulting detective. As usual, she speaks with hard, good sense, tempered by a dry wit that flickers like imp light around her remarks. She has long since discovered that you may boldly speak personal truths if your voice is suitably ironic.

Unmarried, Madame Storey began her series in the 1922 *Argosy All-Story Weekly* and unmarried she left *Argosy* in 1935. She appears in about thirty novelettes and short stories, one short novel, and four serialized novels. Her adventures, written by Hulbert Footner, were collected into ten books that contain all the novels and most of the shorter material. During this professional activity, her heart was touched several times. But beautiful detectives who carry series do not easily love and marry. Not if the series writer were alert. And Hulbert Footner was most alert.

Madame Storey makes her first entrance as a smiling and enigmatic figure, dressed in high fashion.

She was very tall and supremely graceful. It was impossible to think of legs in connection with her movements. She floated into the room like a shape wafted on the breeze. She was darkly beautiful in the insolent style that causes plainer women to prim up their lips.

She wore an extraordinary gown, a taupe silk brocaded with a shadowy gold figure, made in long panels that exaggerated her height and slimness, unrelieved by any trimming whatsoever....snuggled in the hollow of her arm she carried a black monkey dressed in a coat of Paddy green and a fool's cap hung with tiny gold bells.[19]

She arrives like cultural shock. Let the women prim up their lips. Their reaction acknowledges her skill at displaying exquisitely calculated glimpses of a unique professional image. She has coolly planned the effect of her appearance, her offices, her eccentricities. For she is a businesswoman, selling her intellectual skills to a society which prizes the unique and expensive. A society, also, where women are rarely granted more than secondary partnerships. Her image is of serene competence, remote and imperturbable as the floor of Heaven. "It "kept fools at arm's length," and it drew the wealthy clients in.

Their image is enhanced by various theatrical devices. These range from her jewel-box office suite to her monkey and her cigarettes.

Cigarettes: She smokes constantly and her ashtray overflows. This is suspect behavior in the 1920s. Women enjoyed such minor sins only vicariously ("Blow some my way"), since use of cigarettes implied inoperable turpitude. Not that smoking was her consuming vice. Two puffs and she was done. Her cigarette was less an artifact of Hell than a suggestion of strangeness and giddy depths.

As is her monkey, Giannino. He is a little black nuisance, trained to take off his hat and bow on command. He is customarily dressed in costumes that complement Madame Storey's clothing. Part of his life is spent sitting on her shoulder, part sitting on top of that large picture in her office. From here, he descends discreetly to steal the cigarettes smoldering away in her ashtray

Giannino affords a touch of the bizarre. He is a sort of living accent, his presence emphasizing the beauty of her office, as a painter's single touch of red focuses a composition. And her office is very beautiful. It was

more like a little gallery in a museum than a woman's office; an up-to-date museum where they realize the value of not showing too much at once. With all its richness there was a fine severity of arrangement, and every object was perfect of its kind... It was only as I came to know it that I realized the taste with which every object had been selected and arranged.[20]

Taste, Discrimination, Perception, Control: Characteristics more appropriate for a Roman senator than a feminine detective in a pulp magazine. However, Madame Storey rises above her virtues. Within that darkly shining exterior prances a joyous girl, delighted with her own effects. Not that she is overwhelmed by her own image. If the essence of French salon glows about her, it is not only for her private enjoyment, but because it is indispensable to the conduct of her business.

Behind the gracious facade, she runs a tightly controlled establishment. She employs a permanent cadre of investigators. She has direct ties in the District Attorney's office and police headquarters. She is constantly embedded in crime investigations of freshly murdered folk, under-world characters, and glitter-eyed geniuses gone bad.

For all this, she does not consider herself a detective. She is, she says, a "practical psychologist specializing in the feminine." As a psychologist, she is intensely sensitive to the small change of human interaction—the face's movement, the voice's hesitation and slur, the unconscious drives that shape dress and conduct.

She is extraordinary and unique. No other heroine in popular literature approaches her. Through the series she slips with self possession and wit, exquisite and unapproachable. She attains a stature rivaled by no other feminine investigator until the rather different flowering of Jane Marple, six years later in 1928.

By the time Madame Storey arrived, the woman investigator was solidly established in the world of detective fiction. It was a world gravely distorted by the fad for intensely feminine female detectives and by the care taken to shield these ladies from reality's sharper edges.

It was also a world purged of most adult emotions and only hinting at human complexity. This neglected area, Hulbert Footner noted and attempted to fill.

Hulbert Footner (1879-1944) was another of those Canadian-American writers who contributed so weightily to the American pulp magazines. Born in Ontario, Footner attended high school in New York City and became a journalist there in 1905. He moved to Calgary, Alberta, in 1906, to begin his professional writing in earnest. After publishing a number of short stories, he sold his first book to the *Outing Magazine* in 1911. Thereafter his work— short stories, novelettes, and serials—appeared steadily in *Munsey's, Cavalier, All-Story Cavalier, All-Story, Argosy All-Story Weekly*, and, later, *Mystery.*

His first novels dealt with adventure in Canada and the North West. These were partially based on his experiences in the North woods. He moved back to New York City about 1914 and, for a period, played parts in a road show of William Gillette's play, *Sherlock Holmes*.[21] Footner later used this experience in writing and producing his own plays. By 1916, he had also written the first of his mysteries. A few years later, he bought a 17th Century house in Lusby, Maryland (the general scene for several later novels). There he lived until his death in 1944.

The Madame Storey series started in the middle of Footner's career and continued for almost fifteen years. The series shows considerable stylistic change. It begins with a strong emphasis on character and problem, featuring those usual 1920s elements, a detective of dazzling ability scoring off police who barely get along. As the 1930s are reached, the stories shorten, becoming increasingly active and violent. The character portrayal and complexity of character interaction also simplify, and the problem mystery is converted to brisk mystery adventure. It is not necessarily a defect. But it is a measurable change.

Technically, all stories may be classified as mysteries and it is true that most propose a mystery to be solved. This is not always the most important element. Frequently the identity of the criminal is known before the mid-chapters. The balance of the story then concentrates on that intricate duel between villain and Madame Storey as she seeks to complete her case before its fragile strands are destroyed by her opponent.

The initial stories depend heavily on character interaction. The people of the story constantly respond to each other, forming opinions and reacting as dictated by their personalities. The solution of the mystery, is first of all, a matter of psychology. Personal motives are of importance. Clues, as such, are distinctly secondary.

The continuing characters, themselves, are fully developed by 1924. They do not essentially change afterward and are treated warmly in stories rich and various.

The first of the series was "Madame Storey's Way" (March 11, 1922), published in *Argosy All-Story Weekly*. It is a surprising fiction to discover in that bastion of action adventure, for the story contains about the same amount of physical movement as an essay by Emerson. "Madame Storey's Way" is presented in two distinct parts, like an apple sitting on an orange. In Part I, Bella Brickley, narrator of the series, answers a newspaper ad for a job, competes with other women for an unknown position, and is selected as Madame Storey's secretary and Watson.

In Part II, we are presented with the first mystery. Ashcomb Poor, a wealthy philanderer, is found shot dead in his home. His wife's secretary is arrested for the murder. The Assistant District Attorney permits Madame Storey to interview the girl in that glamorous office. (Like Nero Wolfe after her, Madame Storey recognizes the positional advantage in having police and suspects come to her.)

By this time, Rosika has privately visited the scene of the crime and removed certain clues overlooked by the police. After a series of interviews with major witnesses, she calls all together in her office and the guilty party is revealed.

Most of the story occurs within five long scenes. Madame Storey is always before us. The dialogue is crisp, clear, glittering with sudden wit. Sequences of sentences fly past, terse as in a dime novel. Whole pages of dialogue are used. You have the feeling of strong movement. Yet the characters, peering intently at each other, barely twitch. They act and react upon each other. It is a remarkable *tour de force*.

—Madame Storey conducts a satisfyingly high-handed interview with a room filled by job applicants and speaks candidly with Bella.

—She fences astutely with Assistant District Attorney Walter Barron, who has illusions of matrimony.

—She serves tea and cakes to the secretary accused of murder.

—She consults with the murdered man's wife.

—She allows two lovers to explain to each other their bizarre behavior.

Talk scenes. But not static. It is like watching planes of colored smoke drifting one through the other, the immediate interplay of character. Each scene fulfills a triple function: to elaborate the characterization of Madame Storey, to provide necessary facts about a main character, and to clarify another scrap of the puzzle.

The second story of the series, "Miss Deely's Diamond" (May 26, 1923) differs radically from the first. This is filled with movement. A large diamond has been stolen; the gem has an intensely romantic history which reads as if composed by Conan Doyle. Its history aside, the diamond seems to possess certain supernatural attributes. It is said that, if you look directly at it, your unrealized self will fully develop, like a photographic print in solution. Whether that development is for good or evil depends on the hidden state of your psyche.

Superstition or not, that personality alteration is the chief means Madame Storey uses to trace the diamond as it is carried among the small towns and rural houses of New York State, through a series of owners and violent episodes. Finally the diamond is traced back to New York City where it is recovered. Madame Storey does look full upon it. She remains unaffected— except that she spends every loose dollar of her fortune to purchase it, a matter of $150,000. Practical psychology applied to the feminine seems a rewarding profession.

Bella Brickley, however, positively refuses to look at the diamond. She clasps hands over eyes and turns away. But then, Bella is not all that secure in herself.

Secure or not, Bella is one of the most interesting narrators of a popular fiction series. In person, she is freckled, red-headed, and plain. These characteristics scald her, and she has rigidly schooled herself to accept her lack of beauty.

"I am so plain," she writes.

Or she remarks, flat-voiced: ". . . having no pretensions to beauty, I don't have to be jealous of other women."

Those splendid men who step into the consultation room pass by her with only cursory glances. Their indifference is recorded in icy slivers of prose.

At their first interview, Madame Storey tells her:

"...you are suffering from mal-appreciation. Those two ugly lines between your brows were born of the belief that you are too plain and uninteresting ever to hope to win a niche of your own in the world... Think that cross look away and your face will show what is rarer than beauty, character, individuality."[22]

When it suits Rosika's purposes, she is nothing if not plain spoken. It is sour medicine, administered with the knowledge that Bella will not crumble under it.

That Bella eventually rid herself of that cross look and stopped dragging her hair back from the roots may be inferred. Nature provides other compensations. She is remarkably perceptive and her tart, good sense, crisp as fresh lettuce, makes her prose a constant joy. Her opinions sting. Even plain, even red-headed, she is appealing.

She is the key to the series. All events filter through Bella. Like other Watsons, she is easily puzzled. Unlike most Watsons, she has a deadly accurate eye:

On a chauffeur: "one of those exalted creatures with the self-possession of a cabinet minister."
On an elaborate mansion: "The richness of it all was simply overpowering, but I could not conceive of anybody being at home in such a museum."
On a wealthy wife: "She looked as rare and precious as a bit of Venetian glass. This ethereal exterior covered very human feelings."
On hotel hangers-on: "They were divided mostly into two classes: philanderers and pan handlers."
On a ball: "All the family jewels in Newport were given an airing it seemed—mostly decorating the bodies of dowagers that they could do very little for."
On meeting a fancy man: "He whirled around and bowed... My hand was horribly self-conscious in the expectation that he might offer to kiss it. I wondered if it was quite clean."
On a foolish client: "...in an overstuffed baby-blue armchair sat Mrs. Julian, overstuffed herself, and enveloped in God knows how many yards of lavender chiffon."

These terse assessments glint through the stories, leaving painless cuts, as if the prose were sprinkled with delicate crystals of glass. From the beginning to the end of the series, you see through Bella's eyes. And what you see, from the homes and habits of the wealthy to the home and habits of the underworld, is rendered in clear little terse images, delicately polarized. Miss Brickley is artlessly candid in describing her reactions and she responds to each person and event. But be cautioned. Although you read her remarks with pleasure, remember that they are part of her characterization. Behind them lurks the amiable intelligence of Hulbert Footner, and the story told by Miss Brickley has been filtered through her and colored by her understanding.

Those things that you most devoutly desire have a way of arriving spangled with things you don't ever remember wishing for. Bella wants an interesting job working for a supremely beautiful woman. That she gets. She also gets a continuous stream of adventures dangerous enough to gray that red hair.

Bella does not like adventures. Field work leaves her edgy. She does not think clearly under stress. At the moment of action, she functions in a numbed calm. But before that moment, she has the shakes and, afterward, the hysterics.

Madame Storey, on the other hand, relishes action and searches eagerly for excuses to leave her 1850 French Drawing room suite to travel underworld ways, hip-swinging and shrill. Since women jaunt about most invisibly by twos, she carries Bella along—and into astonishing situations.

Madame Storey's predilection for adventure explains why Bella finds herself sitting in a hardcase speakeasy with her hair clipped short ("The Under Dogs"). Or fleeing through a deserted mansion with gunmen straining after them ("The Butler's Ball"). Or looking down Mafia pistols ("Taken for a Ride"). Or tied and gagged in an automobile being driven over a cliff ("The Richest Widow").

Bella: I was trembling like an aspen leaf... By a little catch of laughter in (Madame Storey's) breath, I knew that she was enjoying every moment. Well, that is her way.

At first, the adventures are less harrowing. "The Scrap of Lace" (August 4, 1923) and "In the Round Room" (March 1, 1924) are problem mysteries, not quite as formal as those of Agatha Christie. In both cases, the investigation is conducted at vast mansions, amid the odor of money and the flat stink of relationships gone wrong. "Lace" requires a murder method somewhat too elaborate to be practical and ends with Madame Storey revealing the killer before a group. "Round Room" contains a murdered woman, a secret door, and a lot of confusion about who did what. The murderer (who turns out to be insane) has a marvelous alibi. Madame Storey must lead the county prosecutor around by the ear, since, being congenitally defective, he can do nothing but bluster and blow.

The prosecutor is an early example of the species *officialus boobus* that swarms densely through the series. Most of these are political law enforcement hacks, otherwise depicted as mincing popinjays distended with conceit. They are blood relations to the officials who swaggered brainlessly through those low-budget mystery films of the late 1930s.

Not all law enforcement people are fools. Inspector Rumsey, New York Police, a solid, sharp professional, is Madame Storey's main link to police headquarters. The Crider brothers, both investigators employed by the Madame, never miss a lick and are competent clever men. Of the various sheriffs, coroners, police commissioners, and district attorneys, the less said the better. A more appalling aggregation of blow-hards has rarely been assembled.

Footner uses these dolts to make Madame Storey's life less easy. However, their presence also illustrates his unfortunate tendency to cast characters as representatives types—unfortunate because he was a singularly persuasive writer who could almost make one of these hollow figures come alive. Almost.

Besides the dreary catalog of law enforcement types, other standard characters pepper the series. These include the villain, whose intelligence is dangerously quick and, often as not, has an uncontrolled yen for Madame Storey.

And there are the low-echelon men and women of the underworld. Most are practicing criminals, crude, violent, and fundamentally decent. If the truth must be told, Rosika has a sneaking fondness for them. Since they are impossible socially, she can like them and, as in "The Black Ace," find her heart twinged by them.

Other standard characters include tainted society flowers; the arch-wealthy, decayed by possessions; and clever older men and women, like parental echoes, who support Rosika, no matter what the occasion.

"The Viper" (April 12, 1924) is one of the high points of the series. The story has great force. On the surface, it seems the investigation of a series of crimes committed by a thieving secretary who has murdered her boss. Under the surface, it is a leisurely exploration of a murderess's strange character. Footner's handling of interpersonal nuances is graceful and exact. The story's action is split between New York and Paris. Bella has the joy of going to France and is decidedly deflated when she is sent home, in a couple of days, to run the American end of the investigation.

But she gets over it. And, in "The Steerers" (August 2, 1924), both women are off to England on a cruise ship. En route, they meet a merry pair who spend all their days traveling the liners, making friends with susceptible marks and leading them to another set of friends, the fleecers of these sheep. This comfortable arrangement is shattered when they befriend Madame Storey.

"The Under Dogs," the first novel of the series, was published as a six-part serial in *Argosy*, January 3 through February 7, 1925. Much of the adventure occurs in an underworld only slightly modified from the Jimmie Dale model described by Frank Packard back in 1914. On the whole, the criminals are more believable than those appearing in Packard's work, and they are at least as vicious. The serial also considers the links between crime in the social deeps with crime in the city's high places.

Matters begin with violence. A girl, promising sensational revelations, is on her way to Madame Storey's office. Before she arrives there, she is clubbed down and kidnapped. Attempting to search out the girl, Rosika and Bella (who is horrified by the idea) move into the underworld. The cool, high-fashion Rosika suddenly shows a genius for disguise and an ability to shine in low company, down among the East-side gin mills.

Her investigation gradually narrows to a house on Varick Street, populated by very hard cases, male and female. There are dead men under the basement floor, a chained prisoner in the attic, and a reluctant gang of crooks being blackmailed to work the will of a master mind, dimly seen.

Masterminds, rather. The pair of them get busted in a melodramatic finish and off they go to Sing Sing. The Big Boss, an attorney, is understandably irritated at being foiled by that "tall, skinny woman." While glooming in his cell, he works up a magnificent plan.

This drops upon our heroine in "Madame Storey in the Toils" (August 29, 1925). The frame-up is thorough. Rosika is accused of poisoning a woman with frosted cakes. The motive: to marry the woman's husband. Unfortunately for the plotters, Rosika slips gracefully from poor old Inspector Rumsey's clutch; she conducts her investigation, and routine office business, while a fugitive, and nails to the cross the entire batch who attempted to do her in.

Then back to England, on business, in "The Pot of Pansies" (April 30, 1927). This lightly science-fictional episode turns upon the development of a colorless, odorless, fast-acting gas by a scientist who wishes to end war. Instead he gets murdered for the secret. It does the killer no good. Madame Storey is on him before he can draw an easy breath. Naturally he is upset:

"That woman is a she devil!" he screamed. "She's not human. She kept at me and at me till I near went mad. She ought to have been in the Spanish Inquisition, she should! What's she doing over here anyway, plying her trade? Aren't there enough murders in America?"[23]

That odorless, colorless, quick-acting gas is one of the more durable devices of pulp fiction. Those with long memories will recall that the famous costumed mastermind, Black Star, used a similar gas to steal and rob through the pages of *Detective Story Magazine*, way back 1916; that jolly fellow, the Crimson Clown (also featured in *Detective Story*) had been using a similar gas since 1926; and Doc Savage, the bronzed scientific adventurer, would use an identical gas throughout his career, 1933-1949. Whether 1916 or 1949, this gas was a science-fictional device used to accomplish the impossible and speed the action. By the time Footner incorporated it into "The Pot of Pansies," the marvelous gas was a fictional convention, accepted if not believed, like egg-carrying rabbits and Yuletide spirits. Footner uses the invention as a reason for the action, not as a device to advance the action. In so doing, he enhances the probability of his story, although not by very much.

"The Black Ace," a six-part serial, January 12 through February 16, 1929, was later published as a book titled, *The Doctor Who Held Hands*.

Of this novel, the *New York Times* remarked:

...not only is the plot utterly preposterous but it is so clumsily constructed that the saw marks are apparent to the most inexperienced eye.[24]

More moderately, "The Black Ace"/ *The Doctor Who Held Hands* is not the very best of the series. The plot (which is apparently what stuck in the *Times'* craw) is one of those revenge things, requiring that the villain be insane.

There is, you see, this brilliant psychologist, Dr. Jacmer Touchon—Madame Storey's teacher and rejected suitor—who has simmered for years over the flame of her growing professional reputation. Touchon has made a nice thing out of blackmailing patients. Now, hankering for ever greater achievements, he plans to bring Rosika to her knees. To crush her pride. To dominate her soul. To whomp up on her spirit. After she is well tamed, he'll marry her and show her off.

To such plans—had she been consulted—Madame Storey would have responded by puffing out a cloud of smoke and remarking, in her driest tone: "Ah, Jacmer is a most incorrigible man."

Having thoroughly misjudged his prey, Dr. Touchon puts his dream into operation. First, he sends a minion to hire Rosika to investigate the great Dr. Touchon, himself. Then he proceeds to discredit her by organizing a gun attack in her office. Two men are killed in this action.

Newspaper sensation.

Touchon's manipulations permit an extraordinarily bone-headed detective to solve the murders. Rosika doesn't believe the solution for a second. But she pretends to accept it, and, while being courted by Touchon in the evening, is slipping out late at night to scour the underworld, hauling poor, quaking Bella along.

They are hunting for a young man with a scarred face, the third member of Touchon's gang.

Scarface doesn't know this. His boss (Touchon) has kept well concealed, known only as a mysterious voice. Scarface would, in fact, like to kill the man (Touchon again) who shot down his best friend in Madame Storey's office.

Once more disguised as flowers of the night, Rosika and Bella go forth into a gay round of night clubs and gambling joints. Eventually they locate Scarface and, after harsh adventures, maneuver him into Touchon's presence. Thereupon all the cookies fall off the tray and Touchon, having been choked black, goes up the river to a quieter life.

The story really isn't full of sawmarks. But parts need a lot of lubrication to get down.

"The Butler's Ball" (June 28, 1930) is one of those Agatha Christie things where one person, of a group sitting at a table, shot the victim. It doesn't help that all are in costume. Madame Storey and Bella are on the scene hunting for jewel thieves.

The women find the jewel thieves, indeed they do. They end up fleeing for their lives through a deserted mansion, the gang all pistoled up and hot after them. They escape with the help of the fire department, and Bella has a fine case of hysterics when it is all over.

She really does not enjoy action.

But action is increasingly her lot, for the series has entered the 1930s.

In "Easy To Kill" (six-parts, August 8 through September 12, 1931), Rosika is hired to deal with a Newport extortionist. He turns out to be a wealthy young genius. Gloves come off immediately. At various times, the women are 1) in jail; 2) tied hand and foot, waiting to be wrapped in sheet lead and dropped into the Atlantic; 3) locked into an upper story of an old wooden hotel set afire by fiends.

They escape and take refuge in the rat-hole of a room rented by two small-time street crooks. In a charming scene, Rosika and Bella, bedraggled in their ruined evening dresses, sit on an unmade bed and gobble ham and scrambled egg sandwiches, three inches thick. The stick-up boys eye them tentatively. But Rosika is too skillful a hand to let sex surface. How adroitly she converts their benefactors' half-awakened lust to friendship. How swiftly she dominates their minds and enrolls then in her cause.

Next day, helped by a rich old recluse, she sets a trap for the villain. And through the swirling mist he comes. Is trapped. But the local police fumble his capture. He flees to his yacht, on which he suicides, aided by half a ton of TNT.

So much violence, so many escapes, so many guns and gunmen, clear indication that the 1930s are well upon us.

No time, now, for formal mystery problems and psychological studies. The stories are bright red, rushing furiously forward amid a high metallic whine. Descriptions are pared to the quick. Bella's annoyances more rarely reach public print. Calculated suspense rises shimmering from the super-heated narrative. Again physical danger threatens, and still again. Once more they are captured, tied up, helpless in the power of...

Now it is mid-1933 and Madame Storey makes a major sortie from *Argosy*. She bobs up in *Mystery* in a lightly inconsistent series of short stories.

Mystery was a fancy, over-sized, slick paper publication which had begun life as *The Illustrated Detective Magazine.* It was distributed through Woolworth's 5 and 10 cent Stores and was aimed, with great precision at a feminine audience. The magazine was lavishly bedecked with photographs of consummately 1930ish models posing rigidly in reenactment of story scenes. Madame Storey is not successfully impersonated.

The series' premise is that Rosika has been retained by the Washburn Legislative Committee to investigate the Police Department, city not really stated. In performing this ambitious assignment, she spends much of her time handling problems that the Chief of Detectives, Inspector Barron, has fallen flat on. As is the case with so many other males in the series, Barron takes one long look at Rosika and his voice drops two octaves. While he regards her presence as a professional insult, yet he is smitten. He babbles. He is all hamhanded gallantry, dismal to see.

In "The Sealed House" (July 1933), Rosika pries open the so-called suicide of a "bad woman." Within the woman's home, sealed by court order until legal machinery moves, there are traces of repeated break-ins and searches. Madame Storey deftly locates a blackmailing document and the whole case suddenly pops apart.

It pops in a matter of paragraphs, with a speed characteristic of the series. The stories are compressed as dried fruit bars, and the endings seem breathlessly rushed.

"Which Man's Eyes?" (December 1933) begins with Rosika and Bella being warned to drop their investigations of the local drug ring. When they don't, four gunmen invade the Storey premises, one night, and machine gun Rosika's bedroom. But she wasn't in the bed and nabs the scoundrel responsible, right in the heart of police Headquarters.

Through all this action, Inspector Barron is making over-ripe sounds at Rosika. She finds him intensely repulsive. Somewhat later, she finds that he is connected with the drug ring and that his soul is blotched black.

At this point in the series, the drug ring decides to discredit our heroine, since she has made such a nuisance of herself. In "The Last Adventure with Madame Storey" (May 1934), she is framed for murder—how these themes do repeat—and for narcotics distribution from her own home. Detained by the police, she demands an immediate preliminary hearing and whisks her usual dazzle from the air. Suddenly the evil are confounded. Suddenly all is wonderful. Barron is bounced from the force and the series, with a final breathless lurch, stops as abruptly as an airplane flying into a cliff face.

Slightly before the *Mystery* series ended, Rosika returned to *Argosy*, her one true love. The women go off to summer in France ("Wolves of Monte Carlo," August 5, 1933). Immediately they are abducted, tied up, nearly thrown from a cliff. And that's only a warning to keep their noses out of other people's business. They don't, with success.

Another month, another abduction. In "The Kidnapping of Madame Store" (December 2, 1933), gangsters carry her off. And also Bella. As you may have anticipated, the crooks are suavely outwitted.

The final Madame Storey novel appeared in 1934. "The Hated Man" (six-part serial, July 14 through August 18, 1934) was later published under the title, *Dangerous Cargo*. In this, Madame Storey is retained by a rich pain in the neck. He wants her to keep him from being killed during an extended cruise. She does not quite succeed. The murderer is caught after an extended game of thrust and counter-thrust. During these proceedings, Bella finds a body in the swimming pool; you can imagine what that did to her composure.

"The Cold Trail" (January 12, 1935) tells how a tricky lawyer decisively fools Rosika. His baleful touch leads her case wildly astray and only desperate measures retrieve the situation. It all comes back on the rascal, at last. But it is her worst setback of the series.

To cool her humiliation, she takes Bella on a cruise to France. ("The Richest Widow," August 31, 1935). Promptly up jumps a murderous young man who has found a swell way to vanish himself and wife from a ship in mid-ocean. Rosika finds him out. Whereupon he sets blood-thirsty French killers to catch both women and murder them and chase after them in motorboats. They escape back to the ship, if narrowly. And justice is, after all, done.

There the series ends and there we leave them after stressful triumph. There, the darkly splendid Rosika, her mind shining, and Bella, plain, red-headed, aware. Around them lift the 1930s, a black and scarlet haze, no proper place for a practical psychologist specializing in the feminine. For this time, a coarser meat was carved.

Madame Storey had, however, made the transition to 1930s fiction more gracefully than you might imagine. She retained her intelligent audacity. And if her stories had thinned, they had remained literate and witty, generating pleasing excitement.

But Rosika's real place was in the 1920s, a less convulsed time. There, in a setting of her own choice, she performed her gilded miracles; there, she slipped casually between the social classes, welcomed by Newport wealth, accepted by the underworld. It is the same social flexibility shared by all great detectives, from Nick Carter to Lew Archer.

Perhaps Rosika Storey was flexible, perhaps ambivalent, in her role as a goddess of detection. Hers seemed the world of wealth and taste, where the golden apples glimmered, quietly rich and discreetly arranged. But she required more. Some turmoil in the blood teased her. Taste, discrimination, perception, control, those laudable virtues, lacked a nourishment vital to her mind. That nourishment she sought in the underworld, plunging into it like an otter into a pool, swimming down among the dreadful shapes there, refreshed by their rude simplicities.

She is more complex than Footner bothered to tell us. But writers do not tell everything. Even if they know.

So we end as we began, not quite understanding her. Which is entirely proper.

No woman of any sense reveals every last thing about herself. There must always remain a final question.

6-

From the deeps, we return to the shallows.

From the figure of Madame Storey, drawn in silver and shadow, we turn to a simpler figure—another brilliant female detective, also capable, also admired, also deriving from Sherlock Holmes. But, for all that, also another study in wish fulfillment, with all the curious variations of character and eccentricity omitted in favor of adoration.

Heavens, how Dr. Nancy Dayland was adored. Her series is an extended excursion through pink sugar land.

In an early appearance, Dr. Nancy is "a slight, girlish figure, clad in a long gray coat. A scarlet tam was pulled tightly over her unruly bobbed hair." Her face is delicate with "finely moulded features." Dark eyes glow under delicate level brows. Her musical voice speaks in gently pedantic diction, as if her veins were filled with liquid synonym.

She is Nancy Drew grown up, every girl's dream of what she will be when she becomes a famous criminal investigator.

In less than a year, Dr. Dayland has solved twenty major crimes. When she comes tapping at the door, big coarse tough lawmen crumble and turn over all their professional troubles to her. Before she opens her mouth (delicate, sensitive, red), they begin sniveling with gratitude.

The world, in general, until lately, had been particularly chary and slow to accept the unusual ability of a feminine criminologist. Yet this Chinese sluggishness of mind had monthly been dissipated by the girl's real achievements, her service to the safety of society.[25]

That is the authentic and real opinion of Florence Mae Pettee (1888-?), writer of the Dayland series, grasping in deep and profound admiration, as she doubles and repeats her words and qualifiers again and also still once more.

Pettee's work is scattered across the magazines of the period. Her fiction has been noted in *Black Mask* (1920), *Action Stories* (1923), *Argosy All-Story* (1923), and *Flynn's* (1924). The stories are third-generation Sherlock Holmes and second generation Lady Molly, with a killing dose of girls' book fiction stirred in.

The earliest Nancy Dayland story reviewed is "The Scarlet Spider,"*Action Stories* (March 1923). In this, a fellow rows out alone into the bay, while three witnesses watch. Suddenly he is mysteriously dead, a heavy knife rammed into him. And there, freshly painted on the side of the rowboat, where nothing had been a moment earlier, is what seems to be a scarlet spider and the number "13."

What can it all mean?

What invisible hand slew this man?

It takes Dr. Nancy a single day to uncover the meaning of the painted symbols (which is "July 13"). She also identifies the weapon (a bow gun that hurls knives) and the motive (revenge for "playing the cad").

All perfectly clear—providing that you have straight slim brows and access to the dead man's diaries.

You will be pleased to learn that the murderer never sets foot in the story.

"The Mystery of Voodoo Manor" (which even sounds like a Nancy Drew title) ran in the *Argosy All-Story Weekly* as a four-part serial, July 21 through August 11, 1923. The cast includes "a creature dark like a shadow, yet so transparent that the moon shone through it, lining out, in spectral ghastliness its bone structure beneath..."

In addition to that bit part, there is a murder, a vanishing knife, a corpse rolled over in the coffin, a mysterious peddler who keeps altering his disguise, and an old lady with a pet bat. Nancy discovers the meaning of each and every one of these wonders. Madame Pettee grows hoarse telling us how exciting it all is.

And it may well be. But very soon, one Nancy Dayland serial begins to resemble another.

Murder is done. Black menace looms out there, wuffing and snorting offstage. Dark figures stalk. Weird noises chill.

All this is stage dressing. Actual violence is meticulously avoided. Nancy must be protected at all costs. She may be baffled, but Pettee never allows her to be endangered. In consequence, there is essentially no physical conflict and no rough stuff at the end of a story to boost the adrenalin.

Absence of a concluding action scene leaves a distinct hole in the story. This is filled by the terminal conference scene, familiar to lovers of B movies and the adventures of Craig Kennedy, which established this sort of ending back in 1912. What the scene amounts to is that the detective calls all the suspects together, dazzles them with dramatic pyrotechnics, and exposes the guilty. "Thou art the man!" Consternation! Amazement! Drama after a fashion.

Dr. Dayland is partial to such endings. At the end of each serial, she calls in all the suspects and numbs them with her mind. (She is above the more conventional feminine wiles.) Beneath the prose, the breathless gigglings of a pre-teen girl is clearly audible: See me, Daddy, how clever I have become; see how they admire me!

Nancy explains in detail how she discovered who did it. Then the murderer explains that he did it that way. Then all the characters allow that they will be happy all the rest of their lives. It's heart warming.

At these feasts of reason, very little hard evidence is presented. Nancy is rather above evidence. She doesn't need it, for the murderer will confess, once he learns how that delicate little girl with the bobbed hair has seen right through his complicated scheme.

At times, his bafflement is so complete that he commits suicide. That's as good as a confession—and with suicide, you need no proof at all.

Not that proof is needed. Dr. Nancy says it's so, and it's so. She does not fail. The poor child is not allowed to fail. Failure might press wrinkles onto her delicate, olive-skinned face or thin those bright lips. Florence Mae Pettee has the warmest regard for Dr. Nancy Dayland, famous criminologist.

Not only is Nancy not allowed to fail, she may not even be successfully challenged. If a maid answers her pertly during an interview, Nancy daunts the saucy thing with the power of her eye, leaving her trembling and subdued.

If a jealous police detective scoffs at female investigators, the Chief of Police immediately recognizes that the fellow is dangerously unstable.

If, during a fencing exercise, Nancy's opponent unleashes a fancy attack, Nancy adroitly flicks the foil aside and touches the heart.

Can't fail. Can't be challenged. Has personal force. Has beauty, talent, respect, admiration...

Drusilla Deming admires Nancy without reservation. Drusilla plays the part of Dr. Watson in these chronicles, being much slower than the reader and sugar-mouthed when speaking of the excellence that is Dr. Dayland.

A tiny, gray-eyed girl, Drusilla is younger than Nancy, her closest friend, and as much of a caricature. "Her mind," we are told, is as "unscientific as Nancy's was the reverse. Still the paint-daubing art student often quite naively hit upon a question that set Nancy's train of thought in the correct direction."

For perhaps five years, Drusilla has been prancing along in Nancy's wake, extravagantly admiring. It makes you feel a little sorry for clever Dr. Dayland. All day long, she thinks in a beautifully decorated office, exquisitely feminine in the Russell/Storey tradition. Clients enter. Drusilla bounces in. But clients are business, and Drusilla is a lightweight. Nowhere is there a hint of an equal.

No man engages Dr. Nancy's interest. No social life mars her magnificent isolation.

Does she like music, do you suppose? Does she dance, drive fast, shop for improbable antiques, like books or birds? Has she ever heard a jazz band? Some fine bands in town in 1923. How does she feel about jade or Scott Fitzgerald or the *Smart Set*? Has Drusilla ever mentioned Paul Klee? Do they giggle over "A Nude Descending A Staircase"? Does she like franks with chili, Florida land investment, Charlie Chaplin, beaded lamps?

Why does she have to sit in that tastefully appointed office and never touch the rich world that flashes and crackles just outside the window? Out there, it is the 1920s. Inside poor Nancy sits, supremely perfect, waiting for her twenty-first major case and the adulation she must have grown to resent.

A few weeks after Voodoo Manor, another case begins. This was published as "Marked Down," a four-part serial in *Argosy All-Story Weekly* (September 29 through October 20, 1923). Outside a medium's office in a tall building sprawls a man stabbed to the heart.

"I killed me," he gasps—and dies.

The police fumble. It is Nancy who discovers the diamond-set miniature concealed in a secret drawer of the decorative Chinese dragon. She alone inspects the floor where the body lay and discovers the tell-tale dent. Just as she later discovers the fragment of a will, the blotter stained with dead man's blood, the significance of a cut-out muffler on a passing automobile. It is a straight-forward mystery solved by intelligence and blame few hard facts.

At first glance, the murderer wears such a familiar costume that you blink. Here, at the climax of the story, is Dr. Dayland telling him how he went about his fiendish deed:

"Your clothes were black throughout, even to your long overcoat, your soft black hat and a wide silk muffler bunched high, covering the lower part of your face and any chance gleam of white from your shirt front.

"On your hands, you probably wore thin black gloves. Your hat was pulled low over your face. You were dressed like the prince of darkness, like the lurking shadow of impending evil."[26]

Before this quotation generates a brand new theory of the origin of *The Shadow Magazine's* lead character, it might be well to remark that Bruce Graeme (Graham Jeffries is the real name) had published the first Blackshirt stories in the English *New Magazine* in early 1923. Blackshirt was a slick gentleman crook who wore dark clothing, his wonders to perform. His working attire closely matches Pettee's description of the "prince of darkness." The influence of Graeme is probable, although not proven.

A four-part serial, "Death Shod," ran in *Flynn's*, November 8 through 29, 1924. Someone bad has stabbed a young woman and hurled her over a sea cliff to the beach. The sheriff, a shrewd fellow, swiftly gets out of his depth. He engages Nancy's services. —Can't offer you much but glory, he says.

But Nancy is uninterested in money:

"It's the spirit of the chase—the ferreting out of the obscure that is ample reward."

Nancy spends most of the novel in disguise. The story is another wonderful stew—family insanity, a wealthy counterfeiter, a murder weapon concealed in a jar of strawberry preserves. And secret passages and a secret door concealed in a cliff. And suicide disguised as murder, and suicide disguised as suicide. It is every bit as interesting as Nancy Drew, and much longer, too.

In this serial, as in all the others, the prose is elliptical and full of gas. Madame Pettee is unable to approach a simple word head on: Thus:

Newspapermen	Carrions of morbidity
Blood	Life-giving fluid
Boast	Flagrantly and defiantly flaunt
Killing	the annihilation of life
Looks like	Typifies the picture in every essential
Conscience will hurt	The weight of the knowledge will become burdensome
Thought something wrong	Surmised that something untoward had occurred

Nouns are richly dressed in adjectives:

An old lantern cast a weird light through its elaborately carved and silk-shaded sides.

High-sounding language displays itself:

He, too, had not yet learned the fallacy of fatuous regrets and petty jealousy.

And sentences are decorated until their knees buckle:

> The rolling of the boat in the angry sea will preclude the possibility of striking so tremendous and so unerring a death-wound.

That last quotation means that a man swimming beside a boat couldn't have stabbed the victim because the boat pitched so. (The problem is found in "The Scarlet Spider.") Therefore, the murderer must have stood on shore, 200 yards away, in a cross wind, and fired a knife with the wind profile of a billboard, into a victim seated in a rolling, yawing, pitching rowboat...

"The cryptic and the unusual," says Nancy, "always fascinates me."

Such a sweet girl. And just in her twenties.

7-

The number of pulp magazine series featuring detecting women was distressingly few. This was, in part, a consequence of publication policies which combined conservatism with timidity. In part it was a reflection of editorial indecision, teetering endlessly on its fence of knives, hoping to win women readers but fearing to frighten away male readers.

The most fundamental cause, however, seems to have been the belief that, although some women might glance at the adventures of a female detective, all women would be magnetized by a love story. Did you wish to lure a vast feminine audience? Then pepper your magazine with love stories and romantic serials.

Unfortunately, love stories and detective series fiction are not entirely compatible. The love story is a self-contained unit, rounded as a pearl. It moves from the first meeting of strangers to the first embrace of the engaged couple. Romance peaks. Nirvana is achieved. The courtship and the story end together. Or so it was in simpler times.

If the love story is a closed unit, the detective story series is an open chain—a succession of problems linked by the detective's intellectual agility. Romance might intrude. But it was incidental to the mystery and its elucidation.

Writers, those troubled spirits, had worn away generations testing ways of combining romance and detection.

The most popular and widely used solution placed the love interest squarely among the secondary characters. As a result, love took a heavy toll of narrators and support figures.

Still another approach used love elements which, like traffic on a one-way street, flowed in a single direction. As in the Nan Russell series, where the lead character is loved extravagantly. Her heart remains untouched, as smooth as oiled glass.

Other detective stories faced up to the possibility of marriage, a state of rapture entered only after terrible trials. Once married, one of the partners promptly died, amid high drama, the survivor then being freed for further adventures. The Blue Jean Billy Race series used this approach.

The solution has its disadvantages. You can lose only a few husbands in the service of literature before the process become ridiculous.

An alternate approach—found in the Honeymoon Detective series— permits both partners to live. When the story begins, they are separated by some paltry excuse and investigate separately. Only at the end, only in peril, do they reunite forces.

All these devices injected romance into the detective story as water is injected into a ham. No device worked effectively for long. The simplest solution eventually proven the best: The lead detective, male or female, was simply given no emotional life.

It was a severe omission. But who noticed, during the heat of the chase, that no one kissed Sherlock Holmes?

In spite of writers' tricks, in spite of inserted romance, the detective story was not considered a strong vehicle for drawing the feminine audience. Even the stratagem of making the lead detective a woman did not seem to thrill women.

The wonder is not that there were so few female detectives but that there were so many.

These silent dynamics, like undetected laws of nature, worked under the surface of the series detective story. They seem to have restricted the population of female detectives to modest numbers. And after Nancy Dayland, even this limited presence waned.

Then, in the middle of 1928, *Detective Story Magazine* published six Miss Marple short stories. With that, the greatest of all woman detectives stepped forward. And after her came the renaissance, which led by crooked steps and slow to the plethora of female detectives in the 1970s and 1980s.

But the present is future. In our present, which is the year 1928, *Detective Story* presented Miss Marple. She was a curious detective and the stories were presented in a most curious manner.

8-

Let us amuse ourselves with crime.

Stealing frightens; murder is tacky. Since real crime is tedious, let's devise a game.

During the 1920s, they played The Murder Game. Young ladies who went all funny at a trapped mouse, blandly plotted the extinction of the Rich Old Man or the Crafty Lawyer. On a rainy afternoon, any game is more acceptable than thinking. And you can't decently play kissing games until dark.

If games jade, and the prospect of kissing is remote, perhaps a light discussion group. Let's arrange it this way: Each week, a member will recount a crime of which he has personal knowledge. The others will attempt to solve the crime and unmask the glowering criminal.

What fun!

What shall we call ourselves? We include Raymond West (young writer), Joyce Lempriere (young artist), Sir Henry Clithering (ex-Scotland Yard Commissioner), Dr. Pender (clergyman), and Mr. Petherick (lawyer)...

That's five. Hardly enough. Miss Marple, will you join us? You need only sit and listen. I'm sure it will be educational.

(Miss Marple, elderly spinster, blushes faintly, lifts one hand from her knitting in a depreciating gesture, acquiesces.)

Fine, fine, fine. We are six. We shall call ourselves The Solving Six. How fine. Tuesday night, then. And each Tuesday night thereafter.

That is the premise of The Solving Six, a short story series by Agatha Christie which began in the *Detective Story Magazine,* June 2, 1928, and continued for six stories through the July 7 issue. Three stories were reprinted in *Great Detective* at the end of 1933. After various title changes, the stories were collected as a part of *The Tuesday Club Murders* (1932), and the English title being *The Thirteen Problems.*

To say the worst immediately, the series' premise is artificial. It is one of those cute situational idea things that the 1920s relished so much and which later incited such commentators as Raymond Chandler to flights of lyrical venom. Then too, although each story is partially narrated by a different person, most of them sound like Agatha Christie, being articulate, sensitive, cleverly obscure.

And, finally, all the participants—defying nature's probabilities—have personal knowledge of murder. The sheer volume of delivered death will astound those Americans who consider England a bastion of placidity.

These trivial quibbles voiced and forgotten, the series is splendid. It represents the problem mystery story in full flower, the puzzle, the twist, the dazzling ending being of prime importance. Christie's inventive mind flickers brightly above the limitations of the form.

There is a reason for these stories to be narrated, rather than unfolding as experience. The whole purpose is to display Miss Marple in action. Aunt Jane Marple is, at this time, about sixty-five or seventy and seems everybody's grandmother. But even brilliant grandmothers rarely go rushing across the countryside sniffing out crime. Realistically (in 1928) they sit knitting, listening, understanding.

Jane Marple is the classic armchair detective. Compared to her, Dupin is stagy and the Old Man In The Corner merely quaint. Rarely does Miss Marple have to seek out clues. By a fortunate stroke, each person narrating a story will mention precisely the correct clue to unravel the whole thing.

Miss Marple needs only that single clue. She is inhumanly quick. Her mind is utterly clear, utterly rational. No illusion dims its luster. Untroubled by bias or romanticism, she embodies Victorian discipline without Victorian evasiveness.

Her field is people: Their motives, their actions, their unexpected similarities. For years she has studied the people of St. Mary Mead, the tiny village in which she lives.

For if you spend "a lifetime in a small village, and observe people carefully—you will know the essence of human behavior and motivations the world over. Details and scales of expression differ, and this is what confuses most people."[27]

So intensely has Miss Marple observed village life that nothing surprises her; not evil; not even good. "There was no unkindness in Miss Marple," Christie remarks, "she just did not trust people." Observed experience is the basis for her detective work. She reasons by analogy: Similar circumstances breed similar results.

Thus, there was once a husband who murdered his wife in a very tricky way, using poison. And why? He was a sexually aggressive fellow and in the house was a pretty young girl servant. That basic situation, Miss Marple understands instantly. The tactical detail of how the poisoning was accomplished takes only a fraction longer.

That story, the first of the series, is titled "The Solving Six" (June 2, 1928, *Detective Story Magazine*). For later book publications, it was retitled "The Tuesday Night Club." The problem of the lethal husband is fumbled at artlessly by the other club members. They are sophisticated people of the world, having seen Paris, London, and perhaps Beale Street. But they have not observed people—not the way that this nice old lady from St. Mary Mead has observed people.

That is the silent joke of the series. This tall, thin old lady with her faded blue eyes, this unworldly spinster, her hair piled in white masses, is the real sophisticate of the group. Of them all, she is the only one to understand the human heart.

Besides which she is "full of curiosity, knowing everything, hearing everything; the complete detective service in the home."[28]

She wears an old-fashioned black dress, favors quantities of lace. Her fingers dart nimbly through the knitting as she listens.

She is old-fashioned enough to say a prayer when baffled. She has no high opinion of doctors, finding the best medication in a cup of tansy tea.

Nor is she convinced that the world's excellence has increased with more powerful automobiles and hotter jazz.

She sits quietly there, gentle ineffectual harmlessness, fingers flickering among the wool strands. While her level mind, entirely aware, listens, fearfully dispassionate and sensitive, reasoning from observed similarities and finding the truth unchanging.

Detective Story Magazine did a service to the American mystery reader by printing the Miss Marple short stories. But it did no one a favor by fiddling around with the titles. The "Solving Six" tag was hooked to the next two stories and the titles clumsily changed. The June 9 story was "The Solving Six and The Evil Hour," later published as "The Idol House of Astarte." This was followed by "The Solving Six and The Golden Grave" (June 16, later retitled "Ingots of Gold"). The magazine titles show a certain deficiency of imagination that is, most certainly, not Mrs. Christie's.

The equally unfortunate title, "Drip, Drip" (June 23, elsewhere "The Blood-Stained Pavement") is attached to a splendid story. Miss Marple is in rare form. The mystery she penetrates at once, the instant she hears that a woman in vivid clothing returned alone from a walk. The whole point of the problem (she says) is serial murder by a bigamous husband killing for insurance. Her conclusions leave the others quite flabbergasted. Dear old ladies are not supposed to know about serial murder for profit.

Miss Marple: "Mrs. Green...buried five children—and every one of them insured. I always find one thing very like another in this world."

Later she remarks to her nephew, Raymond West (whose worldly views of life have washed gloomily through several books): "I hope you dear young people will never realize how very wicked the world is."

"Where's The Catch" (June 30, later retitled to "Motive vs Opportunity") concerns a will that vanishes from a sealed envelope in a lawyer's safe. Only a blank sheet of paper is found. And how are we to explain this? Miss Marple can do so easily, drawing upon her recollections of youth. For the record, the lawyer, being a fictional character, is entirely innocent.

"The Thumb Mark of Saint Peter" (July 7) is Miss Marple's own contribution to the Tuesday Night club meetings. The wife may, after all, have murdered her husband by feeding him poisonous mushrooms. He died, muscles knotted, muttering weirdly about a heap of fish—a pile of carp. Miss Marple must resort to a drug index before she understands. Again she is far ahead of the other Solvers.

By this story, the limitations of the Solving Six were being discreetly ignored. New characters move in. The sessions became ever less formal. The convention of a narrated story remained—that and the unchangeable fact that Jane Marple, alone of the group, saw to the heart of each problem before anyone else could turn it around in his mind.

Six stories and then the series was cut off. But six stories were enough. Jane Marple, so quietly launched, moved on to later fame, looking reality squarely in the face, buying baby presents, earning the reputation of the greatest natural detective in England. Her cases appear in five collections of short stories (although not all the stories are hers) and twelve novels. Her final appearance was in *Sleeping Death* (1976), the last new Christie published. In this novel, Aunt Jane is extremely old and physically feeble. But her mind still sheds its steady silver light, incredibly clear and undiminished.

9-

The year 1928 is an appropriate time to terminate our visit with the feminine detectives. Immediately ahead loomed the frightening changes and deep regrets of the next decade. But the special problems of 1930s detective fiction must be reserved for a later study.

Enough that female series characters continued to appear in detective fiction. Ahead were the Norths, Hildegarde Withers, The Domino Lady, Miss Pinkerton, Violet McDade, Grace Culver, Carrie Cashin, Bertha Cool— another full chapter in the story of the woman detective. Of these, some were talented amateurs. Others, the decorative part of a married detection team. Some detected by intuition; others by psychological insight. Most were private detectives—for it was a time of private detectives, their adventures violent, indeed. No longer were women shielded by their sex from the fist, the bludgeon, the knife.

These new characters continued as those familiar detective types established generations before. In doing so, they also continued yesterday's familiar problems. The female detective's hard common sense, her professional skill, remained secondary. The emphasis was still on the woman who happened to be a detective, not the detective who happened to be a woman. The female detective remained an interesting counter melody, not a major theme.

Chapter IV—After Baker Street

1—

Baker Street is a state of mind, as much as anything else.

It was always three-quarters dream. But at that, it was more real than London. London is a geographic place of roofs and people and windows. It has reshaped itself repeatedly, in the manner of living things. But Baker Street, the dream, exists independent of time; it remains undimmed, untarnished, inviolate. The dream of London in 1891, of Baker Street in London, of Holmes and Watson of Baker Street, has grown more permanent than reality.

Return to Baker Street. You are friends with every person there. In those tobacco-scented rooms, you find a sense of place, secure against the turmoils of the night.

You relish the fogs and the deductions. The clients at the door. The white spark of danger in streets of sooted brick and cobblestones glistening in the rain. The sense of fulfillment as the familiar story resumes again. The wonderful meals at case's end.

All this is dream stuff, revealed in the lightning stroke of the precise image, the concrete phrase.

Come to Baker Street and be refreshed. Touch a world less transient than your own, more stable than your own experience, which is gossamer enough and fragile, as you well know.

Baker Street is a white enchantment, deeply satisfying.

2-

The world of Sherlock Holmes spanned forty years, extending from *A Study In Scarlet* (1887) to *The Casebook of Sherlock Holmes* (1927). What began with gaslight and hansom cabs ended in electric light and automobiles. But Holmes entered the Jazz Age only by an accident of publication, and The Science of Deduction remained uncompromised by either hard-boiled detection or experiments in Prohibition.

Holmes influenced an entire sub-branch of the detective story—that group of stories dealing with the exploits of a one-man private detective business. That form was not unique to Holmes. Other detectives had practiced long before, some amateur, some professional, many associated with agencies. None exerted Holmes' influence.

The sheer inevitability of the Holmes figure impressed itself so deeply on fiction that it seemed the only possible way to present a private detective. The Holmes image, powerful as sunlight, shone in the story papers and dime novels of the late 1890s. No sooner were there pulp magazines, than they featured variations on Holmes. And as the number of pulp magazines increased, so did the number of characters reshaped from the clay of Baker Street.

Some of these later characters respectfully imitated Holmes, in the manner of Ashton-Kirk. Others borrowed a characteristic, a relationship, a device from The Sacred Writings. Others were their own man, but because they appeared at a time when Holmes stood so large against the sky, they reflected Holmes in every atom, adapting to him as a plant adapts to the environment in which it lives.

As in the instance of Felix Boyd.

3-

The appearance of the Felix Boyd stories in *The Popular Magazine* should have been celebrated with massed brass bands, fireworks, and free beer.

Boyd was dime novel through and through, dime novel pressed down tight and concentrated, fifty years of dime novel distilled to a simple figure. His presence in *Popular* demonstrates that the dime novel strain, vigorous and kicking, had entered mainstream pulp magazine fiction. Considering the social status of these two forms, that is like saying that a ditch digger had found a job as a minor clerk. But it was upward mobility, no matter how slight.

It was 1904, the dime novels' Golden Age, when the February *Popular* published the first Felix Boyd story. As so frequently happened back then, that story was the first of a loosely linked series, collectively known as "Below The Dead Line."

What does "Deadline" mean? It was a line arbitrarily established as a crime control measure by Inspector Brynes, New York City Police. Officially it was the North side of Fulton Street. Any known criminals found south of the deadline, in Wall Street and the Maiden Lane diamond district, would be arrested on sight. Thus the series title.

Felix Boyd was a one-man private consulting detective whose clients—bankers, stock brokers, jewelers—contracted with him for protection against the Forces of Crime that roamed south of the Deadline. These roamed freely, in spite of Inspector Brynes, and so the stories accumulated, month after month.

That first series ran in *Popular* from February 1904 through January 1906. The stories were collected into two volumes of the Magnet Library, the Street & Smith paperback reprint series, as *Below The Deadline* (ML

428) and *On The Trail of Big Finger* (ML 429), both published early in 1906.

The series continued in *Popular* without a break, from February 1906 through January 1908, under the new general title, "The Adventures of Felix Boyd." These adventures were collected into three paper-bound volumes: *The Adventures of Felix Boyd,* (New Magnet Library 603), *Felix Boyd's Revelations* (NML 615), and *Felix Boyd's Final Problems* (NML 627).

This was a staggering run. Moderately successful series normally contained from four to six stories. Very successful series, stimulating readers to shouts of glee, might run a dozen stories. Even fifteen. The Boyd series, forty-eight in all, was obviously incredible.

Unfortunately, paper covers do not preserve reputations as surely as cloth bindings. In hardback, Boyd may have received recognition—or more recognition than he currently enjoys, Ellery Queen being one of the few commentators to cite him. As it is, cloth-bound immortality was denied Felix. For all practical purposes he was gone by the 1920s. The story type that he represented—hard-nosed action in realistic surroundings against New York City toughs—lasted into the 1930s. But then the ripple effect goes on forever.

The name signed to the series was Scott Campbell, pen name of Frederick W. Davis. (That's *W.* Davis, not the F. C. Davis of the 1930s.) F. W. Davis, a highly experienced dime novel author, was strongly influenced by the popularity of Sherlock Holmes, then King of the World. Felix Boyd not only embodies many of Holmes' characteristics but the stories, themselves, are strongly flavored with second-hand Doyle.

Here is Boyd at work:

> ...had there been an observer...he would have seen personified the relentless sleuth of blood-stirring fiction, the man metamorphosed into the hound, with both the hunter instinct and the human acumen stimulated to supernatural activity.
>
> With lips compressed, with features drawn and white, with eyes that gleamed and glittered as if with fever under his knit brows, Boyd threw open the nearest window and looked out...
>
> Dropping to his hands and knees upon the floor, he took a lens from his pocket and began to study the carpet. Inch by inch, foot by foot, yard after yard, he wiggled over the floor, with the lens at his eyes and his face nearly touching the carpet.
>
> Now and then he lingered over some particular spot, now and then a muttered word escaped him, or an impulsive gesture, indicating his constant mental activity; yet, for the most part his work was done with amazing rapidity and in utter silence.[1]

He lacks only Watson and a deep-stalker cap.

Boyd is not nearly as detailed a personality as Holmes. In the first stories, only his "keen, gray eyes" are mentioned. Later we learn that he has thin, firm lips and thin features, forceful and clean cut. It is little enough substance from which to construct a personality. Like Holmes, he smokes a pipe, is a fine actor, and a disguise artist.

He is, of course, blessed with a brilliantly active mind, perceptive, rapid, piercing:

Boyd occupied a class entirely his own... (His) detective acumen was a gift rather than an acquirement, and was not a fair standard for measuring that of others.[2]

Boyd's clients are stuffed shirts, all. Not so his opponents. The people he most often battles are underworld riff-raff—thugs, dissolute ruffians, casual murderers. Since the stories stand on a massive dime novel base, you can be sure that there is swift, violent crime, rapid chases, searches against time, successful disguises, bar-room confrontations with roughs, and climaxes where the guns go off and the wicked drop shrieking. More often than Holmes, Boyd is in physical jeopardy. For that reason, he carries two revolvers and will shoot down his man without hesitation or regret.

The ruffian crossed the foul yard, and pushed open the door of the stable, into which he hurriedly plunged, with Boyd close behind him. The place was damp and lighted only dimly...

Boyd followed for a step or two—then heard the stable door close with a crash behind him. Like a flash he wheeled sharp about, only to quickly dodge the arms and blows of three others...

"Nail him! Nail him, you fools!" Finley fiercely cried as Boyd leaped aside and brought his shoulders to one of the walls. "If he...

But there his voice was drowned by the ringing report of Boyd's revolver, and one of the gang, who had sprung nearer with a bludgeon, went to the floor with his wrist fractured by the bullet.[3]

The first series is lightly knit together by the lurking menace of "The Big Finger, that obscure genius for crime," whose criminal gangs operate secretly below the deadline. The Big Finger is Boyd's Moriarty.

He is a man of power, of vast criminal resources, a man to be feared, and a man whose misdirected genius one cannot but respect.[4]

For twenty-four stories, Boyd nibbles away at Big Finger's power, confronting him repeatedly, as repeatedly in his power, ever escaping to clash again.

"The Case of the Missing Magnate" (August 1904) tells how a Wall Street financier is kidnapped in an effort to drive down the value of his stock. Boyd deduces that the detective who guarded the financier was part of the plot and takes his usual vigorous steps. He allows the detective to lead him into a trap set in an old stable. There he corners the gang, after some spy work, freeing the financier in time to save the stock market.

The experienced reader, full of acumen, will have already realized that The Big Finger planned the coup. Once more the arch criminal is foiled. It is admitted that, in this case, Boyd had a bit of help. This was supplied by his friend, Jimmy Coleman—a detective out of the Central Office, NYC Police. Coleman was the fellow who came bursting in through the stable doors while Boyd held a pistol on the crooks.

Coleman occupies the traditional position of the slow friend. Not that he is particularly stupid. But Boyd's flashing mind leaves him staggering, and it was, after all, the convention of the period, that all the glory be kept for the lead character. For a secondary character to show the least flush of intelligence would diminish the lead's hot shine.

"The Case of the Under Secretary" (September 1904) begins in Boyd's Pine Street office, then flies off to the docks, from which the daughter of the English Counsul General has been kidnapped. Working alone, disguised as an Irish cab driver, Boyd traces her across the city, rescues her smart as paint. As soon as the guns stop blazing, in burst Coleman and the police, ready to count the dead and book the living.

Well, as you have surmised, The Big Finger planned that matter, too. Boyd tells us so at the end of the story. Not that it matters. Each story is complete and interesting. To have The Finger's menacing shadow hovering over the series only salts the action.

"The Case of the Boss Mason" (October 1904) concerns a purposeless street explosion and a double murder. The trail leads to a secret subterranean chamber where lurks The Big Finger, himself. He is a hard-faced man of iced gray eyes and a treacherous smile. Sad to report, he escapes Boyd's trap. In pour the cops. But they arrive too late, as cops will, and catch only three minions.

After The Big Finger and his operations are finally broken up, Boyd finds that routine work has lost its savor—as anyone might who almost got himself killed once a month. So he tosses over the Pine Street office and his limited practice. From now on, he will accept problems all over New York City, and on Long Island, Staten Island, and the Battery, too.

As a result, Coleman sees Boyd so seldom that he is filled with obscure pangs. He wangles a transfer closer to Boyd's new operations, and the friendship proceeds as before—Boyd providing the pyrotechnics, and Coleman carrying in the broom to sweep up the breakage.

"The Crimson Flame" (February 1906) is a large diamond that glares red when viewed at a certain angle. It vanishes from the jewelry store while being examined by a customer. After the disappearance, she is, also, examined. No soap. The diamond is completely gone. Gone completely.

It's deeply mysterious.

No, not at all. Boyd located the stone within ten minutes of arriving on the scene. (It has been attached by chewing gum to the bottom of the lady's chair.) But it isn't recovered for another three or four pages. First, the thief's confederate must be collected and, beside, a Felix Boyd short story normally ran 11-3/4 pages, double column. You just don't end a story on page 9 because the detective is very clever.

The following stories, if somewhat slight, sparkle with impish vitality. "No Waterloo" (August 1906) describes how Boyd tracks down the miscreants who robbed the closed mansion and almost brained the young man with a bottle. "A Transatlantic Crime" (October 1906) opens in the throes of intense overwriting. Boyd is white-faced, sweating, staring, since he has been thinking all through the night. By sheer mental power, he has solved a London theft and is able to collar the crooks before they disembark in New York City. "An Oriental Episode" (July 1907) takes him to Turkey to pit his wits against an evil sultan.

There are not many of these overseas adventures. Most stories are set firmly in New York City, described in as intense detail as Doyle ever lavished upon London.

It was at this time, on a warm, unseasonable night, well along in December, that Mr. Felix Boyd finally got at his work.
A damp mist was in the air, lending a sickly yellow glare to the street lights. The pavements were wet and slippery and all that was left of the last fall of snow lay foul and black here and there in the gutter.[5]

It is half Nick Carter and half Sherlock Holmes: a hyperactive, deducing genius prowls the mean streets, one hand gripping a pistol, the other clutching a disguise. All around him that vanished world shimmers to hard form: ramshackle stables, clay alleys greasy in rain, over-decorated drawing rooms dense with possessions, construction sites...

Similar scenes had appeared for years in various dime novel series, although without the intensity of selected detail or the urge to social reform which heated the Naturalists' prose. So it is no surprise that the Felix Boyd stories borrow the Naturalistic School's manner without adopting its purpose. Scott Campbell is writing adventure fiction, not social criticism. But he contrives to play the hot orange action against backgrounds reflecting social degradation and despair almost inadvertently, as his melodrama hammers along.

This mixture of realistic detail, toughness, and melodramatic action is interested in several ways. It is a clear example of the dime novel making the transition between a 32-page pamphlet and a family-oriented magazine of general fiction. And it also permits us a sharp look at the hardboiled detective at the larval stage of his development. Felix Boyd may mix Sherlock

Holmes and Nick Carter in equal proportions. But he is also a forerunner of characters and literary forms to be more elaborately developed in coming decades. The literary line of which Felix Boyd is a part would flower in unexpected ways, leading to heroes working outside the law and tough guys clashing on city street—into *Black Mask's* unsentimental harshness and the romanticized violence of the 1930's single-character pulps.

For these, you can't blame Boyd.

He didn't create the trends; he was part of them, way back then, long ago, before the distant future had become the past.

4-

The Honorable Stanley Brooke and Mr. Thorndyke Flint are dissimilar characters from dissimilar fictional worlds.

Brooke appeared in *Munsey's Magazine* in which articles, illustrations, and consciously quality fiction were carefully mixed. It was the first successful monthly magazine that was priced at ten cents and offered to a general audience.[6]

Flint appeared in Street & Smith's *Detective Story Magazine*, a fifteen-cent, bi-weekly publication still bearing the brand of its dime novel origin.

The magazines had little in common but paper and ink. Separating them were immense gulfs of editorial policy, audience, publication runs, and sales. That they shared even one common link seems improbable.

At this time in the early Teens, however, the influence of Sherlock Holmes radiated everywhere. It touched high and low. It joined magazines even more dissimilar than *Munsey's* and *Detective Story*. Where detective stories were published, there the shadow of Holmes fell. All else might differ, but Holmes was a common quality.

His traces may be found even in such an odd mixture as the series about Honorable Stanley Brooke.

Brooke is the lead wonderful in one of those short story series so plentifully supplied by E(dward) P(hillips) Oppenheim (1866-1946). As often happens in an Oppenheim series, the story line reels wildly about, streaming sparks. By jerks and deflections, it unfolds, amazing the reader and surely astounding the author.

The series began in *Munsey's Magazine*, December 1913, under the general title of "The Deliberate Detective." That title dropped away as promptly as an exhausted rocket stage. The series continued monthly through July 1914, changing its character and direction every second story, consistently inconsistent.

Brooke begins as an inefficient amateur detective. In rapid succession, he becomes an adventurer and a professional detective. Is supplemented by a woman detective. Becomes a love-smitten non-entity, mumbling feebly in his own series. These events occupy eight stories, loosely chronological.

In them, flecks of Sherlock Holmes appear, plus dots of Sax Rohmer and bits of Edgar Wallace's Just Men. These influences cling like wet confetti to the story line.

The initial two stories are titled "The Rescue of Warren Tyrrwell" (December 1913) and "The Princess Pays (January 1914). They are less mystery than adventure, as the Honorable Stanley attempts to help people out of difficulties he does not quite understand.

With the third story, "The Other Side of the Wall" (February 1914), variation begins. Constance Robinson is introduced. With that perversity characteristic of an Oppenheim series, she gradually grows as a character until the series lies helpless in her hands.

At first, Constance is merely a drab young woman wearing an old-fashioned, very shabby, red serge dress. She types for a living, knows her brother to be a crook. And she is hostile, suspicious, and several social steps beneath Hon. Brooke.

The brother calls on Brooke for unspecified assistance. Wants him to come to the Robinson apartment and listen to confused noises on the other side of the room wall. Brooke sensibly enough recommends that Robinson call the police or Scotland Yard.

The brother demurs, hesitates, is found dead in the street.

Rattled by conscience, Brooke returns to the Richardson apartment. There he finds the wall shattered open, and Constance abducted. Shoving through the ruins, he finds her in the hands of a criminal pack. They are preparing to murder her during weird rites.

Brooke blasts away with his revolver, kills one fierce fellow, escapes dramatically, girl limp on his iron arm. Very traditional.

After all the action, Brooke offers to aid the girl. But she spurns his help, being proud, contemptuous, grim.

"The Murder of William Blessing" (March 1914) opens on a liner to America. By a helpful coincidence, Brooke meets Constance on board. She is as impervious, mysterious, sharp-tongued as ever, resentful of his every offer to aid her. She is seeking her fortune as a secretary to a rich man, who is instantly murdered. Brooke solves the crime with little trouble, using real clues and psychology. Made brave by success, he offers her a partnership in the new detective bureau he plans to open in London. He will detect; she will type.

By the sixth story, "The Spider's Parlor" (May 1914), the detective agency is a success. Love's sweet anguish now wastes Brooke. He proposes to Constance and is coldly rejected. She is burdened with some mysterious secret, which is none the less mysterious for never being explained.

Love's pain aside, Brooke and Constance foil a murderous doctor who lurks like a piranha in the deeps of an unsavory cafe. The story also introduces

Inspector Simmons of Scotland Yard, the official policeman for the balance of the series.

"The Silent People" (June 1914) are operating in the style of the Four Just Men to avenge social wrongs. Brooke and Constance investigate, easily locate. The Silent People. That they escape immediate death is apparently because The People don't consider them worthy prey. By this story, Brooke is following Constance's advice and has melted intellectually into something vapid and limp. As he dwindles away, she gains in beauty and grace. No longer is her temper loutish. She even has a new dress. But still she rejects Brook firmly, *a la* Nan Russell, no, no, and no. If the reader peers closely, he will see an amused twinkle in her eye.

In "The Glen Terrace Tragedy" (July 1914), Brooke is doubled up with jealousy. Constance has been having quiet dinners with an older man. No need for panic. The fellow is nothing to her personally—merely a suspected wife slayer. Constance is seeking evidence of his guilt. But there is no evidence.

On the contrary, it turns out that he is as noble as a man can get and not ascend into the sky. He is willing to risk arrest and trial to protect his wife's name.

According to the wife's diary (which Constance finally reads), she killed herself, poor thing. Suddenly she realized that she had become old and ridiculous—and that the world was laughing at her, an old old woman in clothing and makeup thirty years too young. It's all in her diary—the sudden self-understanding, the shame, the humiliation. For her sake, the husband is determined to suppress these feminine revelations. Fortunately, Constance persuades him to let Scotland Yard read the diary.

At the close of the story, in the final few paragraphs, Constance agrees to marry Brooke who has, by this time, degenerated into a simpering ninny. There's no reason for her capitulation, other than that the series is at an end and it's nice to tie up all the loose ends.

After these sweet little cakes, nicely decorated and sugared, even the erratic Thorndyke Flint series gives the impression of substance.

Flint was a brilliant private detective, residing on Madison Avenue, New York City, and conducting an extensive practice in the pages of the *Detective Story Magazine* from about 1915 to 1925. In his exhausting work, he was aided by various assistants, Roy Norton and Frank Judson being the most visible. A cool, efficient woman, Nora Books, also aided him.

Flint was a tower of strength. He carried two pistols, disguised himself with ease, and had such a reputation that New York police tumbled over themselves to help him out. In numerous other ways, he resembled Nick Carter.

As a matter of fact, he was Nick Carter. Sometimes.

It is an involved story. The situation seems to have been this. Street and Smith, that famous publishing house, found that they could sell more Nick Carter adventures than even their fiction factory could supply. So they employed Samuel C. Spalding, a crippled Unitarian minister, to rewrite a number of Sexton Blake stories.

Blake had first appeared in an English boys paper, *The Halfpenny Marvel*, December 20, 1893. He soon transferred to another paper, the *Union Jack*, took up residence on Baker Street, and so reflected the glory of Conan Doyle's famous detective as to become known as "the office boy's Sherlock Holmes."[7] By the time the English and United States publishers got together on an international exchange agreement of detectives, an enormous number of Blakes existed. According to Spalding, he rewrote some of these into

...a little over 100 Nick Carter full length novels (for the New Magnet series of paperbacks)... They were always a little over 200 pages in length (about 60,000 words) and I did, as a rule, two a month.[8]

Some of these rewritten stories went directly into the *Detective Story Magazine*—but not as Nick Carters. The name was changed to Thorndyke Flint. Other than the name change, and a certain bland inefficiency in Spalding's concept of an omniscient detective, there is no difference between Flint and Carter. Nor is there a difference in the assistants. You may read Patsy Garvan for Roy Norton, Chick Carter for Frank Judson, and Ida Jones for Nora Brooks.[9]

The name change to Flint may have been intended to reduce the colossal volume of Nick Carter material then appearing in *Detective Story*. From 1916 through 1918, the magazine reprinted 44 Nick Carter short stories from the 1895-1896 *New York Weekly*, crediting these to Sgt. Ryan. Simultaneously, at least thirteen of Spalding's rewritten Sexton Blakes appeared as serials, running almost back to back from 1915 through 1918. Most were signed Douglas Gray.

The first Thorndyke Flint appeared as a 5-part serial, "Clew Against Clew" (April 20 through June 20, 1916).[10] Marching right behind came "Snarled Identities" and "A Battle for the Right," all in 1916. During 1917, the magazine published "The Sea Fox," "Partners in Peril," "Hidden Foes," and "The Broken Bond." And, in 1918, "The Threefold Disappearance," "A Spinner of Death," "The Secret of the Marble Mantel," and "Wildfire."

After these four to five-part series ran in *Detective Story*, they were thriftily reprinted (following a lapse of two or three years) as Nick Carter stories in the New Magnet series.

What an imposing lineage. From Sherlock Holmes through Sexton Blake and Thorndyke Flint to Nick Carter. Granted that the Nick Carter who appeared one year before Sherlock Holmes was not the Nick Carter of 1915.

Times changed relentlessly, and Carter was a most plastic character. But what an extraordinary history. What a glorious line of detection down the years.

5-

Mr. Terry Trimble, the criminals' terror, seemed no more than a clothes-mad dandy:

> ...the loungers beheld a young man, dressed in the acme of style. Coat and trousers and hat were faultless. His waistcoat was a poem, and his cravat a sight worth seeing. He wore a monocle, and he carried a stick.
> One lounger snorted and another sniffed. The young man stopped, and through the monocle one gray eye glittered as if with fine particles of steel. Before that glittering orb the two loungers seemed to wither and blow away.[11]

Once more we are in the presence of a man's man, masquerading, for reasons unexplained, as the traditional fop. We have met him in an earlier chapter. His exterior, all polished frivolity, conceals his astonishing abilities:

> ...He moved languidly, and generally when he spoke it was with a slow drawl, that indicated nothing except extreme boredom with the world and everything in it.
> Appearances may be deceptive, however, as many a gentleman had learned to his cost regarding Terry Trimble... He could think fast and move swiftly when occasion demanded; but Terry Trimble had learned the secret of conserving energy. He didn't make a business of indulging in useless motions, useless talk, or useless thinking.[12]

Useless affectations are another matter. Mr. Trimble is a seething mass of affectations. He lounges bonelessly. He fusses with his clothing. He prattles of poetry and bemoans those tedious hours wasted in investigation. When crisis spreads its red wings he meanders vapidly to action:

> He arose and bowed, and left the (police chief's) private office. He walked through the assembly room languidly, and stopped to chat for a moment with the lieutenant about nothing at all. Twice he actually yawned, and he spent fully a minute adjusting his monocle before he left headquarters and stepped into the street.
> His demeanor indicated anything but speed. Yet, as Terry Trimble had said, speed was his middle name.
> But the speed in this instance was in those glittering gray eyes, and in his nimble and reasoning brain.[13]

You might suspect that, when this glamorous apparition glides onto the scene of a crime, the police would vie in throwing him downstairs. You would be wrong. In Trimble's word, the police split their trousers deferring to him. When he appears, they cast aside organizational discipline and beg for his direction. When he winds up a case, all parties assemble in the office of the police chief. And there, basking in authority's admiration, Mr. Trimble unwinds the problem, assigning blame and praise, fingering the guilty.

It is the difference between art and realism.

These endings are much like those terminal seances concluding the early Craig Kennedy cases. Except that the masses of pseudo-scientific equipment are omitted. Trimble is not rabid about scientific equipment, although he is fond of fingerprints. Rarely does he wind up a case without hauling in fingerprints. They are his basic evidence.

He needs some form of evidence. For his investigations are either illegal or intuitive. His methods is to dive in and stir around until he understands what is going on.

Trimble: "Do you know why people make such a fuss over these so-called mystery cases? It's because they look at 'em from the wrong angle. There is no such thing as a mystery, if a man refuses to believe that one exists. No human being can make a move, either good or evil, without advertising it in a hundred ways. All a person has to do is to read the advertisements."[14]

Although Trimble acts like an eccentric amateur, he is a formal private detective, charging large fees to the large corporations and wealthy individuals who are his clients. The fees are really secondary.

Some two years before the series opens, his rich uncle died, leaving Terry vast sums. No longer needing to work, he set up as a detective. Not that he considered himself a detective. Oh, no. He termed himself a "trouble maker for unscrupulous persons who annoyed others."

This sentiment now induces exquisite mental pain, but it must have been wonderously amusing in 1917.

As if to underline the difference between a detective and a trouble-maker, Trimble lives in a pretentious apartment house. There rooms lead to rooms, an affluent maze—consultation rooms, sleeping rooms, a room for dining. A music room where Mr. Trimble plays brightly upon the piano. A library where he reads all the new poetry "for the purpose of criticism." The necessary laboratory where he fusses over fingerprints. A well-appointed gymnasium in which to stretch and strain.

After the fine example of Ashton-Kirk and Jimmie Dale, Trimble is well staffed with aides. Billings, his secretary and general assistant, can research a will or shadow a suspect with equal facility. Ella Norton, his stenographer, introduced in the second story, "Germs of Bedlam," is

...an admirable young woman. She was small, dainty, with pretty eyes and an abundance of wavy hair, but she was not a girl of the doll variety. One hour daily in the gymnasium...kept her fit. She had a grip and muscle. Her wrists and arms were hard as her hair was soft. She had keen intelligence, could think and act quickly, and possessed a great deal of courage.[15]

Ella spends considerable time saving Terry from doom. As you might expect, she has a fond warm feeling for him. As you also might expect, the astute Mr. Trimble doesn't appear to notice this. Proving again that men are fools.

Although the household must contain numbers of butlers, maids, cooks, and trainers, the only other person mentioned is George, the chauffeur. He pilots the gleaming Trimble limousine, its doors monogrammed, its appearance snooty. In shining splendor, Trimble is whisked all about the city, from slums to police headquarters to the abodes of the mighty rich.

Terry Trimble added a new twist to the limousine convention. This twist rang brazenly down the years to reappear, almost unchanged, in most single character pulp magazines of the 1930s.

The limousine started down the street. Terry Trimble drew all its curtains and snapped on a tiny electric light. He pressed against the seat ahead, and an aperture appeared before him.

From a hidden closet there, Terry Trimble drew out a suit of old clothing, a soft cap, a wig, and a box of make-up. Within ten minutes he had donned the old clothing, and his stylish suit was in the closet. He applied the make-up and he adjusted the wig, looked at himself in a small mirror, and closed the closet.[16]

As would The Shadow, the Phantom Detective, and the Spider, long after, wealthy men and dual-identity heroes that they were. While details varied, the secret automobile dressing room remained a viable device until time swept away the single-character magazine.

Johnston McCulley created Mr. Terry Trimble for the *Detective Story Magazine*. About a dozen Trimble stories were published in two groups— the first appearing in 1917, the second in 1919. Rising around these stories were the formidable heights of McCulley's other series. For McCulley poured forth series fiction with the fecund zest of a grunion fertilizing the tide.

Terry Trimble's adventures are sandwiched between those of Black Star and the Spider, the wonderful detective flashing silver between the darkness of the two criminals. In the initial story, "Trimble, Trouble Maker" (March 5, 1917), a joke goes horribly wrong. Young Selbert, angry at his acquaintance Lawrence, plays a malicious practical joke—he telephones the police that a murder has been committed in Lawrence's office. From his office across the street, Selbert plans to watch with police make things hot for Lawrence.

Instead, the police find Lawrence stabbed to death. Tracing the phone call back to Selbert, they haul him off to jail. His father promptly hires that famous detective, Terry Trimble, to investigate.

Although he looks like a dude and postures like a idiot, Trimble conducts a suitably orthodox investigation. At first. He moves grandly here and there, inspecting Selbert's office, visiting the scene of the crime. With little difficulty, he picks up a bucketful of clues overlooked by the police. In these stories, the police would overlook a fire in the palms of their hands.

By the time Trimble interviews Selbert in that cold cold jail, he has located four new suspects.

At this point, orthodoxy goes out the window and Nick Carter flies in. Away with monocle and cane. On with wig and ragged clothing. Decked out in full disguise, Trimble charges off in the racier tradition of the dime novel. Across exciting chapters, he chases a hot lead. His investigation includes breaking and entering, robbery with violence, theft of personal property, and personal assault. Naughty of him, of course. If he weren't the hero, we should scold him severely.

Now the drama thunders to its climax. A snarling ambusher blasts a shot at Trimble. Misses, though, since a hit would be inopportune. After this action peak, Terry assembles the cast in the police chief's office and separates the guilty from the innocent. Fingerprints reveal the amazing truth.

It was all because a clever fellow was blackmailing a pair of thieves for everything they could steal.

"Germs oî Bedlam" (April 5, 1917) is a merry little tale about four tubes of madness germs. These have been smuggled in from China, where they are all mad. Now the United States is threatened. Riots rock New York City. People scream and froth and fall down. It is clearly time to call in Terry Trimble.

Before the action raves to an end, Mr. Trimble has been captured twice, nearly hung once, gassed, chained to the wall, threatened by an injection of madness, and confronted by the crazy professor who was the cause of it all. With considerable last minute help from his stenographer, Ella Norton, Trimble handles all problems with a nice efficiency.

More than fifteen years later, similar stories would rave among the single-character magazines. Such antic fiction, lubricated by blood and violence, would develop to a distinct form, unique to the 1930s. It is curious to see so well developed a specimen of the future appear in 1917.

It is equally curious to find devices from the heart of the 1930s foreshadowed in the Terry Trimble adventures. At various times, Terry encounters quick-acting gas (a standard McCulley device), a paralysis and disintegration beam, and a radio-activated, wireless, listening device. We call it a bug; Trimble called it a "disk"—a short-range sound transmitter. None of these devices were original with McCulley. Most had dime novel roots, for Nick Carter had long since encountered them. But McCulley seems to have inserted them into Street & Smith's mainstream fiction, where they remained, like malaria in the blood, down the decades.

"Seven Circles" (May 5) concerns murder, the theft of The Seven Circles of Flame—a $150,000 diamond collar—and faked fingerprints. Trimble chases ferociously about, fist fighting and overwhelming the evil. And once again, Ella manages to appear in the nick of time, just when needed, and covers herself with glory.

"Four Squares" (July 5) is the name signed to a series of menacing notes. These declare war on automobiles. Garages all over the city proceed to explode and burn to the chagrin of the Automobile Association. Mr. Trimble is hired to probe these outrages. After thrilling adventures, during which his clothing gets very dirty, he uncovers an intricate blackmail, extortion, and insurance fraud—and a secret master of crime manipulating a poor crazy fellow.

A story with similar internal mechanisms next. The August 5, 1917, "The Lost Disk," tells how Billings manages to lose the transmitting disk of the wireless dictograph. When they tune in on the disk, they overhear an angry man plotting murder. Where or when they can't tell.

Murder he said. Murder it is. People die incredibly, a neat hole seared into their flesh, as if they had been stabbed with a white-hot iron. Off Terry charges, neither eating nor sleeping, as is his custom when engaged in an investigation. Before long, he is on the trail.

And before long, he is treated to a series of highly unpleasant experiences.

First, he is seized by a gigantic steel arm. Then he is paralyzed by an electric ray, tied up, and comes that close to having holes disintegrated through him.

He is saved by Billings and together they capture the mad scientist responsible for these outrages. Once lodged in jail, the rascal escapes, using thermit concealed in his shoe heel to burn away the cell bars. Scampering off to the business district, he sets up his terror machine and starts to work:

Across the street, windows in the big buildings were shattered. Casements were broken down. The face of the building was scarred with holes in the masonry. Down in the street, nocturnal pedestrians fled in panic... Showers of glass fell to the street, bits of brick and stone rained downward.[17]

No one, however, is hurt. This is because the scientist is only peeved—since he has been cheated by those businessmen whose machinations so often set off the plot of a Johnston McCulley excitement.

Before the city is much damaged, Terry recaptures the scientist. All characters now come together in the police chiefs' office, where the greedy, unscrupulous manipulating mind behind the crimes is exposed. He is not the scientist, who is forgiven everything on the modern grounds that his nerves were in bad condition .

At this point, Terry's adventures are interrupted until "Terry Trimble and the Imposter" (December 18, 1917). No further stories appeared until mid-1919. By then much of the sassiness had leached from the series. Trimble's mannerisms had grown pale and dim, in the manner of a *Weird Tales* spine, and the stories seem pale and dim in sympathy.

"Murderer's Mail" (June 3, 1919) concerns the murder of the pretty wife. She licked a poisoned stamp, poor thing. The addled police cannot begin to cope. However, Terry soon discovers that the butler did it. Oh, yes. She was having a torrid affair and he wished to save the family honor. A noble gesture.

"Tragedy Trail" (August 5, 1919) is a long series of mysterious deaths. Who knows why they happened or how they happened. The police certainly don't. While they stumble about waving their white canes and tin cups, Terry takes up the trail...

Comes September 2, 1919, and the same thing happens all over again. It is not murder this time but robbery. That crafty thief, The Fox, is stealing everything loose and writing nasty, sneering notes, too. "Terry Trimble's Fox Hunt" tells how this smirking wretch is run down. No mean task, since the trail leads through trap doors, old sewers, secret passages, and involved such fascinating side issues as a beautiful, if misguided, young woman and a tricky criminal who wears a false beard and fools the world.

"Terry Trimble and the Hidden Tube" (December 9, 1919) is a routine mystery ruthlessly inflated till it can barely waddle. A wealthy financier is mysteriously killed while traveling in his limousine in his Long Island mansion. At the time, he was carrying $100,000 cash.

The secondary plot is an elaborate distraction involving two young suitors of the rich man's daughter, each seeking to ruin the other. One is pretty much a snake, but the other is nice. The financier was bringing the cash to help one of them. So which one did it?

To find out, Terry comes secretly by night to slip silently beneath the limousine. And there he discovers something important. You don't learn what he discovers until the climactic scene. And you wouldn't want to know either, for that would spoil the point of the story. There would be nothing to look forward to if you learned that the chauffeur piped the automobile exhaust into the sealed rear seat. He also left his fingerprints on a chemical device under the car. You couldn't get reliable help back then, either.

Needless to say, the police noticed none of these clues. You can easily excuse them, since they knew Terry Timble was going to solve the crime in nine or ten chapters. So it was not worth the trouble of mounting an investigation.

How clearly the Terry Trimble stories foreshadows one branch of 1930s action fiction. Within fifteen years, New York City would be routinely shattered by criminal geniuses and their quasi-scientific devices. Through the night, the disguised hero would race to confront forces of evil, while forces of the Law whirled ineffectually. There would be detection of a rudimentary sort. Eventually the real identity of the crime master would be laid bare. Prior to that modest revelation, the hero would be trapped repeatedly, threatened by death in uncommon forms, and escape to later traps and later threats.

Terry Trimble was far removed from the two-gun justice figures who shot down chaos in 1930s streets. He was a caricature, not a character. His dizzy mannerisms reflect the dime novels of twenty years before, with their bootblack detectives and Irish detectives and one-eyed miner detectives.

If Terry were overly mannered, in the old style, he was also, like the first robin, an indicator that something new was coming. Change resulted the sleepy surface of the *Detective Story Magazine*. It was not yet time for change. But change was coming.

In the meantime, however, the spirit of Sherlock Holmes moved through the magazines, and wonderful were the figures called up by his name.

6-

The sign "T. Ashley, Investigations," appeared in golden letters on the door of a second-story laboratory-office. The room inside smelled of pipe and cigar smoke and through the windows, you could look down on Albermarle Street in Boston.

There at his desk sat T. Ashley, an investigator who specialized in "the detection of crimes which...lie beyond the usual reach of the law."

Few physical characteristics are given. He has steel-gray eyes and austere lips. It may be suspected that a certain amount of skin and gristle held these components together, but nothing more is described. You may imagine that he looks like Sherlock Holmes. It is likely as he is one of the reflections from the great Holmes ocean. He has also heard of Craig Kennedy. With a trifle more science, he might be a scientific detective, for resolution of his early cases depends heavily upon science—particularly that science so cheerfully written up in the Sunday magazine section.

T. Ashley is in business to amuse himself. His fees range from $5.00 (when the case fascinates him) to $2,000 (if it is dull routine). If he succeeds or if he fails, payment is required. But he has never failed.

The total number of T. Ashley's cases to reach print is not known. The author, George Allan England, placed the stories casually, where he could. They appear in *All-Story Weekly*, *Detective Story Magazine*, *Best Detective Magazine*, and *Detective Fiction Weekly*, and almost certainly in other titles not yet noted. The stories are widely scattered in time, being published from 1918 to 1936.

George Allan England, born in Nebraska, 1877, was of an Army family, moving through the normal rotation of military posts during his childhood. After the family moved to Boston, England worked his way through Harvard, acquiring not only "some degrees and things (but) incipient T.B., and a nervous breakdown."[18] While convalescing in the Maine woods, he began to write "on a busted typewriter and the backs of old letters."

His first story sold and he was soon under contract to the Munsey Corporation, writing for *The Cavalier, All Story*, and the various *Argosy* titles, as well as the detective story magazines already mentioned. He was one of the early greats in magazine science-fiction. His major novels in this genre, "The Elixir of Hate," "The Flying Legion,""Darkness and Dawn," "Beyond the Great Oblivion," and "The Afterglow," received book publication after magazine serialization, and were later reprinted in such magazines as *Air Wonder Stories, Famous Fantastic Mysteries*, and *Fantastic Novels*. He died June 26, 1936.

During the 1920s, England turned increasingly to mystery fiction. His major series detective character was T(homas) Ashley, whose earliest case noted, "Ping Pong" (September 28, 1918), was published in *All-Story Weekly*. It tells of a poor fellow who fell from the window of his home and so died. None of the officials involved, thick as usual, pay any attention to the head wound that did not bleed. Ashley does. (He is Tom Ashley in this story.) He finds clues all over—ping-pong paddles bearing only one set of fingerprints, a tiny bit of glass vial. (England relished the bit of glass clue and worked it into several stories.)

All clues indicate murder. And finally, when the murderer lights and inhales a poisoned cigar, thus evading the law, that proves it.[19]

Around mid-1922, a light dusting of T. Ashley stories began to sift into *Detective Story Magazine*. As detective fiction, the stories are neither distinguished nor bad nor novel. Merely competent carpentry using second-hand wood.

"A Worthwhile Crime" (August 19, 1922) presents T. Ashley a nice problem. While he is investigating a robbery at the home of a political boss, he discovers finger prints on the broken window glass. Ashley checks these with the police, discovers that they are the prints of a man electrocuted six months earlier.

Four days later, the same fingerprints again. This time, they show up on the window sill of another political boss' home.

Challenged by the impossible, Ashley straps on microscopes and magnifiers and glares fixedly at the prints. His fabulous store of knowledge suggests that gloves have been made of the dead man's finger skin. Once that is determined, you have a fair idea who did it.

Sure enough, he's right. It was the attending prison physician.

Motive? The best in the world. The politicians were so busy stealing public funds that they wouldn't support building a charity hospital. So the doctor decided to rob them of their fair share.

Ashley smiles in agreement, leaves the handskin gloves with the doctor, and ambles cheerfully away.

September 2, 1922—"On the Turn of a Test Tube." A rich woman dies before including her good friend, the housekeeper, in her will. She died after a transfusion of blood from her shifty, worthless, weak-chinned nephew.

The blood transfusion gives T. Ashley ideas. Disguised as a fast-talking safety razor salesman, he gets a sample of the nephew's blood in a comedy scene that must have been sure fire, down at the local ice-cream parlor.

After that, the investigation requires only a few interviews, check of a reference book, a lab test—and it's all up with the criminal doctor who transfused the old woman with the wrong blood.

In 1922, you could commit that medical crime with no one catching you up. According to the story.

"When Sleep Spelled Death" (March 17, 1923) is a mild effort that strains to be a suspense story, as a bunny rabbit might strain to be a wolf. T. Ashley is trapped by a pair of ex-convicts who are annoyed with him. They are rather slick ex-convicts and talk as if education has affected their minds:

Convict (explaining to Ashley why he is doomed): "It isn't so much personal revenge, you know. It's more a matter of removing a disturbing factor. You rather interfere with the legitimate law of supply and demand. The world of silly and over-rich individuals demands a certain supply of artists like us to relieve it of its surplus and unearned increment. You disturb the process. So, without malice, but equally without any false sentiments of humanity, we remove you, and there you are."[20]

These literate convicts lock T. Ashley away in a private cell of a private house. He may stay alive until he falls asleep. Then they will kill him. It is an old Chinese torture.

Ashley stays awake for five days, passing time by smoking cigars and working on a dreadful oil painting which, according to one of the convicts, "looks like Hell on moving day." Before he dozes off to death, Ashley lures both convicts, Seagrave and Hann, into the cell to examine his painting. Then the attack:

With a swift upward dash T. Ashley hurled the whole cupful of stinging, blinding, choking turpentine fair into Seagrave's eyes. Even as Seagrave yelled, staggering, clutching, Hann jumped back and jerked out his gun.

One long-armed swipe across the palette, one throw and Hann's eyes and most of his face vanished under an oozing, strangling, fistful of paint. Both (men) were wholly blind.[21]

Ashley now beats them down. He takes a bullet in the shoulder which bothers him no more than a splinter in the finger, locks them in the cell, and calls the police.

In spite of the thundering triple adjectives and flossy dialogue, the story swings merrily along. But even a middling suspense story failed to give direction to the series. England had tried deduction in the manner of Holmes and scientific detection in the manner of Craig Kennedy, neither with particular success. The imagination which buoyed up England's fantasies in *All Story* and *Sea Stories* lifted his detective stories less lightly. These often contain fantastic elements that are later dispelled by reason and a scientific gadget. If the reader is sufficiently uncritical, the stories work and T. Ashley is seen as a wonderful fellow. The trick is to hold reality at arm's length; its least touch would be fatal.

At the beginning of the 1930s, Ashley moved from *Detective Story* to *Detective Fiction Weekly*. It was a move to a new environment. *Detective Fiction Weekly* had discarded most of its English flavor and now teetered between hardboiled detection and action melodrama.

Mr. Ashley likewise teetered. He became very breezy. His prose was purged of adjectives, his sentences of length. And a fine array of gadgets, dimly scientific, strewed the stories.

"The Moving Finger Writes" (October 31, 1931), *Detective Fiction Weekly*, uses seismographic data to fix the time of murder in a museum and break a neat alibi. In deference to the period, a bad gangster appears.

About the same time, England decides to affix a descriptive tag to T. Ashley's name. The tag, a sort of sub-title, was used after a heroe's name as a hook to snare the dullest reader's interest. Thus "The Long Arm of Justice," "King of the Jungle," and "The Edina Terror." England joined the pack by calling Ashley "The Connoisseur of Crime," a title so grossly inappropriate and self conscious that we are embarrassed for both of them.

Unfortunately, T. Ashley has grown almost beyond shame. Become slangy, brash, brisk, adapting himself ruthlessly to the slangy, brash, brisk environment of *Detective Fiction Weekly*, he investigates the "Crystal Clues" (July 28, 1934). The story is one of those problem dramas rigged to display gadgets of murder and detection, none probable.

There sprawls the diamond merchant before his looted safe. The police fail to recognize that he has died by hydrogen cyanide gas. T. Ashley does. He proves it with The Osmoscope, a device he must have borrowed from Craig Kennedy—it concentrates little tiny odors or some such thing. With that instrument, plus bits of glass picked up around the merchant's office, Ashley deducts the true story. The murderer is dragged down, as he waves a hydrogen-cyanide bomb.

T. Ashley begins in the shadow of Baker Street, gravitates to the fringe of the scientific detective school, and finds himself, at last, neither one thing nor the other, peering wistfully through the window at the hardboiled detectives. So many deflections rather stunt his character. He cannot grow, being so much occupied with imitation. Unfortunate. For at his best, T. Ashley is an interesting and sympathetic character. He deserved better than this shadowland.

Other characters to whom Holmes was an ancestral memory also had difficulty. Some managed to pull free and set up in business on their own terms. Other tried without much success.

Consider, for example, the detective heroes of two books published during 1920. Of these, *The Mysterious Affair at Styles* opened the illustrious career of Hercule Poirot, whose name spread through the years. The other, *Garnett Bell: Detective*, appeared, amused mildly, and vanished, leaving no issue. But then Bell never tore himself from the Holmes orbit, or really much wanted to.

Garnett Bell was a detective created by Cecil Henry Bullivant, English author and editor. It is almost certain that Bell first appeared in an English magazine; in the United States, however, he was published in *Detective Story Magazine*—five novelettes, June 24 through September 23, 1919.

Bell is a London private detective, one of those big, young, successful types who would make Philip Marlowe snap with waspish wit if their worlds somehow touched. Bell lacks a Watson and Holmes' flair for drama. He has, however, deep-set eyes, an alert manner, and an apartment in Baker Street. (Sexton Blake couldn't have lived too far away.) He loves tobacco, fine furnishings, open fires, and the quiet of his rooms on the second floor, attended by his man Peters.

He also loves Natalie Gray, a lovely young thing he saved from a murder charge. They get engaged, in a bloodless sort of way, at the end of "The Other Pistol" (June 24, 1919), the first of "The Exploits of Garnett Bell, Detective."

A terrified note from millionaire Marcus Hannaford brings Gray to the man's home—just as a shot rings out. Hannaford lies dead, shot through the head; he holds a pistol and on the floor across the room lies a second smoking pistol. Bending over the corpse is beautiful Miss Gray. From that moment on, it is Bell's job to keep her from being arrested and jailed by Detective Inspector Barkleigh Fox.

Fox does not much care for Bell; Bell adores Natalie on sight; and Natalie, with the imbecilic perverseness of a heroine at the center of a mystery, refuses to explain why she was in that room at that time.

As Bell discovers, her motives were noble. He also discovers an exceedingly complicated and chancy death mechanism of the sort which operates only in 1919 detective stories. The mystery is solved and Fox is only too glad to apologize to the glorious Miss Gray.

"Behind the Green Door" (July 15) concerns the loss of a most highly secret, sensitive paper of the utmost delicacy from millionaire's vault. If the contents of that paper were to become known, he would lose his wife's esteem. And a hateful blackmailer has it in hand. But he reckoned without Garnett Bell...

"Through the Reading Glass" (September 23, 1919) tells how an unpleasant fellow was shot by an antique pistol hanging on the wall. Turns out that it was exploded by the sun focused through a magnifier. Scotland Yard was unable to discover that. They couldn't catch the murderer, either. Nor did they lay a finger on Mr. Bullivant, who seems to have lifted the central device from the Uncle Abner story, "The Doomsdorf Mystery."

Bell is a mighty clever fellow. Bullivant treats him with all the respect due a detective of his powers. But then, everyone treats Bell with respect. After an initial coolness, Scotland Yard takes to calling him in whenever it is oppressed by lack of success. And Natalie—recognizing that the hero never marries till the final story of a series—is only too glad to remain engaged for ever and ever. Or at least until the end of the book:

Natalie: "My dear Garnett, you're far too closely engaged to work and wedded to your profession even to think of another and more binding union."[22]

You can't tell from that remark whether she's had second thoughts or whether she's being the perfect story book heroine. You wonder what Bell made of it.

You know precisely what M. Hercule Poirot would have made of it. No delicacy of emotion was too fragile or too furtive to escape his attention. No nuance of behavior failed to be observed and recorded in the machinery of his mind. Did Miss Natalie speak enigmatically? Then Poirot must test her words and inflections, her expression, her relationships with others, her stated hopes and beliefs. Until the little gray cells do their work and he understands.

Like Poggioli, Poirot detects constantly. It is a way of living. Curiosity plays a part, but more basically he requires order. The neatness of his person, the order of his personal life, are outward signs of his inner precision. It is a cool inner life, almost mechanical, touched by compulsion. We can forgive him that. We can forgive Poirot much.

Beside such a Gibson illustration as Bell, Poirot is a ridiculous figure. This green-eyed little dandy, tubby and self important, his egg-shaped head carried a little to one side, his enormous moustaches stiff with wax, is a figure of broad comedy. When we meet him, he is already old. His great days were long ago, 1904 or 1910, when, as a member of the Belgium police, he was acknowledged as the greatest detective in Europe. After he retired, the glory faded, as glory will. Now reduced by the tricks of time, he has become a refugee, one of many, driven from his country by the German invasion during World War I. When we first meet Poirot, he is living with other refugees in Essex in the tiny town of Styles St. Mary, a point of destiny. At Styles Court, a manor house in that town, he will open and close his career.

To repeat, he is old. Old. Pitying smiles follow him. He must be ga-ga with age, senile, touched. Look at him—an ancient dandy and as comic as ancient dandies have ever been.

Christie uses Poirot's age and appearance to remove him from that state of inhuman perfection which curses story book detectives and freezes reader sympathy. Like Christie, and unlike most fictional characters, Poirot also uses his age and appearance for carefully calculated purposes.

These are thoroughly ambiguous. Poirot does not wish to change his appearance. He is himself, incomparable and unique. That other see him differently, he understands. Their misapprehension of his qualities he exploits, as he exploits his accent and his presumed inability to understand English customs. If he is underestimated, he can collect information more easily. He may even disarm an adversary. Valuable enough advantages in exchange for a few smiles.

He is, as mentioned, intensely aware. Neither age nor pride dull that precise mind. It remains to the end the most sensitive instrument in detective literature.

At the beginning of the series, the debt to Holmes is immediate and clear. In *The Mysterious Affair at Styles* (1920), Captain Arthur Hastings promptly assumes the Watson role. He does Watson poorly. For, as Hastings draws himself, he combines vanity with self absorption and stupidity. He is so immensely thick that we can hardly understand Poirot's affection for him. But there it is. At the opening of *The Big Four* (1927), we find Poirot preparing to endure the horrors of ship travel; he is planning to move to South America and live near Hastings. This suggests that Hastings is a different man than presented in the books and short stories. Perhaps it is a case of the narrator caricaturing himself, which we have also noted in the Poggioli series.

Holmes had Lestrade and Poirot has Detective Inspector Japp of Scotland Yard—a "little, sharp, dark, ferret faced man." Rivalry burns half acknowledged in Japp's heart. He is not of Poirot's ability and the knowledge makes him at once condescending and eager to pick Poirot's brain. In early stories of the series, he serves as the useful official contact without which the private investigator of fiction could not easily function.

Other Holmes' touches fill the text. Poirot has a London apartment on Farroway Street and a kindly landlady named Mrs. Pearson. To these rooms, the clients come tripping in the accredited Doyle fashion, accompanied by a rattle of deduction. It is all quite classical.

Poirot entered the American pulp magazines in a series of short stories that began with September 1923 issue of *Blue Book* and continued through August 1924. A second series, "New Exploits of Hercule Poirot," began in December 1924 and continued to the end of 1925. These stories were later collected in various volumes, including *Poirot Investigates* (1924), *Three Blind Mice* (1950), *The Under Dog* (1951), and *Double Sin and Other Stories* (1961).[23] (Further details on the *Blue Book* Poirots are given in the checklist, Appendix.)

During 1927 Poirot returned to *Blue Book* in the series published as *The Big Four* (1927). The story, a wild and wonderful melodrama, features four masterminds of crime controlling an international organization of evil. Accompanied by Hastings (here at his most stupid), Poirot solves a series of minor mysteries while evading death traps galore. Eventually there comes one too many traps and Poirot vanishes, undoubtedly dead. He is replaced by his smooth-shaven brother Achille, whose identity need concern no one long. The Big Four are obliterated by explosion and the world is pure once more.

There is something irresistibly enticing about international syndicates of crime. Authors from Nick Carter and Doyle to Sayers and Maxwell Grant have attempted the idea, usually to their regret. The mountain of criminality conjured up fails to remain menacing; during the course of the story, it gradually shrinks from a mountain to a hill, from a hill to a rise, and reduces from that to a rabble of people who have forgotten where they left their secret hideout. The Fu Manchu epics show similar internal shrinkage.

The Big Four are as inept as any other collection of criminal geniuses. With all the money in the world and all the manpower to do their evil will, they manage to do little but kill a few walk-on parts. They can't seem to harm Poirot; they are almost unable to touch Hastings. Their immense schemes vanish like a soap bubble in a cactus hell. Given a touring car and a few boys from Cicero or Jersey City, you could take over the whole conspiracy right after breakfast and have plenty of time to wash up for lunch.

The Big Four is not properly a novel but a loosely associated series of short stories. That's the way *Blue Book* published them. This results in an episodic novel in which the parts are better than the whole. And on the whole, the book is one of the lesser gems in Mrs. Christie's crown.

7-

Poirot began in Holmes' image and through a brilliant series of transmutations became his own man, original and an influence in his own right.

A similar development may be followed in the career of Jimmie Lavender. Less vividly drawn than Poirot, far less influential, Lavender still remains one of the finest 1920s detectives to follow in Holmes' footsteps. He is an admirable figure.

He was the creation of Vincent Starrett (1886-1974), a passionate Holmes addict. Starrett was also a writer about books, a lover of books—particularly detective stories. A newspaperman in 1920s Chicago, Starrett's "Books Alive" column in the *Chicago Tribune* became nationally famous. Like his friend, Christopher Morley, Starrett lived his days in bookish pleasures and bibliophile's delights. The elusive first edition called him. He knew that clear fragile joy of holding a book whose covers are pristine stiff, the paper untouched by light. More important, he knew the pleasure of used books, old books, books triumphant in their soil, foxed paper and warped boards. Starrett, of all men, could describe that flick of the heart that surpasses all things when, from the 25 cent table, you draw a title long sought. Such moments separate the book lover from the collector, whose shelves accrue mere value.

A bookman then of experience, deep into Sherlock Holmes. Starrett published that fascinating study, *The Private Life of Sherlock Holmes* (1933) and from Holmes extracted a more modern hero. Jimmie Lavender's adventures appeared in a variety of magazines, including *Short Stories, Real Detective Tales*, and *Mystery Magazine*, from 1923 to about 1939. In 1944, a dozen stories were collected in *The Casebook of Jimmie Lavender*, reprinted in 1973.

Lavender is a self-employed private investigator. He is too specialized to be referred to as a private detective. He lives in a third-floor apartment on Portland Street across from an elevated station. You enter a "rather dingy corridor," climb a great many stairs, knock. Enter a room having an open fireplace (but without correspondence pinned there by a jackknife). The room is crammed with books and chemical apparatus. Selected souvenirs of past cases decorate the cheerful mess.

Lavender's outstanding characteristic is a solitary lock of white hair which thrusts "upward like a heron's plume in his tangle of dark hair."[24] Other physical characteristics are evasive. He smokes cigarettes, plays piano fairly well. Is an intense golfer. His thinking is quick, sequential, less romantic than Sherlock's. Between cases, boredom is apt to roll in and he groans, like Holmes:

"Upon my word..., I am often tempted to turn criminal myself. Detection is a 'busted' bubble. It is only the sensational masterpiece of crime that make the game alluring."

As a murderer once wrote to him: "You are really much too clever, my dear Mr. Lavender. They should put you in a book."

His attitude toward the law and criminals is as flexible as that of Holmes. He is not above jiggling the evidence slightly to force a murderer to reveal himself. Or he will suppress the guilt of a particularly decent person, if no one else will be harmed.

Lavender is on a first-name basis with major figures in Scotland Yard, the New York Police Department (where he can have a job whenever he asks for it), and the Chicago police. He has been practicing for about twenty years and is, therefore, contemporary with Nick Carter and Felix Boyd. He is called in on a surprising number of police cases. As he remarks in "The Case of the Two Flutes," he is merely "augmenting the official investigation." The police accept him as an equal and an insider. You have none of that objectionable deference to him, the private investigator, which makes the Bell stories so irritating.

The Watson of the series is Charles Gilruth, called Gilly, a name with lightly sardonic overtones. Gilly modestly effaces himself. He has little dimension and less presence, unlike Watson, whose presence filled the Holmes stories. Watson is a figure of personal history; his opinions and thought lend weight to the fiction. But Gilly is transparent. He is a voice without history, a presence without a shadow.

Like Gilly, Jimmie Lavender's series leaves no substantial feeling. It is filled with a delicate, silvery light, passionless and cool. But there is no doubt that the stories occur in the real world of human passions and foolishness.

When Starrett shows us that world, he has scrubbed it of all extraneous detail. Few colors and odors intrude. It is an interesting world but remote, vital but bloodless. The characters talk American and are alive. But they appear at a distance. You cannot quite make out whether they live or are images projected on the silver light.

The stories, themselves, represent the transition from the strictly formal problem of deduction to the action detective short story. Gangsters frequently appear. These generate significant moments of peril. They are willing to blow off heads or batter down the hero with metal-encased fists.

The bad women of the stories show a remarkable tendency to shoot when matters get tight. Lavender is a frequent target. If they don't shoot, then they are clever in other ways, and are capable, for example, in poisoning successfully under the noses of the detectives.

The scene is contemporary 1920s and favors upper class sites—nightclubs, country clubs, millionaire's penthouses that are jammed with rare curios and problems that defy solution.

The adventures that certainly not hidebound. A sealed room problem evolves into exposure of a gambling ring and official police corruption. A blackmail case that begins in farce ends, late at night, with the blackmailer being coldly battered by fists.

In a crashed airplane is found a man who does not know how to fly. From a Chicago backyard is dug the headless skeleton of a man insured for $100,000. Murder in the night club: as two guns blaze at him, the victim tumbles dead. But without a mark on him.

Murder aboard the ghost ship, afloat three years after it was believed sunk, drifting the ocean in a Hodgson-like atmosphere, and carrying a withered corpse with a knife between the ribs.

To these problems, Lavender brings a Holmes logic and a Holmes flair for the theatrical. It isn't Baker Street but you can read the stories without feeling that you have been cheated.   Granted that it was not always the case. Life has its downs as well as its ups, and the pulp magazines never managed to circumvent that rule, no matter how breathless the editorial promises. Those pulps that flirted so roguishly at you from 1920s news stands had their own problems. Few of them were specialized titles. Most still attempted to appeal to every reader in the world. This optimistic effort insured that each issue contained one story which acted on the reader as briskly as a dose of ipecac. Such was the art of the editor that no ever agreed which story was terrible and which superb. Readers are a contentious lot.

Some readers expressed rare delight in the detective fiction of Florence Mae Pettee. We met her feminine version of Sherlock Holmes in an earlier chapter. She had a few masculine versions as well. These were published by gifted editors in popular magazines, and readers bought the magazines, and the characters appeared so frequently, they became series characters. It is remarkable.

Early in 1923, *Argosy-All Story Weekly* began the short series, "The Exploits of Beau Quicksilver".…

8-

Beau Quicksilver was known to the underworld as "that damned dude dick". At least that is what Florence Pettee said, and she wrote the series: Seven stories from February 24, 1923, through April 7. Considering all the worthy material that *Argosy All-Story* did publish, you wonder why the magazine bothered with Beau Quicksilver. The editors must have owed Madame Pettee money.

Back in her innocent girlhood, Pettee surely read Nick Carter or Felix Boyd instead of Jane Austen and Bertha Clay. The traces linger in her prose:

From object to object, Quicksilver's steady gaze coursed. He was like some superb bloodhound, nostrils aquiver for the first scent of the truth.

Her head is full of melodrama—mysterious poisons—mummy cases—stupid police—weird menace—penetrating geniuses—elaborate murders—the works.

The adventures are described in a prose written by a girl who has spent her life reading very fast. Beyond the covers of a book, she has had no experience.

Alertly Quicksilver strode to the door, a cigarette clamped between his teeth...

She has never listened to people talk:

—"...subterfuge is useless before blighting facts."
—"Quicksilver, you're barking up a wrong tree."

And her grasp on the meaning of words is highly tentative:

—Quicksilver sat immobile. He might have been carved from joss.
—"It will revolutionize present day fallacies..."

Nor does she hesitate to dress her sentences in silks and laces and send forth her words highly rouged:

Just as the bluecoat raised gnarled knuckley fingers for a more violent summons, the door opened.

Quicksilver remained fiction's most acute pain in the neck, until the coming of Philo Vance. In appearance, Quicksilver is a toff, a dandy, a dude of Terry Trimble class, a glowing testimony to smart men's furnishings. He lounges into the story so bored that he can barely tap an imported cigarette against his monogrammed silver cigarette case. By some fugitive humor his speech is slangy, crisp as celery:

"Swing in the facts from the start. Cut the frills."

By labored contrast, his friend, Police Chief Cartman, speaks sentences as can scarce be articulated by the human tongue:

"The door refused our shoulder third degree; so I shot my way in. And, gad, Quicksilver, 'twas some dope dream I stumbled into."

Cartman, an "elephantine" fellow, speaks in "staccato brusqueness." He is Chief of the C.I.D. (the scene is in America) and he serves nicely as the pitiful foil who does not know what it is all about. He is one of the new breed of police chiefs who goes investigating on his own—no patrolman or detective is ever in sight.

But who needs detectives, policeman, the cumbersome apparatus of a police force, as long as the Chief can persuade Quicksilver to investigate. Why, that man, that man...

...was an enigmatical crime chaser—a mercurial mystery master. Like a chimerical will-of-the-wisp, he lunged to the answer in each cryptic case. No wonder they dubbed him Quicksilver. He ran through a fellow's fingers just like mercury. There had never been another sleuth like him... No one could fathom how he landed the goods. His methods were just that elusive.

And finical! Why, a spoiled operatic star couldn't equal him for temperament! That fellow wouldn't touch a case with the tip of his nobbiest cane if the thing didn't interest him. They couldn't beg, hire or steal him to it.

"Nothing doing!" he would call back with languid insolence, as he irritatingly slipped the ashes from some imported cigarette end. "That crime smells stale at the outset. It's racy Roquefort or nothing!" And when Beau Quicksilver opined thus it meant finis. The case was dead for him. But when some baffling mystery turned up! Ah, then the scintillating sparks flew! There was a flash of Quicksilver. Followed by the startling showdown![25]

The image of Quicksilver varied slightly from story to story, depending upon which classical detective Pettee happened to be thinking of at the moment. In the initial story, "A Tooth for a Tooth," Dupin, Holmes, and Nick Carter are shredded and tossed together like ingredients in a garden salad. You are never sure which detective will glimmer in the next paragraph.

As the story opens, Chief Cartman drives to Quicksilver's residence to implore him to investigate the murder of wealthy Cyrus Whitney. Shunta, Quicksilver's adoring servant, conducts the Chief to the dim room where the great man sprawls, exhausted by a recent case:

A figure lay on the luxurious couch. There was a tall glass on the taboret beside him. He was clad in the most elegant of silk pyjamas. Imported Chinese embroidered sandals covered the feet... The dead white (of the high forehead) accentuated the smoldering, almost feverish brilliancy of the tired gray eyes. The purple shadows of complete exhaustion lay beneath the fiery orbs. Despite the fatigued and fretful lines of the oval face, the features stood forth delicate, sensitive, but baffling in their elusive suggestions of hidden strength. And the jaw whispered of the martial force of a Napoleon.[26]

Like Napoleon, Quicksilver is small, a rather short, thin man, who weighs about 155 pounds. He is a giant of action, however. No sooner does the Chief catch his interest than they are off to the scene of the crime. There lies the millionaire, shot dead amid the fragments of a luxurious meal served in his study. Tooth marks on a piece of cheese lead to a frame up with a pair of false teeth, a crooked dentist, a mysterious plotter known as The Falcon, and a greedy thief who eats whenever his mouth is empty.

The reader who wishes to detect along with Quicksilver is going to be disappointed. The story intends to show the excellence of the detective, not to let every seedy reader with ten cents get into the detection business. The few clues have meaning only because of Quicksilver's special knowledge; he shares this with neither reader nor police. Most of the detection takes place off the page. Even Quicksilver's assistant, Penn Markham, fails to understand what's going on. Under the circumstances, that's all right, for this is decidedly a one-man show.

In"The Hand of The Hyena" (March 17, 1923), that ferocious killer-robber-and universal fiend, The Hyena, warns Quicksilver to keep his nose out. He does not. With the immediate result that he is hanged by the neck from a tree on an island. Easily escaping from this contretemps (he wears a flesh-colored steel throat protector), Quicksilver maroons the gang and puts an end to their reign of evil.

"The Green Rajah" (March 24) is an immense emerald stolen by that devil of crime, The Chameleon. The owner only laid it down, turned away a moment, turned back to find it gone. In a closed room. Could this be magic. Quicksilver, who appears in only the final pages, proves it was nothing but disguise and trickery.

"Blistering Tongues" (March 31) features the Chief and Quicksilver investigating the death of an eccentric professor. Poor fellow was found dead in a mummy case on a blazing hot afternoon. The furnace had been turned on, which turns out to be a clue.

After Quicksilver has found other clues shared with no one, off he goes to the home of another professor. There, with the author's approval, Quicksilver enters the house without permission, searches without authority, opens the professor's safe without difficulty.

Chief Cartman stands mildly by watching all this. Nor does he wince. Not once. A very broad-minded man and a credit to the force.

Now it is time for the final dramatic scene. Quicksilver and Cartman confront the guilty party—a jealous professor. Seems that he painted the mummy case (in which his rival was in the habit of sleeping) with cyanide paint. This vaporized in the heat of the furnace.

The guilty wretch attempts suicide with a poisoned paperweight. Unfortunately he is prevented from doing this. It puzzles the heart to think how he intended to accomplish the dire deed.

Surely, surely, you say, this must be satire. Parody, at the least. But apparently not. It seems merely inept.

The final story of the series, "Murder Incognito" (April 7), concerns another dead millionaire. He's been found in a sealed room in a sealed cabin of an isolated island. Suicide, obviously, since an open gas jet has filled the room solidly with gas. Quicksilver proves murder in short order, by the evidence of a stopped clock and a Kurdish rug that has been hung over the fireplace.

After this case, Quicksilver vanishes from view, with all the trappings of his highly formalized world. The Pettee fiction machine continued to pour forth stories and characters, and, within two months, she had introduced Digby Gresham to *Argosy All-Story* readers.

Gresham is a milder fellow than the high strung, arrogant Quicksilver. Gresham is a transparent Holmes types, investigating lightly bizarre problems amid a cloud of author adulation. The stories are thickly caked with words that need scraping off.

The earliest story noted, "Ashes," appeared in the June 1923 *Detective Tales*. Other stories were published in 1923 and 1924 issues of *Argosy All-Story Weekly*. In 1925, Gresham's adventures shifted to *Flynn's Weekly*, where they appeared intermittently into 1927.

No matter where he appeared, Gresham didn't change much. He remained constant—thirty-five years old, broad shouldered, above medium height. He is cast in Beau Quicksilver's mold, having a "high forehead, the almost feminine delicacy of the features belied by a strong chin and a firm, invincible jaw." Madame Pettee just loves him.

He is a private investigator like Philip Marlowe. Unlike Marlowe, the police are so fond of Gresham that they tumble over themselves to serve him. As a result, he can do almost anything that would land the rest of us in jail. To his most startling transgressions, the police respond with gurgling admiration. Clearly, superiority tells.

"Dead Men Tell Tales" (*Argosy All-Story Weekly*, March 1, 1924) describes how vengeance-mad Nolan Dent stabs his enemy, Amos Vance, and pitches him into a vat of molten steel. No one notices.

Gresham is employed to discover what happened to Amos. He suspects Dent but can prove nothing. Days pass. Dent packs up and moves to another town. Gresham follows. Nothing happens. Then a new town bell is delivered. The author does not tell us that the bell contains the metal in which Mr. Vance was blended. But apparently so. No sooner does it dong than Dent falls to pieces:

"Can't you put me where I won't hear it—that tolling thing? Yes, I killed him! God! Can't you lock me up away from the sound of that devilish death chant!"

The Pettee stories in *Flynn's* are usually less volatile than this. They have expanded, as rice in water, until they fill the pages with a flat, frantic prose. Within this, ghosts peers, secret doors gap in fireplaces, sinister cloaked figures glide blackly, weird voices laugh, bodies appear, murderous automobiles dart from the darkness. The stories contain almost everything but a coherent narrative line.

Through it all strides Gresham, bursting with information that he got someplace and is keeping to himself. He shoves imperiously into other people's homes. He orders the police to come and go. He is very bossy, but they love. it.

In the "Touch of the Dead" (*Flynn's Weekly*, January 10, 1925), Steven Allenby, a policeman, suns Gresham up exactly:

"...that real crime-scout, old Digby... (is) a human barometer..., a regular seismograph, for carrying scrawled on his solar plexus all atmospheric shindigs surrounding the scene of the crime."[27]

Allenby is described as having a "slapstick nonchalance." Apparently a goblin has cursed him so that he is unable to speak English.

The story tells of a deserted old mansion in which a dead body appears. Under the nails of its right hand is a mysterious powder. Then there isn't any powder. Instead there are ghost voices, terrorizing family and servants. Gresham goes in and out of doors, and the police gape. After a very long time, Digby discovers that the crazed social worker did it. By then, the story has been so distended with hokum, we don't care.

As the characters of Beau Quicksilver and Digby Gresham demonstrate, the influence of Holmes persisted, although sadly diluted and diminished. The Pettee characters are hardly characters at all. They are presented with a raw directness of a child's fingerpainting: a few flashy traits, a few admiring gasps from admiring secondary characters. Insufficient material from which to construct an enduring, or human, or interesting figure. Around them reels a jerry-built structure intended to be a mystery, but which fails to be anything but a series of galloping events, only loosely associated.

Lacking characters or a coherent structure, the story relies on movement and constant surprise to sustain itself. The effect is of someone setting off fireworks in a small room. It is startling, if not exactly fiction.

While these variations on Holmes stumbled about the market place, another group of figures was developing in *Flynn's*. That magazine was, in 1925, still struggling for an identity in the face of powerful competition. Its pages were dense with English mystery fiction and many of its series characters were not so far removed from Baker Street that they did not reveal gleaming splinters of Holmes and Watson.

Some of the variations worked on that respectable influence were interesting and successful. Other were grotesque.

As was Inspector George F. Hopper of the Queen City Detective Bureau.

9-

In a previous volume, we caught a glimpse of Inspector Hopper being a scientific detective. Always interested in science, George was. He enjoyed a brief, merry career in *Flynn's Weekly*: Three years or perhaps a trifle more. Bertrand Royal wrote the series.

The stories are inflated with wind, and Hopper, for most of the series, is only crudely realized. He is presented as a genius but succeeds only in being ridiculous. He does represent an early instance of the Sherlock Holmes line trying, without much success, to blend with the professional policeman story.

Hopper does. He is Chief Inspector as the series opens. He specializes in abstract reasoning.

Query: Are Hopper's deductions genuine?

Deduction: It seems that the author does not know what a deduction is and, therefore, is putting us on.

Corollary: The rest of Mr. Royal's story is fake, too.

The "Query," "Deduction," "Corollary" routine is used by Hopper whenever he finds a piece of paper and a pencil. With these simple tools, he pours out pure twaddle. Admittedly he has one major success. In the short story, "When Time Stood Still" (June 20, 1925), he reasons accurately enough to free himself from a jail cell and a rather nebulous murder charge. He is also able to tell investigating officers exactly where to look for fingerprints and other physical evidence. All this he worked out mentally.

At series' beginning, in 1924, he drivels and babbles as if a seam had burst in his forehead. He has been in police work for seven years. In spite of that experience, he talks in supposedly sparkling sentences which make him sound demented:

Hopper: "I'm a little late. Got interested in a problem involving time. Worked it out, but forgot the flight of time. Did you ever know, Mr. Commissioner, that time, although unseen and invisible, may yet be anticipated and an event depending upon time foretold?"

You might foretell that the police commissioner, to whom these veering remarks are directed, is going to relieve Hopper because of mental collapse. Nothing so sensible happens, and Hopper continues in full spate:

"I have just figured out when the two hands of my watch would be together—practically eclipse each other. Interesting little experiment. I'll show it to you someday. You see, all you have to use is a ghost—only we don't call it by that name. We call it 'X' because it is unknown. It's a handy thing to know in police business..."[28]

He is obviously addicted to something very strong.

As usual in the early Hopper stories, the first chapter is a crude recap of some scientific theme that the author has been reading. In "The Handcuffed Ghost" (November 4, 1924), Hopper lectures his detective squad on the philosophy of perception according to Hume. Thereafter, the theme is leadenly inserted into the story—which concerns the attempted shakedown of an Italian storekeeper. The critical clue (part of a man's finger hanging from a telephone pole), isn't mentioned till the final moments.

As you might suspect, the squad members admire Hopper intensely. Miss Florence Jones (who will soon become Mrs. Flory Hopper) thinks he's just sweet.

Others do not. Professional jealousy within the police department shortly bring him up on faked charges. This occurs in "Through To a Showdown" (November 22, 1924). His investigation of a gambler's murder gets mixed up with politics. (Or perhaps not politics; perhaps his superiors just got fed up with his pretentious language and lack of consecutive thought.) Anyhow, he is charged with something or other, but resigns. Goes back to the vine-covered cottage his old mother willed him, in which lives his sweet, 7-year old adopted son. As an afterthought, he solves the murder case, shaming the corrupt officials.

Following this triumph, he marries Miss Jones and, for the rest of the series, is referred to as ex-Inspector Hopper. He continues as a private consultant, becoming one of the very earliest to have some sort of police background. He continues to write those cockeyed analyses to himself. These thoroughly impress his friends, one of whom refers to him in this fashion:

"What a brain! A golden bowl brimming with mental nectar."

By the end of the series, Hopper has become a lawyer and is making a success of it, thank you.

Essentially he is a lone wolf private detective. While in the early stories, he has subordinates to investigate elements of the problem, all threads—and all deductions—remain in Hopper's hands. At this time he is 28 years old, gray eyed, smokes cigars, and has a brain like a golden bowl filled with mental nectar.

"Across the Border" (December 27, 1924) concerns a tricky stock swindle across three states. Hopper goes forth investigating and is killed by electric shock. He gets it off a door knob. He stays dead twelve minutes. Then an interfering doctor brings him back to life.

The 1924-25 stories are great soft gigantically inflated and mushily wobbling bags of tumultuously inapplicable verbiage excessively elucidated in an expository manner, very gassy. Bits of semi-scientific concepts float in the prose as bits of carrot in the gravy.

The prose does not remain this disastrous throughout the series. In later stories, waste wordage is sheared away. The characters begin to talk like people and even Hopper grows human. He is reasonably competent in "When Clews Converged" (September 26, 1925), when he recovers a stolen diamond necklace, clears three framed crooks, and crushes an arch plotter, all by reasoning.

"Clews Concealed" (September 11, 1926) is a very long novelette. Hopper is now an attorney-at-law and solves a robbery, plus long-range murder by rifle. The prose is tight and clean, the action line strong, and the dialogue sounds as if flesh and blood could speak it. The fiction is far superior to earlier inanities.

For all the drivel of the 1924-1925 stories, they include certain interesting elements of police inter-departmental rivalry, political interaction, and personnel administration during criminal investigation. These factors were almost unknown in the mysteries of the period. Royal handles them badly, but they are mentioned at all is encouraging. You needn't look for the police procedural in this place, however; the fiction lacks all feel for the realities of police work. They are simply problem stories with a pseudo-official setting.

A more flamboyant private investigator than Hopper is Henry Rood, a big, beaming country boy come to the city to get into *Flynn's*. Henry is a certified graduate of the "Eureka Correspondence System of Crime Detection, specializing in Finger Printing and Deduction."

His education did him little good. He pays out $1000 to buy the Argus Detective Agency, run by a shabby old swindler who immediately decamps. Then the men come for the unpaid office furniture; the landlord wants all that back rent.

Henry finds himself stripped and standing in the street with the agency secretary, a Miss Mildred Canby. She is a brightly tinted young woman with short black hair. She regards her new boss with less than admiration, referring to him as "The poor simp."

All this is told in "Henry Rood—Successor" (September 12, 1925) by Jack Bechdolt. Although matters look dim for Henry at this point, the sun returns in the final pages. Henry stumbles over a holdup man, captures him, earns a $2000 reward.

These pleasant events place Henry squarely in the mainstream of filler detective stories—the kind that bulge their cheeks and stamp their feet to make the reader laugh. Most of the humor in a comic detective story lies in watching the writer struggle to be funny. In his role as the dumb cluck who makes good, Henry Rood is mildly amusing. Very mildly.

As usual, the massive hand of coincidence falls freely. It is the sure way to a happy ending.

"For Twenty Grand" (October 10, 1925) tells how Mildred rescues Henry from a gaggle of crooks, chiselers, and a beautiful blond—all gathered on a small Atlantic island. By this time, Mildred is in love with Henry and proposes to him at the end of the story.

About a year later, "The Plague of Cats" (September 18, 1926), they are still engaged. By this time, the original joke—smart girl, dumb boy— has been exhausted and Mr. Bechdolt, with the slyness of his kind, has quietly reversed the roles. Mildred has become a flighty sweetie who, for reasons of comic characterization, ispermitted torun allherwords to getherin to clusterslikethis.

Although Henry is still not bright, he has developed a trace of detective ability. He detects a murderer who has filled an old skinflint's home with cats, the better to terrorize him. The situation is pleasingly bizarre. It is not enough to save the series, which vanishes soon afterward.

Some fairly bizarre things happened to Derek Trent, too. He was a diluted essence of Sherlock Holmes, transposed to New York and given the benefit of a friend named Edward Santry. Santry is a lawyer and he is not denser than a stone wall. Trent is another amateur who is said to be a private investigator. He has private means, assuring that he won't starve while practicing his profession.

Trent receives minimum characterization. He has a pointed chin, long fingers (which drum as he thinks), and a remarkable memory. In deference to Holmes' musical ability, he plays piano—not righteous, God-fearing jazz, but forgotten hymns. He plays these very slowly in a variety of keys, causing intense depression in the listener.

Trent's brief series appeared in the 1924-1925 *Flynn's Weekly* and was written by Charles Rodda, later a collaborator with Eric Ambler. Like other *Flynn's* fiction from these dark times, the stories are strong on odd devices and hyper-activity, whatever they lack in reasoned structure.

In "The Mark of the Paw" (November 22, 1924) some fiend is hurling a cat with poisoned claws upon his victims. That's what the police think. In these stories, the police think strange things. Trent suspects that the police are wrong. One dark and stormy night, the fiend drops a tree across the road and, when Trent attempts to move it, the fiend fires point black, three times. Misses every shot. Thereafter, Trent proves that the murders were committed with a device that left marks like cat claws. He is shrewd.

"The Seventh Mandarin" (December 27, 1924) is that ever popular idea of something valuable being hidden inside one of a series of statues. To locate the valuable, the villain must steal one statue after the other. In the Sherlock Holmes version, the valuable was hidden in a bust. In the Trent version, it is inside the figure of a mandarin. The sneering, merciless Yung Hsi has learned this secret and is collecting mandarins. He is very bad, and when Trent and Santry fall into his clutches, he leers:

"...neither you nor your friend will leave this house alive."

Remarks Santry: "The situation was growing more tense."

"The Sign of the Serpent" (January 17, 1925) introduces a deadly black swollen horror that walks by night. It hurls curses and feathers dipped in blood and is pretty scary. Under its curse, old John Halcott is fading away. Trent enlists the aid of a friendly voodoo doctor to save the old boy and then reveals the plotter's identify by the matter-of-fact method of shooting a hole in him.

"The Prince of Euralia" (January 24, 1925) is enriched with borrowings from Holmes. A sure-enough prince, engaged to a swell girl from Oklahoma, has abruptly pitched her over in favor of champagne parties and chorus darlings. Trent makes a shrewd deduction, couched in the Holmes' vernacular:

" Is his Highness fond of chocolate eclairs...? I can only impress upon you the importance of finding the answer to my question."

And further, in the fine old tradition of thumping Watson on the head: "Santry, I fear that you are unobservant. The garden path has told us quite a story."

"The Haunted Swamp" (April 11, 1925) features a glorious gigantic snake about 99 feet long and with blazing green eyes. It appears in a swamp at the exact place where a beautiful girl and her fool father are trying to start a housing development. Other people select beaches or lake fronts for development; these people like swamps. But in this swamp is something that doesn't like housing developments. And so the scene thickens with bodies half buried in mud, while the snake rises fierce on dark nights, its eyes glaring brightly. The only clue is a bloody hat and a razor blade embedded in that tree limb, up there, directly over where the snake was seen to rise.

Immediately Trent sees through the whole thing. The menace is ended and the developer, freed from danger at last, clutches Trent's arm to babble:

"...if you want a bungalow site at any time, there's no place to beat the Haunted Swamp."

Amusing slight stories. If there is little character development and less believability, the gimmicks are still interesting. Trent is hardly taken as seriously as, say, Dr. Nancy Dayland. And the villain is often hard to detect—unless you cheat and select the least likely man.

Another detective afflicted with acute Sherlock Holmesitis was announced in the September 11, 1926, issue of *Flynn's Weekly*. Walter Archer Frost, we are told, had prepared a series to be entitled "The Benevolent Sins of Ruggles," a thoroughly 1915 title. The idea seems to have been that a character with a shady past has reformed sufficiently to go around doing good—using shady methods. A semi-justice figure, a detecting Robin Hood; something like that. Ruggles is dedicated to helping the innocent, even if he breaks the law. "I'm a near crook," he tells his assistant, "but I wear better."

That remark must mean something for he keeps repeating it—to the bafflement of assistant and reader alike. When the agenbite of inwit nibbles powerfully, he also remarks: "There are pages in my life I'd give my soul to blot out."

No direct information is given of these pages. From broad hints, we gather that he must have been at least a Mafia Don. He has detailed knowledge about organized crime and its leaders. He knows all about the situation in New York City. Also in Mexico, South America, and Europe. About sixty different crooks want to kill him, a circumstance which makes him very careful. He carries two automatics and is referred to as the underworld's "most dreaded enemy." It is hard to understand why.

Ruggles is a great bull of a man, very powerful, with characteristics of this detective and that, and some of Bulldog Drummond, and a lot of Sherlock Holmes. Of himself (he says), I am "an amateur detective or volunteer criminologist." More accurately, he is a professional private investigator. His business is located on 86th St., New York City, in a first-floor apartment that has a device for viewing clients as they enter. Perhaps to count their machine-guns.

His assistant, Dan Crane, has been with Ruggles ten years and is all weak-kneed admiration.

Small wonder. Ruggles (by the way, he doesn't seem to have a first name) is adept at all Sherlock Holmes' little amazements:

"I can't say I know much about (the murderer) beside the fact that...he is tall and unusually powerful...(and) a recent injury to his left hand has not healed yet, favors English tweeds and knickerbockers... (His) right leg is somewhat stiff in the knee..."[29]

Then, dazzling all, he details how these conclusions were reached.

His deductive abilities are coupled with a fearsome range of information. In the first chapter of his first appearance, he discourses on:

—reptile poisons
—Pliny natural history
—habits of the red squirrel
—spider communication
—hearing range of the human ear
—the China Sea as a cyclone producer

For his part, Dan Crane salts every story with references to other cases from the past. Very Holmesian, indeed.

The series begins with a two-part serial, "The Garlic Bulbs" (September 18 and 25, 1926, *Flynn's Weekly*). This is a tale of grim revenge, all taking place out in the country. The adventure has been expanded from a short story to a two-part serial by packing in scenes, some of which are necessary to the action, and introducing quantities of alarms and excursions.

It is hard to tell who is doing what and why. This scared fellow is being pursued by someone with a trained *karait*—a mean snake. Since garlic bulbs drive away snakes, he is anxious to get some, and goes slipping out at night to dig for garlic in other people's gardens.

Instantly detecting what all the fuss is about, Ruggles prescribes a nice *ichneuman* (mongoose) as a specific for *karait*. Then the mongoose is killed by hands unknown and black horror walks...

Dan: "Who and what is this fiend, Ruggles?"
Ruggles: "There's no time to go into that now."

If he did, the story would end with Part I.

"Trapped" (October 2, 1926) takes place out in them West Virginyer hills. It features a diabolical frame-up, a framed prison guard, an unhappy ex-NYPD detective, and a savage outlaw. The innocent man is jailed. Ruggles promptly slips him from jail by forging a release order from the Chief of Police. It's as easy as that. This benevolent sin is proved justified, after the terminal gun fight brings down the true criminal. In the final column, the guard is saved from disgrace and Ruggles from blame.

"The Van Holberg Tragedy" (March 12, 1927) begins a rapid movement away from the mystery story toward the story of adventure action. It begins with Ruggles' client being found dead in his bed, all crushed. The cause was vengeance—Malay vengeance. The Malay servant is immensely strong and, what's more, has filled the food with chopped human hair, an additive reputed to cause death and such. Ruggles eventually ends this fellow's career by breaking his neck in a hand-to-hand finish. In spite of the action orientation, the story is simply littered with deductions.

Later stories leave the United States for romantic Java. Van Holberg hires Ruggles and Crane to protect him. He needs it. He is menaced by Chinese pirates, ex-cons, and torturing natives in "Jungle Hate" (March 19, 1927) and from a murderous anthropologist in "The Glavis Affair" (June 4, 1927).

Let's leave them at this point, far from home, sweating and deducting. Closer subjects call us.

Like so many other private investigators of the 1920s, Ruggles remained an inspired amateur yearning for a deerstalker hat. This yearning was endemic to the *Flynn's* of that period. Other magazines bowed gracefully to the English mystery school. *Flynn's*, however, worshipped at the shrine.

As in other forms of worship, there was loud public outcry calling attention to the superior qualities of *Flynn's*, even as in the magazine itself, less visible change shuddered and eddied through the pages like currents of air in a haunted room.

A watcher out of time may note a tendency to violence, rather than deductive talk, at story's ending. That Ruggles and other of the detectives face physical violence and use muscles, as well as intelligence. That the puzzle situations they face are complicated by measured injections of melodrama. That focus of attention was gradually shifting from problem to action, from polite middle-class murderers to more rugged social types.

Quiet change. *Flynn's* public face remained fixed on the English mystery and it loudly worshipped on the street corner.

Arthur Morrison is generally conceded to be one of the world's greatest masters of the short story.

His "Tales of Mean Streets" are everywhere regarded as classics. By a freak of fortune there have been unearthed recently the lost manuscripts of six splendid stories by Mr. Morrison.

Probably no other detective story magazine has every been able to offer such a literary feast to its readers.

Only Flynn's Weekly, edited by the greatest head the United States Secret Service has ever known, would be likely to show the enterprise that is represented in the acquisition of publication rights to these stories.[30]

Morrison had previously appeared in *Flynn's*. His deaf and dumb detective, Queg, had glowed palely in late 1925 issues. The scene was London; the time that never-never period when a householder, discovering murder, would call a private investigator, rather than the police. If they called Queg, they got a clever fellow. Two clever fellows—since Queg had an assistant named Ruff. No other names are given. The stories are slight and thoroughly improbable. Their main point of interest is that Queg is deaf and dumb, blindness having been already used by Max Carrados.

Queg investigates like a storm, scribbling endless cryptic shorthand notes to Ruff and staring hard at people's lips. "It Takes A Detective" (August 29, 1925) tells how poor Queg falls into the hands of vicious crooks. If only he could call out. But he can't. Instead he leaves his fingerprints all over things, as the criminals haul him (for ill-explained reasons) from crime to crime. The fingerprints represent a simple code. Ruff translates this and comes raging to the rescue.

"Louder Than Words" (September 26) features a wonderful murder gadget—a chair decorated with a carved dragon. Sit down and the dragon puffs a poisoned needle into you.

These stories are fragile as tissuepaper kites. They exist for the device, even then stale, and the spectacle of the severely handicapped detective rising above his problems. Queg ran his course and disappeared, but the idea of a handicapped detective floated around the periphery of mystery fiction until revived by *Dime Detective* and *Dime Mystery Magazine* around 1940.

A more enduring English detective than Queg, and with an equally interesting twist, began in the mid-1925 *Flynn's*. The detective was X. Crook, a self-explanatory pseudonym, since he was a reformed criminal become a successful private investigator. The series continued on and off into 1927 and later stories may exist.

The writer was J. Jefferson Farjeon (1883-1955), then beginning a long career as an author and dramatist. Born in London, son of a novelist, he was named for the American actor Joseph Jefferson. His first book, *The Master Criminal*, was published in 1924. From that date to the late 1940s, Farjeon turned out more than a book a year, many published under the name Anthony Swift. He specialized in mysteries with horror backgrounds, described as "the grandly sinister."

Not much of this is found in Fargeon's early mystery fiction. It was published in *Argosy*, *Flynn's*, *Detective Story Magazine*, and can be described as "the grandly conventional."

His character, Mr. X Crook, was an astute, middle-aged gentleman, pallid and gone iron-gray at the temples. Such symptoms of old age were caused by twelve years in prison. The sentence reformed him. He selected the name X. Crook to announce to the world that he had reformed. His true last name does not seem to have been given, although we learn that his first name was Henry. He is given to deep remarks: "A man who has found his conscience never goes back on anybody."

He opens for business in a quiet Hampstead street (a suburb in north-east London). His door is painted green and on it is mounted a brass nameplate.

Scotland Yard does not believe he has reformed. So little do they believe, so highly do they regard his skill at mischief, that Detective Edgar Jones is planted as Crook's butler. He calls himself William Thomas, as in Doubting Thomas.

Thomas watches Crook and boils with dire suspicion. Particularly since he attracts one crook after the other, all glitter-eyed with hope that Crook will rejoin them. The first to show up is Vera Norrington, Crook's ex-sweetheart. She arrives in "Red Eye" (June 20, 1925), the first of eight stories in the initial series.

Vera casts her spell, but Crook is untouchable. He is able to persuade her to disgorge the huge ruby she has just stolen and, by a series of manipulations so easy to heroes of short fiction, prevents a deadly Burmese from killing her. After all, the fellow only wanted to reclaim the ruby and stick it back into his favorite idol.

More glib crooks come calling in "Thomas Doubts No Longer" (July 11, 1925). They can't tweak Crook back to crime. Naturally it follows that they try to frame him. Can't do that either, although it's a near thing. Crook guns down the lead villain, just as he attempts to shoot a small boy obstructing his escape.

That good deed convinces Thomas that Crook has reformed. Filled with admiration, he allows that he is eager to cooperate on Crook's future cases. But he soon vanishes from the series. It was a stupid thing to pay a Scotland Yard man to do—even as, a few years later, it would be equally stupid to pay a New York City police officer to spy on Lester Leith.

The small boy saved by Crook's gun work is named Ernest Price or Pip. Being dirty, ragged, and clever, he serves Crook as all small, dirty, ragged boys serve the great detective—providing an eye in the streets, a little information, and a great deal of hero worship.

Still another frame-up is attempted in "Elsie Cuts Both Ways" (August 29, 1925). Crook gets out of the toils gracefully and again saves a young woman from a life of evil. On this inspiring note, the series ends.

And after a pause for inspiration, a new series begins. The stories concern a number of unorthodox mysteries in remote locales and improbable circumstances, including

—an elaborate plot to convince a Lord that he is a kleptomanic ("The Kleptomanic," September 18, 1926).

—an hotel thief who pretends to have been robbed ("The Hotel Hold-up," November 20, 1926).

—an amnesia victim who has forgotten that he murdered a fiend ("The Man Who Forgot," September 3, 1927). In this story, Crook agreeably helps conceal evidence of the crime, since the victim deserved it.

The Crook epic ran through 1927, paused to reflect and test the air, began a later group in September 1928, and shortly thereafter melted away to wherever series go when discontinued.

It was a long sequence of fiction. Plainly Mr. Crook possessed appeal, although its nature eludes us now. The stories are slight and conventionally handled. The crimes are elaborately arranged, like an Eighteenth Century hairdo, and the deductions are more so. It is all mannered and self conscious. Which could be forgiven, it the characters were not ciphers. Mr. Crook, himself, is as faceless as a No. 2 pencil.

10

To be faceless is an occupational hazard of a copy.

These faces from the Twenties and earlier are a varied lot. But at their base all are connected to Baker Street and the towering figures of Holmes and Watson astir in legendary London.

The personalities that Doyle built exerted a force anticipated by no one. Who could have predicted the persistence of these phantoms? But as long as Holmes—derived character types pleased readers, the magazines were pleased to offer monthly variations on the great originals.

Each writer created his own set of variations. The detective behaved as a preening fop, as a slangy romantic. He was crippled by physical defects or haunted by a criminal past. He was an ex-policeman hounded from his job, or a would-be scientist, or a two-gun thinker.

He was everything but a character whose peculiarities rose naturally from within, a personality alive in his own right. To the extent that his traits were imposed from without, as clay is applied to a wire form, to that extent he was artificial, a construct that moved and mouthed. And rarely lasted more than half a dozen stories.

The basic mystery narrative received as many self-conscious variations as the detective figure. Love interest was inserted, under the reasonable assumption that the reader would warm to the detective's affair of the heart. Humor was tried. Supernatural elements were included, so that they could be explained away, with impressive rationality, at story's end. A welter of miscellaneous scientific facts were added, as salt to the main dish, so that, for a few years, no detective dared venture forth without his microscope and bundle of litmus paper.

And into most stories was stirred increasing action and violence. The emphasis on action was a direct carryover from the dime novels, which never erred on the side of dullness. The dime novel style slipped directly in *Detective Story*, itself the standard against which later detective magazines competed.

Detective Story was influential. But it was certainly not the only influence. The action story was a familiar offering in the general fiction pulps, as it had been in the dime novels. That a strong action line would be transferred to the magazine mystery story could have been predicted by the dullest reader—even one who had never touched a dime novel.

Action story is a generic term for any fiction stressing movement and conflict above all else. It is orchestrated for trumpets and drums. The action story sets up a goal and piles the road to it with obstacles; over these, the hero struggles and groans. These obstacles include violent physical encounters and dangers and high speed chases through the scenery.

However, the pulp magazines elevated action to a major element of the mystery. Not just intellectual activity but physical movement, and plenty of it. In time, the mystery-adventure story emphasized action to the point of becoming lop-sided. The crime problem became a minor part of the adventure; all the rest was muscle, gun, and the threat of death.

The new magazine, *Clues*, which began in 1926, was a major vehicle for the action mystery-adventure. The magazine did not begin with such a clear-cut editorial policy. *Clues* groped around for almost a year before you began to hear its unique voice. By then, *Black Mask* had opened the hard-boiled era and *Flynn's* was feeling the first symptoms of the changes that would alter it to the tough, fast action *Detective Fiction Weekly*.

11-

Clues...just now is especially interested in detective or mystery novelettes, containing from 15,000 to 20,000 words. The editor prefers the mystery type of story, with a great deal of suspense and incident matter, and he does not object to a very slight love interest.[31]

The date was 1927 and *Clues*, in a word, was in the market for red-hot mystery adventure and action and thrilling events and action and peril terror thrills action. What was published was not quite as sensational as the editor might have wanted. The magazine fiction jittered nervously, glancing toward *Black Mask*, *Detective Story Magazine*, and *Flynn's*. The focus was on action, although action diluted by description and quantities of stiff dialogue. Improbable gangsters appeared and toughs who parsed their sentences. The pages creaked under the weight of police who performed in the brave, single man tradition.

Granted that the stories flouted police procedure and gangster procedure with sublime disregard for the real world. It wasn't important. A hot-running story that got off fast and was studded with violence—that was the point.

And at this point, one of *Clues'* first series characters turned from Baker street to what would soon be mainstream detective action fiction. His name was Barron Ixell, a sleek man of the world and a roving, consulting detective. His stories were written by Oscar Schisgall and were published from 1927 through about 1932. Four early stories were later collected in *Barron Ixell: Crime Breaker* (1929).

The name Ixell did not choke readers with indignant rage that they should be so trifled with. The name had a noble foreign ring. Readers instantly understood that they were in the presence of a superior being.

Superior he was. Mr. Schisgall freely admitted it. Ixell was the conventional rich fellow whose genius brings police fawning to his feet. He calls himself a criminologist. That is 1920s code for a wealthy individual who doesn't have to work and has taken up crime detection as a hobby. He may be a professional but he certainly receives little pay for his exertions.

You are well acquainted with the conventions of the figure—a man tall strong impeccably dressed. As to specific detail, his face was long, his hair brown, his age in the middle thirties.

An upper-class genius then, detached from society, stepping in to correct these little problems, then stepping out again.

The difference is that these stories are not the tame landscapes of the English mystery writers. Remember that *Clues* wanted suspense and incident. In practical terms, that meant someone got physically damaged every chapter. Or that the narrative stopped frequently to accommodate explosions of violence.

Ixell's little problems are not routine. No friendly murder puzzle at St. Mary Meade here. Ixell must contend with criminal geniuses whose schemes have tied the police in knots. The boss criminal lurks unknown beneath a fancy pseudonym—The King of Crime, Monsieur Satan, The Circle of Terror. Like the earlier criminal masterminds of *Detective Story Magazine*, these people reign in secret, usually operating with a small group that includes their woman, a lieutenant, a nimbus of hangers-on.

All have savage ways. Pal around with Ixell long enough and you will be hit on the head, tied up, pounded. Your nights will be sleepless, your days exhausting. It is a criminologist's life.

During the early stories, Ixell is traveling through Europe to study police methods. What he learns is that police are boneheads, whatever their nationality. In the fine old tradition, the police leap at Ixell's direction. They gawk at his accomplishments. They fumble all the important points. How else is a professional policeman supposed to act in the presence of the gifted detective.

Granted that Ixell's methods are original. His problem is always to close with the master criminal.

In "The Circle of Terror" (the scene is set in Brussels), Ixell poses as pickpocket to infiltrate an association of ferocious thieves. This is the usual pulp magazine gang—a gigantic glow of menace obscuring a tiny group.

Ixell is accepted into the group. Immediately he presses his luck, which has been simply marvelous, and presses it too far. Learning that the criminal top echelon is attending a fancy ball, he goes there undisguised, is recognized, and now violence comes frothing and shrieking from the monochrome prose.

With that authority vested in him by the author, Ixell orders a police raid on the criminals' hideout. Sooner than you would believe, the pages swarm with people waving guns. Then it's down down down the mandatory secret passage. Gunfight in the blackness. Mr. Big's right hand man is shot dead.

It is the action climax of the story, although not the end.

Another chapter remains. For nothing yet has been explained; and it is difficult to unravel a confusion like this in only a sentence.

So here we are again, cops and crooks grouped like schoolboys around Ixell as he lectures. Nostalgia blurs our eyes. It is the ancient Craig Kennedy terminal seance, revived for a new generation of readers and complete to the final detail. The detective is as brilliant, the police as dumb, the witnesses as fascinated as in those glorious days of 1912 when the world was new and tomorrow's war casualties merry.

Even by *Clues'* standards, these endings were unmercifully sluggish. Ixell explains for half a dozen pages of straight narrative and gradually works around to the true identity of the crime genius, exposed in the final words.

A similar structure is followed in most of these stories, for this is formula fiction, entirely without shame. The narrative bones are large and well marked: The police are baffled by a super criminal. Ixell thinks up a cunning trap which doesn't quite work, although it yields a lead. Then follows the search, the burst of violence, the gathering of the cast for the final revelations.

Formula it may be, but the situations are cleverly worked up. Ixell is pleasingly fertile in contriving tricks to expose that concealed criminal identity, the basic mystery of the story.

Monsieur Satan ("The Devil's Pigeons") is a Paris extortionist who promises to shoot you dead unless you part with your jewelry. Just drop it all in this bag and fasten it to the leg of a carrier pigeon, thoughtfully delivered to your room.

Ixell plans, conceives a clever trap, gets rapped violently on the head. Undaunted by failure, he tries again and still again. And finally the gang's hideout is located. Ixell ties a long string to one of the pigeons and he and the police go racing after the bird across French fields. It is an extraordinary scene.

"The King of Crime" reigns in Berlin. He is a slick thief who drugs and gasses his victims. Ixell positively scintillates. First he discovers the stolen gems (which the police promptly lose); then he follows the clue of the red clay—the only clay of its kind—to the suburbs.

There he is gassed and tied up. Burns himself free. Subdues four men. Nabs The King with his own gas bomb.

The police assist by exclaiming "Achtung," "Schnell," and "Herein aus."

In "Follow The Red Line" (scene, Geneva), Ixell unravels the problem of the kidnapped Russian diplomat. The ransom is to be delivered by an automobile driving across Switzerland, following the route on a red-marked map until a light is seen. Then five-million francs are to be dumped along the roadway.

The automobile is tracked from afar by airplane, a distinct technological advantage. But only Ixell deduces where the money drop is to occur. Then action, violence, thrills—all talked to tedium, as usual, in the final chapter. To that point, the story is one frantic chase.

The Barron Ixell series is a hybrid. Part is blood-hot action, part the conventional detective-as-genius school. From such mixed heredity sprang this variation of the lone-wolf private investigator. He was influenced by the tradition of Baker Street, if dimly. He displayed a trace of *Black Mask* toughness, but lacked its realism. He prowled the pages of *Thrilling Detective, 10 Detective Aces, Popular Detective*, those flawed jewels of the Thirties. And he remained jaunty and accomplished as melodrama swirled red about him and violence racked the story.

No matter how cunningly packaged, the present never quite cancels out the past. Nor did the action story succeed in eliminating the classical mystery. In the face of grave competition, Baker Street persisted. It persisted so vigorously that, with the help of August Derleth, it recreated itself in the figure of Solar Pons.

Derleth had written the first Solar Pons adventure when he was a nineteen-year old junior at the University of Wisconsin.

At the outset, I wrote to Sir Arthur to ask whether he intended to write more adventures of Sherlock Holmes... Early in autumn of 1928...he replied—by means of a terse message scrawled upon my own letter—that he did not. He seemed, as I recall it now, unnecessarily emphatic about it, as if this decision, made once previously and set aside, were now irrevocable, and no amount of persuasion would this time cause him to change his mind.[32]

Since Doyle declined to do so, Derleth resolved to write another Holmes story. The scene would be London, the time immediately after the retirement of "The Master" (as Pons referred to Holmes), and the characters those appearing in The Sacred Writings. They would include Dr. Lyndon Parker (narrating and performing Dr. Watson's function), Mrs. Johnson (housekeeper at 7B Praed Street, as was Mrs. Hudson at Baker Street), and Baron Ennesford Kroll (an arch-criminal of the Professor Moriarty class). And there was, chief among these, Solar Pons, not quite Holmes and yet a recreation of him.

I needed first a name, syllabically similar to that of Sherlock Holmes. So Solar Pons was born because I though of Solar in its suggestion of light, and Pons as the bridge—"bridge of light" seemed to the adolescent mind singularly brilliant, which, of course, it was not.[33]

Not brilliant but thoroughly durable. The first Pons adventure, "The Adventure of the Black Narcissus," was written in an afternoon and evening. Submitted to Harold Hersey, who had just started a new pulp magazine group, the story was promptly accepted—payment was $40—and published in the February 1929 issue of *The Dragnet*. Three additional stories appeared in *The Dragnet* before it was sold to A. A. Wyn's Magazine Publishers in 1930. Two other Pons stories were published in *Detective Trails*, December 1929, and *Gangster Stories*, March 1930. After this, Derleth's interest deflected in other directions, and Pons did not appear again in print until *The Misadventures of Sherlock Holmes* (edited by Ellery Queen) was published in 1944. In 1945, Derleth published the first Pons collection, *In Re: Sherlock Holmes*, under his own imprint of Mycroft & Moran. Later Pons adventures were published in various digest mystery magazines, including *Ellery Queen's Mystery Magazine*, (1950), *Nero Wolfe Mystery Magazine* (1954), *The Pursuit Detective Story Magazine* (1955-1956), *Double-Action Detective Stories* (1956), *Hunted* (1956), *The Saint Mystery Magazine/Detective Magazine* (1954-1964), and *Alfred Hitchcock's Mystery Magazine* (1961-1966).[34]

The series is charming and if the pastiche is a trifle thinner, a trifle less vital than the great original, and touched by an occasional Americanism that raises the eyebrows of purists, it is still wonderfully pleasing. Since we can have no more Holmes, Pons will do nicely.

12-

We have lingered overlong with the ghost of Sherlock Holmes. His influence was pervasive as air, relentless as gravity. So many investigators, male and female, amateur and professional, begin with Holmes. So few of these departed Baker Street for less traveled roads.

Holmes and his admirers are unique. But they represent only one strand of many in the fabric of the detective story. Other investigators contributed with equal enthusiasm and with almost equal force, way back there.

Among them you find uniformed police and police detectives, investigators from the government and business world, hardboiled manhunters, representatives of private agencies.

Each bright strand added its trifle. Each, in its time, was freshly vivid. Each made a unique and personal contribution to magazine fiction.

Chapter V—The Professionals

1-

Watts, The Unriddler, worked openly for the United States government in the 1911 pages of *Blue Book*. He assisted the Attorney General on matters concerning trust busting, a popular indoor sport of the time.

The series was created from scraps of headlines and torrents of imagination by Guy C. Baker, a prolific writer of fiction for *Blue Book*, *Popular, Short Stories, Detective Stories*, and other magazines during the Teens and Twenties. He grew to specialize in high-tension adventure novelettes where the girl ended up facing danger but was finally saved, without moral damage.

Baker's earlier work was less tense. His character, Unriddler Watts, was a small, slight, blue-eyed, fragile fellow with a thin, pale face. He is described as "quaint" and "whimsical," and appeared in slender little whimsical stories pervaded by a dry, cute feeling.

For all his slightness, Watts seems about as dainty as a sackful of iron knobs. His assignment in "A Tempest In a Trunk" (April 1911) is to locate a trunk located with revealing documents. These prove that the National Pharmaceutical Company has been price fixing "in restraint of trade." The documents were collected and shipped by whistle blower Stevens. But now the trunk has vanished.

Watts methodically checks railroad records, finds no trace. From this point he returns to first causes and interviews Stevens. Immediately he detects a false note in the man's voice. By bluff and strength of will, Watts forces Stevens to admit that he thieved back the trunk because the Company offered him $50,000.

And thus, in the fullness of time, an extraordinary apparition appears in the office of Attorney General. There is the trunk and perched on it is Watts, dangling his legs, playing with a cigar, and looking all-fired droll.

Cute detectives must be taken in stride. Even when they are a combination of Old Sleuth and Peter Pan. Most of the professional investigators were of less frivolous stuff. They were employees, earning their bread and wine by representing such monoliths of stability as the Government, or insurance companies, or large detective agencies. Organizational discipline gripped them. They had no immediate ties with Baker Street. Not even a faithful friend to record their successes.

Instead they drew salaries and reported to superiors, that unfortunate condition to which so many readers are reduced.

Since fiction is less formal than the world it describes, the professional investigators do operate rather casually. If they are organizational men, their hearts remain free, their expense accounts unlimited. They report casually, if at all. And their employers, generous to madness, require little more than a post card every other week, just to keep in touch. You can barely distinguish some of these professionals from private investigators with one-desk offices.

That air of blithe independence glows from most of Edgar Wallace's professional detectives. They are as improbable as Watts. Yet you cannot bring yourself to care. Wallace's least efforts are wrapped in prose so warmly ingratiating that you feel obligated to believe what is unbelievable. That does not mean the sun ever fell upon a detective who looked and acted like some of those strolling Mr. Wallace's pages.

His early fiction teams with young men of heart-breaking superiority. Competent, achingly assured, they dress with tasteful richness and restraint. They are airy, omniscient, aggressively spritely. These luminous geniuses are sometimes noblemen, sometimes Scotland Yard men, sometimes both. They have been known to pursue other professions, including that of insurance investigator—a profession of high glamor to non-insurance investigators.

Whatever his specific profession, it is the same young man. Only his name varies and his choice of gray-eyed sweetheart.

An early example of this paragon appears in Wallace's 1918 series, "The Lapses of Larry Loman," three related short stories in *The Popular Magazine*.[1] Larry is a particularly unfettered member of New Scotland Yard's Criminal Investigation Department—the famous C.I.D.

Before the story opens, he has been roving foreign climes and caught a spectacular malaria. It has affected him strangely. Without warning, weird buzzings thrill in his head. Then forgetfulness. Later he wakes—four hours, or six, or eight, have passed. He remembers nothing. His memory has completely lapsed.

It is an unfortunate condition, at an unfortunate time. For Larry is deep in single-handed battle with "The Crime Trust," (April 4, 1918).

The Trust has united every major crook in England into a coordinated group. The premise is capable of generating a shelf of books. Why it produced so few stories is incomprehensible.

Nor it is comprehensible why Scotland Yard, in all its glory, can assign only one man to battle all the crooks in England. Either we misunderstand, or Mr. Wallace did, or Larry Loman heard it wrong.

Larry is confident that, in spite of his lapses, he can break up the Trust and expose its evil leader. Larry's doctor, Sir George Grayborn, speaking with the assurance of the unafflicted, tells him that he will improve. Only a matter of time, my boy.

But then, once again, behold! Larry blanks out while the focus of a silenced pistol fusillade. When consciousness returns, he finds himself in complete white face, wearing a Pierrot costume, and with a handcuff dangling from one wrist.

This will be the general series format. Larry sets off to smash some part of The Crime Trust. Then blackout. He wakes in unorthodox circumstances. Later he learns the details of what he did while lapsing and discovers that the mission has been completed with a maximum of drama.

The adventures continue through "The Affair of the Stokehold" (April 20, 1918), and, all too soon, "The Cure" (May 7, 1918).

In this final story, $185,000 (not pounds) vanish from a solid steel safe. It is a devilish trick engineered by that arch fiend of crime, leader of The Trust, honorable doctor Sir Grayborn. This revelation, he sneers into Larry's ear as that young man sits lapsing and blank-eyed.

Alas for The Crime Trust. Larry is faking his symptoms, the illness having cured itself. He arrests Sir Grayborn and the whole conspiracy goes bust.

Charming. If not entirely convincing.

When Al Capone went to jail, his business interests did not falter. They rolled along, bribing, slugging, bombing, as lethal as ever. For any large organization, criminal or otherwise, possesses a self-sustaining command and operations structure. This persists. Ridding the world of a single master criminal does not destroy, or much inconvenience, his organization

Wallace certainly knew this. He merely ignored his knowledge while writing fiction for the popular magazines. Not that Wallace was the only writer to ignore the facts of organizational persistence. That the crime master's empire collapsed with his death or arrest was purely a convention. It provided an artistically crisp ending, rather than a realistically messy one. It was as useful in the *New Nick Carter Weekly* as in the *Phantom Detective* and *Spider*. A single bullet invariably annulled national conspiracies.

No sooner had The Crime Trust dissolved than Wallace introduced another—The Big Four Syndicate—to the pages of *Argosy All-Story Weekly*.[2] The Big Four was a loose associate of criminal gangs, gathered together to rob and steal efficiently. Once again this criminal mass was opposed by a single detective, Robert Brewer, "The Policy Sleuth."

The Policy Sleuth series reflects the bibliographic complexities usual to a Wallace series. Eight adventures were first published in the English newspaper, *The Sunday Post*, September 28 through November 16, 1919. The series was titled "Crooks of Society" by John Anstruther.[3] During the 1920-1921, the series was republished in *Argosy All-Story*. About eight years later, the stories were reprinted as a book in the Reader's Library under title, *The Big Four*.

The *Argosy* stories were partially Americanized before publication and Brewer's appearance lightly reworked. In *The Big Four*, he is described as having "a tiny, well-regulated moustache; in his eye was a monocle." The book states that his father was a Scot, his mother a Macleod.

Argosy varies the facts with utter indifference to higher truths. In these wholesome American pages, Mr. Brewer, clean-shaven, un-monocled, is from New York City. His father was a naturalized American, his mother a Scot.

These cosmetic changes are not essential. Brewer is about as American as Windsor Palace. But if he is an imperfect American, he is a perfect example of Wallace's bright young man. He has a roving commission, expensive tastes, and the habit of success. He is foresighted. He out-thinks, out-maneuvers, out- points a succession of clever criminals, never spoiling the faultless crease in his trousers. An admirable man.

Brewer works for the Federated Assurance Corporation, an organization of independent insurance companies. The Chairman and General Manager is Douglas Campbell. He is oppressed by the knowledge that Federal Assurance has many idiotic clients, all wealthy, all excessively social. These persist in crusting themselves with insured gems and rushing forth to frolic in Soho and the Casbah or other places where no sane person goes without an armed escort.

What is worse, four separate criminal groups are prowling about. They glow with plots to steal insured jewels, thereby lowering the dividends of Federated Assurance. It is a dreadful situation.

So Campbell has hired Brewer to foil these thefts, Brewer rejoices in the title of Temporary Chief of the Federated Assurance Corporations' Detective Department—or the T.C.F.A.C.D.D., a collection of letters which gives him unholy glee. The F.A.C.D.D. is a one-man department.

His work requires Brewer to travel throughout England and Europe. That provides Wallace unending glittering backdrops against which he works his wiles. The series opens in Monte Carlo ("Reddy at Monte Carlo," December 25, 1920, *Argosy All-Story Weekly*.) There Brewer traps wicked Reddy Smith in the act of cleaning out a simple-looking young society fool— later revealed to be Mr. Brewer in his role as the gilded simp. (It is a role that The Saint would lift to shining heights.)

Brewer is gifted with a trick memory. It allows him to recognize almost every active criminal on the European side of the Atlantic. He knows their personal characteristics and all their professional histories. So much data would puzzle a computer. But not Bob Brewer. From his specialized knowledge of the criminal, he reasons out the crime to be committed. Then he sets an artistic trap, garnished by masses of police to make hard the transgressor's way.

In "The Burglary at Greenwood" (January 1, 1921), Brewer spoils wholesale theft of jewelry from an impregnable safe. Thereafter, at weekly intervals, he rescues Federated Assurance clients from such menaces as:

—a lovely young woman singularly skilled at cards. ("Baccarat At Cowes," January 8).

—a slickly fraudulent horse race ("A Race At Ostend," January 15).

—a necklace which is disappearing pearl by pearl ("The Heppleworth Pearls," January 22).

In his spare time, Brewer also saves the tenth largest diamond in the world from knavish fingers ("The Star of the World," January 29). And he prevents that association of criminal gangs—The Big Four, headed by Reddy Smith—from cleaning out a bank by craft and chloral hydrate ("The Big Four and the Bank," February 5).

"The Lucky Dip" (February 12) tells how Brewer finishes off the Big Four. These rascals plan an Enormous Robbery of society women come to the Hospital Ball. All the glittering ladies are to be admitted, by special ticket only, to an isolated room for a special drawing. Once inside, they will be shown the hollow end of a pistol and urged to rain diamonds. The plan works well—to the point where Mr. Brewer, in blond wig and evening dress, shoots down the main gunman.

In 1929, these stories were collected as a small, purple volume of the Readers Library, *The Big Four*. Several chapter titles were changed. (Refer to listing in the Checklists.) With the usual perfidy of the times, the stories are run together like chapters of a novel. Individual story openings have been slashed, hacked, deleted, and rearranged. The original stories open and precede with beguiling charm; the book "chapters" stumble because the deletions have harmed the sense of each opening scene. It is not Wallace at fault in *The Big Four* but barbaric editing.

These stories are fluffy entertainments, giving all points to the hero. They glitter and sparkle, bright with banter and Wallace's cheerful asides. Brewer is wonderfully effective, if inhumanly knowing. But you don't care at all. He may be a fancy dresser and a pseudo-American, but there is nothing wrong with his head.

Nor is there anything wrong John Richard Plantagenet Bryce—Captain Jack Bryce—Wireless Bryce. All names of a splendid young officer demobilized into post-World War I joblessness. Thus he joined the two Anthonies—The Mixer and The Brigand—on the pavements of London.

Bryce did not turn to the gentlemanly occupation of robbing thieves. Instead he foraged for work until his possessions were in pawn and his pockets contained only lining. At this point he applied to law firm of Hemmer & Hemmer for employment. And, at this point, the series "Wireless Bryce" began in *The Sunday Post*. The author was said to be John Anstruther. The series ran weekly, ten stories from November 7, 1920, through January 9, 1921. Later lightly revised, they were published in the Readers Library as *The Iron Grip* (1929)[4]

Bryce finds employment as a trouble shooter for the law firm.

James H. Hemmer (Senior Partner): "We have a very large clientele and we are constantly getting into difficulties from which private detectives and the ordinary resources of the law cannot extricate us."[5]

Bryce can, however. Not only is he a fine young man, just under six feet tall, but he is extraordinarily, abnormally strong. He is another representative of that line extending from the dime novels and Nick Carter, through The Night Wind, Tarzan, and Polaris Janess, to Doc Savage and Superman. All were inhumanly powerful.

Bryce stands modestly among these giants. His strength is entirely natural. He exercises only casually, tossing a living room divan from one hand to the other. Snapping off the end of a 1-inch dowel with his fingers. Holding up 200-pound prize-fighters at arm's length before hurling them through windows. Casual little exercises. They keep his muscles toned.

Since he is so exceedingly powerful, he prefers the direct confrontation to intellectual subtlety. In the first story of *The Iron Grip*, "The Man From 'Down Under'," his assignment is to free a stupid young fool from the grip of a gambler. This he does by getting himself invited to a gambling hell, noting that it is crooked and announcing the fact. Then action:

(The gambler's) hand was on Jack's arm, but the next instant he went down to the ground with a smashing blow to the face.

Instantly there was pandemonium. Four attendants rushed at the young man: the first he picked up and flung against the wall; the second he lifted bodily above his head; and the other two stopped in their tracks.

He took a quick glance round, then flung the man upon the green table, which collapsed with a crash under the impact, scattering cards and money in all directions.[6]

A few well chosen punches and slaps bring the gambler to reason and he hands over the young fool's losings. A simple assignment.

In later cases, he cows a bully who has entranced an inexperienced girl. Intervenes between a timid woman and her ferocious brute of a husband. Saves a secretary from her crooked boss, and recovers a stolen diamond, out-thinking a slick lawyer. The list is long, the criminals unpleasant, and their downfall complete. Jack Bryce is exceedingly personable. Rarely does he use his strength more than twice a story, and always in such situations as you would yourself, if your desk job hadn't left you a little out of condition.

In the tenth story, Bryce meets the beautiful Miss Molly M'Greggor who has shot, not mortally, a wicked Frenchman. The scoundrel forced his attentions on her and accused her of theft. It would upset even Maigret. The Frenchman slips into London and kidnaps Molly away. But Jack Bryce recovers her during certain violent activities on a Channel steamer, and they are engaged to be married in the final paragraph. Which is a good enough sign that the series has ended.

Captain Bryce's exploits do not seem to have appeared in American magazines. None of *The Sunday Post* fiction seems to have crossed the Atlantic until it was included in various Readers Library volumes. Fortunately, Mr. J. G. Reeder arrived promptly. He illuminated the pages of *Flynn's, Detective Story, Dime Mystery Book*, and other magazines from 1924 to 1922. Reeder was quite a different person from the powerful Captain Bryce but even more engaging.

Mr. John G(ray) Reeder, Public Prosecutor's Office, London is a towering figure in crime melodrama. You turn to his stories again and again, each time with satisfaction. Each time wishing that Mr. Wallace had written fewer racing novels and many more Reeder adventures.

Mr. Reeder was something over fifty, a long-faced gentleman with sandy-gray hair and a slither of side whiskers that mercifully distracted attention from his large outstanding ears. He wore half-way down his nose a pair of steel-rimmed pince-nez through which nobody had ever seen him look—the were invariably removed when he was reading. A high and flat-crowned bowler hat matched and yet did not match a frock coat tightly buttoned across his spare chest. His boots were square-toed, his cravat—of the broad, chest-protector pattern—was ready-made and buckled into place behind a Gladstonian collar. The neatest appendage to Mr. Reeder was an umbrella rolled so tightly that it might be mistaken for a frivolous walking cane. Rain or shine, he carried this article hooked to his arm, and within living memory it had never been unfurled.[7]

The costume varies slightly, but remains obsolete, twenty years out of style. However the large calibre Browning automatic in his pocket is very modern. The long blade concealed inside his umbrella is fine steel. For all his mild ways and gentle speech patterns, Mr. Reeder is a cold-eyed realist, entirely able to take care of himself. The strange clothing conceals a frame of hard strength. That limp handshake and air of fumbling, apologetic ineffectivity coats a competence crisp and vigorous. He is no softer than a steel birthday cake.

It is Reeder's affection to appear old and slow, as it is his affection to punctuate his remarks with a succession of "um's" and "er's." This is determined eccentricity, laid on with lavish hand, both on the part of Mr. Reeder and Mr. Wallace. Beneath the mannerisms glows the mind of an informed man—informed in elaborate, specific, exhaustive detail about criminals and the world of crime.

Exact knowledge is a wonderful help in crime detection. But Mr. Reeder modestly disclaims personal merit. He succeeds, he whispers hesitantly, because, er, ah, he has a criminal mind.

"I have that perversion. It is a terrible misfortune, but it is true. I see evil in everything...in dying rose bushes, in horseshoes—in poetry even. I have the mind of a criminal. It is deplorable!"[8]

Reeder is Chief Investigator for the Public Prosecutor's Office, roughly analogous to a super District Attorney's office. In law enforcement circles, he exerts remarkable influence. Scotland Yard welcomes him, for he is a professional, long seasoned. In the past he has been a Secret Service agent, a Scotland Yard officer, and for a brief period, a private investigator.

His connections are strong, if used rarely. He can exert considerable political influence, most peculiar in a man who spends much time alone in his room, amusing himself, over tea and muffins, by thinking out horrific variations of current crimes.

Having no wife, he is under no obligation to accept invitations. These he refuses with gentle melancholy, remarking that the invitation coincides with a sad personal anniversary. Alas. Downcast eyes.

He is the world's greatest authority on counterfeit money, a lesser authority on poultry. In addition to these admirable passions, he has a guilty fondness for fairy stories and joke books and a ravening interest in criminal records. And he claims to have the thickest skull of any man on the police force.

Compared to this quaint, apologetic, devious, lethal figure, Terry Trimble and Watts have the reality of cereal box cut-outs.

Mr. Reeder first appeared in *Room 13* (1924) as a secondary character.[9] Immediately he moved into short stories, eight being collected into *The Mind of J. G. Reeder* (1925). *Terror Keep*, the second and last Reeder novel, appeared in 1927. Two years later came a collection of three novelettes, *Red Aces* (1929) and four novelettes, *The Guv'nor* (1932) (US title: *Mr. Reeder Returns*). All novelettes were originally published in *The Thriller*, a large, flat, multi-columned English publication dedicated to the mystery-action story. First issued in February 1929, it serialized *Red Aces*, the best possible introduction for a new magazine.

J. G. Reeder was well represented in American detective fiction magazines. They include *Detective Story Magazine, Dime Mystery Book, Clues, Flynn's,* and *Star Novels Magazine.* (Refer to Checklist.) The stories are filled with excellent things. "The Poetical Policeman" (*Flynn's*, November 8, 1924) tells of a bank robbery. The watchman is found tied, chloroformed, dead, the bank manager in the act of bolting. The manager, an ex-convict, is arrested for the deed. But Mr. Reeder, ever curious and observant as an electronic device, pieces together a different story from a sick rose bush, scratches on the dead man's hand, an old horseshoe, and a policeman's love poem wrapped around flower stems.

"The Treasure Hunt" (Flynn's, November 22, 1924; reprinted *Dime Mystery Book*, January 1933)[10] is based on the criminal belief that law officers—and particularly Reeder—have secreted vast stores of bribes, blackmail profits, and associated loot. Reeder plays skillfully upon this belief, manipulating a pair of thieves so that they open a concealed place that the police may not legally investigate. To their horror, the thieves discover where the nobleman's wife had gone.

"The Troupe" is a gifted group of confidence artists. They appeared in the December 6, 1924, *Flynn's*, and the February 1933 *Dime Mystery Book*. Mr. Reeder, becomingly hesitant and soft spoken, steals a pickpocket's watch and disrupts an exceedingly slick con game.

During the course of "The Stealer of Marble" (*Flynn's*, December 20, 1924), Reeder meets Margaret Belman, a lovely young lady of about twenty-three, with strong good sense. She lives in a boarding house a few doors from Mr. Reeder's home on Brockley Road, out on the Kent edge of London.

To the regret of his housekeeper ("They all go wrong at seventy"), Reeder sees much of Margaret. He escorts her to her job (typing) in London each morning. Sometimes he escorts her home. ("There is no fool like an old fool," remarks his housekeeper, handing down a cup.)

He saves Margaret''s life—for the first time—in "The Stealer of Marble." At the time, she is locked into an indoor telephone booth, while a mad-woman pours bottled carbon monoxide down over her from the room above.[11] Later he provides a similar service in "The Investors," when both of them are locked in a basement filling up with river.

To Mr. Reeder's considerable surprise, they become engaged at the conclusion of *Terror Keep* (1927). Wallace does not tell us that they actually married. It must have been reasonably serious, since Reeder shaved off his side whiskers before storming forth to rescue her.

"The Green Mamba" (*Flynn's*, March 14, 1925) refers to Mr. Reeder. He is astoundingly devious as he manipulates the downfall of an untouchable criminal king, reducing him, in a matter of weeks, to a convicted felon with a severe knife wound. Yet it seems that Mr. Reeder, that mild gentleman, never raised a hand.

The Reeder novelettes are rather superior to the short stories. There is more of them, for one thing. Your satisfaction increases in direct proportion to the quantity of Reeder available. All stories have that touch of melodrama which so irritates some and makes the story even more satisfying to the rest of us.

"Red Aces" is nearly a formal mystery, although its trappings are bizarre—a little, armored, cement-block house in snowy country, the Ace of Diamonds and the Ace of Hearts pinned to the door, mysterious blood stains, a dead policeman, and um—Mr. Reeder—er—performing wonders. "Kennedy the Con Man" returns to the days when Reeder was a private investigator, just before moving to the Public Prosecutor's office. His photographic memory never performed more brilliantly. Although bedeviled by a brash young secretary, he breaks up an elaborate mass kidnapping plot and stage manages a dazzling finale. It only appears that the mob has him at their mercy.

"The Treasure House" (*Star Novels Magazine*, Summer 1933) tells of an elaborate fraud, murder, and identity substitution, whirling away about two and a half million dollars locked in a castle's strong room.

These stories race along, lit irregularly by the eerie blue flare of violence. Plots are substantial and complex. The characters interact and there is blood and emotion in them. The lead girl is as often in danger as Mr. Reeder. The chief villain is never wholly despicable. Humor lightens the intense proceedings.

Nor is Mr. Reeder always the omniscient and invincible master detective. Twice during "The Case of Joe Attymer" he is nicely caught by an amateur villain—to Mr. Reeder's great disgust. As a character, he is nicely measured blend of superiority and unworldy innocence, his idiosyncrasies carried to the point of caricature and perhaps a trifle beyond. Yet he lives splendidly.

Edgar Wallace is known for the high excitement of his fiction. He does not hesitate to entice the reader with all those worn devices of yesteryear—trap doors, death traps, hidden rooms, sinister masked figures, silenced pistols, deadly gases, and such artifacts of bloody action as have kept his novels condemned by academic halls. Beneath these gaudy decorations, you come to a more substantial world. Wallace uses the devices of melodrama to emphasize normal situations gone sick and strange. The real world surrounds the melodrama as an apple its seeds.

It is the same with his characters. They are simplified figures, rarely geniuses, nor often fools. They stand firmly in the real world. Unlike the characters of the 1930s magazines, Wallace's people do not live amid enormous events and perform enormous exploits. They remain in human scale, human beings in a firm world.

Even when excitement and mortal danger, like night flares, turn that firm world to something momentarily strange.

"Terror Keep" (*Detective Story Magazine*, five-part serial, November 6 through December 11, 1926) shows Wallace at his richest. The melodrama boils up thick as buttered cream against sharply pictured backgrounds. Crazy John Flack has escaped confinement. He is out to get Reeder, to steal the bullion, to avenge himself on several nervous parties. Margaret Belman,

lured to that murderously lovely castle by the sea, is to be the bait by which
Reeder is to be destroyed. And so we come to pure joy—a high melodrama
of secret stairs, spring guns, vast caverns below, death traps, hidden stores,
murder, abduction, escape. All the elements that compensate for a lack of
philosophical speculation on the nature of reality.

Scene follows excellent scene. Reader putting aside the poisoned milk
with gentle apologies. Reeder kneeling in his bed, waiting in the intolerable
darkness for the maniac with a knife. Margaret sliding tumbling rolling
twisting down the sloping cliff face, four hundred feet above the beach.
The ponderous slow inexorable collapse of the immense sea cave, as Flack's
boat heads toward a collapsing wall. Reeder sighting his pistol on Flack,
reluctantly deciding that he can't assassinate the man.

Sharp, strong scenes. Melodrama—meaning scenes and emotions
overplayed, exaggerated, overblown, spuriously heightened.

Well, well. Yet Mr. Wallace's story blazes along in the real world. The
grass smells warm in late afternoon. The sea is icy and filled with cold
grating stones. The familiar sun shines on familiar objects. There go rather
old-fashioned automobiles being driven rather fast. There, angled against
the wall, is a substantial divan. The scene is filled with familiar objects
and well-known sights. The world, sound and real, moves at its familiar
pace.

No miracles here. Except, perhaps, in the agility of mind shared by
the main characters. We recognize this world. In spite of its concentrated
dangers and actions, we could step into it now, as Alice stepped into the
mirror, and feel—however we customarily feel. We will grant some personal
variation of feeling.

Only remember, please, that you have, after all, stepped into melodrama.
Heightened and improbable situations. That divan angled against the wall,
for instance. If its hidden latch is loosened, you may tip it so. It moves
back, revealing a narrow stone staircase leading downward. God knows what
lies off down there at its end. Or what thing breathes, down in the silent
dark.

2-

One of the more popular themes of the 1920s was the gathering of
jolly souls to play at solving crimes. Several of these we have already met.
There was The Tuesday Club come together once a week to speculate on
the latest crimes, and a stronger concentration of worldly wisdom and pomp
you never did see, although most of the actual detection was performed
by Aunt Jane Marple.

Another such group, of less sedate activities, was the Scientific Club.
We have previously met this group, estimating the volume of water displaced

by a corpse, when they were not taking pills and shrinking away into golden rings.

Other groups interested in crime detection organized formally, rather than informally. Some formed themselves into a business. Others united to provide justice in an unjust world. Three such groups were The Shadowers, The Justice Syndicate, and The Adjusters. All were different. All created by the 1920s passion for organizations.

Certain things these groups had in common. All were secret. Two were directed by women. And all, at different times, considered the letter of the law to be constructed of rubber bands.

The Shadowers left behind them such a trail of deflated laws that this group might, more accurately, be classified as Bent Heroes. It is expedient to insert them here. Since expediency lay at the core of their operations, we can honor them obliquely by ignoring the cold logic which has, to this point, informed the structure of this work.

Ruthless accuracy demands the admission that The Shadowers were a prize collection of crooks. One distinction places them in a discussion of detective agencies: They had discovered that by combining their illegal talents in a legitimate business, they could earn more than by slipping forth, dark lantern in hand.

The Shadowers was the idea of Rex Powell, an attorney with a highly detailed, first-hand knowledge of the criminal world. Unlike his associates, he had never been convicted. He is the central, male lead and, therefore, his eyes are grey, his poise that of an aristocrat. He is lean, dark-haired, in the mid-40s (temples just touched with silver), and he is intense. All customary attributes for heroes with a past.

His associates are cut from equally familiar stock.

"Professor" George Roper, stock swindler and fake medium, is also tall, lean, graying. His face, deeply sad, is lighted by an "ascetic" dignity. This apparently means that he looks hungry. At one time he ran a carnival shell game.

Lucian Baynes is an expert in many fields—jewels, art, smuggling. He wears a small blond mustache and is neat.

His good friend, Clifford Nichols, a one-time forger and counterfeiter, is a hand-writing expert. He wears a small dark goatee and those slender fingers still perform marvels with a pen.

Philip Howe, the safe expert, is a retired cracksman, locksmith, and tough guy. His taste is clothing is unsubdued. Perhaps his face is a trifle weak, if handsome. He observes delicate moral distinctions. He has refused to work on any case that might send any ex-friend to jail. (These stories were written back at the time writers believed in The Code of the Underworld.)

And finally, the office manager and secretary is blond Ethel Jepson. Barely twenty, she is the brightest little delicate self-depreciating shoplifter. My goodness. A slum girl, she was trained by the notorious Lefty Jane, herself. You know what that means.

The others regard Ethel uneasily. She is a gifted and nonstop liar. Her function in the novels is to make them twice as long. She does this by constantly flying off at a tangent: "It's only a hunch but... Trust me!" Thus knocking all their plans to pieces. Always fortunately.

As the stories progress, Rex grows to love her. What is a novel without a love story, even when the woman is a stranger to the truth.

The Shadowers' stories were written by Isabel Ostrander (1885-1924) under the name David Fox. The scene is New York City; the setting, a lavish office suite in the Bolingbroke Building. The suite is constructed in the form of a hexagon—six offices surrounding the central office where Rex receives guests.

In one office, Henry Corliss operates his laboratory. In another, Cliff Nichols keeps his acids, inks, and reference books. No doors connect the rooms. Silent sliding panels are used instead.

In the office that connects with the corridor sits Ethel. Dictaphones connect her room with the other, for The Shadowers sternly preserve their anonymity. They listen in silently to the client, are rarely seen.

Under Ethel's desk is a concealed keyboard. As she talks with prospective clients, she also types out her impressions of them. From the typewriter, a printed paper tape feeds back through a slot in the wall to where Rex and company fall greedily upon it. Somewhere in this vast world, there is, quite possibly, another equally ridiculous way of running a business.

Rex's office contains a large table, a large desk, and a large screen. Behind the screen are heaped mounds of golf clubs, rifles, paintings. All this is window dressing.

It is Rex's theory that the room should be decorated in a manner to ease the mind of the client. Within seconds he can whip out books or art objects or framed pictures of John L. Sullivan—whatever makes the client feel at home.

Needless to say, the place smells of money. It is somberly luxurious. And for a reason: The Shadowers do not aim at the usual rag-tag client. They are content only with the best—the Blue Book social figures, Wall Street's most towering financiers.

Their initial professional announcement consisted of five hundred engraved notes sent to substantial society matrons. An additional five hundred circulars were also sent to wealthy business leaders.

Should you find yourself in need of any discreet, strictly confidential investigation by a private corporation of gentlemen, not blackmailers or inefficient bunglers, send your visiting card to "The Shadowers, Inc." and an expert will call upon you at once. No divorce evidence or investigations of a scandalous or trivial nature will be undertaken. We have positively no connection with any so-called private detective agency, give no information to the press, permit no publicity, and never carry our results to the authorities unless expressly requested to do so by our clients. If you miss any documents, jewels or other valuables of great importance, if any one of your acquaintance is being subjected to blackmail, if you handwriting has been forged or you fear for the safety of some one near to you, communicate with us.

Most Respectfully Yours,
The Shadowers, Inc.[12]

Their first case, "The Man Who Convicted Himself," was published as a six-part serial, April 3 through May 8, 1920, in *All Story Weekly*. After a large opening, heavy with explanations and character introductions, we sweep grandly into a tangle of blackmail, robbery, amateur seancing, mysterious drugged figures, and those mysterious gems, the Three Burning Black Pearls.

To investigate these wonders, The Shadowers have developed investigative techniques that are fully as eccentric as their office layout. After considering all available facts, they gather around Rex's table and discuss which of them will take charge of the case.

It depends on whose speciality is most involved. Once the leader is selected, all others subordinate themselves to his, usually, freakish directions. All but Ethel. You can't do much with Ethel.

"The Super-Swing," a seven-part serial, ran October 29 through December 10, 1921, in *Argosy All-Story Weekly*. A rich fellow calls in The Shadowers to investigate some threatening notes. Thereafter, The Shadowers are shadowed. They meet a miser who collects murder weapons and strain to locate a secret safe that has somehow disappeared.

Action lines jam the story. Each Shadower proceeds on his special business, meets his own special adventures and dangers. To these activities are added numerous blind trails and equally unrewarding conferences around Rex's table. Threading through the confusion is the story of a nice young fellow, wrongly suspected. The story contains so many names, so much unculled description, that the waters recurrently close black over your head.

During their investigation, The Shadowers perform in the time-honored bent hero style. If they work for the good of society, they are unbound by most social constraints. As a matter of routine, they commit crimes sufficient to sent them all up for 3,147 years.

They plunge with gusto into safe cracking, suppression of evidence, forgery, and conspiring to conceal murder. They remove an embarrassing corpse by forging a death certificate and organizing a burial at a distant cemetery, way way in the middle of the wilds, out around Newark. Yet police never come to call and detectives are pleasingly dense.

The Doom Dealer'' (six-part serial, February 26 through March 30, 1923, *Argosy All-Story*) pits them against a "Dealer in counterfeit death.'' This menace, disguised by wax masks and artificial hands, permits himself to be buried alive in the place of men wishing to vanish.

In uncovering this fascinating business, The Shadowers are shot, drugged, knocked out, and imprisoned. Rex ends helpless in the hands of the crooks. But Ethel saves him, quite unexpectedly. For by this time her crackpot activities have got her banished from the organization. In the nick of time, she returns gloriously, smashing into Rex's prison, waving guns and knives and screaming and slugging crooks with a bag full of iron.

Very thrilling. Unfortunately her scene isn't dramatized. We are told about it. This technical defect is common to the series. So many action scenes are told about, at third hand, that an evasive haze dulls the luster of the chapters.

One final novel was written. While it was still being serialized, David Fox died, concluding a series which might otherwise have continued until the sky cracked.

The final novel was "The Handwriting on the Wall," a six-part serial, March 29 through May 3, 1924, *Argosy All-Story*. Ethel has returned from an unexplained absence. She has been off learning how to spell and dress, those requisites of civilization. No sooner has she seated herself in the council room (blushing fetchingly under Rex's gaze), than we learn that old De Puyster Monckton, millionaire, lies murdered before his safe. On the wall is scrawled the figures 6099.

Could his son have done this terrible thing? Certainly possible. But the son tells a fantastic story of how he has been hounded through Europe by minions of a powerful financial syndicate. So improbable a story convinces us at once that some devil's plot is aimed against this innocent lad.

Off The Shadowers scatter, eager to find out. They are not uniformly successful. One is drugged. Another finds a French maid. At length, all obstacles overcome, they gather in that richly paneled room where Rex's interpretative genius (and Ethel's lucky hunches) reveal those sinister threads which...

You must admit that The Shadowers are an unique investigative group. With what agility do they toil and spin, filling up space between the first paragraph and the last, until a new six-part serial plops out, steaming hot, to delight mystery fans. Who, God knows, never object to dreary prose and padded narrative.

At the end of 1920, that busy author Hugh Kahler began a short series for *Detective Story Magazine*[13]. The subject was another investigative group, this one thoroughly illegal, which called itself The Justice Syndicate.

The Syndicate is nothing more than a conspiracy. A conspiracy to see justice done, admittedly. But a short-circuiting of due process, regardless. The principles are the Chief of Detectives (of the Pittland Police), Olaf Larsen, and successful lawyer, young Walter Enfield.

The concept was Larsen's. It was based on his experience with criminal law as administered in the Norway of his father—a process utterly foreign to the American-English system of trial by jury.

...criminal law as administered here became, nearly always, a battle of wits between two lawyers, one of the defense and one for the State, a kind of superchase, in which...justice was too easily neglected for the mere games' sake.[14]

That was in 1920; how different matters are today.

So Larsen has made a private deal with Enfield to share information:

(Thus) he brought about the offensive and defensive alliance later known as The Justice Syndicate, with the object of combining the forces of defense and prosecution in an honest attempt to establish the truth in each case on which they worked.[15]

The result being that lawyer Enfield is always on the side of the angels: He gets free access to evidence available to the police. He will not accept a guilty client; or, if discovered to be guilty, the client is dropped or told to take a plea.

The snare in this Eden is that it is hard to determine where the angels are. The real world lacks the clear assurance of fiction. So there is disagreement.

When there is disagreement, Charlotte Gray arbitrates.

Charlotte is the third member of The Justice Syndicate. An ex-school teacher and amateur investigator, "Her instinct, her habit of ignoring facts and dealing with convictions, had an uncanny way of hitting somewhere near the head of the nail."

It must scald women to be reminded that, while they are incapable of consecutive thought, they have a mystic feeling for the truth. If that convention can't be swallowed, the bulk of popular 1920s fiction will gag you.

To her credit, Charlotte is tough-minded, as well as intuitive. She also has a rare temper. Her associates enjoy stirring her up to watch the blue and green sparks flash.

The three represent the brains of The Syndicate. The body and feet are provided by Silvio Farone, a smooth little Italian researcher who appears to work for Larsen's office. Farone is never invited through that private doorway to Charlotte's office, where The Syndicate deliberates.

When they have gathered together, they make an odd group, almost like characters in a fiction. Larsen, a big, solid man, is a well-to-do bachelor; like most bachelors, he has a Chinese servant. Lawyer Enfield has a crippled leg which gives him constant pain; his face is romantically pallid, touched by lines of agony; he speaks slowly, relaying upon "intellect and precedence and law."

By contrast, Charlotte, is "vividly healthy and alive and eager and keen and (had) surrendered without a struggle to governance of intuition and emotion."

Contrasting characters provide the stories with built-in drama—sickly reason opposing healthy intuition, with a Norwegian referee.

"No Man's Hand" (November 23, 1920) concerns the murder of a tightwad's young male friend. After the murder, a poor dub of a fellow is found hiding in the room. Off there in the fireplace, sizzles a revolver. But the dub swears he didn't do it. Nobody did. Nobody was there. Yet the victim's face is powder stained.

Charlotte eventually senses parts of the true answer. The reader gets there before her. If the story is slow, it is also complicated and interesting. Not enough characters appear to obscure the guilty party, but in spite of that, the characters compel attention. They are more complex than usual. There are interesting viewpoint reversals, during which the despicable, by revelation of an unsuspected motive, become less despicable.

In true justice figure style, The Syndicate conspires to protect the murderer:

Charlotte: "Let's have a little justice for the living, for a man who's done something for the biggest kind of motive..."

Meaning that he was protecting his wife's reputation. Well, well. The Just Men would probably have approved.

"Purely Circumstantial" (January 1, 1921) tells how a loathsome little rat learns the secret of The Justice Syndicate and goes blabbing it all over. In consequence, an enormous political scandal develops. An honest politician attempts to aid the three and his re-election grows doubtful.

To this point, the story seems fairly rational. The nasty fellow was accused of using a cyanide cigarette to murder a fine citizen. The Syndicate suspects otherwise. It is to their advantage to let this wretch go to prison. But it is not Justice. It is a reasonable, if obvious, moral dilemma. You can almost believe.

Then appears that good politician; he is wearing his own pants and acting for the good of the people. At once your belief ceases. If writers realized the effect such incredible characters have on readers, they would cut them ruthlessly from the story.

It all ends satisfactorily. The Syndicate, however, has received so much publicity that it fades from the scene with this story—or soon after. The series has not been traced further.

Secret groups pursuing justice marched bravely on through late 1920s magazines. During 1927, *Flynn's Weekly* featured a story series by Valentine (Archibald Thomas Pechey) concerning The Adjusters, a mysterious detective agency that succeeds where the police fail. (It was another of *Flynn's* imported series, the book *The Adjusters* having been published in England in 1922; earlier magazine publication is suspected but not known.)

The aims of The Adjusters are disinterested. They are funded by unlimited capital. At the helm stands iridescently lovely Daphne Wrayne— only daughter of Col. Wrayne, V.C., D.S.O. Daphne has a flat in Brook Street, a luxurious home in Maidenhead, and her recreations—significantly— are hunting, shooting, tennis, and golf. She's a whizzer, and not yet twenty. Smokes cigarettes, too.

To tell the truth, she may not be iridescently lovely. Valentine has forgotten to describe her. Since, however, his story is on the level of an advertising cartoon about mouthwash, we can assume that he will provide all the usual cliches.

The Adjusters include four other members.

(Perhaps you would like to skip this and go do something else? You go right ahead. This will only make you terribly angry. You don't care? Well, you are certainly brave enough; imagine deliberately swallowing all this guff.)

The other four Adjusters are:

Sir Hugh Williamson, a tanned explorer, who wears a gold monocle and derives, fairly directly, from the more obvious characteristics of Doyle's Lord John Roxton (*The Lost World*).

James Plantagent Ffolliot Treviller, a young nobleman, tall, powerful, thewed like a young giant, etc.

The handsome lawyer, Martin Everest.

The red-faced theatrical man, Alan Sylvester.

There is, you see, a personality for each emergency.

Their purpose is to see justice done. Unlike the Just Men, or any of the other groups we have seen, they will not *countenance* breaking the law. Bending it, perhaps. Just a little.

They meet in concealment at 179 Conduit St., W., in London. At that address stands the North Western Trading Syndicate. But go inside. Enter the Board Room—respectable—solid marble mantel—solid marble clock—solid mahogany "official-looking table" and "official-looking chairs."

Here The Adjusters meet to plan their coups—four men sitting around a table listening to a slip of a girl half their age. Plenty of pluck, you know.

The series began September 10, 1927, in *Flynn's Weekly Detectives Fiction*. The story, "The Case of Richard Henry Gorleston," concerns a wicked Lord who assumes another identity in order to cash a check that he as written oddly, in order to make it look a forgery. This is to incriminate a nice young fellow. And so it does, and matters seem black, until The Adjusters strike. All got up in different clothing to disguise their identities, they get the Lord drunk, convey him to the apartment he used in his alternate identity, and call in the police to catch the rascal. Trapped, outplayed, by a dainty little nineteen-year old cigarette smoker, he signs a confession and creeps away. A solid triumph.

"The Lighting Returns Company" (September 17) tells how The Adjusters recover the sum of 1,004 pounds, 4 shillings, and 6 pence. It was swindled from an old sea captain who stepped right out of a Sunday school paper.

It is a legal swindle. No one can help him. But Daphne finds a way. She arranges that everywhere the swindler turns, he finds signs reading "1004 4 6." They are in his wallet, his bedroom, outside his window.

The harassment breaks his will and he refunds the money. At a rough estimate, this exploit cost The Adjusters 8,002 pounds, 3 shillings, 9 pence. They also bent a few laws, including those relating to pickpocketing, breaking and entering, robbery, harassment, and blackmail. Didn't kill anybody, though.

Yes, yes, it is thin. Improbable. Nor is it improved by being written in the prose that refers to a butler as "the stalwart commissionaire."

But then not all series please everyone. Somewhere lives a reader who enjoyed The Adjusters, who laughed at the situation, who delights in pretentious prose, carbon-paper characters, improbable action, hollow concepts.

These discordant characteristics seem to have assured The Adjuster's later success. Daphne and her four friends stepped grandly into books that were widely distributed in England. For more than forty years and at least forty-six volumes, they continued to prosper. The series was signed by Mark Cross, apparently another Pechey pseudonym. The first volume of the Cross series, *The Shadow of the Four*, reintroduced all the characters and plunged furiously into plots and counterplots, all nimbly negotiated by the wonderful

Daphne. It is minor league Edgar Wallace. But it is also far more interesting than the mannered cavorting of the *Flynn's* short stories.

3-

Few detective agencies would recognize The Shadowers, The Justice Syndicate, The Adjusters as being other than amateur. These groups are whimsical, rather than professional. They are as specialized as that little shop around the corner which sells handmade copper jewelry this month, stained glass suncatchers the next. The third month, it is gone. But there are always other little shops, endlessly hopeful.

In magazine fiction, as in shop keeping, amateurs find endless opportunities to sport as professionals. It is sport, not work. Their fees are often high, their official-looking tables polished. But rarely are they in business as Pinkerton's understands the term.

Consider the Malcolm Steele National Detective Agency.

Steele is the sole owner and director. He was formerly in the Secret Service and, after leaving, founded a detective agency to keep his hand in. For Steele is independently wealthy and indifferent to money.

So indifferent that he prefers to work for small fees. Inexpensive quality bears its own reward: He is able to pay high wages to his three office managers (the agency has branched out successfully) and a fleet of investigators. He is out to make the National Detective Agency the best in the country.

In person, Steele is a tall man, massively built, rather forbidding in appearance. Even among friends, his "manner is of distinct reserve and aloofness." He has gray eyes, since all characters of impeccable moral and ethical position have gray eyes. His dress is slightly more idiosyncratic. He wears an "inevitable long, dark, heavy raincoat...with its collar tightly buttoned, and a slouch felt hat...pulled down over his eyes." It is 1928 and the trenchcoat is already a cliche.

Steele appeared in *Flynn's* from 1924 to around 1928. The series was credited to Mansfield Scott, almost certainly a pseudonym. The scene is the United States but the tone is English. As director of a national detective agency, Steele is right out there in the field, conducting his own investigation. Directors have that right.

Steele reasons from sparse clues to surprising conclusions. Much dialogue is used. Various narrators observe his work and write about it, first-person. They do not appear to very astute. The small amount of action is consumed in interminable cross-examinations, discussions, and interviews.

The backgrounds are interesting, the plots intricate, the clues honest. These virtues cannot give life to narratives choked by words. A vigorous lead character might have breathed fire into the proceedings. Unfortunately, Steele is barely alive. He presides over the series like a gigantic statue staring blankly across ruins sunk in the sand.

Steele's initial appearance is as a casual presence in "Horror of the Crags" (November 29, 1924). He does little and the detection is up to the narrator—one of those nice fellows who lurches along making shocking discoveries. He finally learns why two, three, four people have plunged at night from a cliff.

By January 3, 1925, Steele has become a functioning detective. In "Footprints of Guilt," he proves that his client did not murder. Although the client's footprints lead across a snowy field to the murdered man. The client says that there wasn't a dead man there. Or footprints, either.

(Authorship of "Footprints" is credited to Melville Hume, since Mansfield Scott began a serial in this issue.)

"Shadow of a Shade" (March 14, 1925) is a mystery problem. The background is elaborately tangled. A pulp fiction story, maliciously based on an actual incident, is the root cause. Now a man sits dead in his chair, a contact powder burn over his heart. The significant clue, as Steele discovers, is the amount of cream remaining on the blancmange.

Cream on the blancmange. Footprints in the snow. Horror at the cliff's edge. Dr. Eustace Hailey would feel comfortable with these problems. Murder among polite folk, the clews genteel. The detective is no coarse intrusion upon those enjoying English manor life in the 1925 United States. Although he wears a trenchcoat and slouch hat (charming eccentricities), his conversation is delightfully poised. He has the breeding of old wealth and position. His mind darts lightly across the puzzle. Here is the murder, grotesque enough. Sad. Very sad. And here a fact, there an inexplicable incident. All bits that the investigator's mind will assemble. Until the hidden truth stands clear.

The murderer, revealed, pats his lips with a linen napkin. By Jove, Inspector, I confess myself bested at the game.

In other magazines, the fiction had a different sound. Over at *Black Mask*, the prose was less formal, less mannered. The fiction was ever tighter, more intense, steadily more violent. It was couched in language that grew more colloquial, packed with the broken rhythms of speech, not the formal cadences of writing.

Gangsters appeared among the clipped sentences. The characters carried guns and whisky glasses. More action pushed into the stories. The atmosphere was dangerous, aggressive, a lot colder and harder than 1923. The characters moved about. They didn't sit in soft chairs talking at each other. They conflicted. Occasionally they hit each other.

By 1926, the *Black Mask* touch began to show up in *Flynn's Weekly*. By mid-1927, change to the fiction style was apparent. The magazine title was modified to *Flynn's Weekly Detective Fiction*. Title changes, like adrenaline, are specifics for weakening circulation. As are action stories.

And abruptly the Malcolm Steele series shifts from the problem story to mystery adventure.

In the five-part serial, "Defenders of the Law" (August 27 through September 24, 1927), Steele and his agents assist the anti-vice forces of Boston in a battle against organized crime. The story is self conscious in its new clothes. The action is harsh and continuous. The subject matter—familiar enough to us now—is of dives, gambling joints, gang crime tied in with city officials. It is a hot, hard adventure in the urban jungle.

By late 1928, *Flynn's* had become "Formerly *Flynn's*" and carried the new title *Detective Fiction Weekly*. The Steele series has moved closer to the *Black Mask* sound. "Death Dealers" (January 21, 1928) concerns crooks and police corruption and heady quantities of violence. Steele, himself, barely escapes a machine-gun trap:

As he dropped to the running board, two vicious yellowish-red, continuous tongues stabbed forth from the black windows, and the street echoed back and across with the savage rat-tat-tat-tat-tat-tat of machine guns.

The crash of glass mingled hideously with the *thrum* of drilled metal as the rain of death poured down upon the body of the sedan...[16]

A violent story is not always a hardboiled one. "Hardboiled" refers to character attitude and decision, not to events. Guns may go off and bodies fall in every paragraph; characters may swill straight rye and pound each other with blackjacks and brass knuckles. Those are events of an action story. The hardboiled story comes into being only in the character response to the pounding and shooting and killing. The response may be sadistic. Or it may be unsentimental detachment, cold-eyed as an insurance adjuster assessing your second fire. Whatever drives the character, the story shows his attitudes and decision concerning events. The story is more than action scenes.

This is a weakness of the modified Malcolm Steele series. It converted to *Black Mask* action without *Black Mask* substance. it demonstrated, by this oversight, that guns and gangsters could be as tedious as another murder in the vicar's library.

Although Steele is imperfectly hardboiled, he came a long way from his origins as a 1924 genius investigator. His series did manage to convert to a more contemporary style. And it did take a few wobbling steps toward the routine violence of 1930s fiction.

Steele was not the only *Flynn's* character to adopt violent ways. The editor seems to have decided during 1926 to vary the deep English hues of his magazine. He tentatively introduced a few stories of contemporary American action. Not realistic, you understand. But brisk, with action-oriented characters. Among these were Ranger Jack Calhoun, a formidable man.

Calhoun's official titles varies slightly from story to story. Most usually, he is Chief Inspector for the U.S. Rangers stationed near the Sunken Lands of Northern Arkansas. He is an official investigator and a ferocious manhunter. His series, written by Edward Parrish Ware, ran from 1926 to 1935, from *Flynn's Weekly* to *Detective Fiction Weekly*, from The Jazz Age to the Depression, almost a decade of brutal action.

4-

The Sunken Lands of northern Arkansas lie west of the Mississippi—a swampy tangle of mud, snakes, vines matting together a density of bushes and trees. Here channels of black water wind. Mosquitoes cloud. There are shanties by carpets of lily pads and shabby boats. The sun is heavy. The humidity strangles.

Through this tangle prowl quaint old backwoodsmen, "swamp rats," inseparable from their rifles. Here slink thieves, murderers, and such blood-soaked riff-raff as add violence to a frontier environment.

The scene is ferocious; the stories are the same. They are cast in that simplest of forms—the tale of the single good man against the forces of lawlessness. Packs of human vermin, in this case. Out into the wilderness paddles Ranger Calhoun. His mission is simple: Bring in those killers.

Since their condition on return is not specified, Calhoun brings them in dead, often as not. He wears a pair of .45 revolvers and carries a rifle. Since these are stories of danger and violent action, his weapons grow white-hot through the chapters.

At the series' beginning, the action is not so lethal. In "One Good Man" (September 18, 1926), Calhoun goes after a pack of thieves fled into the swamp. Sheriff Lundsford, the resident thick-headed, red-necked blow-hard, collects a posse and paddles fiercely off in the wrong direction.

Calhoun reasons out where the quarry is, then slips upon them by night. He slugs them down, one by one, shooting only once. Then brings the whole batch back to the glory of the U.S. Rangers.

You expect this sort of competence from Calhoun, who once remarks that he is "hard-boiled without much conscience." That isn't Calhoun's real opinion of himself. It's something Edward Parrish Ware read in *Black Mask* and thought it would be nice added to Calhoun's character. Calhoun is tough but not hard-boiled. Not really. He is too sympathetic to young love and feminine feelings to be without conscience. On the whole, he is a competent professional of the type described as "bad news."

In "The Negative Clue" (November 20, 1926), he Sherlocks around the swamps, pondering why Old Razorback, who has been arrested for a double murder, didn't just throw the bodies into the mud. Why did he try to bury them?

Because he didn't do it, obviously.

If that story is run-of-the-mill, "The Panther" (July 9, 1927) is hard-nosed, unblushing suspense. It moves at an unrelenting pace—no introspection, no psychological finesse, no complex character building. Just a continuous pressure of danger, fear, and physical violence.

That infamous outlaw, The Panther, is running amok in The Devil's Bowl region. Calhoun is ordered to bring him in. And the Panther's gang, too, while he's at it. Thereafter, Calhoun:

—finds a wounded man, almost dead, marooned on a mud island in the swamp.

—is shot at by an ambusher with a rifle.

—disguises himself as a swamp rat and bluffs his way into The Panther's camp.

—is interviewed by the tough leader, who conceals himself in the shadows, only his white hands showing.

—discovers an imprisoned woman.

—gun fights his way free of the camp.

—returns with a troop of Rangers for a brutal fire-fight and slaughter of the outlaws.

—discovers that the man he saved on the mud island was actually The Panther, displaced of command by the more bloody faction of his outlaws.

—allows The Panther and his sweetheart to escape, since they assure him that they have reformed.

Although faint mystery elements appears, this is basically an old-fashioned adventure story. In another climate, Hopalong Cassidy could have handled the same assignment in the same way and with equal gusto.

"The Grave on Number 10" (August 10, 1929, *Detective Fiction Weekly*) tells how an old drunk sees a night murder and burial out on a mud island. He blabs about this at all the bars, ends up in the same grave. Calhoun, full of intuition, located the grave and uncovers a clever identity switch and a second murder.

From mid-1929 on, the stories cease their effete posturing and hunker down to straight blood and violence. "The Red Record" (September 14, 1929) suggests that Dunn had been mightily impressed by Hammett's 1925 "The Gutting of Couffignal." The Jungle Butcher, a crazy outlaw, has declared war on the Arkansas river counties. He is methodically murdering and burning his way along the Mississippi.

The first part of this story sounds as if it were rewritten from a *Western Story* novel. It is packed with horses, six-guns, posses. Horsemen gun down the only witness. In an old, wooden hotel, Calhoun walks into a gun trap. Pistol battle in the halls. A henchman grips his bullet-smashed arm. From a horse-drawn cab, a treacherous shot. Then the mysterious girl is whirled away.

So far, this is another job for Hopalong Cassidy. Now, however, the story veers toward the Mississippi. Trailing the girl, Calhoun comes to a wharf, is attacked by a gang. He battles free, escapes in a boat. Is alone on the River.

Almost drowns.

Blunders into the Headquarters of The Jungle Butcher. It is improbable luck but essential to the pace of the story. He is captured, tied.

The Butcher announces that he will attack and destroy Barfield's Point. After that, he will cut off Calhoun's hands and nail them above his door.

Down the river the fiends swoop, about 150 men on a pair of riverboats.

At Barfield's Point, they rage ashore.

To meet what Jesse James met at Northfield, Minnesota. The Rangers are waiting there, a rifle in every window.

Massacre.

While the streets fill up with smoking brass, Calhoun saws loose his bonds on broken window glass. Grabbing up a gun, he cleans up on those of the gang surviving the ambush. He captures The Butcher and the story ends with the banners of Good floating high.

As the 1930s progressed, the Calhoun stories gradually shortened. Stripped-down plots packed in ever more action. In "Calhoun's Way" (January 18, 1930), the sheriff suspects a meek bookkeeper of robbing a bank. But Calhoun grows a set of whiskers and runs down the real robber, just as he's sailing off for a new and merry life.

"Satan's Sink-Hole" (August 25, 1934) reduces the opening of "The Panther," although in summary. A masked man has marooned this poor naked fellow on a mud island. "Sign these papers or die!" But Calhoun has been investigating back at the poor fellow's cabin. Through the swamp he comes, just in time to gun down the leering fiend and save valuable timber rights.

Now the stories are published less frequently and with more familiar material. They melt into the great pulp magazine sound. Violence haunts Calhoun. Everywhere lurks danger. Let his attention wander and at once his skull is slugged.

Searching the swamp for missing men, he finds a dead man peacefully leaning against a tree ("Killer In the Cane," January 19, 1935). Immediately Calhoun is slugged, pitched into a bottomless bog. Using his belt, tie, and a helpful tree branch, he barely escapes. Is immediately recaptured and imprisoned in a shanty. There, a smart city gangster has terrorized a girl and her father into hiding him out. He is running a buried treasure racket, luring fools into the swamp and killing them for their money. Just the thing a big city gangster would plan.

The girl frees Calhoun. But they are trapped in the cabin. The gangster has set fire to the place and lurks outside, his weapon cocked. While the murderer gloats, Calhoun slips through the roof and kills him with a single, long-range pistol shot.

Let us leave Calhoun at this point.

Down into the black swamp water the blood runs. Over the corpse stands Calhoun, tanned face expressionless. In the silence, a fish splashes. Circular rings spread silently across polished water. Another cartridge, another death, another triumph for Inspector of U. S. Rangers, Jack Calhoun.

It grows dark. Over the body, Calhoun stands motionless. He will not move until the next story. He stands immobile, without feeling, lifeless as the corpse at his feet. In 1926 he was a vigorous, if shallow, figure. In 1935, he is an efficient killer, one among many in the bloody pulps. Here he will stand, unchanging, waiting, until Edward Parrish Ware feeds another sheet of paper into the typewriter and the story begins again.

5-

We began in 1911 with Watts and end with Calhoun in 1935. Both were government investigators. But how different their techniques. How divergent their stories. The air they breathe is not the same, and between them, raw and deep, gapes an immense chasm, torn by some convulsion of fiction.

The differences between Watts and Calhoun have been exaggerated by time. But it is true that professional detectives of the Teens seem far more obsolete than the detectives of the late 1920s. War and social change have intervened between these two extremes. War and depression, joblessness and inflation, a dazzling upward spiral of invention and mass production, technology's searing kiss, and the utopia hopes of Prohitibion which had deflated, by 1926, to public gun fights between contending packs of criminals—all this change, all this anxiety, was compressed into fifteen years, 1911 to 1926. It was a modest fraction of time to contain such a seething mass.

Under all these pressures, magazine detective fiction changed. It changed rather gradually, for the magazines were conservative. While they were willing to try the new, they never risked much new at any time. They were daring by the teaspoonful.

And so, while time gestated the new, the magazines continued to present the formal problem story: crime, investigation, solution, the detective seining up clues like a fisherman netting baitfish.

The action story also continued, its movement-danger-suspense well salted by devices from the dear dead dime novel days. Time only stripped and intensified the action story. By the 1930s it had become a major component of the single-character and weird menace magazines. Glittering with violence and fantastic elements, preoccupied with criminal conspiracies, the form remained viable until the early 1940s.

Another story form, the hardboiled detective adventure, had begun development during the early 1920s. Like the DNA molecule, the hardboiled form was composed to two linked strands, two divergent ways of looking at the world. Of these, one is best described as melodramatic fantasy; the other, objective realism. The fantasy was sometimes very real; the realistic story was often highly romantic. But the two elements are reasonably distinct.

Both were violent. Both were written in colloquial language, flaring and crackling like ball lightning. Both appeared in *The Black Mask* and, by 1926 (before either strand had reached maturity) both would exert a terrible pressure for change on competing magazines.

The Black Mask hardboiled story was narrowly focused. Its subject was carefully selected, a single slice from society, one cut of the apple. But its view, although restricted, was intense as laser light and savagely compelling.

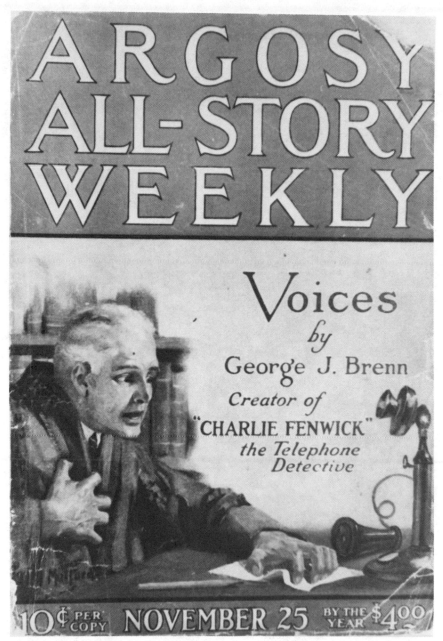

Argosy All-Story Weekly, November 25, 1922. The pulps routinely transformed technology to fiction. In the Charlie Fenwick series, endless adventures boiled from that fascinating gadget, the telephone.

Blue Book Magazine, September 1912.   The sedate cover camouflaged a brisk selection of adventure fiction, intermixed with short mystery series.

Flynn's, January 24, 1925.   Initially filled with English authors and fiction like stale popcorn, *Flynn's* transformed itself to the 1930's *Detective Fiction Weekly*, a violent, worldly delight.

All Story Cavalier Weekly, April 17, 1915.   Grace Duval, the important half of The Honeymoon Detectives, a married detective team, contemplates a clue in the only unreprinted serial of the series.

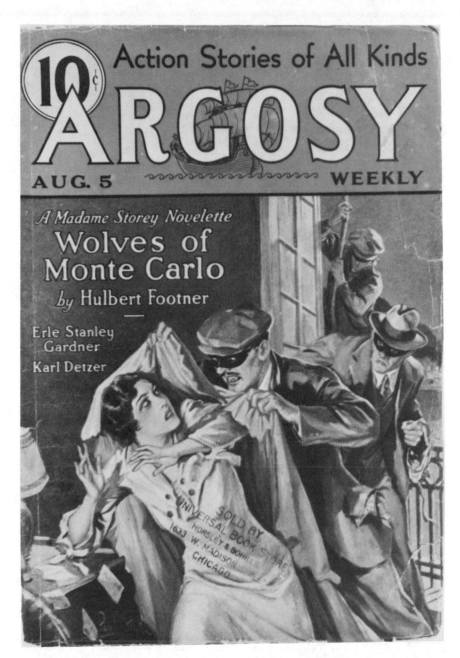

Argosy, August 5, 1933. As Mme. Storey's series entered the 1930s, the stories shortened, became more violent. But her charm never waned.

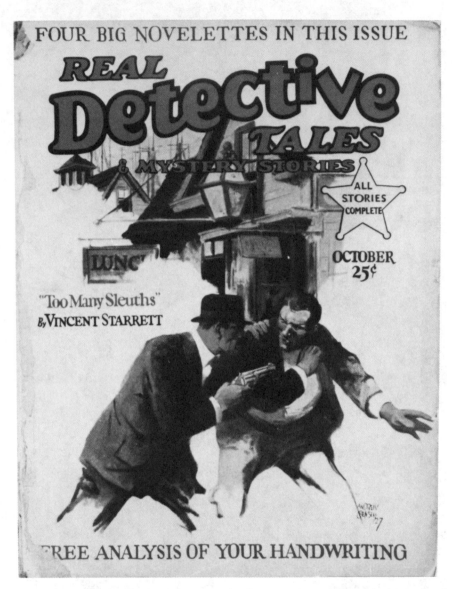

Real Detective Tales and Mystery Stories, October 1927.   The magazine evolved from the 1922 *Detective Tales*, companion publication to *Weird Tales*. It continued to the early 1930s, gradually transforming to a true-detective magazine.

Argosy All-Story Weekly, February 24, 1923. The popular Shadowers serials told the adventures of a pack of crooks operating an honest private detective agency.

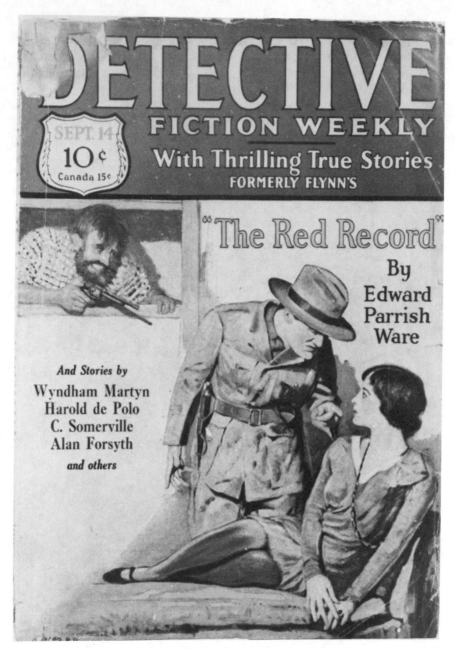

Detective Fiction Weekly, September 14, 1929.   Hardboiled Ranger Calhoun battered his way through scarlet cases, mixing wild west violence with mystery action down in the Mississippi River swamps.

Black Mask, June 1930.   That tough-talking private investigator, Race Williams, blasted away in *Black Mask* from 1923 to 1934, and popularized detection by gun fire.

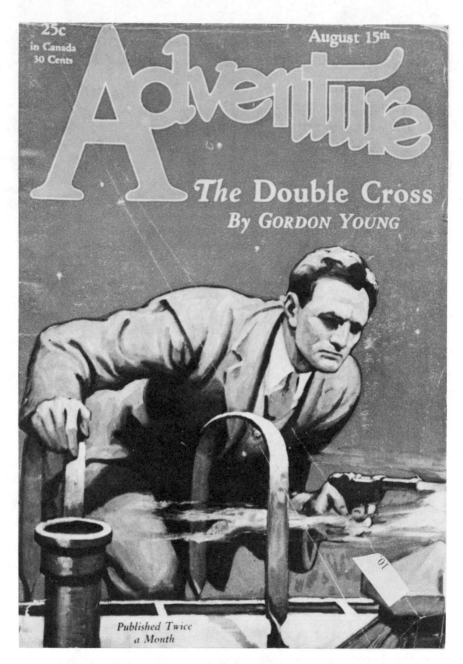

Adventure, August 15, 1929.   Don Everhard, gambler and gunman, began his hardboiled career in 1917, continuing in *Adventure* until 1936.

Black Mask, August 1934.   Even the deadly Flame had moments of difficulty. She persisted in marrying the wrong man, although she loved Race Williams. None of her husbands survived.

Flynn's, October 24, 1925.   Captain Brady and Sergeant Riordan led the action in a fine series of pre-police-procedural police procedurals.

Chapter VI—From the Mask

1-

The Black Mask was created because the *Smart Set* magazine was financially ill. It had not always been that way. But massive editorial shuffling, an editorial policy during 1913 which terrified advertisers, and crumpling sales had left the magazine wan.[1] Even a new owner, Eugene F. Crowe, and the appointment of George Jean Nathan and H. L. Mencken as co-editors in 1914, failed to cure the magazine's woes.

In 1915, still oppressed for operating funds, Mencken and Nathan decided to fish the rich water of the cheap popular magazines. They discovered that, by creating a pulp magazine, then selling it as soon as it caught on, they could generate funds to revive *Smart Set* still once again.

Thus they created, nourished, and sold the *Parisienne*, a magazine pandering to the intense popular interest in all things French. The fiction was drawn from the *Smart Set* slush pile, with the setting, what ever it might have been originally, altered to France. First issued July 1915, the magazine was sole to Crowe in November 1916 for $5,000.

A second magazine, *Saucy Stories*, whose fiction also originated in the slush pile, was issued August 1916 and sold four months later for $10,000.[2]

Some portion of this money remained with the co-editors, who were receiving only token amounts for their labors on behalf of *Smart Set*. The rest was applied to that languishing magazine, which continued to absorb funds and look pallid. (*Parisienne* and *Saucy Stories* continued to show bright profits long after being sold.)

In March 1919, Mencken remarked in a letter to Ernest Boyd that he was "thinking of venturing into a new cheap magazine scheme..."[3] He had noted the success of Street & Smith's *Detective Story Magazine* and the ever-faithful *Smart Set* slush pile contained about one mystery manuscript for every five submitted. Later Mencken would write:

I could get out a 128 page magazine at a cash outlay of no more than $500. As a matter of fact, Nathan and I did it in the case of the Black Mask.[4]

The first issue of *The Black Mask*, dated April 1920 and issued, as usual, the month before, was immediately popular.

Mencken to Ernest Boyd, April 3, 1920:

197

Our new louse, the Black Mask, seems to be a success. But the paper famine may murder us at any moment. The thing has burdened both Nathan and me with disagreeable work. The Smart Set bonds fall due next year, and we must do some hard sweating to avoid bankruptcy.[5]

In November 1920, *The Black Mask* was sold to Crowe for $5,000, plus a later, undisclosed amount of about $7,500. Mencken seemed glad to get it off his hands:

The Black Mask is a lousy magazine—all detective stories. I hear that Woodrow reads it. Reading mss. for it is a fearful job, but it has kept us alive during a very bad year. The *Smart Set* makes expenses, but very little else.[6]

Mencken and Nathan viewed their three pulps with raucous contempt. That people would pay to read sub-literary swill merely emphasized that the national taste was degraded beyond salvation. Since this could not be cured, the intelligent man would set about to draw a little personal benefit from the national calamity.

So *The Black Mask* began as a cynical exploitation of the public enthusiasm for detective stories. Filled with *Smart Set* culls and showing irremediable marks of its *Smart Set* origins, *The Black Mask* carried itself with a self conscious swagger. Its nose lifted high. Not the slightest glimmer of coming greatness warmed its pages. Now and again it glanced back at Mencken's formidable figure and muttered under its breath that no intelligent man could take detective fiction seriously.

Certainly no intelligent man could take *The Black Mask's* detective fiction seriously. Most of the stories were written by unknowns who stayed that way. Not only were they condescending about mystery stories but they were unaware that they did not know how to write this form of fiction.

From "The Silver Lining" by John Baer:

Most stories start in one of two ways. The hero is either in love or in debt. Often he is both. So is our hero, and in this respect he is therefore not in the least original.

Meet him. At this particular moment he is in his bedroom, and in no mood to be introduced to strangers. Take a look anyhow.

He is standing before his dresser-mirror, fitting a mask. The mask is black and covers his entire face; there is a slit only for the eyes. On the dresser is a revolver. Oh, yes; it is loaded.

Now, putting two and two together, as the saying goes, we arrive at the total four. The young man anticipates a lively evening. He needs money and he's going to get it....[7]

He attempts to rob the heavy winner at a gambling joint. In the scuffle, they exchange straw hats and, since our hero's hat contains his initials, he must exchange hats again at gun point. Some months later, our hero had become a bankrupt. Then, the other fellow, knowing him to be the unsuccessful robber, tells him that the gambling winnings, $11,000, were concealed in the lining of the first straw hat, which our robber had given back.

"The Bamboozler" by J. R. Ward:

Out of the underworld, like a groundhog fearing its shadow, came, on a night when the moon was hidden by heavy clouds, Sleepy Norton, bad man. Like a rat suddenly finding itself in the open he scampered along in the shadows, a crafty rodent of that part of the city where the shady side of life is prevalent and where the scum of humanity finds its plane.[8]

A crooked lawyer conspires with an incompetent sneak thief to fake the robbery of a movie star. The thief's tough pal turns the fake into a real robbery. At the end of the story, all the criminals are arrested by accident.

"Bram Dwyer's Bonfire" by Ward Sterling:

Jones rolled over and leaned on his elbow. Consciousness returned slowly. His head ached. Chairs, tables—all the furnishings—were doing a grotesque dance before his eyes.
Was it time to get up? He rubbed his fingers across his throbbing brow... The cobwebs dissolved slowly... Someone was pounding on the door... He must have overslept.[9]

He is a bank employee, regaining consciousness in the aftermath of a robbery that has left all employees unconscious, the bank looted. The sheriff believes it was an inside job. But astute man-hunter, Bram Dwyer finds slivers of glass on the floor, tampering at the skylight, and the loot concealed in some bales of hay. Instant deduction. How did he know that it was in the hay? Well, it happened in a small town, and everyone but the feed-store operator came to gawk at the robbery scene.

"The Door" by John Hanlon:

The door to the terrace opened, slowly, softly, remained wide for a moment, showing a patch of inky night between the white walls of the bedroom; then it closed again, slowly, softly.
So still was everything that the faint click of the latch sounded as loud as toppling towers.
The woman watched, eyes widening, temples throbbing, a scream welling in her throat.

The door had opened, the door had closed but no visible hand had touched the knob...[10]

Someone is in the room with her. No, no, she is only overwrought from the funeral. Yet there—on the bed—she can see him clearly, lies an old man; there, she sees herself bending over him, relentless, a hypodermic in her hand. Then the images vanish. "Don't torture me," she moans. "I'll tell everything—everything!"

Outside the door listen two detectives. One grins at the success of the magnet they had placed on the door lock—a trick to terrify her to confession. The other detective stammers in horror. He had not activated the magnet. But the door opened by itself.

Eight to twelve stories appeared each issue. Serials were soon added. At 20 cents an issue, the fiction cost less than 2 cents a story. This explains a great deal.

For some years, the table of contents included a small sketch of a domino mask. Behind this crossed a dagger and a flint-lock pistol. Beneath the magazine title ran a line specifying the type fiction offered— "A Magazine of Mystery, Thrills and Surprise" (1921); "Romantic Adventure, Mystery and Detective Stories" (1923). By 1927 it had stabilized as "Western, Detective and Adventure Stories," a promise retained on the covers into 1930. For *Black Mask*, the foremost hardboiled magazine of the decade did offer some western action, as well as tough, urban investigators.

At the beginning of its life, however, *Black Mask* was anything but hardboiled. Its fiction featured incompetent crooks, a few genius investigators, a lot of dumb police. The stories were written by the usual unfamilar 1920s names, all sounding vaguely spurious and suggesting wry editorial jests.

The Black Mask may strike us now as being barren, but even barren fields may eventually bloom. A few traces of living prose stirred in the October 1922 issue of *The Black Mask*, which published Carroll John Daly's first story, "Dolly." At the same time, the October issue of *The Smart Set* offered Dashiell Hammett's first story, "The Parthian Shot."

Simultaneously, two writers had appeared who would embody the two major elements of the hardboiled school: the dual lines of objective realism and melodramatic fantasy.

Two months later, in the December 1922 issue of *The Black Mask*, both men again published stories. Daly contributed "The False Burton Combs," the stone which began the tough dick avalanche. Hammett, writing under the name Peter Collinson, published "The Road Home."[11] That story foreshadowed those ethical ambiguities and moral rigidities later characterizing the best work of the hardboiled school.

Coincidence plays strange tricks. For more than two years, *The Black Mask* had ambled along, placidly conventional. Then, in a single issue, it went mad. It spit out two powerful lines of development, one of which changed the face of mystery fiction. Granted that *The Black Mask* was only an accidental vehicle for a pair of particularly strong writers. If Hammett had not been selling to *The Smart Set*, then he might never have sold to *The Black Mask* and it is possible that the hardboiled school, or some variant, would have evolved in another magazine. The development of any major literary line seems inevitable only after the fact. At the time, it is all a series of non-repeatable accidents and coincidences so improbable that the least deviation would have aborted the whole flimsy process. If, if, if...

But Hammett did first publish in *The Smart Set* (with excursions into *Brief Stories*) and did find a toe-hold in the *Mask*, rather than *Adventure* or *Detective Story Magazine*. Daly did find *The Black Mask* receptive to his violent fantasies. And both men appeared in the December 1922 issue of *Mask*, one of the key issues in pulp magazine history. Much began here.

2-

Race Williams began here.

Race Williams is often credited with being the first hard-boiled detective. That strains the definition of detective. Williams is a hired adventurer who may occasionally detect if he blunders into a clue the size of a bathtub and painted bright pink. He has little use for clues, even less for chains of reasoning.

Thought is not required in a Race Williams investigation. Iron-headed determination, the ability to soak up punishment and give it, straight shooting—those are the basic requirements. Especially straight shooting:

Williams: "That's my racket. Meet lead with lead, violence with violence, and death with death. This working on the side of the law may have its advantages, but it has its disadvantages, too. The law is always looking for evidence; legal evidence, when a few corpses decorating the scenery would be much more effective and certainly quicker."[12]

It is all pleasantly uncomplicated. Crime is clearly visible. Evil is obvious. Evil stands there trying to shoot your head off. But you are half a second faster with your gun. What could be simpler. No crooked courts and biased judges; no shyster lawyers squirming through gaps in that raddled tissue, the law. You meet crime. You defend yourself, and the cops may bellyache, the way cops will, but you solve all the problems at once:

It may be conceited—but truth is truth. I'm a Private Investigator who doesn't believe in red tape. I never did object to a little gunplay. I shoot fast and hit what I shoot at. The police know that. The papers know that. And most of all, the professional murderers know that. I'm a lad, who after the shooting takes place, likes to have his picture taken standing up—not laid out on a slab with a medical examiner pointing out to the boys just how it happened.[13]

This way justice is served as surely as if there had been trial. And much more completely.

When I put a .44 in a man's forehead—he stays dead. At least he always has.[14]

The author of these admirable sentiments, Race Williams, is a big, hard, casual fellow, who carried his two .44 revolvers through thirty years of battle and sudden death, from 1922 to 1952. He stands a little under six feet tall, weighs 180 pounds, has black hair, dark skin, high cheekbones. He is of Scotch-Irish extraction. Unlike later hard-boiled investigators, he rarely drinks and avoids sex as carefully as he avoids thought. Instinct, he remarks, has helped him more times than reason. He is one of the earliest of the writing private investigators, turning out his adventures in a brisk, first-person narrative, glinting with wise cracks, slang, and a casually crude prose not far removed from illiteracy.

The stories sound as if they have been transcribed from speech with all the colorful speech and bragging preserved intact. The flavor comes over strongly in the first paragraphs of the first Race Williams story, "Knights of the Open Palm."

Race Williams, Private Investigator, that's what the gilt letters spell across the door of my office. It don't mean nothing, but the police have been looking me over so much lately that I really need a place to receive them....

As for my business, I'm what you might call the middleman—just a halfway house between the dicks and the crooks. Oh, there ain't no doubt that both the cops and the crooks take me for a gun, but I ain't—not rightly speaking. I do a little honest shooting once in a while—just in the way of business. But my conscience is clear; I never bumped off a guy what didn't need it. And I can put it over the crooks every time—why I know more about crooks than what they know about themselves. Yep, Race Williams, Private Investigator, that's me.[15]

Race Williams and his adventures were created by Carroll John Daly (1889-1958). Born in Yonkers, New York, Daly was a slight, small man who lived musician's hours, writing all night and going to bed at dawn. He began writing when he was 33, after holding a wonderful miscellany of jobs—owner/operator of the first moving picture show in Atlantic City, manager of a theatrical stock company, salesman for real estate and stock, and manager of a fire-alarm company. After his first story in the 1922 *Black Mask*, his crime and adventure fiction was published in such pulp magazines as *Argosy All-Story Weekly, Flynn's Weekly, Detective Story Magazine, Dime Detective, Frontier Stories, Detective Fiction Weekly, Clues, Thrilling*

Detective, Popular Detective, Famous Detective, and *Smashing Detective.*
His series characters stretch across the decades: Race Williams (*Black Mask,*
Dime Detective, and others), Satan Hall (*Detective Story, Black Mask,*
Detective Fiction Weekly, Famous Detective), Clay Holt (*Black Mask, Dime*
Detective, Famous Detective), and Vee Brown (*Dime Detective*). There were
others.

Most series characters and most stories were chopped from the same
tree. The fiction was rough, violent stuff from the beginning, and rough,
violent stuff it remained. Only slowly did his style change. The fiction he
published during the 1940s was a paler version of his 1920 successes. He
never lost his ability to sustain suspense through a story of frenzied action.
But, by the late 1930s, magazine mystery-action fiction was seeking other
channels. Daly's popularity waned sharply. As the pulps began to fade, his
markets fell away. He attempted, uneasily, a less heated style. He left New
York for California, hoping to break into television. Without success. The
short story market was gone. His books no longer sold. He remained in
California and, at the end, wrote a few scripts for comic books. He died,
January 1958, flat broke and forgotten.

How different his first fifteen years of professional writing. Then he
gleamed and glowed. Readers applauded. Sales leaped at his name on the
cover. Race Williams was echoed by other characters in other magazines.
His world of melodramatic violence, more fantastic than realistic, echoed
in *Clues* and *Ten Detective Aces, Thrilling Detective* and *Spicy Detective,*
and some dozens of similar magazines that whooped through the 1930s,
each borrowing and modifying Daly's vision of bloody menace and
unrelenting gun action. More than any other writer from *Black Mask,* Daly
influenced the direction of the 1930s detective-action pulps.

He has received little acclaim for this. The lesser detective magazines
of the 1930s are not well examined. Critical comment has tended to fix
on Hammett and Chandler, whose objective realism, glittering about a
romantic core, could be tied to more familiar literary lines. They could be
associated with such respectable names as Hemingway. But Daly was down
in the bargain basement of literature. He was noticed but not acclaimed.

In part, this neglect is because Daly wrote violent fantasy during a time
when realistic prose was a major literary current. From any rational
viewpoint, Race Williams' world was fantasy, no matter how clipped his
prose and contemporary his scene. The hero is beaten and shot to extinction
and rises refreshed. He litters the city with corpses, with no deleterious effect
on his license. He never misses, with either hand, with .44 revolvers, in
combat, which is fantasy in itself. He pounds punches slugs speeds breaks
into breaks out of escapes by coincidence and returns again. The police
scowl at him. The politicians grumble. But he remains unchecked,
undisciplined, and richly rewarded by his clients.

Fantasy. The action occurs in our familiar world. But it is a world almost devoid of consequence and emotional reactions. It is all busy fun. A pleasant savage game. Fantasy.

The first Race Williams, appropriately enough, appeared in an issue of *The Black Mask* (June 1, 1923) as fantastic as *Amazing Stories* managed to publish. This issue was devoted to Ku Klux Klan stories. What the authors lacked in specific knowledge of the Klan was compensated for by imagination and research in the newspapers. The Daly story, "The Knights of the Open Palm," is no more authentic than other stories of that issue. It is a great deal more vigorous and it prances merrily.

It is, in fact, a vibrant wild west thriller with automobiles and the East substituted for horses and the West. It could have been converted to a Hopalong Cassidy adventure in a single revision.

The story, told by Race Williams, himself, is breezy, vernacular, and full of rude humor.

Race Williams, Private Investigator (he prefers Investigator to Private Detective) is hired to find a kidnapped boy. The KKK got him after he had seen and heard too much. His father, Earnest Thompson, is full of fear. Williams can't understand it. "Imagine if it had a been my boy—blooey—I'd of bumped that gang off one, two, three, right down the line."

So Williams takes the train to Clinton—after a brief delay to look up a minor crook who has been kicked out of the Klan. The crook is that valuable adjunct to a writer; he is a Plot Enabler, providing the hero with all the information needed. If you got off the train at Clinton, you would know nothing of Klan structure, nomenclature, or passwords, and would be forced to stalk fruitlessly about, your .44s rusting under your coat. But Race gets all the needed information and off he goes.

No sooner is he in Clinton than three Klansmen visit his hotel room. They are very tough and greatly surprised when Williams lets them look down his gun while he jerks the hood from the leader's whiskered face. He drives them out of the room. "And the next time you come around here I'll take that nightshirt off you and shove it down your throat-whiskers and all."

Next morning, the hotel manager, looking white, asks Williams to leave. At that moment enters tough farmer Buck Jabin and his two tough sons. Jabin wants to shake Williams' hand and offer him a place to stay if he needs it. The Klan has written Jabin a few letters but he is too much a hard case for them to fool with. Before marching back to the farm, Jabin speaks privately to the manager, turning him whiter than ever. Shaking and sweating, he assures Williams that he can keep his room as long as he likes.

All minor plot elements now in place, the action begins.

That night Williams heads for a Klan rally. He borrows a bicycle, clubs a watching Klansman, and rides off to the meeting. There he ties up another guard and borrows his robe to attend incognito. Too soon the tied guard is discovered. Williams escapes and follows a mysterious group of Klansmen to where the kidnapped boy is held.

Yes, of course it's coincidence. How on earth do you expect a story to flow from event to event without coincidence?

The Klansman prepare to kill the boy. Their mistake.

Crack!
Yep, it's my gun what speaks and that lad goes out like a light. The other lad draws a gun and looks around him bewildered. But he don't see nothing; leastwise in this world he don't. I get him right through the head—there ain't no mistake where I land in that distance...

Oh, I ain't a killer, but remember, there were four of them, and that left two more to be accounted for yet..."[16]

The third one soon dies, but the fourth, the bearded tough of the hotel room, shoots at Williams from the rear, creasing his head. He wakes up in jail, is swept off to trial. But Buck Jabin and his boys drop by to see that justice is administered, and the judge squashes the indictment—after the kidnapped boy has testified that he saw KKK members murdering and robbing.

By this time, the Klan membership in Clinton is melting away. Thompson thinks it would be a good idea for Williams to leave town and drives him to the depot.

It is a dark and stormy night. At an isolated part of the platform, Williams unexpectedly comes face to face with the bearded Klansman.

Was he quick? Well, he never had no chance. Mind you, he had his gun in his hand, but he never used it. Just as clean as a whistle I had pulled and shot him straight between his bloodshot eyes.[17]

A nice quick, easy case, and a healthy score of bodies, for a Private Investigator who ain't no killer.

Race Williams was Daly's fourth gun-free adventurer to appear in *The Black Mask*. All characters are as similar as cartridges from the same box. The unnamed narrator of "The False Burton Combs" (*The Black Mask*, December 1922) sets the tone for the group:

I ain't a crook; just a gentleman adventurer and make my living working against the law breakers. Not that I work with the police—no, not me. I'm no knight errant, either. It just came to me that the simplest people in the world are crooks. They are so set on their plans to fleece others that they never imagine that they are the simplest sort to do.[18]

To earn your living skinning crooks is to walk the shadow line with The Brigand, John Doe, and other luminous gentlemen crooks discussed in the third volume of this luminous series. Except that these gentlemen crooks were not lethal. Daly's hero is.

I'm mighty quick with the artillery myself.
And that gun is always with me. It ain't like I only carry it when I think there's trouble coming. I always have it. You see, a chap in my line of work makes a lot of bad friends and he can't tell when one of them is going to bob up and demand an explanation. But they all find out that I ain't a bird to fool with and am just as likely to start the fireworks as they are.[19]

After "The False Burton Combs" (which left its hero quivering on the brink of matrimony), Daly produced a second nameless quick-gun hero in "It's All in the Game" (*The Black Mask*, April 15, 1923). The following month, he introduced Three-Gun Terry Mack—a private investigator with a small gun up his sleeve—in the first of two stories: "Three Gun Terry" appeared in the May 15, 1923 *Mask*; a second story, "Action! Action!," followed in the January 1, 1924, issue.

By then, Race Williams had arrived and these initial finger exercises were dropped.

3-

Literary forms do not leap spontaneously from the vacuum. Yearn as we will for simple origins, we find the new emerging only slowly from the heart of time, that cool green heart which contains no true beginnings or endings but only continuations.

The hardboiled style, which energized 1920s mystery writing and spread its vivid stain across the decades, was one such continuation.

Hardboiled fiction was a lesser branch of American realism, practiced by talents as diverse as Howells, Stephen Crane, Jack London, Upton Sinclair, and such later modernists as Hemingway and Faulkner—all writers alert for echoes of the human heart while, at the same time, describing, with immense precision, reality's glittering shell. Or describing how they, personally, saw that shell—a qualification that leads to surprising complexities.

Popular magazine fiction was never overly concerned with realism, objective or otherwise. It was, however, a long-standing convention of that fiction to twine exact descriptions of place, personality, and atmosphere in among highly seasoned bursts of dialogue and action. When framed by familiar detail, even high melodrama can seem possible.

As mentioned in earlier volumes, bursts of realistic description chatter through the adventures of Nick Carter, Felix Boyd, and Jimmie Dale. Those adventures were far from being hardboiled. For the hardboiled story is a consequence of character, the attitudes held and the decisions made—so often unsentimental, pragmatic decisions, strongly flavored by self interest.

Turn-of-the-century magazine fiction showed only fitful traces of hardboiled attitudes: a few paragraphs in Nick Carter, a few pages in Hopalong Cassidy and the Lone Wolf. These traces were the precursors of a more acrid strain which rose about 1910. At that time, the family-type magazines discovered the delights of fast-gun, hard-nosed adventurers, foreign legionnaires, and soldiers of fortune. These characters radiated a qualified amount of personal harshness and violence, although not intensely enough to disturb the tranquility of the family reading circle.

When the new magazine, *Adventure*, was introduced in 1910, its fiction turned sharply from the family circle to that more curiously specialized audience, men. *Adventure's* fictional arena was the world and its subject, all the human conflicts that could be imagined upon that agreeably wide stage.

One of the first major series characters in *Adventure* was a professional gambler who had, quite incidentally, killed more frequently than any man in the United States. His name was McDonald Richmond, familiarly known as Don Everhard. He seems to have been the first major hardboiled series character of the pulps.

Everhard was created by Gordon Young, a prolific writer of action fiction, who published his excitements in *Adventure* for almost thirty years. Young combined a number of the story types then popular—adventure stories with tough heroes, crook stories with bent heroes, and crime stories with revelations of life in the underworld. All these forms, Young combined with the image of the frontier gambler and transplanted the composite figure to a contemporary urban scene.

However mixed his origins, Everhard was a fresh and interesting character. And one of considerable influence. For many of Everhard's qualities, developed in shining detail between 1917 and 1921, gleam equally bright in early Race Williams novelettes. Whether Everhard directly influenced Daly's early adventurer-heroes is a moot point. In five years, a very strong character creates his own environment, becoming so persuasive and so inevitable that, like Holmes or Tarzan, his features are permanently stamped on a particular fictional form.

However his influence was transmitted, the Everhard series contained much that later found its way into the hardboiled convention.

Everhard, a first-person narrator, is an adventurer who is not a criminal, is not a friend of the law, and is not very respectable. His friendship is given sparingly:

The code I try to live by has been a simple one; and I have made but few friends, for in that shady borderland between the upper and the under world and in a life of semi-outlawry, friendships are as exacting as in a blood-brotherhood.... The only Phythian friendships that remain in the world are among the soldiers of fortune, adventurers and outcasts—the brotherhood of the damned.[20]

He earns his living in that borderland, a shark preying on sharks:

...I am, or was in those days, as dexterous a card-shark as there was anywhere; but to the best of my knowledge I never fleeced an honest player.[21]

His reputation is violent:

"Take a good look at him if you want to see the most famous gunman in this country. His name is Richmond, calls himself Everhard. He has killed more men than any other fellow in America—and is proud of it."[22]

It is a reputation earned by his quickness and accuracy with the .45 automatic and his willingness to shoot:

One of the reasons I am progressing nicely toward a quiet old age is because I have always taken the trouble to shoot first. "Draw last and shoot first" is as good a health maxim as I know. And one of the reasons certain persons have knocked on my door in the quiet hours because they thought I might want to see who was there before I was ready to shoot.[23]

Everhard enjoys action more than thought:

I don't know why it is, but I never seem to have any better ideas and plans by thinking the matter over for a long time than I get by taking the first thoughts that pop into my head....[24]

His life is emotionally austere, no self-indulgence being permitted and few emotions. "I am cold-blooded and not easily excited." In a crisis, he is frigidly wary:

It is true that I had a flashlight, a small one. It is also true that I was not the sort of man who would hold up a flaming beacon to invite from complete darkness the guns of possible marksmen. Who cares to distinguish that caution by an offensive name is at liberty to do so.[25]

And he cannot be deflected from his purpose by personal danger, gunmen's threats, or feminine wiles:

I told her, not bitterly and certainly with no kindliness...that like all pretty women she thought she carried a pardon in her face, that, after all, the fault was not entirely hers because every man who saw her, and other pretty women as well, pretended it was a privilege to dance to the snapping of their gem-studded fingers....

"Oh, you are cruel—cruel," she said, looking up with something painfully wistful in her eyes. "Don't treat me this way—as if you didn't care. Oh, say something—*do* something! Strike me—beat me—kill me or—Don, kiss me!"

How much of that was art and drama, how little was meant, I do not know. I did not try to keep away the smile. There was no other answer.[26]

Gunplay does not bother Everhard, nor death. But it must be straight, honest gunplay, gun for gun and bullet for bullet:

...I had a name as a "killer," which was little unjust to one of my peaceful disposition; but the facts as rehashed in the papers made me out as an extremely dangerous sort of person.

And as far as (he) was concerned, those facts were true. I intended to kill him when I had got a confession out of him. Not shoot him down like the dog he was; no. But to force a duel out of him and after the stern justice of the Middle Ages settle the matter in a trial by ordeal....[27]

There would be many such trials by ordeal, for the series was long.

Gordon Young transferred the gun artist from the western saloon to the city and set him adventuring along the dark fringes of the underworld. Carroll John Daly took the adventurer and converted him, after trial and error, to a private investigator. Between the two characters lay trifling differences: Everhard, the black sheep of a wealthy California family, was literate, polished, restrained, a rather slender man of medium height. Williams, a great, solid, lion of a man, was partly literate, crude, often violent, occasionally sadistic. Both were men of honor. Of the two, Williams is the more famous. Fame is one of the fringe benefits of appearing in *The Black Mask*. History has reserved no special honors for a hardboiled gambler from *Adventure*: but it showers laurels on the first hardboiled detective.

4-

The Race Williams series started with deceptive slowness—two stories in 1923, three the year after; five and a serial in 1925. Thereafter, a modest mixture of novelettes and serial parts that totalled about five items a year—for the serial parts, only loosely connected, were as much novelettes as pieces of a larger work. Most got assembled into hardbacks, where they were presented as novels, a feat equivalent to presenting a patchwork quilt as a lace tablecloth.

The Williams machine ground methodically on through 1935. At that point, it transferred to *Dime Detective* and four long short stories a year. So matters continued to 1940, when the stream thinned to occasional contributions in *Detective Story, Thrilling Detective, Dime Detective*, and lesser markets. More than fifty-five stories and nine serials (one of them incomplete) were published, covering, Mr. Williams' career as a gun-swift on the wicked city streets. In thirty-two years, he showed little detective ability but an extraordinary skill at shooting people in the head. People who deserved it.

The initial stories are preoccupied with elemental violence. The mystery element is trivial, being reduced to these simple bones—What on earth is going on? Who is the concealed crime master?

The story seems to have spurted from the typewriter in flaming jets:

Race is hired to recover the papers, save the kidnap victim, bring in the killer, avenge a friend.

At the scene of a crime, he meets a deadly killer, a tricky woman, or both.

Soon he has been slugged or shot and taken prisoner.

By luck or coincidence, he escapes.

Immediately he lunges back into danger. The tricky woman works against him, evading, obstructing, protecting someone else. If she would cooperate, the story would be over in 2,000 words. Often he is manipulated by the brilliant master criminal, who correctly assesses Race's intellectual force but incorrectly estimates his tenacity. The mastermind's terrible gunman, a fearsome, swaggering killer, leers and sneers.

Williams is trapped. The forces of evil hold him tied, wounded, disarmed. As fingers tighten on triggers. As the atmosphere grows tense as an IRS audit.

Then a wild reel of action. The concussion of heavy caliber pistols. And Mr. Williams, smeared with gore and painful dents, tucks away those smoking guns and departs, leaving a stack of corpses for the Medical Examiner to marvel over.

"Half Breed" (*The Black Mask*, November 1926) is a wild west story that begins with two Indians killed in New York City. Both are Williams' clients and he follows an involved trail, something about oil leases, to Oklahoma. There he impersonates the half brother of a beautiful Indian girl worth perhaps 999 millions, who may be menaced. Maybe not; who knows.

Suddenly she vanishes. And here lies Race, arrested, tied, jailed, as the posse pounds all about the sage-brush. And peering in the jail window at the helpless Race is an evil face, knife in hand....

All leading to a fine duel in the dark and a surprising disclosure of identity. Mr. Williams' fee is $10,000, a respectable sum.

"The Hidden Hand" appeared as a five-part serial in *Black Mask* (June through October, 1928). This is a serial by courtesy only, each part complete, all loosely connected, and each with its own title.

Williams is employed by a philanthropist who has the idea that he can eliminate a criminal organization, The Hidden Hand. This is terrorizing Florida. The Philanthropist gives Williams the names of four criminals. All are leaders in the crime ring. Each knows the name of the mysterious mastermind directing activities.

Williams goes after each leader in turn. Four crooks, four serial parts. In each, he is captured and almost killed before he cuts down this issue's gloating menace. This naturally narrows his available leads. During these startling activities, Williams' life is repeatedly saved by Tina Sears, an enigmatic beauty, who consistently lies to him and otherwise confuses matters. Williams' bone-headed vigor is played off against the pompous, self-seeking, publicity-wise Gregory Ford, self-acclaimed as The Greatest Detective in the World. Ford is a continuing character appearing irregularly to series end.

Eventually Race shoots down all the crime leaders in self-defense. Then, in the fifth serial part, he learns that the mysterious Hidden Hand was the Philanthropist, himself. He was using Race to get rid of all those selfish criminals who wanted to share the gang's stealings. After these revelation, the Philanthropist gets shot. Of course.

In "Tags of Death" Williams is in a three-way competition with Ford and Detective Sergeant O'Rourke of Headquarters. They are attempting to track down The Tag, a highly competent murderer who is slaughtering criminals. Or their bodies, he leaves a yellowish-brown metal disk. Some tags are large and some are small, leading Race to suspect that a second murderer is helping out. This minor murderer, Race traps while cleaning up a bloody jewelry store holdup and murder. After that, he guns down the Tag's top aide in a theatre, having thrust his way on stage in the middle of a performance; the aide, costumed up like The Shadow, has just fired a rifle at his intended victim. Race blazes away and down the fiend tumbles from his box into the musicians' pit:

I was looking at the face of the man who lay dead, stretched out on his back over the bass drum. And I was getting a kick out of the three holes in the side of his head. A pretty bit of shooting, that—considering the conditions.[28]

The scene is neatly bloodless, and the prose, smirking with self-satisfaction, gives no hint of what really happens to a head hit by one or more .44 slugs. Daly is thinking in terms of hitting a tin can with a .22. It is much less messy to shoot a tin can.

Although Race is not a fast man with a compliment, he is fond of precise professional work and comments on skilled gunmanship wherever he finds it, whether by criminal, policeman, or himself. It is part of the craft to shoot economically and with exactness. You duel, not murder. You face your opponent and, when the weapons slip from the leather, you don't wave them above, orating—you use them competently, as a craftsman uses a chisel and a plane.

Formal ritual? Perhaps. Borrowings from silent western movies? Maybe? Echoes of Owen Wister's *The Virginian?* Certainly.

All the formalities of the western's climactic gun-scene are here: the quick draw, the confrontation with evil, the extraordinary accuracy with either hand, with large-caliber revolvers. Hopalong Cassidy didn't get to New York City, but he didn't need to. Race Williams got there first.

After the shooting in the theater, the Tag offers $100,000 to the man who shoots Williams down. Killer Lu Roper from Philly is to do the honors and Williams is to be lured into a death trap by a woman.

A woman who looks like a young girl. She seems to be about sixteen years old, her face young, innocent, clear. Until she begins to talk. Then "her face set tightly—hard, appraising, intelligent—strength of character— sureness of purpose." She is the brains behind the Tag. She has planned his crimes. She is The Girl with the Criminal Mind, The Flame, less dramatically known as Florence Drummond.

Florence and Race share interesting times together in *Black Mask.* She will appear again in "Tainted Power" (three-part serial, June through August 1930); "The Flame and Race Williams" (published as *The Third Murderer),* a three-part serial, June through August 1931; and "Six Have Died" (published as *Murder From the East),* a three-part serial, May through August, 1934; and later in *Dime Detective.*

Their relationship is ambiguous. He grows to adore her, and she is intensely fond of him. Or perhaps it is love. Whatever the emotion, it doesn't prevent her from leading him into a series of murder traps. At the same time, she makes certain arrangements so that, with luck, he can walk out again. She has great faith in his skill with a gun, if little confidence in his intelligence. She is evasive and slippery. She is two-faced and treacherous. She persists in using him as a counter in her own schemes. And she repeatedly throws down her life to save his. It is a complicated relationship, once nearly ending in marriage.

Florence personally kills Roper when he attempts to ambush Race in Pennsylvania Station. And she is shot almost to death in the next part of Tag case, which concerns the kidnapping of a judge's daughter. After extraordinary dangers, the daughter is saved. Florence will recover after all. And the Tag dies, a nice bullet placed, with precise craftsmanship, between the eyes.

In "Shooting Out of Turn" (October 1930), Race leaves New York City to help a small town District Attorney capture a murderer, John McCue. Every step of the way, Race is obstructed by the Chief of Police, who is either corrupt or has concealed reasons for keeping McCue from arrest. Race learns the reasons—McCue has a confession proving that the DA's father was a thief. The Chief and the father were good friends, explaining that part of the matter, more or less. Race burns the confession, which ends the matter, since McCue has stopped a .44 with his forehead and will cause no further trouble.

Friendship is the spring that drives "Death for Two" (September 1931). Williams' old pal, Detective Sergeant O'Rourke, has been shot by Killer Mertes. Race announces to the papers that he's going to stand in for O'Rourke: He'll report to the wounded officer, take his orders, and bring Mertes to justice.

The papers promptly announce that Williams is willing to shoot it out with Mertes and has information that he can lay hands on the Killer in twenty-four hours.

All this is merely to stir the bottom of the creek. But it brings Ed Kranze, a hired killer, grinning on Race's trail. And it leads a blond Broadway star, glowing with wet-lipped sensuality, to lure him into a death trap in an old house. Race goes. Prepared:

Glorious Blond: "You'll help me. I'll do anything—pay anything—for your help. But you're so cold and unsympathetic. Most men—It's as if you knew something about me; think I'm bad. But I'm not—I'm not. I don't want to be bad."

Race is unimpressed.

Hysterical? Possibly. Acting? Probably. Tricky? Certainly....
As to the sex interest, if we must have that in life. Well—she was a rare trick, as women go.... The proximity of that beautiful, youthful body...the over-powering perfume of the East...and her soft breath upon my cheeks, should have sent my head swimming. And I daresay there is a place and time when they would have. But this was decidedly not the place nor the time....

(She is trying to turn him so that his back is to a suspiciously quivering set of full-length curtains.)

So, as far as I was concerned, let me say that she hung to me like a wet blanket—and to make the simile quite correct, she turned on the water works and began to make monkeys out of a tie I had a particular bit of fancy for.[29]

It is Race's melancholy fate to be clung to by a succession of desirable young morsels, tender, fragrant, and pressing themselves tightly against him. Nothing of interest ever happened. Only The Flame caused his pulse to jump, sometimes.

Race is, however, a man with organized priorities. Sex is nice. Staying alive is nicer. When Kranze pokes his gun through the curtains, Race nails him.

What does it all mean? Well, the blond charmer had been blackmailed by Mertes; she was to lure Williams to doom. Now Williams offers her a choice: reveal Mertes' address or go to the police station. That produces an emotional storm:

(She) dashed forward into my arms.
Those next few moments are best to forget. The woman was distraught; irresponsible for what she said—what she promised. I let it all slide over, and forgot it afterwards. But I gave her the truth just the same....
"You don't know what you're saying, and neither do I. But if I fell for every—" And I didn't add that in my game I could have enough beautiful women to establish a harem. I just said: "This is business with me. I'll break the law right now, and not only let you go but see you clear, if—if you tell me where Mertes is...."
I looked straight down at those curved, red, cupid-bow lips—or whatever the hell the literati call them. The soft lure of deep... But, anyway, I gave her the glassy eye.
"You haven't lived the life you've lived, jumped the hurdles you must have jumped to reach the place you've made without knowing the rules of the game. You get exactly what you pay for in life. I'm asking you for no favors—I'm giving you none. I want Mertes. If you turn him up, you go free."[30]

These are familiar fields. Hammett had already explored them with the Continental Op and Sam Spade. And before Hammett, Gordon Young and his tough adventurer, Don Everhard, met similar situations with similar self control. Both Young and Hammett invest the situation with ethical overtones, sifting through shades of meaning to judgments about personal responsibility and self respect.

Daly's net is less sensitive. His violent fantasies were not built for delicate discrimination. They settle for accessible virtues—craftsmanship, straight-shooting, friendship and its obligations, keeping your word no matter what the personal price. Valuable virtues all, fitting to the prose in which they are embedded.

Williams' friendship for O'Rourke demands that he bring in Killer Mertes. He will do so, no matter how many blond girls, clinging like wet blankets, offer him wonders to do otherwise. So he prys loose the address of Mertes' apartment. Goes there. Finds it surrounded by police, with the Killer holed up inside, holding a young girl hostage. But not for long. After considerable drama, Race enters the apartment. Mertes wounds the girl, then surrenders before Race's gun.

Can Race shoot down an unarmed man? Certainly not. But he can give Mertes a chance to shoot him in the back with a concealed gun. Which proves immediately fatal to the Killer.

The procession of death continued into the 1930s. Action burns surplus wordage away. Race's larger illiteracies have long since disappeared and the prose is increasingly spare, increasingly harsh:

I was doing pretty well. The temptation was to drag my gun across Eddie's face, stop it at his mouth, shove a few teeth into his throat and finally kick him around the room until he got lost. And a very laudable temptation, you've got to admit."[31]

This inspired posturing is an imitation of the authentic hardboiled stance, not the real thing. It is the reverse side of hardboiled, whose more notable practitioners were taciturn men, touchy of their reputations, coldly pragmatic. They thought spare, sudden thoughts and took spare, sudden action. They never bothered to share their hardboiled thoughts with the reader. The tougher a character is, the less he talks about it.

Race consistently talks large, violent stuff. He has in him some traces of that savage river roustabout, Mike Fink:

I'm Race Williams, I am. I bite off mountains and spit out cliffs. I'm an iron-headed, steel-fisted, brass-nerved, flashing, flaming, .44-fingered bad man with death in my eyes and destruction in my trigger fingers. I'm the original terror. I'm the biggest, meanest, hardest private investigator standing between the roots of Heaven and the flaming vaults of Hell.

Which is not to say that Race's adventures are altogether counterfeit. He is one hard pilgrim, and his activities are violent, often brutal. His investigations are primitive as a Stone Age hunt. But each time Race slugs an enemy or blasts him away, he must discuss the act with the reader, his tone a curious mixture of apology and pride which give the *Black Mask* stories their distinctive sound:

I brought down my right hand and pounded the nose of the gun across her forehead. Blood flowed into her eyes....

As for crashing her on the head! Did I have a touch of conscience about that? Don't make me laugh. I know, according to the accepted formula for heroes, I should have waved her gun aside, taken her in my arms and kissed the murder out of her eyes. But I didn't. That's why I'm alive to tell it. Any explanation for my brutal act? Sure! She had it coming to her.[32]

Violence comes easily to this prose. In other *Black Mask* fiction, violence defines a character, resolves a climax, illuminates the mores of a class. Violence is a natural consequence of the story, generated by special characters conflicting in special situations. In Race's adventures, no special situations exist. Violence is the normal condition. The story progresses by violence through violence to the ultimate violence. Violence is the major response permitted the characters. Already as shallow as saucers, they are further limited and dehumanized, for Daly's narrative allows little behavior more sophisticated than clubbing, stabbing, torturing, shooting.

During 1933-1934, Race William's final years in *Black Mask*, the stories begin to cannibalize themselves. Repetition thrusts from the narrative like fragments of a recurring dream: The shoot-out with the hired killer. The blackmailed beauty. The $10,000 fee. The kidnapped child tormented by fiends. The blow from behind. The murder trap baited by woman's tears. The search against time. The scene in which Race, disarmed, wounded, tied, facing the killer's gun feels his bonds loosen....

"The Death Drop" (May 1933). Race investigates a horrid mess in a company mining town where the miners have been locked out, big city gunmen are strike breakers, the sheriff is crooked as the Snake River, the secret boss plots unchecked, and all the wholesome citizens sit inert. It is all cleared up by shooting the right people.

"If Death Is Respectable" (July 1933): Beautiful society queen, Gladys Drake, hires Race as her bodyguard. Well, she needs help. Well, she is being blackmailed. Well, she was in a hotel room along with a young gunman. Well, he is dead. Well, she shot him, you see.

From these twisting lies leads a trail to letters written by gangster leader Eddie Kean. They would convict him of murder. The letters are found, then lost. Gladys is blackmailed to marry Kean, her cheeks flushed with shame. But Race follows the trail to the Philadelphia office of a murdered doctor. And, with Kean's gun in his back, Race pulls a trick shot that settles everybody's problems. Especially Kean's.

"Six Have Died" was three-part serial (May, June, and August 1934), later published as *Murder from the East* (1935). The story consists of three loosely linked novelettes, unified only by recurring characters and a central situation of no great probability.

The deadly Count Jehdo of Astran, a mythical country, heads an enormous organization which has infiltrated the United States. Jehdo's agents murder and torture, steal government secrets, prepare "to strike simultaneously through the entire country," leaving it an easy victim for conquest. Fortunately for the United States, the organization has been penetrated by the unknown Agent No. 7. Against this secret burrowing stand the Count Jehdo, the Countess Jehdo (none other than the Flame, new married to the title), and the frigid Eurasian, Yarrow, Deputy Chief of the conspiracy.

Into this seething pot plunges Race. He has been hired to save the darling kidnapped child with blue eyes and golden hair, such a picture of sweetness. Either her father reveals government secrets or the child dies.

As Race conducts the investigation, it is a simple matter. You begin by slugging heads with gun barrels, then club out some teeth and shoot holes in selected foreheads. He proceeds with enthusiasm. By an unfortunate turn of events, he ends tied to a chair while Yarrow prepares to slaughter him. Since it is only the first part of the serial, it is not altogether surprising that he is saved by Agent 7. Agent 7 seems to be a woman. Could it be that... The gold-haired little dear is saved. Yarrow glowers in the hospital, all shot up. And, for the balance of the serial, Race becomes Jehdo's chief target. How lightly he prances among murder traps, as the cast is thinned by death, the guns crash, the bodies tumble. Between killings, the principal characters face each other and growl grittingly between their teeth.

Race gets captured and tied up once again and saved, once again, by Agent 7, now revealed to be Florence. She is working in her own way for her country, expiating the excesses of her criminal career.

But she has saved Race once too often. Yarrow identifies her as Agent 7. She is manacled to the bulkhead of a yacht, her delicate back bared, slashed with a whip, while Race rages in his bonds. Then Race is loose and Yarrow dies unshriven, mourned only by C. J. Daly—who had been using Yarrow as an elastic bandage to hold all these plot fragments together.

For the third serial part ("Murder Book," *Black Mask*, August 1934), a new elastic bandage is required. Daly constructs one from a venerable cliche of popular fiction...the book which contains all the names of the spymaster's lieutenants. Could this book, the Yellow Book, be delivered to US authorities, the Count's organization could be crushed.

Florence promptly arranges that Race steal the volume. By now, the Count has also learned that Florence is Agent 7. Unless Race returns the book, Florence dies.

That being the case, Race rips back the book from the authorities, ignoring their pitiful cries, and returns it. Shortly after, he finds himself tied up a third time, death seconds away.

With considerable trouble, he gets free, precipitating a crimson finale. Florence is left a widow and the Yellow Book is carried in triumph to the representatives of Virtue, Peace, and Justice.

From beginning to end, "Six Have Died" is a wild, improbably, inconsistent, repetitious, wonderful pandemonium. Pure junk food. But delightful in its own cockeyed way.

The November 1934 issue of *Black Mask* offered the final Race Williams novelette to appear in that magazine. There followed a pause of almost a year before the series resumed in the September 1935 *Dime Detective*.

Daly had already published extensively in *Dime Detective*. Since 1932, the magazine had featured twenty-five of his novelettes, most about detectives Vee Brown, Marty Day, and Clay Holt. These differed from Race in various details of physical description and habits, and resembled him in all other ways. All were accomplished man-slayers, killing, killing, killing.

The *Dime Detective* magazine, through which pulsed this bloody ecstasy, had first been issued dated November 1931. It was the fifth pulp magazine offered by the fledgling Popular Publications and one of the most successful. Over twenty-two years, two hundred and seventy-four issues would be published, the final one dated August 1953. Through these pages streamed an array of writers whose work would shape the direction of mystery fiction for more than two decades, among them Erle Stanley Gardner, Frederick C. Davis, T. T. Flynn, Norbert David, Hugh B. Cave, Max Brand, D.L. Champion, Frederick Nebel, Raymond Chandler, Cornell Woolrich, Robert Turner, John D. MacDonald—to cite a distinguished few of the distinguished many.

During its first years, *Dime Detective* featured what was termed "horror-mysteries," a story form resembling a Gothic thunderstorm—sinister action in sinister surroundings. Hordes of pullulating evil. Specters glowed malignantly and ghouls and ghosts and demonic shapes to their prey did rouse.

In the final pages, the story came thumping back to earth. The wraiths from Hell stood revealed as tricks by assorted lawyers, businessmen, and friends of the family, mass murderers all, avid for someone else's money.

These adventures in fantastic melodrama jostled with classical example of the hardboiled detective story, as perfect representatives of the type as ever were published in *Black Mask*. For *Dime Detective* had wooed contributions from writers steeped in the *Black Mask* style. So irresistible did readers find this harsh excellence that, by 1934, the hardboiled story began to choke out the horror-mystery. Although that form slowly dwindled away, its gory talons clicking with rage, magazine covers and story titles continued to emphasize horror-mystery elements through about 1936. By then *Dime Detectives* had converted to hardboiled action fiction, vivid, contemporary, fresh as new grass.

Williams entered this gaudy world with the September 1935, "Some Die Hard." The story tells of the serial murders committed by a drink-crazed madman. Or so it appears. Race's client is found murdered. He is consistently obstructed by that brutal police inspector, Iron-Man Nelson, a psychopath in his own right. The pace is fact and violent, the story line tricky and rather more complex than usual. Race's familiar asides to the reader are severely pruned back. Race, himself, soon adds a .25 automatic worn up the sleeve, as did Three-Gun Terry Mack.

Race's assurance remains undimmed. In this new environment, he seems less free to shoot and swagger. He seems more sharply drawn, a trifle more substantial.

It is as if the reader had been peering through an unfocused lens toward a towering figure, part mythic hero, part daydream, insubstantial and blurred. Until the focus is abruptly altered. Then the figure dwindles, condenses, resolved to crisp solidity. So, in *Dime Detective*, the Race Williams story complicates, concentrates, takes on a literary weight lacking in such a less casually integrated piece as "Six Have Died."

The familiar sustaining characters of Race Williams' world transfer to *Dime Detective* with him: His office boy and general assistant, Jerry; police detective-sergeant O'Rourke (whose name later simplifies to O'Rouke); and the Flame, her Criminal Mind untarnished by time.

"City of Blood" (October 1936) allows Race to clean up a town overwhelmed by gangsters. He proceeds directly to the task, killing five gangsters in five hours, then loading his guns for the city's crime boss, who has kidnapped the beautiful girl. Race discovers her prison by torturing a captured thug until he turns his own stomach. After this the guns begin to pound.

For cleaning up the town, Race is made Police Commissioner for a week. In keeping with the Hopalong Cassidy atmosphere of the story, he promptly posts signs that, after a deadline, known criminals will be shot on sight. Today an edict would give the Supreme Court colic. But it worked for Cassidy and, in 1936, it worked for Race Williams, within the page of *Dime Detective*, at least.

So the years slip by, a blur of names and faces in this cruel bright world. Men die and women. The Medical Examiner smiles agreeably at a bullet-pierced forehead: "Race Williams does such nice clean work." The .44s hammer and are not satiated. Iron-Man Nelson, vicious, smart, honest, is a looming danger, tied and humiliated by story's end. Gangsters and gang leaders swagger and menace. Blackmailers grin with hot eyes. Killers grin with cold eyes. Corpses fall dull-eyed. Blood stains the crisp sentences. Anger movement violence shakes the pages, a heavy wind whose pressure never stops as years slip away.

December 1937, "The $1,000,000 Corpse": The judge's niece is a respectable girl, isn't she? Or is she Jane Blake, that deadly feminine killer who guns men's lives away? At stake is a $1,000,000 legacy. Which gangster Manning plans to have. And why not, with the girl at his mercy, Race disarmed and tied with wire to a chair, and Race's secret assistant dead on the floor. But things just don't work out the way Manning intends, you can kiss the Book on it. Jane flickers through the series, a .38 in her purse, Race glowing her heart. She is a less savage version of the Flame.

March 1939, "Hell with the Lid Lifted": Disguised as a surgeon, a mad surgeon, Race is brought to a private railway car to amputate a girl's leg. The girl is the Flame, and shortly after, the guns get busy, as Race blasts into the heart of a swindle. Before every last character dies, Race gets married. The bride, a young winsome sweet, is known as The Little Killer because of the clever ways she thinks up murders. And she had to get married that very day to come into her inheritance. The Flame doesn't protest at all;

she knows the whole thing is a hoax. A prior marriage interferes with The Little Killer's hopes of becoming Mrs. Williams, and the wedding night is spend chastely enough shooting down the evil .

After the February 1940, "Cash for a Killer," the sequence of Race Williams stories in *Dime Detective* was interrupted. The day of the detective action melodrama was insensibly closing. No longer could a story sustain itself on a sequence of pretty shots to the forehead, smashed teeth, and gangsters taking the bitter pill. Human emotion had edged into the fiction. Constraints of the real world limited the action. No longer could the detective romp through his bloody fantasy, bypassing law in his pursuit of justice.

Daly was fifty-one years old in 1940 and his fiction markets were fading. That world he had created around Race Williams, and which had so long sustained his fiction, had hardened. Change was essential. But change was difficult.

"Body, Body, Who's Got the Body" was published in the October 1944, *Detective Story Magazine* and reprinted in the 1946 *Detective Story Annual*. It is a relatively subdued adventure. Race undertakes to remove a blackmailer's body from the home of a prominent philanthropist, only to end caught between the guns of a beautiful girl and the philanthropist—himself an emperor of blackmailers.

From 1947 to 1950, only a bare handful of Race Williams stories were published. A few appeared in *Dime Detectives*, most in *Thrilling Detective*. "Race Williams Cooks a Goose" (*Dime Detective*, October 1949), a brisk piece of action, pastes together familiar situations and events. Race's client is murdered, a consequence of ancient crime and blackmail. Jerry is taken hostage and Race, disarmed, must face the killer alone. It is long familiar stuff, but it is wonderful how Daly can make those dry gray bones caper.

"The Strange Case of Alta May" (*Thrilling Detective*, April 1950) is perhaps the only dull Race Williams' story written. A long-lost heiress has returned. Or is she an imposter? Race pecks at the problem through a smoothly complicated narrative about murder and a five-million dollar swindle. In deference to this tame new fiction, Race kills no one, is present at only one murder, and behaves in a sluggishly realistic manner. The story is carefully crafted to avoid melodrama's garish glare. It does.

The detective pulp magazines found the early 1950s a dreadful time, a time of extinction. One after another, the great old magazines were dying. In 1949, *Ten Detective Aces*, Street & Smith's *Detective Story Magazine*, and *10-Story Detective* were discontinued. The following year, 1950, saw the death of *Private Detective Stories* and *15 Mystery Stories*. In 1951, *Super-Detective* and two giants, *Detective Fiction Weekly* and *Black Mask* were cancelled. And the bad news continued into 1953, when such major titles were eliminated as *Dime Detective*, *Detective Tales*, *Thrilling Detective*, *Popular Detective*

The Phantom Detective, and Popular Publication's continuation of *Detective Story Magazine*. One by one they fell, the great and the less, the classic magazine and the faithful copy, a sorrowful litany of failure, as publishers turned to more economically viable slick magazines, digests, paperbacks, comic books.

For a few years, as the walls collapsed, Editor Robert A. W. Lowndes of Columbia Publications stood firm with *Famous Detective* (which became *Crack Detective and Mystery Stories* in 1956) and *Smashing Detective* (which became *Fast Action Detective and Mystery Stories* in 1957). But firmness was not enough. By the end of 1957, the big, rough-paper detective pulps were gone.

As the shadows thickened during 1954-1955, Daly published a few short stories in both *Famous Detective* and *Smashing Detective*. These magazines saw the final stories, one each, about Clay Holt, Satan Hall, and Race Williams.

The last Williams, "Head Over Homicide," appeared in the May 1955 *Smashing Detective*. It is another tightly written, meticulously subdued story, telling how Race rescues a rich kidnapped heiress—who was not kidnapped and didn't want to be rescued. Up whirls an evil fog of murder, concealed murder, a secret ex-con husband, a wealthy suitor, a disappearing corpse. Race misunderstands the entire situation and deduces the wrong murderer. He doesn't sort out matters until a page before the end and by then, a tricky woman has got away with murder. Race fires not a shot. And on this restrained note, his series ends.

5-

Race Williams, Private Investigator, represents the first of two ways that the hardboiled urban detective developed. A curious combination of influences had produced Race—dime novel detectives, silent movie gunfighters, pulp magazine adventurers. Daly blended them all (we may suspect) with private daydreams, creating a hero who was startlingly influential. Race's example set off an astounding number of imitators, quick with the wise crack, quick to draw, quick to fight crime gun for gun and bullet for bullet.

They were not particularly intellectual. But you can think any time.

During the 1930s, these detectives made their homes in *Clues* and *Thrilling Detective*, in *Ten Detective Aces*, *Popular Detective*, *Dime Detective*, *Spicy Detective*, in *Detective Tales*, and in those G-man magazines which came and went like shadows under the trees. All were stuffed with melodrama; a few realistic touches were added to make the impossible seem mildly probable. Through these stories flowed the violence, the persistent attitudinizing, and the absence of consequences which confirm this branch of detective fiction as fantasy.

Four months after Race Williams began his harsh career, a second hardboiled detective made his appearance in *Black Mask*. He was the nameless Continental Op. The force and brilliance of his series, by Dashiell Hammett, would permanently alter the face of detective fiction.

6-

The Op is fortyish and a little heavier than he should be. He appears only in cases which might logically be brought to a private detective. He is on excellent terms with the police. He carefully avoids emotional involvements with the people in a case. He stays sober when working. He is no lone wolf, but a cog in a large and efficient organization. He is tough in self-defense, but completely devoid of sadism. Many of his cases involve no physical violence; in those which inevitably do, the violence is written with taut understatement. He describes one of his most dangerous situations as "a game that made up in tenseness what it lacked in action," and the description fits most of his adventures.[33]

The Op is a solid professional, investigating for a living in the streets of 1920s America. He joined the Continental Detective Agency's Boston Branch when he was twenty. He left in 1917 to enlist in the AEF, and earned a captain's rank in Military Intelligence. After the war, he rejoined Continental, worked in Chicago, then transferred to San Francisco. There he worked for about five years before his series opened in *The Black Mask* ("Arson Plus," October 1, 1923). He was then in his middle thirties, which is not quite the "middle age" he claims for himself.

His career loosely parallels that of Samuel Dashiell Hammett (1894-1961), who joined Pinkerton's Detective Agency in 1915, when he was twenty-one. Eight years later, in February 1922, he finally resigned. His service with Pinkerton's had been repeatedly interrupted, first by enlistment in the Army (in 1918), thereafter by recurring hospitalization for tuberculosis.[34]

From this point, the careers of Hammett and The Op diverged. Hammett became a writer and inadvertently struck a tone and a style which swept the Victorian cobwebs from mystery fiction. The Op—we assume—continued as a detective. He enjoyed the work, was fully aware of the price that enjoyment exacted.

Nothing is free. Every choice leaves its mark. The pleasures of man hunt and problem solving, complicated by occasional violence and frequent boredom, are paid for by accruing emotional frigidity. As Hammett describes it, the profession of detection offers much; it also progressively dehumanizes. The problem is dramatized in the four novelettes from 1927-1928 that were reworked into *Red Harvest*. A strong intelligence can recognize the process and perhaps reverse it. But the struggle against dehumanization is continuous.

The Op's initial fictional career was about seven years long. (That excludes the extensive reprinting of his adventures.) Thirty-four Op cases appeared in *Black Mask*, 1923 through 1930. Single stories were also published in *True Detective* (1924) and *Mystery Stories* (1928). Three full-length books, *Blood Money, Red Harvest, The Dain Curse*, developed from certain story sequences in *Black Mask*.

Much later, in 1941, *Ellery Queen's Mystery Magazine* began reprinting Hammett's short stories, including many of The Op's cases. This led to the publication of nine paperback story collections between 1943 and 1962. All were edited and annotated by Ellery Queen.[35]

By 1962, Hammett was a year dead. He had become a political pariah and a literary icon. His reputation as the principal founder of the hardboiled school was magnified by international acclaim. His fiction was seriously discussed. His major characters were instantly recognized. If he were not a major writer, he was, at least, a major minor writer.

All this recognition was based on fiction written mainly between 1923 and 1933, a thin enough slice of time.

In 1930, Hammett had gone to Hollywood. He was successful there, a valuable creator of story ideas. His magazine fiction had stopped; after "The Thin Man" (*Redbook Magazine*, December 1933), he completed only three short stories for *Collier's*. The Hollywood money poured in, was drunk, gambled, flung away, symptoms of self-destruction that had shown before but now ran unchecked. He separated from his wife and family, began a three-decade relationship with Lillian Hellman. His books became moving pictures. He provided dialogue and continuity for the initial 1934-1935 episodes of the *Secret Agent X-9* newspaper comic strip. He assisted Hellman with her plays, acting as a critic and guide, a fierce judge. He lived locked within self-appointed rules which, never stated, were never relaxed. A rigidity required (perhaps) by a sense of fracture. The forces fracturing him are not known. Other novels became films and the Thin Man was adapted to radio. In 1941 Hammett left Hollywood. The following year, he joined the Signal Corps, was assigned to the Aleutians. Returned, his politics increasingly left wing, he became President of Civil Rights Congress in 1946, the year Sam Spade entered a radio series. Lung trouble and alcoholism. During the black carnival of the McCarthy years, Hammett's reputation was savaged. Refusing on principle to provide CRC documents to an investigating committee, he was sentenced to six months in federal prison. The Internal Revenue Service claimed back taxes, stripped him. He had a heart attack in 1955. It was now a long descent through darkness. He attempted to write novels. All failed at once, or sputtered slowly out. The accumulating disaster of these years, he met with frosty self-possession. His physical condition deteriorated. He remained stubborn, proud, frail, inflexible, with a personal integrity as austere as a Roman patrician. He died January 10, 1961, of emphysema and lung cancer.

He is a figure from Greek tragedy, the golden man immolated by tragic flaw and the malice of gods. No such end is prefigured in the Continental Op series. Matters are not simple there, but doom is not inevitable.

The Op was based on the man who gave Hammett his initial detective training—James Wright, the assistant superintendent of Pinkerton's Baltimore office.[36] The character is colored by traits of other detectives Hammett met during his career and also seems to reflect much of Hammett, himself. The Op, short, stout, stolidly healthy, is a simplified and reversed image of tall, lean, tubercular Hammett.

Whatever his origins, The Op is a well-seasoned professional, thoroughly competent at his job. He enjoys his work and, being a professional, has accepted all the associated responsibilities and restriction. As he remarks, when refusing a massive bribe:

"...I like being a detective, like the work. And liking work makes you want to do it as well as you can. Otherwise there'd be no sense to it. That's the fix I'm in. I don't know anything else, don't want to know or enjoy anything else.... Money is good stuff. I haven't anything against it. But in the past eighteen years I've been getting my fun out of catching crooks and tackling puzzles, my satisfaction out of catching crooks and solving riddles. It's the only kind of sport I know anything about, and I can't imagine a pleasanter future than twenty-some years more of it. I'm not going to blow that up."[37]

The professionalism is a constant. It is a discipline, severe and demanding, unaffected by expediency. A professional has committed himself to a course of action and abides by its terms. If being a detective requires that you sit nine continuous hours in a car, watching a house, then you sit. You may grouch at hunger, physical needs, boredom. But you accept inconveniences. You have obliged yourself. To do less is to betray yourself.

The atmosphere of professionalism in the Op stories is hardened by a constant flow of specific facts about the business of detection.

...a detective can't afford to believe in luck or coincidence, unless he has unquestionable proof of it.

Tracing baggage is no trick at all, if you have the dates and check numbers to start with...[38]

I made a quick inspection of the house and grounds, not expecting to find anything; and I didn't. Half the jobs that come to a private detective are like this one: three or four days—and often as many weeks—have passed since the crime was committed. The police work on the job until they are stumped; then the injured party calls in a private sleuth, dumps him down on a trail that is old and cold and badly trampled, and expects—Oh, well, I picked out this way of making a living, so....[39]

We now dropped that angle and settled down to the detail-studying, patience-taxing grind of picking up the murderer's trail. From any crime to its author there is a trail. It may be—as in this case—obscure; but, since matter cannot move without disturbing other matter along its path, there always is—there must be—a trail of some sort. And finding and following such trails is what a detective is paid to do.[40]

My next play was to canvass the vicinity of where the car had been stolen and where it had been deserted, and then interview the witnesses. The fact that the police had fruitlessly gone over this ground made it unlikely that I would find anything of value; but I couldn't skip these things on that account. Ninety-nine percent of detective work is a patient collecting of details—and your details must be got as nearly first-hand as possible, regardless of who else has worked the territory before you.[41]

There are four rules for shadowing: Keep behind your subject as much as possible; never try to hide from him; act in a natural manner, no matter what happens; and never meet his eye. Obey them, and, except in unusual circumstances, shadowing is the easiest thing that a sleuth has to do.[42]

These are descriptions of personal experience, unsentimental as a recipe. Other professional detectives of the past, Vidocq and Allan Pinkerton, himself, had written of personal experiences from knowledge as direct as Hammett's. They also wrote for the taste of their times. Those tastes emphasized melodrama—chases, disguises, confrontations, emotions snapping in the winds of passion.

Experience, so brightly dressed, transformed to fiction.

In this, these earlier professionals differed from Hammett. In his work, the fiction is concentrated and understated until it resembles fact. Authentic procedure, realistic detail give the narrative the glitter of a dry, bright morning. He, too, wrote for the taste of his times.

Behind his stories stand the ghosts of hundreds of investigation reports. Their cadences linger in his prose. The tone is objective, terse and stripped. He creates a locale in a sentence. Descriptions of people occupy two or three sentences. He tags a personality by the set of shoulders, the shape of the head, a peculiarity of dress.

The physical description is limited because other techniques are used to demonstrate character. It is done with unadorned statements describing motion and attitude, by the choices the character makes, his expressed attitudes, and, above all, his speech.

A Hammett story requires attentive listening. The dialogue seems a simple transcription from reality. It is plain as a curbstone, artless as water. Easy slang tumbles in it and slants of humor.

Sheriff: "We got a city slicker here to catch our firebug for us. But we got to tell him what it's all about first."

Deputy: "Ain't the Lord good to us."[43]

The dialogue conceals considerable craftsmanship. No matter how real it all sounds, this is conversation in fiction, not a slice of life. Each line of dialogue contributes to the overall effect, providing information, advancing the story. It is there for a purpose. It may sound natural, but that is Hammett's skill. Dialogue in fiction is, in this sense, as artificial as a plastic cat.

The Continental Op's first case, "Arson Plus," was published in the October 1, 1923, issue of *The Black Mask*. Like the earlier "The Road Home" (December 1922), an adventure story with a detective, this was signed Peter Collinson. The story describes the investigation of an arson at an out-of-the-way house; the servants escaped but the owner, according to testimony, died in the fire.

The investigation is a joint effort by The Op and a Sheriff's deputy. Cooperation is mutual. The Op gets along fine with the Sheriff and his deputies. No one is stupid. All are competent men, drawn in brief sentences, hard as bone, that catch personality in a casual line:

On the Sheriff: I had never known him to miss an opening for a sour crack; but it didn't mean anything.
On Deputy McClump: a rangy, towheaded youngster of twenty-five or six with all the nerve in the world—and most of the laziness.

Unlike other magazine detectives, The Op does not search out clues and ratiocinate from these. He constructs few chains of deductive logic. But he does read people. This is a major investigating tool—together with the methodical application of routine. Being methodical, he begins his investigation at the crime scene. He goes out to examine the remains of the burnt house. He continues by interviewing a witness and the survivors of the fire and the dead man's few associates. He verifies their stories. He patiently collects facts and meticulously examines these. Very slowly he pieces together an intricate mosaic of information. At last a laundry list reveals an obvious discrepancy. And suddenly, the arson-accidental death case changes to one of conspiracy and insurance fraud. Which ends in a high-speed automobile chase, accident, and brief gun play.

The October 15, 1923, issue of *The Black Mask* contained two Op stories: "Crooked Souls" (later reprinted as "The Gatewood Caper"), was signed Hammett. "Slippery Fingers" was signed Collinson, the last use of the pseudonym.

"Slippery Fingers" concerns murder. Bloody fingerprints are found on the knife. They are not the suspect's fingerprints—and the case that The Op laboriously constructs can't get over those prints. Until, at police headquarters, he discovers that the suspect's fingertips feel slippery.

Examination shows that the fellow is wearing a splendid set of forged prints, prepared to scientific standards that would delight Dr. Thorndyke.

The November 1, 1923, "It" (reprinted as "The Black Hat That Wasn't There") begins as a simple problem. Bonds held in trust have vanished from a safety deposit bank. Zumwalt, responsible for the bonds, has hired the Continental Detective Agency to trace his partner, who vanished when the bonds did. In vanishing, he also jilted the married woman with whom he had planned to run away.

The situation is simple, clear, direct. But it is not reality. It is an elaborate construct of lies and partial truths. Accepting nothing that he is told, testing every fact and statement, The Op works his way to the real situation. Which leads to a horrifying confrontation in a lightless cellar, where the unarmed Op is pitted against a killer with a gun. The "It" of the title refers to a corpse buried in the cellar—solid evidence of murder and found because The Op is skilled in reading men.

(The first-person narrator of "It" is not specifically identified as The Op. Cogent arguments may be raised for and against inclusion of the story in the series. Since, however, the narrator describes himself as "thick-bodied" and both the prose tone and investigative techniques are those of The Op, this discussion assumes that "It" is from his case book.)

"Night Shots" (February 1, 1924): Shots from the window of the sick man's room. Twice it happens, each time missing the sick man. The second time, a bullet wounds the nurse in the next room. Once again, what seems to have happened is a screen of lies. The Op investigates, concludes the case by planting himself in a cupboard and watching for what he has deduced will happen.

A more strenuous case, "Zigzags of Treachery," was published March 1, 1924. A doctor has been shot dead. Maybe suicide. Or maybe his wife did it. No sooner does the Op look into the problem, than a second wife pops up. From that point, shadowing, bluff, and intelligence uncover a fuming mass of identity substitution and murder.

The final scene crisply demonstrates the difference between the fiction of Hammett and that of Daly. Race locates the guilty party—is shot enough to produce gaudy bloodstains—plants a .44 squarely in the forehead of the last second, so to speak.

Hammett does it differently.

The Op reasons that a letter, containing an essential piece of evidence, has been mailed to a con man. He confronts this fellow in a hotel room. There is a brief display of guns, and the Op shoots the gun out of the con man's hand. (He explains this feat by saying that your bullet has a tendency to go where you are looking.) The Op then hears a confession and secures his evidence. At a price—the con man is to get his gun and a fair start. Too good a bargain for a multiple murderer, but circumstances force the Op to close the case quickly.

The con man, not content with his advantage, pulls a flim-flam trick and leaves with the evidence. As he escapes from the rear of the hotel, he attempts to shoot the Op's colleague in this case, Detective Sergeant O'Gar. O'Gar kills him.

The con man's gun would not fire. It had been broken by the Op's bullet. The Op knew this. As he knew that the evidence had been stolen back. That the man would bolt for he rear exit. That O'Gar was at the rear exit. That the con man would attempt to shoot.

All these matters to Op understands without much conscious thought. He grasps the situation as a whole. Then he can feint, maneuver, manipulate, play the odds, nudge the action to his favor. Like a chessmaster, he plays for position, relying on his close knowledge of individuals to force their decisions. Rarely does he find it necessary to duel with .44s.

The Op's manipulative skills show up early in the series and develop until they cause a severe personal crisis in *Red Harvest*. His success in manipulating people and events depends on how thoroughly he understands them. During many of his 1923-1924 cases, he simply does not have time to understand. The case matures too rapidly. Before he has uncovered more than a fragment of the truth, events spontaneously explode, with only the slightest warning.

A Race Williams shoot-out is prefaced by dire snorting and stamping in the dust. These familiar preliminaries to combat are not part of the Op's experience. In his world, no teeth bare, or faces scowl, and the stream of lies does not falter.

Only a minute sign of physical strain signals the flashpoint. An eyes widens, a shoulder tenses. The attack comes with appalling swiftness. Fists, feet, teeth—direct physical violence with all the pain, bleeding, and shock that smashed bone and crushed flesh provides.

In the January 1, 1924, "The Tenth Clue," the Op is slugged and dumped into the middle of the Bay. In "One Hour" (April 1, 1924) he is murderously attacked by four counterfeiters and his face pulped. The violence rises from the situation and the physical effects are not lightly tossed off. A beating requires hospitalization, not a decorative bandage.

The Op routinely meets profound physical danger that bursts unexpectedly from the routine stuff of investigation. No formal duel here between gunmen; that is melodramatic fantasy. The reality is a familiar office with worn furniture and 10 o'clock sunlight through dusty windows and a slight widening of the eye before the attack. Which is the final recourse. Violence does not come until all lies are exhausted.

The savagery of "The House on Turk Street" (April 15, 1924) explodes as the Op is quietly questioning a nice little old man and woman. He is seeking information about a missing boy. Then a gun muzzle prods his neck. He finds himself tied up tight. He has come by accident into the home base of a robbery ring that has just murdered a bank messenger and stolen $100,000 in bonds.

Through a story superbly concentrated and raw with suspense, the Op manages to remain alive, as gang members intrigue against their leader, and he against them. Three people end up shot dead, the leader is captured, a tricky girl escapes. But at the end of the violence, the Op has only the sketchiest idea of what was going on. The gang has assumed greater knowledge and destroyed itself on that belief.

"The Girl With the Silver Eyes" (June 1924) continue the later history of the girl who escaped from Turk Street. The Op investigating the disappearance of another girl, finds himself in a storm of murder roaring around a forged $20,000 check.

At the end of this trail is the girl with silver eyes. She has changed her name and appearance since Turk Street but her seductive technique, once used to con bank messengers, is unchanged, and terribly effective.

She plays her sexual force on The Op. Almost she overwhelms him. Almost. He is not quite romantic enough to succumb, but he comes close enough to be badly scared. The scene is a distant ancestor to that more famous scene in *The Maltese Falcon* when Spade refuses Brigid O'Shaughnessy. The Op's experience in "The Girl with the Silver Eyes" lacks the intensity and the levels of ethical ambiguity reached in Spade's scene. The Op must fend off a sort of sexual hypnosis. When he meets a similar situation at the end of "The Gutting of Couffignal," he is much more in control.

The scene in which male rejects predatory female was certainly not new to fiction. Don Everhard faced those deadly melting charms, as had Nick Carter, of all people. And so back through history to pre-history, where the tale was told while lumps of giantasaurus sizzled over the fire. It is one of narrative fiction's basic scenes. Its popularity has remained undimmed across thousands of years, in spite of woman's unimaginative refusal to pounce upon the timid male and rip away his last shreds of respectability.

Hammett brought a new intensity to this venerable day dream. It leaped revitalized from his stories to Race Williams to the adventures of the hard-drinking, hard-living private detectives of the later pulps. Few of these were concerned with the interpersonal complexities Hammett got into the scene. They kept the action and discarded the content and rewrote Spade vs. O'Shaughnessy as if they had just invented the situation. Some day dreams are immortal.

The force of Hammett's best scenes comes from the reality of the characters. His people are individuals, acutely sensitive to nuances of speech and physical movement. They are aware as a hungry fox. Except for tiny, involuntary physical movements, they give nothing away. That quality of awareness in his characters distinguished Hammett from other detective story writer and is one of the reasons why his work remains alive, long after Race and other hardboiled legions have faded into yesterday.

The Op is nameless, faceless, almost without history. His personal life is barely described. Few first-person narrators have allowed so little of themselves to seep into a story. What gets in is quietly understated:

I'm not what you'd call a brilliant thinker—such results as I get are usually the fruits of patience, industry, and unimaginative plugging, helped out now and then, maybe, by a little luck....[44]

He enjoys poker, boxing, Fatima cigarettes, a little off-duty drinking with friends. He is a bachelor, living in an apartment whose rooms and furnishings remain undescribed. Aside from these meager traces of personality, he is sometimes reflected obliquely in the comments of others— as in *The Dain Curse*, when the novelist Fitzstephen remarks, "You're never satisfied until you've got two buts and an if attached to everything."

The Op's boyhood is not mentioned, nor his relatives, and whatever shape and direction his relations with women have taken, they have been excised from his pages.

In spite of these blanks, the feel of the man communicates through the series. He enjoys the technical exercise of his craft and often comments on it. He keeps his professional contacts brightly polished. He is patient, thorough, objective—above all, objective. His profession is to discover the objective reality of a past situation; this he can only do by a methodical accumulation of facts.

Some facts are hard evidence—bullets or documents or fingerprints. Other facts are less substantial. They are near-facts, distorted facts, or no facts at all. And they are derived from interviews—meaning that whatever The Op learns has been passed through the filter of another's personality. This he must compensate for.

It is the detective's role to sift the blurred information he receives and construct from it an approximation of what happened. He can never close with his rock. However he tries, it will always lie more than an arm's length away, its contours shifting queerly, never entirely firm.

The quest for objective reality is central to Hammett's work. It is also the central problem in every detective fiction. Few writers are willing to press far into these shifting gray planes. Most settle for a central situation obscured by one or more networks of lies and partial truths; these are slowly cleared up, the whole intermixed with agreeable murders and racing about. By the novel's end, the characters and the reader are so exhausted by the activity that they accept the detective's description of the crime's reality. He may be right. But few detectives seem to realize that they are dealing with an image of an image.

Hammett seems always aware of this. It is one of the lessons he learned in the world of professional detection. One of the lessons most of us learn: The world outside of books is singularly evasive.

Deliberately distorted reality is at the heart of "Women, Politics, and Murder" (September 1924, reprinted as "Death on Pine Street"; the story, with the original title, was reprinted in the August 1974 revival issue of *Black Mask*.) A philandering husband is shot on the street. His wife is at one end of the street, his girl friend on the other. The Op repeatedly interviews both women and, through a mist of lies and evasions, slowly pieces together what likely did happen—and what did not. To protect the girl friend, a local politician engineers a faked attempted-rape charge against the Op. All the characters end up at police headquarters. The Op is in serious trouble, until he produces a rabbit from the hat and bluffs a confession from the real murderer. The attempted rape charge is dropped and the Op has the satisfaction of dropping the politician with one nice punch, objectively very real.

"Who Killed Bob Teal?" appeared in the November 1924 *True Detective*. It purported to be a real case written by Dashiell Hammett of the Continental Detective Agency. The case, which has a good deal in common with the earlier "It," concerns the search for the murderer of young Bob Teal, one of Continental's most promising operatives. He is found shot behind a bill board. The situation surrounding his death was later reused for the murder of Miles Archer in *The Maltese Falcon*. The case concerns two partners, one of whom cooked the books and disappeared with perhaps a quarter of a million dollars. The Op investigates briskly and closes the case with admirable speed.

Bob Teal was one of the supporting characters of the series—to November 1924. Other Continental operatives appear frequently: Irish Mickey Linehan, big-bodied, humorous, terse; and little Dick Foley, a dark Canadian, weighing less than 110 pounds, who talked like a telegram and was the best shadower the Op knew. Frequent appearances were made by The Old Man, manager of Continental's San Francisco branch, and as enigmatic a character as appears in Hammett. "A tall, plump man in his seventies... with a white-mustached, baby-pink, grandfatherly face, mild blue eyes behind rimless spectacles, and no more warmth in him than a hangman's rope."[45] Years of detective work have eaten away his humanity, leaving a polite smile over solid ice. Only the murder of Bob Teal arouses any emotion in him, and that is disciplined down to a more rapid tapping of his yellow pencil on the desk. He is the final stage of the professional, where human warmth has been extinguished by the demands of the work, leaving only technique in a frigid silence.

A far more human personality is Detective Sergeant O'Gar of Homicide, a stocky, bullet-headed man, who customarily wears a wide-brimmed hat. He is tough, friendly, cooperative, and, and the Op remarked, easy to work with.

None of these characters change much. Their images, sharply drawn, remain essentially unchanged, although *The Dain Curse* adds a few touches to Mickey Linehan's character. The Op, however, changes, and continues to change. Very quietly.

That extraordinary adventure, "The Gutting of Couffignal" (December 1925) mixes detection, adventure, character drawing, and war drama. It neatly demonstrates how to think consecutively in the middle of action. The Op is guarding wedding presents at a reception on the island of Couffignal in San Pablo Bay, north of San Francisco. The island is attacked by pirates who sweep, with military precision, through the town, shooting, killing, burning, a rage of violence, looting the place to a shell. During the giddy violence, the Op injures his ankle and must borrow a crutch. But the injury doesn't affect his ability to reason to unconventional conclusions. At the end, he brushes aside a massive series of bribes, sexual and otherwise, to bring down the clever Princess Zhukovski with a bullet in the leg.

The idea of organized looting is repeated on a larger, more elaborate, more violent scale with the publication of the two linked novelettes, "The Big Knockover" (February 1927) and "$106,000 Blood Money" (May 1927). In 1943 these were published under the title *Blood Money*. In the first part, a small army of criminals takes over two blocks of San Francisco. They loot a pair of banks with maximum violence, gunning down police and citizen alike. Then vanish.

To admirers of the Gray Phantom, Black Star, and Rafferty, the situation is familiar. In these fantasies, however, no one gets shot and the responsible master criminals glow like searchlights in the night.

In Hammett's world, you find less intellectual brilliance, more treachery, much more blood. No sooner are the banks robbed than planned double crossing turns the criminals howling upon themselves. Mass murder decimates the gang, like a fuse consuming itself. The killing continues until only a handful of leaders is left. By then, the Op has tracked the conspiracy to a modest little house. There a terrified little old man, Papadopoulos, and a ferocious terror of a woman, Big Flora, guard a basement solidly packed with stolen money.

Papadopoulos, the brains behind the crimes, is as far from Black Star as it is possible to get. Without hesitation, he betrays most of the remaining gang. Then vanishes before his identity is known. In the second part of the story, he goes into hiding and proceeds with new schemes. He is aided by a deluded girl who believes in the mythical "Code of the Underworld"—where nobody squeals and all are faithful to the great fraternity of crooks. It is clear that she didn't read the first part of the story.

After prodigies of treachery and violence, Papadopoulos is rooted out. But only after he has corrupted one of the Op's colleagues. In an attempt to save the Agency's reputation for honesty, the Op maneuvers four or five people and sets up a situation where double murder is likely.

The arrangement bristles with angles, like a difficult billards shot. The corrupt agent is killed. The Op has not shot anyone, but he has certainly made it easy for people to die violently. As he explains the matter to the Old Man. "It happened that way. I played the cards so we would get the benefit of the breaks—but it just happened that way."[46]

Soon after this case, the blood bath at Personville.

Four loosely linked novelettes tell of the Personville case. They were published monthly in the *Mask* from November 1927 through February 1928. Later they were revised into Hammett's first novel *Red Harvest*. It is not a highly integrated novel, the original novelettes remaining undigested, but it is one of the finest gangster novels ever written. It is cynical, violent, savage. The characters slaughter each other and are slaughtered as indifferently as one would close a door. On the surface, it is brainless as a dinosaur fight.

Underneath the scarlet churn, there are other, more permanent matters: that corrupt men can die finely, that chaos is close, that death is not the worst fate, that men are ruled by fictions, that power seeks more power, that you can trust only yourself but not too much.

Bitterly cynical views, street wisdom novelized.

The strategic problem of the story is how to break up the criminal combine ruling Personville. The Op does so by setting one criminal faction against another.

He enjoys almost excessive success. As in *Blood Money*, the criminals eagerly turn on themselves. The killing is immoderate, even for the undisciplined pulps. So successful is the Op at maneuvering groups into mutual slaughter that he finds himself reveling in his skill. And having stepped to the lip of Hell, seeing in himself the self pride and power hunger that has corroded humanity from the gangsters, he manages to step back. It is not easy. He forces himself back to humanity by an act of will. All standards of behavior surrounding him, legal, moral, ethical, have failed; but he is a disciplined professional and the professional discipline is what supports him in this melting frenzy of a world.

The Dain Curse looks at this problem from another angle. It is another four novelette group that was published monthly in the *Mask* from November 1928 through February 1929. In its final form, rewritten and revised, the novel remains episodic, linked by characters and by a plot which remains deeply buried until the end. It resembles four separate houses joined by a secret tunnel.

Hammett was dissatisfied with the novel, counting it a failure. Whatever he wished it to be, it is a series of vividly real scenes, realized in detail that shines like plated metal. The continuing story line is a series of tragedies as Gabrielle Leggett's father, step-mother, husband are polished off in dramatic ways. Where she goes, there follows murder, kidnapping, assorted disasters. All attributed to the curse of her Dain blood. She is young, a morphine addict, and believes herself not only cursed but insane.

The Op thinks otherwise—and proves it, after a spectacular series of adventures, melodramatic and violent, each presented with such compelling realism that it seems the only possible way things could have worked out.

The Op is able to suspend activities long enough to stand by Gabrielle while she attempts to quit morphine cold turkey. The episode is harrowing.

Gabrielle is reasonably sure the Op is in love with her, and he is non-committal enough to leave his feelings in doubt. Their relationship seems a great deal more like father and daughter than potential lovers, but whatever the exact situation, it is clearly deeper than anything the Op had previously allowed on his pages. This small amount of public emotion does not disturb the clarity of his mind. Before the book is half over, he knows what concealed hand is working against the girl. But he cannot prove it. Before he can act, the explosion of a bomb spoils the case.

The ending of the piece is a curious business. Each of the earlier parts had ended, after a full dose of dire events, with the Op discussing the case with his friend, writer Fitzstephan—who seems to be modeled after writer Dashiell Hammett. That structure is followed to the end. The Op has a final conversation with Fitzstephan, who is the evil genius of the piece, an insane man who believes himself sane but will try to save himself from the death penalty by pretending to be insane. It is a nicely complicated situation, mentally and legally.

Fitzstephan is a man who came to the same point at the lip of Hell as did the Op in *Red Harvest*. The Op drew back. Fitzstephan did not. He stepped boldly forward into the intrigues, planned murders, manipulation of people, arrangement of lives for his own purposes, until insanity and the final bomb that maimed him. Whether he was insane and chose to dehumanize himself, or whether he made the choice and became insane is not clear. Insanity is the final step, it would seen, the ultimate dehumanization. The bomb explosion left Fitzstephan deformed, his physical condition reflecting his mental condition. The choices presented in *Red*

Harvest are carried to their conclusion in *The Dain Curse*. Under the melodramatic violence of the novels is a silent discussion of the consequences of personal choice. The conclusions are frigid. The deepest part of Hell is ice.

After the latent intensity of *The Dain Curse*, the three final Op cases seem almost conventional—as if Hammett has had something on his mind and has finally said it and is now interested in other problems, other ways.

"Fly Paper" (August 1929) is smooth as a jade figure, the distilled essence of hardboiled investigation. A young girl of good family has run off into the fringe world of crookdom and there dies of arsenic poisoning. Followed by gun violence, murder, and a small-scale man hunt. It is done in concentrated prose that takes amazing stylistic liberties and succeeds without effort:

Babe liked Sue. Vassos liked Sue. Sue liked Babe. Vassos didn't like that. Jealousy spoiled the Greek's judgment. He kept the speakeasy door locked one night when the Babe wanted to come in. Babe came in, bringing pieces of the door with him. Vassos got his gun out, but couldn't shake Sue off his arm. He stopped trying when Babe hit him with the part of the door that had the brass knob on it. Babe and Sue went away from Vassos' together.[47]

We have left the moral shadings and ethical dilemmas of the novels. "Fly Paper" and the following two stories are straight forward investigations in the real world, and the Op distinguishes himself by solid common sense.

In both "The Farewell Murder" (February 1930) and "Death and Company" (November 1930), the Op's common sense cuts through bizarre confusion to the simple bone.

In "The Farewell Murders," terror stalks a scared old man out in the country. Corpses appear and disappear, a pet dog cooks over a woods fire, while a pair of suspects hover ominously. But when the old man is murdered, these artistic trappings are swept aside briskly enough. In "Death and Company," the wife has disappeared and the husband receives notes (from Death and Company) demanding cash for her return. The ransom is placed and vanishes under direct observation. Routine, unromantic investigation leads to a room where the wife's body is found, and investigation cuts through all the melodramatic decorations to a realistic conclusion. Common sense and solid detective work.

How insubstantial the thundering romanticism of Race Williams seems.

7-

Two fictional styles met in the 1922 *Black Mask*. The romantic fantasy of John Carroll Daly and the realistic narrative of Dashiell Hammett. Both were writing fiction for money; both manipulated plot and character, suspense and atmosphere, to construct salable stories.

Of the two, Daly was the most successful as a commercial writer for the short term. His fiction was tied only casually to reality, and, because it was less demanding, could be easily copied in substance, if not in style. From the Race Williams example grew dozens of lesser characters, strong on first-person narrative, on gun action, on bright adventure in a world only casually resembling the one you see out the window.

Hammett selected the more difficult way. He mad no conscious choice. He began in the way most familiar to him, dealing with reality and the people of reality:

This stubborn hewing to the reality of the private detective, based on his own Pinkerton experiences, is what set Hammett's central character apart from all who went before and all who were to come after...

...Hammett was not a writer learning about private detection in order to create a detective hero; he was a private detective learning about writing. This meant that as he wrote, he retained the detective's subconscious attitudes toward an investigator's life. It is this subconscious state of mind, I believe, which separates his work from that of Chandler or MacDonald or their followers. It is this subconscious state of mind which makes Hammett the singular innovator he is.[48]

He innovated. But the lessons he taught, there on the pages of *The Black Mask*, took longer to sink in than those of C. J. Daly. Hammett was handling the raw stuff of personal experience, shaping fictional reality from the reality he had known. It was a road which incidentally led toward literature, although he showed little interest in Literature as such. In spite of the magazine medium, in spite of habitual violence, in spite of the passage of time, something permanent got into his work. He is still read. Not so that other branch of the hardboiled detective story, the melodramatic fantasy, which has gone obsolete and quaint, a museum piece from long ago.

8-

Black Mask: Notable American pulp magazine, 1920-1951. Created by H. L. Mencken and George Jean Nathan; first issue, April 1920; first editor, F. M. Osburn. During its first decade, the magazine offered a variety of detective-mystery-crook-western stories. These gradually replaced as the hardboiled school developed, featuring a variety of detectives and an unique, terse style mingling cynicism, brutality, and romantic idealism in understated and often realistic prose. During the editorship of George W. Sutton, Jr. (October 1922 through March 1924 issues) fiction by Carroll J. Daly and Dashiell Hammett was published, representing, respectively, melodramatic fantasy and realism—although realism slightly tinted by romanticism. Under the editorship of Philip C. Cody (April 1924 through

October 1926), other major writers, Gardner, Nebel, and Whifield along them, continued development of the hardboiled narrative. Joseph T. Shaw (editor, November 1926 through November 1936) further developed and intensified the hardboiled story into a formal genre. At the same time he created a cadre of writers whose imagination and technical excellence profoundly influenced the course of magazine mystery fiction: among them George Harmon Coxe, Norbert Davis, and Raymond Chandler. After a salary dispute, Shaw left the magazine, was replaced by Fanny Ellsworth (December 1936 through April 1940); although featuring other writers, Frank Gruber, Steve Fisher, Cornell Woolrich, who became nationally famous, the magazine slowly turned from the hardboiled story. This had crystallized to formula. On February 1940, the magazine was purchased by Popular Publications. Kenneth S. White became editor, June 1940, adding the work of John D. MacDonald, D. L. Champion, William Campbell Gault, and others who continued to emphasize character in increasingly realistic situations, while turning from the familiar hardboiled atmosphere of despair and moral decay. During the war years, the fiction quality, although patched with brilliance, slowly eroded. The magazine became a bimonthly, May 1953, the magazine was incorporated into *Ellery Queen's Mystery Magazine* which, for some years reprinted fiction by *Black Mask* writers. Twenty years later, a single revival issue of *Black Mask* was published, dated August 1974.

By then time had diffused the shock of its personality. Its lesson had long been assimilated. During its great years, the magazine had provided an alternative to the puzzle mystery, the idiosyncratic investigator. It viewed violent crime and violent justice in realistic settings where ethical problems and actions intricately combined. The *Black Mask* world was always professional, always dangerous, always unstable. Its example lingers, a deep resonance in our present fiction. A result not anticipated by Mencken and Nathan as they searched the *Smart Set* slush pile for appropriate manuscripts.

Chapter VII—Cops

1-

Police Detective Peter Noggins is a very small man. Stoop-shouldered, wearing glasses and highly near-sighted, he looks like "an overworked bookkeeper." He seems to apologize for taking up space and breathing valuable air. When he talks, his head hangs bashfully; his hat twiddles round and round in apologetic fingers. Several years before, his wife (a perfume expert) died, leaving him all her stock. This he sold, becoming wealthy. After becoming wealthy, he joined the police force.

How this fragile little retiring fellow ever became a detective is not known. If he lacks most qualifications for the job, he excels in one: He has intelligence. Real intelligence. "Brains," as they say throughout the series.

He performs almost daily miracles.

"Noggins simply looks around, listens a bit, gets his common sense working, and brings in his man."

Noggins was featured in half a dozen stories published in the 1920s *Detective Story Magazine*. The author, Harrington Strong, is better known as that sparkling plot-master, Johnston McCulley.

As mentioned earlier, McCulley poured forth series characters with easy facility. When Peter Noggins first appeared ("Initiating Noggins," April 6, 1920), McCulley was juggling Thubway Tham and Black Star and would soon begin The Thunderbolt series. He had tried and terminated a series featuring the genius private detective, Terry Trimble; with Noggins he now attempted a police detective series, six short stories being published between April and October.

McCulley was an admirable technician of light fiction. His stories twinkled and swirled like fireflies in the wind, lightly improvisational. It was a style sufficient for the adventures of an amiable crook or a bent hero but rather too informal for the adventures of a police detective.

"Noggins Shows His Nerve" (April 20) is a bright little set-piece, hollow as a ping pong ball. The Chief of Detectives opens these proceedings by wondering if Noggins has nerve. Brains, of course; but nerve? Who knows. Alerting us at once that a tale of courage will follow.

Noggins goes forth alone to investigate the brutal beating of an old pawnbroker. (For purposes of the story, Noggins' partner, Merriwale, is nowhere to be found.) The pawnbroker accuses the Grale gang before he dies. Off Noggins goes, all by himself, into the deeps of the slums, wandering among the pool halls, asking for Grale. Huge, muscled thugs in purple-striped shirts and yellow ties sneer down on him. At last he traces Grale to a back room down in the stews, where he slouches, a muscled mountain, with two big mean friends. They promptly lock the door, take away Noggins' gun and handcuffs and hit him twenty or thirty times.

Then, as people do in a Johnston McCulley story, they all leave the room to get a drink, planning to come back and batter him some more. Before they return, Noggins escapes through a window. He reels staggering through the neighborhood until he can borrow a gun from a storekeeper.

Then back to the pool room. A few shots are exchanged. Noggins is wounded in the shoulder, but captures Grale, ties him up, and calls for the wagon.

And isn't the Chief of Detectives delighted that Noggins has shown he's really got some nerve.

In "Noggins' Souvenir" (June 8), a thief known as The Fiend has been striking at will. Success after success. No clues. Except that, after each robbery, a strong perfume lingers in the air.

Noggins is detached from Homicide to assist the investigation. He has no more idea than you or I what to do. While wandering around pathetically during lunch hour, he detects a heavy French perfume. Shadows the wearer to an hotel. Discovers that he is a vaudevillian in reduced circumstances.

Noggins shadows him from the hotel, but loses him.

Returns to Headquarters. Great commotion. The Fiend has struck again. Off race Noggins and another policemen to the scene of the crime. Immediately they are knocked senseless by the thief, who seems to have been hanging around, waiting for them.

They awake to a terrible display. Through the room in which they lie tied, The Fiend's minions parade, one by one, uttering vile threats. Then Noggins and companion are drugged and released.

As soon as he can walk without wobbling, Noggins arrests the vaudevillian. Down at headquarters, he sternly accuses the wretch of being The Fiend. No one seems to notice that there is no evidence, least of all The Fiend, who promptly confesses.

And what was the key clue? As the gang members paraded back and forth, Noggins noticed that they all wore the same pair of shoes. Thus, not a gang but a one man in many costumes—a quick-change artist.

How simple these problems are, when explained.

"Noggins Sees It Through" (August 24) concerns murder. That glinting musical comedy star, Rosa Nebbler, has been strangled. Noggins and Merriwale go forth, all by themselves, to investigate—no photographers, no fingerprint experts, no doctor, no ambulance. Just the two of them nodding sadly over the body.

Then a call from Headquarters. A Pedro Vega has come in and confessed to the murder: He did it because she toyed with his affections. Noggins doesn't believe the confession, not for a moment. And within a few pages, he has uncovered the deceitful, wicked plot of a wicked, deceitful man. Who is arrested, handcuffed, and then eats a poison pill. No one had thought to search him for a poison pill. But then no one thought to search him for machine guns and trench mortars, either.

Which is the main problem with this series in particular and most early 1920s police stories in general. At that time, police operations were more informal than at present, less polished and less technical. But they were not totally bereft of sense.

But you would never guess that from the fiction in *Detective Story Magazine* or its competitors. In those casual pages, no glimmer of understanding lighted the writers' black ignorance of police problems, police procedures, police attitudes. The uniformed cop, the headquarters plain clothesman, consistently received short weight. It had been so for year after aching year.

Said literary convention, the police are dull and thick. They are loud-mouthed igorats, all, and the pilot light of their intelligence flickers low and blue. They are blundering and crass, their derbies stained, their chewed cigars foul. Their massive feet lumber from the humiliations of the past to the follies of the future.

Or so it was in ten-cent fiction.

Out there in the bad world, matters were different, as matters frequently are. The police did have their problems. They lacked manpower, training, equipment, facilities, and public support. Salaries were low and communications chancy and finger-printing was still suspect. Laws varied widely from state to state, almost from county to county, as laws will. A Federal Bureau of Investigation was not to be thought of. And professional capabilities varied madly, from hard-rock organizations of trained men in some big cities to small town constabularies where law enforcement meant catching a tourist driving 21 miles an hour.

To some extent, this crazy patchwork was reflected in pulp magazine and dime novel fiction. More often, what was reflected was the literary convention. Few enough writers were as familiar with the police operations of their day as was Charles Dickens with the police and detective officers of his day. From the time of Poe, writers had used that venerable device of letting their investigator shine against a field of official stupidity. That tradition was one hundred years old and respectably seasoned.

Few writers realized how many hard-minded men, competent and astute, filled the police departments of the nation. Few realized that a police investigation bore little resemblance to the activities recorded in *Detective Tales* or *Mystery Magazine*. Or that police operations differed so completely from the magazine descriptions: that masterminds were few and most deaths senseless and genius investigators in permanently short supply; that the police are men with the faults and problems common to men, and with common excellences.

It would take decades for that enlightenment to seep through magazine fiction.

The adventures of Bill Lawson represent one tiny step in that direction. He is an over-aged headquarters detective, twenty-five years on the force. His paunch sticks out. His bald spot stretches from front to back, bordered with gray hair. For the entire term of his service, he has roomed at the Caliph Hotel, across from Headquarters. He is a bachelor. Twenty-five years ago died Nora, his sweetheart. Since then, he has not cared for women

An odd man, Lawson. He cares for little. But he cares for shoes. Owns fourteen pairs. These he polishes continuously, compulsively—groom, polish, brush. It keeps his hands occupied while he thinks out his current case.

Never lived a man so dedicated to shoes. Whatever pair he wears glitters with polish as glassy bright as a metallized surface. He constantly fusses with them. Dust, rub, wipe—continuous reflexive motor discharge. While he thinks. Sometimes when he is not thinking.

Or so author Louis Lacy Stevenson tells us. Stevenson had a lot of stories in *Flynn's Weekly* and its avatar, *Detective Fiction Weekly*. These stories deal most often with crooks, criminal plots, violent action. Only a few are reserved for the investigations of Bill Lawson, whose cases are thinly scattered from 1925 to around 1928.

Since they are so spread out, their style and content vary largely. As a group, they present a little sermon, for those clever at listening, on changes in magazine fiction styles over four years.

"Cold Storage" (January 24, 1925, *Flynn's*) is a curious story. To begin with, it is awful. It is one of those filler fictions that stuffed up surplus space in all the detective magazines of all the publishers. Its elements are utterly simple: The hero must catch the dangerous fiend. The fiend catches the hero. By a trick, the hero escapes to catch the fiend. Between 2500 and 3500 words and with all the individuality of a pickle in a bottle.

Since Stevenson's story was written in 1925, "Cold Storage" opens at leisure. First you must plough through pages of background information,

Therefore...

The Bat, murderous safe-cracker, dope addict, escaped fiend, with long yellow teeth, is after Lawson, who had once captured him.

Lawson is after The Bat.

Lawson's pal, Gold Front, a valiant negro shoe-shiner with a gold tooth glittering in the front of his mouth and the hope of bettering himself in his heart, only he is humorously lazy and will not study, a grave mistake but typical of the race, is protectively watching Lawson. Gold Front is that familiar figure, the peculiar friend.

A second friend, Michael Terry, is a genial, red-faced truck driver. He has married The Bat's ex-wife. Terry is that ever popular figure of inconsequential fiction, the low-brow pal. He is true to Lawson as the stars above.

The story is simplicity. The Bat hits Lawson on the head and ties him up. Then Gold Front and Terry are hit on the heads and tied up. The Bat stacks them all in a warehouse on a sub-zero night and waits for them to freeze.

Before the series ends at its beginning, in pops Mrs. Terry with the police and story ends triumphantly.

Lawson does absolutely nothing but get hit on the head.

Now step forward to 1927: March 5, "The Square Emerald" (*Flynn's*). Here is an entirely different story. Called to a mansion to investigate the theft of an immense emerald, Lawson plunges boldly into evasion and trickery among the wealthy. Beneath innocent smiles lurk criminal minds. About every two chapters, Lawson is nearly killed. Twice he is almost crushed by immensely powerful arms, once nearly drowned, once shot down in a swamp. In spite of these trials, he reasons out the solution, using four cans of ox-blood and a soft cloth. He never does get around to calling Headquarters for assistance.

Gold Front and Terry seem long forgotten. This is taut, sober, intense narrative, stripped of eccentricity, other than the shoe gimmick.

Now, again, forward to "Green Eyes" (six-part serial, December 16, 1927, through January 21, 1928 *Flynn's Weekly Detective Fiction*). Still another world has appeared. In this one, the gangster element is uppermost. Through a haze of digested Hammett, Lawson stalks the killers who gunned down two men and two girls at the Hollis Tool & Machine Company. From crook to crook, Lawson hunts, amid a foam of violence.

Now a little girl is kidnapped. She once called Lawson "Uncle Bill." His flinty heart scalds, his pale blue eyes narrow. He hurls to the floor his favorite reading, the newspaper column, "Advice to the Lovelorn," and darts away after the disguised criminal.

At last to run down the kidnappers and save the little tot, way out in Denver, a long train ride from New York City. Uncle Bill came through, dear.

These touches of pink sugar to one side, it is a stripped, hardpressing narrative. There is in it none of the *Black Mask* color or the feeling of reality and tension that *Black Mask* stories radiated. But it is a story from which the last drop of English influence has been squeezed—an indicator of a remarkable change in *Flynn's*.

Lawson works so much on his own that he might as well be a private detective. For the sake of variation, he is given a badge and a job with the city, but he is a loner. With his habit of not writing reports and never keeping in touch with the Captain, you wonder how he survived for twenty-five years.

You wonder some about Inspector Hickmott, too. His stories, however, are so interesting you find it easy to forgive the improbable investigative procedures used. Hickmott is an English Detective Inspector. The writer is announced as R. M. Freeman, a name to be considered warily. For it is so very close to that of R. Austin Freeman, whose Dr. Thorndyke stories were *not* appearing in *Flynn's* at this particular time. The burnt reader smells editorial trickery.

Whatever the truth of authorship, the adventures of Detective Hickmott begin with the September 5, 1925, *Flynn's*, "The New Half Crown" being the initial story.

An incomplete skeleton, acid burned, is dug up from the back yard of a house from which a woman has vanished. All evidence points in one direction. Yet Hickmott wonders: her purse contained new half crowns, not released for public use until after the murder. Once you begin thinking along those lines, you reason out an entirely different story...

Hickmott is an acute reasoner. His features are entirely commonplace, but the intelligence behind is supremely sharp. In "The 'd' Mark" (September 12, 1925) he explodes a frame-up by noting the use of the delete sign in a column of numbers. "The Joined String" (September 26) begins with theft of a diamond necklace and expands steadily to the exposure of a crooked insurance company. "The Wax Match" (October 3) leaves a slight oily stain around a burn on a note and so exposes a clever forgery plot. "The Shirt Stud" (October 31) is a complex business of robbery, assault, and embezzlement. Nothing makes any sense, until Hickmott discovers a little gold shirt stud at the scene of the crime.

These are not realistic stories, but they are crisply written, interesting, each with a pleasing little twist. Although little is made of formal police activities—Hickmott still seems more like a private detective than a policeman—no one is outlandishly stupid. Each story turns on a crucial clue, just one. As soon as Hickmott gets his eye on this, everything falls into place.

Nothing dramatic, you understand. These are carefully constructed problem pieces, emphasizing questioning, thinking, watching. Hickmott doesn't make you tingle with glee. But he is certainly able and it's a shame to leave him unreprinted.

It is an act of Christian mercy not to reprint some of the other characters from *Flynn's*. Douglas Greer has not been reprinted. He was a police detective in a scattering of serials and short stories. These were signed Peter Perry. From 1926 through 1928, you were liable to stumble across a Greer adventure, and begin reading before you were aware of danger, and wake up tightly strapped in a tub of soothing water, while the doctor murmured psychotherapy.

Which is to suggest that the quality of the Greer stories vary. Some are not actually awful. They come in all types and styles. In an earlier volume, we have noted "The Liquid Bullet" (December 4, 1926), a scientific detective thing. Another, "The Radio Fiend" (November 13, 1926) is one of these Hero Battles Into Cavern Filled With Advanced Technical Equipment to Destroy the Fiend's Spy Plot formula stories.

Then there's the one about the sledge-hammer murder in the boiler room, "Blodgett's Return" (January 21, 1928). And the adventure of the evil swami who dies and is then shot in his coffin—"Twice Dead" (October 8, 1927).

No two stories are really alike. The only thing that ties them together is the name Greer. This is possible because the closest inspection has not revealed a shred of personality by which Greer may be identified. As a hero, he is an uncut stencil. Early in the series, the author assures us that Greer is an impulsive and unruly fellow and his "unwillingness to be bound by rules and orders...has retarded his promotion on the force." No indication of this creeps into the stories. Nor any real indication that Greer is a police detective. He is, instead, the standard, free-lance pulp magazine hero, doing what he wants, going where he wants, unfettered by rules and regulations and the organizational discipline that binds small souls.

He is unfettered and consistently heroic. He shoots down the crooks trying to waste him. He saves a trapped engineer from the wreckage of his engine, as the boiler swells and the sentences hiss with deadly pressure.

Greer accomplished wonderful things. But as far as real character goes, Greer has none. His author forgot to give him any. His author was more interested in peculiar situations and weird locales. Look at that insane asylum. What a swell place for a story! It resulted in "The Mad March Hares" (two-part serial, June 5 and 12, 1926, *Flynn's*).

Arch criminal, Lew Bunny and his Hares, have taken over an insane asylum. This is the cover for their planned robbery of a Federal Reserve truck that will be carrying four million dollars. Greer goes it single-handed. Defying a fierce bulldog and assorted homicidal maniacs, he enters the asylum. There he frees a captured brother officer. After a spirited gun fight back and forth across a piano, they overcome the gang—most of it. What's left of the gang then locks Greer and friend into a padded cell. They begin cutting their way to freedom. Before they do so, a madman glides up to

Lew Bunny and slices him absolutely to ribbons with a straight razor.

That appears to solve all problems and the serial ends.

In "The Forty Thieves" (four-part serial, May 28 through June 18, 1927, *Flynn's*), Greer is in hot pursuit of a gang that has stolen 150 automobiles. They wreck two trains in their getaway and escape to their hideout in an abandoned coal mine.

(Look at that coal mine. What a swell place for a story!)

Both these serials have their moments. Ten years later, the pulps would be packed with similar lunatic ideas, inadequately worked out, substituting energy for the illusion of reality, and gore and violence and shock for rational plots. The detectives of these mad whirls would be sharply drawn and influence the action. Greer is not and does not. He is only incidental to the general raving and rushing.

The story pounds along in routine prose, leaping over logical gaps at a single bound and lofting blithely past voids in the narrative. But who pays any attention? Who cares? Peter Perry didn't care. And neither did that hollow police detective, Greer. And neither, apparently, did *Flynn's*.

2-

With few exceptions, police cut a sorry figure in the early magazines. Most wore baggy pants and red putty noses and got hit in the face with pies a lot. They were straight men for the genius investigator, gaping as he explained how the cat drank the milk. Their primary function was to get things all balled up. They were also used to cart off the guilty at story's end, lending an air of spurious reality to the adventure.

In a few magazines, the police performed with slightly more realism. *Adventure* and *Blue Book* occasionally featured police who were human beings, sometimes competent, infrequently living on the page. But these were supporting cast characters, incidental to the pyrotechnics of the vivid young investigator.

Little changed with the appearance of Noggins, Greer, Hickmott, and Lawson. They were called police detectives, but they were police detectives only by courtesy. They were of the police without being in the police. They functioned with delightful independence, as unhampered by rules and regulations as the dime novel detectives before them. And they demonstrated such a casual attitude toward evidence that you cannot imagine their cases being accepted for court.

One and all, they are representatives of that shining group which George N. Dove terms the "Great Policemen."

...the Great Policeman solves the case himself; the other police in the story help him with the accumulation of evidence, but in the resolution the Great Policeman is a solitary figure. Moreover, he typically withholds the solution or partial solution from the reader, though he may confide it to a close associate....

...His work with other policemen is usually minimal, except as he sends them on errands or uses them to collect information. The other policeman may operate as a team, but the Great Policeman is not part of it.[1]

The convention of the Great Policeman, like that of the brilliant amateur or the eccentric private investigator, is deeply engrained in fiction. He is an individualist, and as an individual following his own course he appeared in the early morning of detective fiction: in *Richmond: Scenes from the Life of a Bow Street Runner* (1827), published two years before Sir Robert Peel established London's Metropolitan Police; and in the Vidcoq *Memoires* (1828-1829), through which, as in a dream, shreds of fact and clouds of fantasy swirled melting together.

Back then, emphasis on individual exploits was excusable, for the police were as unstructured as a custard. But as the police organized in the real world, fiction remained fixed to the individual and his marvelous exploits. The comparatively late *Lady Molly of Scotland Yard* does not reflect the glories of Scotland Yard but the glories of the clever heroine, a Great Policewoman in her own right.

More than twenty years later, little had changed. If a professional policeman were the hero of a series, he performed in the tradition of the brilliant amateur, as did Prentice (*The Black Mask*, 1922-1926) or Brian Gridley (*Detective Story Magazine*, 1923).

By 1923, however, change was fermenting quietly in the deeps of detective fiction. Dashiell Hammett presented the first of his realistic supporting police in "Arson Plus." And the following year, in England, Freeman Wills Crofts introduced Inspector Joseph French, whose first case, *Inspector French's Greatest Case*, took a tentative step away from the Great Detective tradition. French would appear in thirty-three books published between 1924 and 1957, puzzling through intricate investigations and methodically developing evidence for the courtroom. While French is the primary investigator in these cases, he invariably acts as a part of a larger organization. The novels make it clear that French's successes depend on contributions from various departments within Scotland Yard and assistance from other official agencies. He is not a lone hand but a part of a much larger organization which surrounds and supports him.

Both Crofts and Hammett moved from the Dumb Cop/Great Policeman story forms to more realistic presentations, shaped and limited by the real world. Not fantasies. Not dreams. But something close to the real thing, with recognizable human beings performing sometimes boring, sometimes dangerous, always demanding work.

Now the literary wind began to shift and the way policeman and police work were portrayed began to change. It is tempting, as over-simplifications are, to credit Hammett for this. But you can't credit the first leaf for the tree's foliage. Hammett was one of several detective story writers beginning to work as objective realists. This was a developing literary form violently energized by the First World War. It spoke to the reader by showing, rather than telling, and produced its effect by a ruthless selection of images and detail. Hammett came to this austere art by way of report writing, field experience, and his personal feeling that the detective story would benefit from fresh, cold air.

Other writers followed. Whether they followed Hammett's example or adapted their work to the larger current of objective realism, in which Hammett is one face among many, is a matter to be discussed in councils of the wise.

Whatever the initiating impulse, a new and distinctly more realistic police series began in *Flynn's* during late 1925. It would continue to 1939. That series featured Sergeant Riordan and Captain of Detectives Brady, and was written by Victor Maxwell, who was almost certainly somebody else.

It is a satisfying series. Humor sparks through the stories. The action flows without high melodrama and equally without that high foolishness used by lesser writers to disguise their lack of control over the material. Riordan and Brady are professionals—tough, unsentimental, competent professionals, the kind that the fiction of the period claimed you only found in a private investigator's office.

In this series, the only private agency—oddly named the Protective Association—gets some vigorous knocks. At one point, Brady tells one of the PA ops: "I always told you that you went off at half cock. That's why you're not on a real force, only playing around with insurance companies."[2]

The Private I lacks professionalism and professionalism is what this series is about. Sergeant Riordan is the lead. He is the aide (persistently spelled "aid") of Captain Brady. For the most part, Brady gives Riordan his head in an investigation. "You're a good boy," he says. And Riordan is that.

For a fifteen-year series, the cast is fairly permanent. Familiar faces stay put: The Chief of Police Roberts; the gigantic Halloran, fat as an Eskimo supper, hard as battleship plate under the fat; neat young Willis, and Stacy and Enright, and Lieutenant Osburn. Good solid men.

Good solid dialogue, spare and exact:

"Take him up to the Bertillion room and mug him, finger-print him, and find out who he is. Then lock him in solitary. He's probably in the picture book. Look back about three years or more. Let me know what you get on him. I'll be in my office."[3]

The speech is slangy and vigorous:

"If he ever got ten thousand dollars, he'd show up like a sky-rocket on a dark night."
...they couldn't start a fire if they had matches and kerosene."

When these police think, they sound like men thinking. They do not sit glowing with solitary genius, winding out chains of exquisite deductions:

Riordan: "Suppose you prowled a room for a suit of clothes and suppose you saw a good-looking suit case...and then suppose you found the suit case was full of kale—what would you do?
    "Knowing you were just a plain bum...what would you do? Remember, we're just supposing. Being a bum, if you had any wit at all, you'd know that ten thousand dollars would be too much for you to handle. Now what would you do?"
Ransome: "Darned if I know, sergeant."
Riordan: "Well, supposing it was Canadian money, what would you do?"
Ransome: "Maybe I'd ditch it—or most of it."[4]

They look in likely places and the money had been ditched.
    It doesn't sound at all like those fictional dreams of police work that *Detective Story Magazine* (or *Flynn's*, elsewhere) had been publishing.

"...in the police business, mister, yuh got to wait till yuh find things. Yuh can look for'em, yuh can know what yuh're lookin' for—but till yuh find it yuh can't move. That's why they say the police are slow."[5]

Nor is police work a matter of some Great Policeman hurdling forth solo, his wonders to perform. The men go out in pairs. When they investigate, they ask questions. And questions. And questions. They look. Then they return to look. They all go down town to the Station and there are more questions. Very frequently, they use the rule that a person may be detained in jail for 48 hours. This tool they use with a precision born of long experience, just as they use a rather detailed knowledge of the law—which no one but Dashiell Hammett seems to have considered needful in a policeman's training.
    In "Staples Case" (*Flynn's Weekly*, March 5, 1927), a rich man, seeking notoriety, has faked his abduction and murder. After a succession of false clues, including a notation on an unchanged desk calendar, a tin-lined room on the waterfront, and scattered blood stains, the rich man is found and marched to police headquarters.
    At this point, the story would end in most series. The man faked his death. The police saw through it. Now close with a few wry words.
    This series handles matters differently.
    The rich man apologizes lightly and edges toward the door.

No, says Riordan, you're under arrest. For the following crimes:

—malicious mischief
—dumping refuse into a navigable stream
—conspiracy to defeat justice
—conspiracy to manufacture false evidence

"Now," says Riordan, "how do you like coming back to life? It's a little different from what you figured, isn't it?" A little different? This is gloriously different. The difference gusts fresh as dawn air through *Flynn's* pages. You even get a hint, in these stories, that the police have something more to do than wander up and down, scowling at crime.

Riordan...slipped into a chair at his own desk and busied himself with routine affairs, which had to be attended to no matter what other matters might be before the bureau.[6]

Routine matters, which had to be attended to, no matter what.

That statement alone is enough to tell you that we are reading here of a different world. The work continues. The routine work, the reports, the comings in, the goings out. Riordan pulls the night shift. Brady goes home to his wife. The men needle Halloran about his weight:

Officer: "You used to be able to stop a longshoreman."
Halloran: "Got one you want stopped?"

(Halloran is slow, ugly, so old in the service they don't look up his age for fear he'd have to retire. He is better than a platoon of infantry in a fight. He waddles. He salutes by hauling one limp flipper up to belt height and letting it flop back. When he takes hold of a case, no mistakes. No holes left to check. No evidence bungled. His imagination is thin about motives and that has held him back. But his investigations are neat, thorough, complete.)

What kind of police are these? Nobody is stupid. There are no clowns or clodhoppers. The most ineffective character of the cast is Patridge, local manager of the Protective Association.

Patridge has no presence. He is a small man, not particularly forceful nor intellectually rigorous. He has no resemblance to the Continental Op. Brady dislikes him. Patridge's Protective Association has commercial security arrangements with certain merchants. If a theft occurs, the Association learns about it first, well before the police. This means that if Brady and company are called in, it is after the fact, when the case is cold toast and cold coffee.

In the story "Something New in Vanities" (October 2, 1926), Brady gives Patridge a night in jail for being a possible accessory. A rash of jewelry thefts have broken out, with the arrival in town of five blonds demonstrating a combination purse, key ring, and make-up kit. Patridge gets conned into certifying that they are bonded, which they are not. For which oversight, he is lodged briefly in a cell while Riordan and the boys run the matter out.

The police in this series do a lot of looking and waiting, as in the September 19, 1925, "Threads of Evidence." Persistent robbery of railroad passengers. Riordan climbs into his uniform—the formal kit—blue and gold and rich braid and a star. Off he goes to the train station, where he is asked two thousand questions a minute by every person who doesn't want to bother walking over to Information. He watches. After several days, he notices that a neatly dressed woman has been there frequently. Loose threads hang from under her hat. It is a small observation, but it leads to the capture of two thieves.

All sorts of cases come along.

Theft: Someone lifted the jewelry sample case, with $50,000 worth of merchandise from the train depot. Riordan goes out. He looks, questions the victims. Then the case turns up with a few pieces of jewelry remaining. By that time, Riordan has got a picture in his mind. It does not say Theft but Swindle. And Swindle it proves to be.

To the unhappy fellow who did not get away with it, Riordan remarks: "Never mind readin' these stories in the magazines. They don't always work in real life." ("Mostly Head Work," *Detective Fiction Weekly*, December 15, 1928)

Hotel Robbery: A visiting Duke is robbed of a suitcase, a suit of clothing, and $10,000 Canadian money. There follows methodical searching and methodical questioning. Finally they locate a woman, an ex-convict, who seems to have some connection with the robbery. They get her by methodically watching the train station. It is hardly a flashy investigation. No master mind wearing a black hood appears in this story. Nobody blasts about with a purple sizzling death ray. The police question the woman, learn that she has befriended by another ex-con. It all comes together, inevitably, unexpectedly. Riordan makes a shrewd guess—it is hardly a deduction. The money is located. The thief is taken not long after. ("A Darned Good Tailor," *Flynn's Weekly*, November 20, 1926.)

Bank Robbery: A fake bomb ticks in a bank. After the panic, $75,000 is missing. No one saw it go. Once again, the police toss romantic fiction out the window and go for the solid bone facts. Which, in this case, include a love-sick messenger, a love-sick banker, and a love-sick delivery driver. All love the same woman. She works at a department store. The store keeps sales slips of employee purchases. Among her purchases are items used in constructing the fake bomb... ("The Bomb," *Flynn's Weekly*, March 12, 1927.)

Murder: A tricky story. Here, a woman dead with an impossibly angled bullet wound in her chest. There, her husband with an equally improbable wound in his leg. Riordan investigates and gets it all balled up; he has one of those days when things do not go click. Fortunately, Riordan can fall back on Brady, who gets it right the first time. It was all a matter of where the shot was fired from. ("The Bullet Holes in the Ceiling," *Detective Fiction Weekly*, October 12, 1929.)

And so through the years. In "The Corpus Delicti" (*Detective Fiction Weekly*, June 11, 1932), the butler finds his employer limp on the floor. But when the police arrive, the body has vanished. Political pressure grinds down on Chief Roberts to straighten it out fast. And so the police do, uncovering a variation on the old badger game. Just as in real life, the rich man responsible weasels his way clear, if barely.

"Death in the Binoculars" (*Detective Fiction Weekly*, March 31, 1934) involves a little fairy tale told by a man who claims to have seen a murder through his binoculars. Riordan takes him apart in short order, since he knows something about fields of view and image size. In spite of it all, everything turns out happily.

A long story, "The Devil Wears Diamonds" (*Detective Fiction Weekly*, July 1, 1939) features Halloran as a major character. In honor of the occasion, he is somewhat reduced in fatness and age, and somewhat increased in general intelligence. All rigged out in an obsolete tuxedo and large white sapphires, he lumbers forth to night club among the roadhouse boys, who live precariously on the gang's edge. Halloran is fishing for information about industrial thefts. He gets plenty, and the police arrive at a plant in time to catch the people involved. Guns go off then. Gunfire is a rarity in this series but 1939 readers did like their violent endings.

At that, only one man gets shot.

"The Devil Wears Diamonds" is a fine story, tough, restrained, the action line pleasantly complicated, the humor sardonic. At this time the police procedural was not officially born. (That would not happen, according to eminent authorities, until the publication of Lawrence Treat's *V is for Victim* in 1945.) But Brady, Riordan, and Halloran didn't know that. They had been appearing in police procedurals for twenty years. While doing so, they made most other police series of the Twenties look like strings of paper decorations.

Victor Maxwell, that mysterious writer, did good work, solid as an oak board. You read his stories with enjoyment and regret that there are no more.

3-

The magnificence that is the Captain MacBride and Kennedy series can hardly be done justice in a handful of pages. A full monograph would be more appropriate. Something bound in leather. radiating the authority of a classic.

Frederick Nebel, author of the series, did not feel that way about the stories. He refused permission for one of the MacBride/Kennedy cases to be used in *The Hard-Boiled Omnibus*, remarking:

The reason why I don't want to see my old Black Mask stuff between boards is because I think it served its purpose well when it was first published but I honestly cannot see what purpose it would serve now.[7]

Nebel is not the first author to object to the resurrection of his youthful work. Nor is he the last author to undervalue his pulp magazine work. There were reasons. Apparently he felt that the work was dated. He was correct . The work is dated, although, in Nebel's case, that is not a serious flaw. It was also melodramatic, highly violent, and the police work is not particularly realistic. Captain MacBride performs as a full-fledged Great Policeman, dragging along a few continuing characters who are less policeman than comedy relief. And the second lead, Kennedy, the reporter, is often so drunk he can barely navigate the paragraphs.

Acknowledge these defects and Nebel was still wrong. The series is brilliant. It contains the distilled essence of hardboiled writing, a curious mixture of complexity, savagery, and pathos. It is austere. It is understated to the point of grayness. It is coldly sentimental. It established at least one—perhaps two—characters who lived on the page and involved the reader with them in the quiet way of pure art.

Thirty-seven stories were published in *Black Mask* between 1928 and 1936. These were written by Louis Frederick Nebel (1903-1967) who had begun selling fiction while still in high school. His first *Black Mask* story, of 67, appeared in the March 1926 issue. He contributed to a number of action and adventure pulps (*Action Stories, Air Stories, Lariat*, and *Northwest Stories*), as well as detective magazines (*Detective Action Stories, Detective Fiction Weekly, Dime Detective*). For these magazines, he created a number of series characters; they include the very hardboiled Donahue (*Black Mask*, 1930-1935) and the extended Cardigan series (*Dime Detective*, 1931-1937).

In 1933, Nebel published the first of three novels, *Sleepers East*, a best seller. It was followed by *But Not the End* (1934) and *Fifty Roads to Town* (1936). At about this period, he began a slow disengagement from the pulps and pulp writing, gradually working into such better-paying slick magazines as *The American Magazine, Collier's, Good Housekeeping, Liberty*, the *Saturday Evening Post, Woman's Home Companion*—a roll call of major magazine markets to which every pulp writer aspired, although few enough ever reached these golden peaks. As customary with these markets, the fiction contained strong romantic lines. Nebel never succumbed to mere sweetness. His romantic lines were embedded in terse, taut prose that promised more fear than kisses.

A selection of these slick magazine short stories were reprinted in the mystery digests of the mid-1950s: *The Saint Detective Magazine* (1955-1956), *Michael Shayne's Mystery Magazine* (1958), and *Ellery Queen's Mystery Magazine* (primarily 1956-1962). The last six of these latter stories were new, and his final published story, Needle in a Haystack," appeared in *EQMM*, August 1962.

Of Nebel, Ellery Queen remarked that:

Although as a career writer he has sold more than 5,000,000 words, he does not consider himself a literary person, and despite his vast experience as a professional he has never spoken or written formally on the subject of authorship, its trials and tribulations, its techniques or terminology. His system of working is his own—the one that suits him best. For example, he does not like to write an outline of a story: once the character and plot are clear in his head, he proceeds to the first, and almost final, draft.[8]

The MacBride-Kennedy series was written early in an extended career, when Nebel was twenty-five years old. The series is brilliant, spare, and exceedingly tough. It contains frequent cadences from the Hemingway school, simple sentences in sequence, joined by "and" to produce a hard, cumulative rhythm:

MacBride had removed his hat but his overcoat was still on and his hands were in his pockets. His face was gray and hard like granite, and his eyes were like blue cold ice, and he stood with his feet spread apart and his square jaw down close to his chest.[9]

He has read Hammett and has caught the terse dialogue sound, suggesting more than it says:

Presently he was aware of Kennedy standing beside him.
"Where've you been, Cap?"
"Places," said MacBride.
"What did you see?"
"Things."[10]

Violence runs just beneath the skin of the paragraphs. It is not gun violence. That is usually reserved for the brief burst at the end of the story, although it occasionally swells to a scene of extended ferocity, as in "Wise Guy" (April 1930). More usually, violence is verbal, as when MacBride tongue lashes an assistant DA in "Take It and Like It"; or it bursts out, coldly savage, as physical beatings. There are numbers of these.

> Weymer took one step, swung. Kennedy was lifted off his feet. He hit the wall. The building shivered. He crumpled and lay on the floor. Weymer, white-faced, started after him. Cohen clipped Weymer with a blackjack and Weymer stopped, stood stupidly in the middle of the floor, his legs sagging but still holding. He rubbed his hand across his eyes, backed up slowly until the wall stopped him. He stood there, still passing a hand across his eyes.[11]

Kennedy gets himself beaten up frequently. But no character, major or minor, is exempted:

> Tom Shack leaned back in the mahogany desk chair, took his cigar from his mouth and watched Testro manhandle the blond boy in through the doorway and across the carpeted floor to a blue leather divan. The blond boy hit the divan on the small of his back, bounced once, then tried to get up. Testro slapped his face flat-handed; first one cheek and then the other. The blond boy stopped trying to get up.[12]

Physical violence, like a hunting alligator, swims just beneath the surface of these stories. The characters shudder with rage held down too long. They are white-lipped with wrongs that cannot be corrected, with personal situations poisoned beyond correction. They explode into frenzy. Frenzy is the only release from the corner in which they are trapped. Frenzy comes often.

The scent of over-heated metal hangs in the air. Thick-chested men stand between you and the door, their eyes remote, their big hands clenching. Fear moves in the sentences. Rage flows silently from someone unseen waiting in the next room.

Which would make for an exhausting and monocolor story, if that were all Nebel offered.

He offers considerably more. That line of impending violence, glowing through the story, is played against a background of dark comedy, often as broad as a burlesque pratfall:

> Moriarity was pacing up and down trailing great clouds of cigar smoke, and MacBride, making a neat pitch, hung his hat on the costumer in the corner and said:
> "Where'd you get the lousy cigar, Mory?"
> Moriarity pointed to a box on the desk. "You ought to know. They're yours."
> "So now you're aping Kennedy, huh? Mooch, mooch—it's getting so around here that anything I don't lock up or nail down—"[13]

The police detectives supporting MacBride, and particularly Moriarity and Cohen, are consistently used as comic characters. They are cheerfully inattentive to the tension and smell of hot iron around them. They wander unconcerned, uncommitted through these taut adventures, practicing back flips, playing cat's cradle, never too involved for dice or cards.

MacBride roars at them, briefly livid. They leap into uncoordinated motion, become effective police for an instant. Until MacBride leaves. Then they lapse back to comedy.

Other scenes are played with less obvious humor:

...a long curtained touring car...took the turn of the driveway swiftly, leaning a bit, and then brakes, sharply applied to wheels with skid-chains, brought the car to a definite, violent stop. Behind, a flivver coupe, squealing, whanged its front bumper into the rear bumper of the touring car. A loud oath was heard within the coupe and then Baumlein, the medical office man, hopped out as Kennedy drifted languidly from the touring car.

Baumlein cried: "You nuts, you nuts, you! What are you doing, trying out new brakes or something?"

"Hey Finnegan," Kennedy called to the touring car's chauffeur, "you trying out new brakes?"

"Yowssuh!"

"Finnegan says," Kennedy told Baumlein, "yowssuh."

"Look at my bumper," Baumlein yelled. "Look at it."

"You look at it. What's the sense of both of us looking at it..."[14]

These comic inventions float serenely on the scalding stuff of the crime and the people involved in the crime. The contrast is intense, and the narrative slips effortlessly back and forth between the two. When the violence comes erupting forth, all teeth and fists, it is doubly terrible because of the laughter in which it has been embedded.

This dichotomy of mood is also reflected in the personalities of the two lead characters, Captain Stephen J. MacBride of the Richmond City police, and John X. Kennedy of the *Free Press*. (The "X" in Kennedy's name means nothing; in "Lay Down the Law," we learn that he added it when he joined the Army and they insisted on a middle initial.)

At the beginning of the series, in the five loosely connected stories under the general heading of "The Crimes of Richmond City," the contrast between the two men is not emphasized. Kennedy is the wise-cracking, hardboiled reporter of *The Front Page*.[15] MacBride is the tough, square cop, doing the best he can in a corrupt city.

It is a highly corrupt city. It seems to be in Ohio, and, in many ways, it resembles Cincinnati, although no one goes so far as to name names. In "Raw Law," the first of "The Crimes of Richmond City," a crooked political boss has the town tied up tight. A bootlegger, Gink Cavallo, controls the police department from the top. The State Attorney, Mulroy, is Cavallo's man. MacBride is eighteen years on the force, an aggressive, smart, honest cop, but he is unable to get his cases through court. When one of his detectives is murdered, the killing is fixed. MacBride rages. He is caught between stone walls. He is failing in his job of keeping the law. He has a gritty feeling of fear for the safety of his wife, Anna, and his young daughter, Judith.

At this point, the murdered man's partner, Jack Cardigan (no relation to the Cardigan of Nebel's *Dime Detective* series) quits the force and proceeds to fight fire with fire. With his savings, he hires six gunmen and sets up a rival bootlegging ring, hijacking Cavallo's liquor dumps and shooting it out with Cavallo's mob until it is shot apart. Cavallo is killed.

The crooks at city hall get to fighting among themselves and end up indicted. There is a grand shakeup, and on to the next installment.

Over the next issues, law by violence is slowly imposed on Richmond City. The offices of the mayor and the police commissioner are cleaned out. Soon a reform mayor is in and a crackdown under way on the bootleggers, while the guns hammer and the corpses pile up so rapidly that the most careful reader loses count.

Cardigan, the good genius who started all this row, early moves on to other things. He has filled the first story, but MacBride grows into the others. MacBride is a "tall, square-shouldered man of forty more or less hard-bitten years. He had a long, rough-chiseled face, steady eyes, a beak of a nose, and a wide, firm mouth that years of fighting his own and others' wills had hardened." He has, as we are told, "windy blue eyes," drinks Scotch and smokes three-cent cigars, when he is not sucking at a burnt old pipe crammed with a rich, heavy tobacco.

> MacBride had never been affluent—he was always in debt, there were always bills to be met; graft lay around him within easy reach but he scowled at it, went on driving a shabby car, went on being in debt.[16]

He is hard-nosed, rigid, not quite inflexible. He is given to monosyllables, unless goaded to a fury. He has the tendency to take an investigation away from his squad, to go out there and do it himself, almost always alone, following the leads with a repressed fury that becomes increasingly visible as the series progresses. He is not fussy about the minutia of the law. He will slap down a suspect or stride into an apartment without a warrant, for he is personally administering the Law as abstract justice. It would get him bounced off the force in about eight seconds, these days.

In "Wise Guy" (April 1930), Alderman Tony Maratelli's boy, Dominick, has been hanging around in the company of bootlegger Sam Chibbarro. The Alderman appeals to Macbride for help. Doubting that he can do anything, MacBride drops into the Club Naples where Chibbarro, Dominick, a welter-weight Kid Barjo, and three girls are partying. Once they spot

MacBride, the party melts away. Leaving, however, Kid Barjo dead of a slit throat in a back room.

Dominick vanishes and stays vanished. As violent things happen. The Alderman's home is bombed. Dominick was hiding there. He is traced down finally at the Club Naples and arrested, but refuses to tell the police anything. Then one of the girls of that ill-fated party, Bunny Dahl, is found in her apartment, almost dead from gas. The pulmotor temporarily brings her back to life. Chibbarro did it, she says. MacBride leads a raiding party to capture Chibbarro:

> Whatever may be said of him, good or bad, (MacBride) never hung back in the face of impending danger. If he planned a dangerous maneuver, he likewise led the way, remarking with ironic humor, that he carried heavy insurance.[17]

After a savage and extended gun battle through a house, Chibbarro is taken. Bunny has died, but not before she has signed a full confession. Fortunate. Without her confession, detailing all the wheels within wheels, it would have been impossible for the reader to unscramble what all the shooting and shouting was about. There is so much action that the concealed story the investigation is supposed to reveal remains concealed to the last.

To sum it all up, Kid Barjo attacked Bunny, who killed him in self defense. Dominick wanted to cover for her. Bunny threatened Chibbarro to get her out of the trouble or she would tell what she knew about his houses of prostitution. Chibbarro decided to kill her and, while he was about it, Dominick.

So crime is confounded and the police close another case. And nobody had the vaguest glimmer of what was going on until Bunny was introduced, late in the story, to pull it all together and clarify the confusion.

It is one of the defects of the hardboiled story from this time that the action obfuscates the story. The individual scenes are vivid; the characters glitter with life; the language is razor sharp; and what has been going on under the surface of the story is either omitted or wrapped in opaque confusion. You ride the tidal wave and hope it will all make sense on the last page.

We first meet Kennedy in "Raw Law." He is a neatly dressed, hardboiled reporter, with a mannerism or two carried forth from earlier fictional characters. A cigarette droops in his mouth. He moves with weary indolence, as if exhausted by life, his smile vague, his face "young-old," and with the "whimsical eyes of the wicked and wise." He attaches himself to the police with the single-minded devotion of an accountant hunting for a lost penny. He lounges with them, rides with them, investigates with them, is never heaved out on his ear, is never denied access to the goriest slaughter or most violent raid. He is constantly talking. Every remark is a wise-crack, most of them funny. He is as hard and bright as a polished steel rod, and as slender. He stands five feet eight inches, weighs 135 pounds, is blond with a sallow complexion.

Now step ahead a few years. Kennedy has changed.

Kennedy is drunk. Kennedy is almost always drunk. He wears a lop-eared hat and a threadbare summer overcoat, even in the worse of Richmond City's sleet storms. He wears one tie until he loses it. "He looked like a scarecrow or like the shadow of an emaciated tree." His mouth is usually slack, his eyes placid. "Once, a long time ago, he had been a fairly good amateur boxer, but he had taken to the primrose path. Only his nerve, his brain, remained."[18]

"Rough Reform" (March 1933). Young Rose Matteo, temporarily blinded during the public murder of a city clerk, is herself murdered by two masked thugs. Then her brother, Nick, vanishes. The killing is somehow tied to those scraps of conversation Kennedy overheard, while drunk in a club—something about ditching the new mayor and MacBride. At the root of the plot squirm the usual corrupt Richmond City politicians. They instigated a strong arm scheme that went wrong, and so from murder to murder, death, savagery, and violence. Until MacBride faces the entire crew alone, gets disarmed, is almost shot, then saved at the final second by the missing brother.

"Farewell to Crime" (April 1933). A woman lies strangled in an apartment in which the police find a cache of heroin and a bank book with a huge balance. Apparently MacBride's close friend, the Chief Medical Examiner, is a dope supplier. Which tears at MacBride, although he will investigate and let the facts fall where they fall. He and Kennedy follow the trail of a sneezing man. It leads into a sewer of blackmail, treachery, drugs, and, of all things, love. And, at the end, MacBride is able to give back his friend's self-respect. Before that happens, several other people find themselves dead.

As in so many of these investigations, Kennedy shines:

"That guy Kennedy uncorks the wildest schemes of any guy I ever knew. First off, they seem goofy—but when you look back, when you check up, you find out how sane they are. Drunk or sober, on his feet or on his back, that guy *always* uses his head."[19]

And so he does. He is the perfect amateur detective. He works in intimate symbiosis with the police; he is intuitive. He understands human relationships with the barest of clues. None of this ability seems conscious. His genius, like that of Professor Poggioli, works constantly, without much conscious thought. Be he ever so drunk, he looks, he hears, he understands.

Because the Kennedy-MacBride series is one of strong contrasts, Kennedy and MacBride are contrasted. This would seem to be the reason for changing Kennedy from the polished steel rod of a wise-cracking newshound to the staggering, threadbare starvling of casual genius. MacBride is hard, positive, uncompromising, rigid; Kennedy is none of these. MacBride is the pragmatic cop, slugging along, link by link, to the end of the chain; Kennedy is the romantic intuitivist, understanding the whole situation and stepping at once from the beginning to the end. They complement each other wonderfully.

"Lay Down the Law" (November 1933). Kennedy, while drunk, meets a drunken woman and, as a result, almost loses his life. She knows the truth about an old murder, and the boys think she told Kennedy. MacBride learns that killers are after Kennedy and has a hair-raising time, chasing after Kennedy, never quite locating him. He finds, instead, some gun-quick red-hots who make that big insurance policy a sound investment.

After endangering his life repeatedly, MacBride cleans up the hunting killers but is unable to find Kennedy. Who comes reeling in, blind drunk, from a Scavenger Hunt party, where he has been swilling away the hours. He passes out.

MacBride looked down at him. He was sorry and angry and bitter. He listened to Kennedy cough and looked at Kennedy's wet shoes, his ghostly face. He used the telephone.

"Jake," he said. "Send a couple of boys up... I want them to put Kennedy to bed. Hot rum punch and so on. Right away."[20]

He is sorry and angry and bitter. He hates the pulped wreck that Kennedy has made of himself. But he honors the mind behind the alcohol haze; he honors the ability. And he is very fond of the man. Not that he likes showing it. MacBride keeps his feelings carefully covered by a lot of growl, but that is his way.

Kennedy is aware of MacBride's feelings. It is the sort of thing Kennedy is exceedingly sensitive to. Almost never does he allude to their friendship, that silent thing between them. He addresses MacBride with a frivolous disrespect:

Kennedy: "Palsy-walsy, I've been places, seen things, met people. I'd like to introduce you to a few of the facts of life, you ripe tomato."[21]

About the time he became such an accomplished drunkard, Kennedy's speech became littered with affectations of English speech, after the manner of Jay Gatsby. "...you do work for the jolly old Police Department, what?" he remarks. Or refers to MacBride as "You old tomato" or "The old potato." It would be irritating, if you didn't feel that he were ribbing himself, the police, *Black Mask*, and perhaps the mystery story—Philo Vance, maybe, who waved even more strenuous affectations in the face of the police department. Whatever he does, it is hard to dislike Kennedy:

There was something ageless about Kennedy—something worn and battered and washed-out; and also, something wise and good-naturedly wicked, like a benign satyr. He took nothing seriously—least of all himself... A little round-shouldered, a little hollow-chested, he looked as if a good wind might knock him over.[22]

Very rarely, Kennedy lets his mask of casual disrespect slip; at least once, he speaks coherently and at length on the subject of MacBride:

"The skipper is a big bull-headed mutt. He's got a one-track mind and he thinks that shield he wears is another kind of bible. It never occurs to him to walk around a tree, he's got to batter his head against it. To him the law, my friend, is the law: good, bad, or indifferent, it's the law. He carries it out as strictly on himself as on any heel that he picks up. Sometimes I think he's goofy. I don't approve of his outlook on life, his foolhardy honesty, his blind loyalty to his shield. But I like him. He's probably the best friend I've got."[23]

There have been worse character references.

"Bad News" (March 1934): Kennedy attempts to do a favor for plainclothes sergeant Joe Marino—a matter of locating a man. He finds murder. He also turns up a teasing female, a pair of men at each other's throat because of her, and a brainless shooting on a sleet-filled night, all for the love of a worthless woman. MacBride is on leave during all this, but Kennedy, going from drunk to dead drunk, handles it nicely enough.

This describes, coldly enough, a story which is one of those minor classics that *Black Mask*, in general, and Nebel, in particular, turned out with so little apparent effort. It contains not only the violence and unsentimental toughness of the story type; it is also filled with that unique mixture of pain and self destruction, love and decency, which stand out intensely against the toughness and violence. "Bad News" is resonant with lives passing, briefly touching, departing again, moving toward life or, just as often, a destined niche in Hell. The story moves, like life, with a sort of random inevitability, a directionless stumbling toward a fixed goal. Its harshness touches.

At the end, Panderoofski, the barman at Enrico's on Flamingo Street, takes Kennedy home and puts him to bed.

He emptied Kennedy's pockets and hung up his clothes. The pockets had given up only six cents, a few keys, a box of matches and a penknife.

Panderoofski set the alarm clock for seven the next morning. Then he took half a dollar out of his own pocket, laid it on the bed table. He stood for a moment looking down at Kennedy's tired, wasted face. He shook his head woefully.

"Jeeze," he said. "Jeeze."

He went out.[24]

Ferocious, circumstantial detail, coldly objective, somehow as violent as a forest fire.

In the August 1934 "Be Your Age," it is murder at the amusement park. A slack-wire artist has been beaten and strangled. The police arrive and do police things. Kennedy has come along with them. He has a terrible case of hiccoughs. (The series is filled with these trivial problems: hiccoughs, bumped noses, bumping into things, stumbling over things—devices all to bring a touch of sunlight to the black story.)

Kennedy staggers off to visit a friend, and get a drink, and also get the word on the dead man and his love life. He joins with MacBride to follow a trail of blood drops, footprints in the sand, and they end, at last, with a woman surrounded by muscled, snarling men. None of it quite makes sense to MacBride, but Kennedy has it all worked out in his head.

In "Fan Dance" (January 1936), the police raid a night club, setting off a riot. After the place is cleared out, there lies a club owner, strangled. For this mess, MacBride gets a 30-day suspension and the whole department gets shaken up. Kennedy goes snooping out of sympathy. He immediately runs into a very violent mother with a knife, a fan-dancing daughter covered with platinum paint, an unwitting father, and a couple of very very tough hoods. Kennedy takes a terrible battering from these. However, aided by an empty pistol and a loaded shotgun, he solves the problem. And apparently salvages MacBride's reputation.

The MacBride-Kennedy series continued to the August 1936 "Deep Red." It was Nebel's last appearance in *Black Mask*, barring a reprinted story in 1951. Cap Shaw was fired as editor at the end of 1936 and Nebel turned to other matters, most of them paying more than *Black Mask*.

The MacBride-Kennedy series is one of Nebel's major contributions to the magazine. Not as poetic as Chandler, not as realistically detailed as Hammett, the series is an extended masterpiece of hardboiled fiction, violence wrapped about a core of pity. MacBride and his wayward cops are unlike any police you meet in more gritty police procedurals. But in spite of their imperfect professional techniques, they come alive. They move through that terrible world you sometimes sense behind the headlines, that fouled place where graft, corruption, and murder are customary. It is hardly a pleasant world or a clean one. It can hurt, deeply and permanently. It hurts MacBride; hurts him but does not corrupt him. There is honor and stubborn decency, even in these deeps.

Over the years as the series matured, MacBride was increasingly edged to the side by Kennedy. Of all the amateur investigators we have met, he is the most vulnerable. He is a drunken failure, broke, fragile, living alone in a single room, often helpless, subject to the rough world's mercy. That steel-rod Kennedy of the early stories is never entirely lost, in spite of all. The nerve and the brain remain. Somehow the calm perception continues, untouched by all the drinks. He becomes, at last, the major figure of the series, a starved little figure in a threadbare overcoat, moving unsteadily through the sleet-whipped streets of Richmond City, his feet sodden, his hat lost, his vision blurred with whiskey. On his way to another glimpse of Hell, another headline.

A curious and a touching hero.

4-

The police story was a minor offering of the 1920s pulps. Among the tumble of investigators, amateur and private, the occasional police detective flickered briefly, his series traditional, its duration brief. Such superior series as MacBride and Kennedy or Brady and Riordan arrived without fanfare, endured without acclamation. They were exceptions. The more usual police series was made of ruder stuff.

Near the end of the Twenties, a number of short-lived series sprang to being. Hardly series. They were more like sparks, flashing to fade out instantly. Inspector Guilfoy, Officer Minter, Inspector O. Rater of Scotland Yard. All in *Detective Story Magazine* between 1926 and 1929. Inspector Fragne and Detective Second Class Jimmy Dugan in *Detective Fiction Weekly*. (Dugan alone stretched into a series.) But other, more durable, police series were under way soon after.

Sgt. Sir Peter, Edgar Wallace's nobleman Scotland Yard detective, boyish and quick witted, performed wonders of adroit, if not realistic, detection in the 1930 *Detective Story Magazine*. Sir Peter was in the older tradition, matching wits with slick members of London's upper criminal classes. Sgt. Sir Peter was followed, in 1931, by violent Satan Hall, Carroll John Daly's version of a police detective.

Hall first appeared in "Satan's Lash" (*Detective Story Magazine*, August 8, 1931), then transferred to *Detective Fiction Weekly*, where he appeared intermittently until 1944. He also made widely scattered appearances in *Black Mask, Detective Tales*, and *Famous Detective*. Hall was ferocious, the Race Williams of the police force. A big, powerful man with big iron hands, he sought out killers and slapped them down. If they went for a gun, he downed them in another way. His killings were always in self defense. He was called Satan because he looked like Satan.

Hall worked almost entirely outside normal police channels. He reported direct to the police commissioner. That simplified matters for Mr. Hall and Mr. Daly.

Still another hardboiled police character from the same period was Captain John Murdoch of *Ten Detective Aces* (1932 into the 1940s). Murdoch worked nominally within the police system, although more casually even than Captain MacBride and with even more personal involvement in the investigations, if that is possible.

But the story of the police series in the 1930s pulp magazines is not to be told here. Enough to mention that they appeared rather more frequently than in the 1920s in such magazines as *Dime Detective, Detective Tales, Thrilling Detective*. During the mid-1930s, stories of FBI agents became popular, a hot new development. They were featured in every magazine, but particularly *G-Men, Ace G-Man Stories, Federal Agent,* and others. These magazines were no more faithful to reality than the usual pulps and they are equally enthusiastic. The excitement never stopped and the bodies never ceased to tumble.

All series, G-Man and police, further elaborated those main story types laid down during the 1920s. Great Policemen conducted their cases with a fine disdain for routine; hardboiled cops shot away and slugged away, enforcing the law with a maximum of muscle; and a tiny number of series edged hesitantly toward the formalities of the police procedural, although realism was never permitted to interfere with the action.

Captain MacBride would have approved. The opinion of the real police has not been solicited.

Afterword...

From Baker Street gaslight to Depression machine-guns is a modest journey. It is only a trifle over forty years across the calendar. But it is far longer than that in the less familiar mileage of cultural and social change. That particular forty-odd years seems to have been of incredible duration. So much changed, so permanently.

Forty cents or forty apples may be understood by the mathematics of counting. Forty years require more than numeration. They must be lived through. If the mind understands forty years, the heart tends to stumble with confusion at that sum.

The forty years after Baker Street are rich in such confusion. Technology rushed forward, wave on wave, unebbing. Yesterday's assurances ran like sugar candy in the rain. Manners changed. Communications changed, and, as they changed, changed all using them. The rituals between the sexes also changed, men and women viewing each other in fresh, and uncomfortable, contexts. As railroads altered distance and time, and the automobile came, and wealth pooled in strange places; as the labor movement rumbled inchoately, and idealism, defeated in the fields of war, rose again, smiling coldly in its shining new cynical shell.

Within the immense turbulence of these forty years, we have followed a single atom of cultural history, the detective story, as it passed through the pulp magazines, themselves transients in the flow of time. They reflected their period casually, accidentally. Their accounts of imaginary crimes provided fugitive glimpses of the thousand-faceted society in which they were embedded. Upon the magazines, as upon everything else, the dynamics of change played.

At the time Holmes stepped forth, the mystery story was already rooted deeply in the past. Through those archaic deeps moved professional police. Amateur and private investigators, vividly eccentric, pursued their wonderful course. Feminine detectives pattered along dangerous ways. The mystery puzzle, the crime story, the action melodrama, all were in being.

The pulps concentrated and exploited these different story types. *Detective Story Magazine* demonstrated that the detective story was commercially viable in a specialized magazine. *Mystery Magazine, Detective Tales*, and the following multitudes, provided a benign environment in which these stories flourished. And at the same time, they developed an audience eager for more and a cadre of writers briskly providing more.

Not that the pulps were the sole vehicles for the detective story. They competed with the mystery play, the detective motion picture, the weekly mystery in the newspaper, the monthly mystery in the slick magazines, the stream of novels which were ushering in the first Golden Age of mystery. The pulps were merely one vehicle among many.

But it was in the pulps, insatiably gulping material, that the pulse of evolution hammered quickest. Here science and technology met detection. Here the married couple, the doctor, the strong man, the professional investigator probed crime for the public's delight. All these were figures from the past, polished and amplified for the markets of the Twenties. They were intermixed with Holmes variants, hardboiled investigators and tough police, insurance representatives, reporters, and government men. Each one made his contribution to the conventions of the detective story. All collectively established a body of work from which the next decades would draw, as the Twenties had drawn from the past.

We have again approached the mountains of the Thirties. And again we pause and turn back. Other unexamined areas invite us.

The detective story was only a part of that incomparable feast offered by the pulp magazines. For every detective story, a dozen adventure stories were published. And now to adventure, we shall turn.

In the next two volumes, we will follow the adventure story through the early magazines. We will meet a brilliant new group of series characters and many of the recurring themes which energized the adventure story across thirty years of pulps.

We will follow the further activities of the bent heroes—from the Night Wind, a figure of inhuman strength and agility, to Zorro, who brought to the pulps the costumed hero battling for justice outside the law. And we will meet such violent gentlemen adventures as Col. Terence O'Rourke, the Irish terror, Captain Bantam, and Bulldog Drummond, whose example founded a new line of heroes.

We will meet Norry, the Diplomatic Agent, a major figure in the early American spy story; Trevor, whose intelligence network shook the world; John Solomon, the Cockney espionage mastermind. And other adventurers: Jimgrim of Arabia and India. Tros, whose activities so curiously involved him with the destiny of Imperial Rome. Tam o'the Scoots, a fighter ace of World War I. And we will join Peter the Brazen to roam China, facing death on every page.

Even closer to home, we will meet a swarm of less familiar people who found adventure on familiar streets, in familiar towns—ball players and gold diggers, bums, political figures, circus front men and vaudeville teams, lawyers, firemen, and secretaries. All adventurers, every one.

Their stories begin in *Far Horizons*, the next volume of *Yesterday's Faces*.

Notes

To the Curious Reader

[1]J. Randolph Cox, "More Mystery for a Dime: Street & Smith and the First Pulp Detective Magazine," *Clues*, 2:2 (Fall/Winter 1981), p. 52.

[2]As an example, Allen J. Hubin lists 632 series characters who appeared in books between 1878 and 1975. Even this immense listing is incomplete. Refer to the listing in Hubin's "Patterns in Mystery Fiction: The Durable Series Character," *The Mystery Story*, edited by John Ball, Penguin (1978).

Chapter I—The Geniuses

[1]Frank Luther Mott, *A History of American Magazines*, Volume IV (1885-1905). Cambridge, Mass., Harvard University Press (1957), p. 114, *fn* #26. *Short Stories* was published twice a month during 1921-1949, and monthly thereafter, surviving as a digest to at least 1957. From 1936 it was edited by Dorothy McIlwraith.

[2]M. P. Shiel, *Prince Zaleski and Cummings King Monk*, Sauk City, Wis., Arkham House (1977), p. 3.

[3]Scott Campbell (pseudonym for Frederick W. Davis), "The Right of Way," *The Popular Magazine*, Vol. X, No. 4 (February 1908), p. 223.

[4]Guy C. Baker, "The Secret of the Rising Sun," *Blue Book*, Vol. XIV, No. 5 (March 1912), p. 1093.

[5]John Thomas McIntyre, *Ashton-Kirk Investigator*, Philadelphia: Penn. Pub (1910), p. 112.

[6] *Ibid*, pp. 168-169.

[7]J. Allan Dunn, "Marked By the Dead," *Detective Story Magazine*, Vol. VIII, No. 4 (August 20, 1917), p. 25.

[8] *Ibid.*

[9]This formal treatment of evidence is well demonstrated in Freeman's Dr. Thorndyke stories and accounts for Thorndyke's over-determined and laborious examination of every scrap on or near the crime scene. Thorndyke was the exception in fiction and often in real life, as well. Between the theory of handling evidence and the way it was actually handled lay a considerable chasm.

[10]Otto Penzler, "Collecting Mystery Fiction: Father Brown," *The Armchair Detective*, Vol. 16, No. 3 (Summer 1983), p. 249.

[11]Ellis Parker Butler, "Bread Upon the Waters," *Detective Story Magazine*, Vol. IX, No. 2 (September 25, 1917), p. 70.

[12]Butler, "Chicken Bait," *Detective Story Magazine*, Vol. XIII, No. 5 (April 2, 1918), pp. 40-41.

[13]G. K. Chesterton, "The Tower of Treason," *The Popular Magazine*, Vol. LV, No. 4 (February 7, 1920), p. 117.

[14]Unsigned, "Heart to Heart Talks," *All-Story Weekly*, Vol. CI, No. 1 (August 30, 1919), p. 174.

[15]Lewen Hewitt, "The Twisted Bullet," *Detective Story Magazine*, Vol. XXXVIII, No. 2 (February 12, 1921), p. 63.

[16] *Ibid*, p. 65.

[17] *Ibid*, p. 68.

[18]These bright little fantasies were collected as *A Houseboat on the Styx* (1896) and *The Pursuit of the Houseboat* (1897).

[19]John Dickson Carr, *The Life of Sir Arthur Conan Doyle*, NY: Harper (1949). Chapter XXII, "The Beginning," discusses Doyle's world-wide lectures on behalf of spiritualism and main elements of that belief.

[20]Unsigned editorial note to "The Ghost Detective: I—The Haunted Policeman," *Detective Story Magazine*, Vol. L, No. 4 (July 15, 1922), p. 51.

[21]Ellis Parker Butler, *Ibid*, p. 54.

[22] *Ibid*, p. 59.

[23]Butler, "Who Killed Dikkory," *Detective Story Magazine*, Vol. L, No. 6 (July 29, 1922), p. 49.

[24]Nancy Blue Wynne, *An Agatha Christie Chronology*, NY: Ace (1976), pp. 172-173. The thirteenth Quin story, "The Love Detectives," appeared in *The Mousetrap* (retitling of *Three Blind Mice and Other Stories*), NY: Dell (1960).

[25]Agatha Christie, *An Autobiography*, NY: Dodd, Mead & Co. (1977), p. 420.

[26]An interesting discussion of the Quin and Satterthwaite series, by Earl F. Bargainnier, may be found in "Agatha Christie's Other Detectives," *The Armchair Detective*, Vol. 11, No. 2 (April 1976), pp. 112-115.

[27]Albert Edward Ullman, "Quick Change," *Short Stories*, Vol. CVI, No. 1 (January 10, 1924), p. 84.

[28]Christopher Morley, *The Haunted Bookshop*, NY: Grosset & Dunlap (undated). Chapters I, II, III, and VI originally appeared in *The Bookman*, the latter chapter in the June 1919 issue (Vol. XLIX, No. 4, pp. 482-491).

[29]T. S. Stribling, "The Refugees," *Clues of the Caribbees*," NY: Dover (1977), p. 6.

[30]Stribling, "Cricket," *Clues of the Caribbees*, p. 268.

[31]Stribling, "The Governor of Cap Haitien," *Clues of the Caribbees*, p. 51.

[32]Stribling, "A Passage to Benares," *Clues of the Caribbees*, p. 311.

[33] *Ibid*, pp. 313-314.

[34]The date of Poggioli's death is given as January 20, 1929. The date refuses to match any date of publication. It appears in a pseudo-biography of Poggioli, written by Stribling, and published in *Sleuths*, NY: Harcourt, Brace & Co. (1931), edited by Kenneth MacGowen. The biography introduces a reprinting of "The Prints of Hantoun." The date discrepancy need not be taken seriously, since the biography is a leg-pull from start to finish. Stribling was determined not take his detective seriously.

[35]Stribling, "The Mystery of the Chief of Police," *Best Dr. Poggioli Detective Stories*, NY: Dover (1975), p. 24.

Chapter II—Detecting Doctors

[1]Chris Steinbrunner and Otto Penzler, *Encyclopedia of Mystery and Detection*, NY: McGraw-Hill (1976), p. 285. L. T. Meade was the pseudonym for Elizabeth Thomasina Meade Smith, an exceedingly prolific writer for the popular magazines (1854-1914). Clifford Halifax was the pseudonym for Dr. Edgar Beaumont (1860-1921). Three cases of Clifford Halifax, M. D. were reprinted in a volume, edited by Alan K. Russell, titled *Rivals of Sherlock Holmes*, New Jersey: Castle Books (1978). Pages ix and x of this volume give additional biographical information on Meade and Beaumont.

[2]Clifford Ashdown (pseudonym for R. Austin Freeman and John J. Pitcarin), *From a Surgeon's Diary*, London: Ferret Fantasy (1975).

[3]A discussion of Dr. Thorndyke and the scientific detective school may be found in Chapter I, *Strange Days*, (Volume 2 of *Yesterday's Faces*) (1984).

[4]David Douglas, "The Pomeroy Case," *People's*, Vol. XXII, No. 5 (May 1917), p. 161.

[5]William Almon Wolff, "The Play Doctor," *Blue Book*, Vol. XXXIII, No. 5 (September 1921), p. 50.

[6] *Ibid*, pp. 50-51.

[7]Unsigned editorial, *Flynn's*, Vol. IV, No. 3 (February 7, 1925), p. 386.

[8]Anthony Wynne (pseudonym for Robert McNair Wilson), "The Double Thirteen," *Flynn's*, Vol. IX, No. 3 (September 5, 1925), p. 334.

[9]Wynne, *op. cit*, Vol. IX, No. 4 (September 12, 1925), p. 556.

[10]Munsey sold a package of five magazines to Popular Publications: *Munsey's*, *Argosy*, *Railroad Magazine*, *Detective Fiction Weekly*, and *All-Story* (which had been converted to a love story magazine).

[11]In Wynne's next Dr. Hailey novel, *The Mystery of the Ashes* (1927), the good doctor once again attends a fancy dress ball as Falstaff. And once again finds himself leaping over London rooftops like a gazelle.

[12]Freeman Wills Crofts, *Enemy Unseen*, NY: Dodd, Mead & Co. (1945), p. 123.

[13]Wynne, "The Double Thirteen," *Flynn's* Vol. IX, No. 3 (September 5, 1925), p. 346.

[14]The Dr. Bentiron series is discussed in Chapter I, Vol. 2, *Yesterday's Faces*, Bowling Green (1984).

[15]Ernest M. Poate, "Satan's Wood," *Detective Story Magazine*, Vol. CXIX, No. 3 (June 14, 1930), p. 42.

[16]Poate, "The Tiger's Touch," *Detective Story Magazine*, Vol. LXXXI, No. 6, (February 20, 1926), pp. 91-92.

[17] *Ibid*, p. 95.

Chapter III—The Clever Women

[1]Baroness Orczy, *Lady Molly of Scotland Yard*, London: Cassell (1926), p. 1.

[2]C. L. Pirkis, "The Experiences of Loveday Brooke, Lady Detective: The Bag Left On a Doorstep," included in *Rivals of Sherlock Holmes*, edited by Alan K. Russell, NJ: Castle Books (1978), p. 19.

[3]Anna Katharine Green, "The Golden Slipper," included in *Crime On Her Mind*, edited by Michele B. Slung, NY: Pantheon Books (1978), pp. 155-156.

[4]George R. Sims, "The Man With the Wild Eyes," included in *Crime On Her Mind*, p. 37.

[5]M. McD. Bodkin Q.C., "How He Cut His Stick," included in *The Further Rivals of Sherlock Holmes*, edited by Hugh Greene, Baltimore: Penguin (1974), p. 191.

[6]Slung, *op. cit.*, "The Woman Detectives, A Chronological Survey," pp. 357-377. The survey extends from Mrs. Paschal to the feminine detectives of the 1970s, and includes author, title of major collection, and a brief commentary on the detective under discussion.

[7]The Dora Myrl-associated books are *Dora Myrl: The Lady Detective* (1900); *The Capture of Paul Beck* (1909); and *Young Beck: A Chip of the Old Block* (1911). Two other collections featuring Dora's future husband, Paul Beck, were also published.

[8]Pirkis, *op. cit.*, p. 18.

[9]Orczy, *op. cit.*, p. 275.

[10]Unsigned Introduction to "The Mysterious Goddess," *All-Story Cavalier Weekly*, Vol. XLIV, No. 1 (April 17, 1915), p. 1.

[11]Arnold Fredericks (pseudonym for Frederick Arnold Kummer), *The Ivory Snuff-Box*, NY: Grosset & Dunlap (1912), pp. 12-13.

[12]Fredericks, *The Blue Lights*, NY: Watt (1915), p. 49.

[13]Fredericks, *The Film of Fear*, NY: Watt (1917), pp. 266-267.

[14]Anna Katharine Green, *op. cit.*, p. 154.

[15]The appearance of a number of feminine detectives close together at the opening of the 1920s was not the beginning of a new trend but the working out of older magazine policy. The extraordinary success of the women's slick magazines, *The Ladies' Home Journal* and others, led some of the pulp magazine publishers to slant their wares toward the women of their audience. From around 1912-1915, *Blue Book*, *The Cavalier*, *The Argosy*, and *All-Story* filled covers with glowing women smiling out, and the fiction presented women in love and women in adventure, their romances endangered till the serials' end. Not all the fiction, by any means, or even a high proportion of it, was slanted toward women. But enough was provided to catch a feminine reader without frightening away the men.

[16]Raymond Lester, "Nan Russell: Investigatrix, VI—The Better Way," *All-Story Weekly*, Vol. CVIII, No. 6 (April 17, 1920), p. 208.

[17] *Ibid*, p. 207.

[18]Hulbert Footner, "Madame Storey's Way," *Argosy All-Story Weekly*, Vol. CXLI, No. 2 (March 11, 1922), p. 220.

[19] *Ibid*, p. 214.

[20] *Ibid*, p. 215.

[21]Unsigned article, "The Fiction of Hulbert Footner," *Argosy All-Story Weekly*, Vol. CL, No. 3 (March 31, 1923), pp. 321-323. Additional biographical material on Footner also appeared in *Argosy*, Vol. 223, No. 5 (September 5, 1931), p. 716.

[22]Footner, *op. cit.*, p. 216.

[23]Footner, "The Pot of Pansies," *The Velvet Hand*, London: W. Collins (1933), p. 84.

[24] *New York Times* (July 28, 1929), p. 13.

[25]Florence Mae Pettee, "The Scarlet Spider," *Action Stories*, Vol. 2, No. 7 (March 1923), p. 73.

[26]Pettee, "Marked Down," *Argosy All-Story Weekly*, Vol. CLV, No. 2 (October 20, 1923), p. 300.

[27]Robert A. Lowndes, "The Editor's Page," *Startling Mystery Stories* #16 (Summer 1970), pp. 5-6.

[28]Agatha Christie, *An Autobiography*, NY: Dodd, Meade & Co. (1977), pp. 420-421. The quotation, while appropriate to Miss Marple, was not made about her, but about Dr. Sheppard's sister in *The Murder of Roger Ackroyd*.

Chapter IV—After Baker Street

[1]Scott Campbell (pseudonym for Frederick W. Davis), "Below The Dead Line: The Case of the Boss Mason," *The Popular Magazine*, Vol. II, No. 6 (October 1904), pp. 168-169.

[2] *Ibid*, p. 171.

[3]Campbell, "The Case of the Missing Magnate," *The Popular Magazine*, Vol. II, No. 4 (August 1904), pp. 144.

[4]Campbell, "The Case of the Under Secretary," *The Popular Magazine*, Vol. II, No. 5 (September 1904), p. 182.

[5]Campbell (October 1904), p. 172.

[6]Mott, *op. cit*, "Sketch 19: *Munsey's Magazine*," pp. 608-619. The magazine began as *Munsey's Weekly* (1889-1891). It was retitled *Munsey's Magazine* in 1891, the first monthly 10 cent issue being dated October 1893. Its authors included O. Henry, who published a dozen stories between 1905-1910. In 1918 the magazine title was again changed to *Munsey*. It became an unillustrated, all-fiction monthly pulp in July 1921, continuing through the October 1929 issue. It was then merged with *Argosy All-Story Weekly*, which promptly became *Argosy* with the October 5, 1929, issue.

[7]Butler, *op. cit.* p. 43.

[8]J. Edward Leithead, "Nick Carter In Another Man's Shoes," *Dime Novel Round-Up*, Vol. 29, No. 11, Whole No. 350 (November 15, 1961), p. 113.

[9]Roy Norton is listed as an author on the title pages of many *Popular Magazine* issues, 1912 through 1920. We recognize that we are in the presence of an editorial joke. What the joke is is less clear.

[10]At this time, *Detective Story Magazine* appeared twice a month. Issues were dated on the 5th and 20th. The magazine became a weekly with the September 4, 1917, issue.

[11]Johnston McCulley, "Trimble, Trouble-Maker," *Detective Story Magazine*, Vol. 6, No. 5 (March 5, 1917), p. 5.

[12]McCulley, "Four Squares," *Detective Story Magazine*, Vol. 8, No. 1 (July 5, 1917), p. 2.

[13]McCulley, "Trimble, Trouble-Maker," p. 9.

[14]McCulley, "Seven Circles," *Detective Story Magazine*, Vol. 7, No. 3 (May 5, 1917), p. 14.

[15]McCulley, "Germs of Bedlam" *Detective Story Magazine*, Vol. 7, No. 1 (April 5, 1917), p. 20.

[16]McCulley, "Trimble, Trouble Maker," p. 17.

[17]McCulley, "The Lost Disk," *Detective Story Magazine*, Vol. VIII, No. 3 (August 5, 1917), p. 27.

[18]Anonymous, "George Allan England," *Famous Fantastic Mysteries, Vol. 2, No. 3 (August 1940), p. 79.*

[19]"Ping Pong" was reprinted in Ellery Queen's 1942 anthology, *Sporting Blood.* The anthology is easier to locate than the 1918 *All Story.*

[20]"George Allan England, "When Sleep Spelled Death," *Detective Story Magazine*, Vol. LVI, No. 3 (March 17, 1923), p. 74.

[21] *Ibid*, p. 85.

[22]Cecil H. Bullivant, "The Exploits of Garnett Bell, Detective: II: Behind the Green Door," *Detective Story Magazine*, Vol. XXIV, No. 6 (July 15, 1919), p. 84.

[23]Nancy Blue Wynne, *An Agatha Christie Chronology*, NY: Ace Books(1976). This invaluable book includes cross references of the short stories to the various American titles in which they appeared. Retitling of the Christie books has been widespread and constitutes a terrible menace to the reader who buys from a mail-order title listing.

[24]The Dedication to *The Case Book of Jimmie Lavender*, NY: Bookfinger, (1973) states that "JIMMY LAVANDER, great pitcher for the old Chicago Cubs, loaned his attractive name" to the detective.

[25]Florence M. Pettee, "The Exploits of Beau Quicksilver: 1—A Tooth For a Tooth," *Argosy All-Story Weekly*, Vol. CXLIX, No. 4 (February 24, 1923), p. 573.

[26] *Ibid*.

[27]Florence M. Pettee, "Touch of the Dead," *Flynn's Weekly*, Vol. III, No. 5 (January 10, 1925), p. 887.

[28]Hopper's gibbering about clock hands and time expanded to almost a full page of narrative in "Clews in Ambush" (*Flynn's Weekly*, Vol. VII, No. 1, May 30, 1925), p. 64. In this, a problem in algebra is laid out and explained in detail, complete with techniques for using the "x." At 1/4 cents a word, Mr. Royal's mathematical abilities earned him $1.75 for that page of published copy.

[29]Walter Archer Frost, "The Glavis Affair," *Flynn's Weekly*, Vol. XXIV, No. 4 (June 4, 1927), p. 606.

[30]Announcement facing p. 321, *Flynn's Weekly*, Vol. XVII, No. 3 (September 18, 1926).

[31] *Clues* fiction requirements as stated in "The Manuscript Market" column of *The Writer*, Vol. 39, No. 10 (December 1927), p. 330.

[32]August Derleth, "The Beginnings of Solar Pons," *A Praed Street Dossier*, Sauk City: Mycroft & Moran (1968), p. 2.

[33] *Ibid*.

[34]The Pons adventures were continued by Basil Copper in a series of paperbacks published by Pinnacle Books: *The Dossier of Solar Pons* (1979), *The Further Adventures of Solar Pons* (1979), *The Secret Files of Solar Pons* (1979), and *The Uncollected Cases of Solar Pons* (1980).

Chapter V—The Professionals

[1]The Larry Lowman series originally appeared in the English *Grand Magazine*

between July 1917 and February 1918. The final two stories, "The Herzeimer Wedding Present" and "Lord Exenham Creates a Sensation" do not seem to have been published in the United States.

[2]P. R. Cousse, "The Argosy and A Dissertation," *Edgar Wallace Newsletter* No. 26 (June 1975), pp. 1-2. This article comments briefly on the *Argosy* and remarks that Edgar Wallace published only ten short stories in the magazine (1920-21 and 1923).

[3]John A. Hogan, "Seek and You Will Find," *Edgar Wallace Newsletter* No. 26 (June 1975), p. 3. The house name, John Anstruther, was used by Wallace for many of his most interesting short story groups, including *Four Square Jane* and the stories comprising *The Mixer*.

[4]Hogan, "The Mission That Succeeded," *Edgar Wallace Newletter* No. 48 (November 1980), p. 3. Hogan reports that he first read Wireless Bryce stories in a 1920s magazine; this publication has not yet been identified.

[5]Edgar Wallace, *The Iron Grip*, "The Man From 'Down Under'," London: The Readers Library, reprinted March 1930, p. 15.

[6] *Ibid*, p. 28.

[7]Edgar Wallace, *The Mind of J. G. Reeder*, "The Poetical Policeman," London: Pan Books (1962), p. 10.

[8] *Ibid*, p. 24.

[9]In *Room 13*, Reeder is vaguely connected with the Secret Service. He represents the law in this interesting story of deceit and violence among high-class crooks. (In 1927, Wallace would redo the first part of this novel and call it *The Squeaker*,) At the very end of the story, it is revealed that J. G. Reeder is not J. G. Reeder but a Secret Service representative named Golden. The real J. G. Reeder is that handsome hero who just got the girl. This bit of foolishness is ignored in all subsequent stories.

[10]For publication in *Dime Mystery Book*, the Reeder stories were edited down and Americanized. Thus Reeder is from the District Attorney's office. Such Britishisms as flats, pounds, lorries, and, we may suppose, Brownings, are banished from the prose. In spite of these cavalier changes, the stories hold up brilliantly.

[11]Carbon monoxide is stated but carbon dioxide is meant, this being one of the by-products of marble and acid.

[12]David Fox, "The Man Who Convicted Himself," *All-Story Weekly*, Vol. CVIII, No. 4 (April 3, 1920), pp. 472-473.

[13]Hugh Kahler (1883-1969) successfully left the pulps for the slick magazines. He contributed to the *Saturday Evening Post*, *Collier's*, and *American*, and, from 1943-1960, was the Fiction Editor for the *Ladies Home Journal*.

[14]Hugh Kahler, "No Man's Hand," *Detective Story Magazine*, Vol. XXXVI, No. 3 (November 23, 1920), p. 46.

[15] *Ibid*.

[16]Mansfield Scott, "Death Dealers," *Flynn's Weekly Detective Fiction*, Vol. XXX, No. 1 (January 21, 1928), p. 23.

Chapter VI—From the Mask

[1]Editor of the 1913-1914 *Smart Set* was Willard H. Wright, later to become famous as S. S. Van Dine. Wright's editorial policies favored advanced sophisticated, often

imported fiction, with the result that advertisers felt "his magazine was printing material that was either incomprehensible or immoral or both." Refer to William Manchester's book, *H. L. Mencken: Disturber of the Peace*, NY: Collier Books (1962), p. 92.

[2]Carl Bode, *Mencken*, So. Illinois University Press (1969), p. 71. *Saucy Stories* was a satirical version of the popular *Snappy Stories*.

[3]Guy J. Forge, editor, *Letters of H. L. Mencken*, NY: Knopf (1961), p. 142. Ernest Boyd was the British vice-counsul in Baltimore from 1913-1918.

[4] *Ibid*, p. 363. The extract is from a letter to Philip Goodman, dated February 24, 1933.

[5] *Ibid*, p. 180. The "paper famine" resulted from wartime production restrictions.

[6] *Ibid*, p. 216. The extract is from a letter to Fielding Hudson Garrison, dated December 31, 1920. "Woodrow" refers to Woodrow Wilson.

[7]John Baer, "The Silver Lining," *The Black Mask*, Vol. IV, No. 2 (November 1921), p. 51.

[8]J. H. Ward, "The Bamboozler," *The Black Mask* Vol. IV, No. 2 (November 1921), p. 65.

[9]Ward Sterling, "Bram Dwyer's Bonfire," *The Black Mask* Vol. V, No. 2, (May 1922), p. 93.

[10]John Hanlon, "The Door," *The Black Mask*, Vol. V, No. 13 (March 1, 1923), p. 27.

[11]In the underworld slang of the Teen, Peter Collins was the slang for "nobody," a "John Smith." By extension, Peter Collinson is the son of nobody.

[12]Carroll John Daly, "The Death Drop," *Black Mask*, Vol. 16, No. 3 (May 1933), p. 33.

[13]Daly, *Murder From the East*, NY: International Polygonics (1978), p. 8.

[14]Daly, "Death For Two," *Black Mask*, Vol. 14, No. 7 (September 1931), p. 32.

[15]Daly, "Knights of the Open Palm," *The Great American Detective*, edited by William Kittredge and Steven M. Krauzer, NY: Mentor (1978), p. 18.

[16] *Ibid*, pp. 32-33.

[17] *Ibid*, p. 38.

[18]Daly, "The False Burton Combs," in *The Hard-Boiled Detective*, edited by Herbert Ruhm, NY: Vintage Books (1977), p. 3.

[19] *Ibid*, p. 13.

[20]Gordon Young, "Bluffed," *Adventure*, Vol. XXVIII, No. 4 (February 18, 1921), p. 10.

[21] *Ibid*, p. 26.

[22]Young, "Dead Or Alive," *Adventure*, Vol. XXXII, No. III (December 30, 1921), p. 142.

[23]Young, "Bluffed," p. 12.

[24] *Ibid*, p. 44.

[25]Young, "Sorcery and Everhard," *Adventure*, Vol. XXX, No. 3 (1st August 1921), p. 118.

[26]Young, "Dead Or Alive," p. 167.

[27]Young, "Crooked Shadows," *Adventure*, Vol. XXXV, No. 2 (June 20, 1922), pp. 21-22.

[28]Daly, *The Tag Murders*, NY: Clode (1930), p. 146.

[29]Daly, "Death for Two," *Black Mask*, Vol. XIV, No. 7 (September 1931), p. 17.

[30] *Ibid*, pp. 20-21.

[31]Daly, "If Death Is Respectable," *Black Mask*, Vol. XVI, No. 5 (July 1933), p. 38.

[32]Daly, *Murder From the East*, pp. 281-282.

[33]Anthony Boucher (pseudonym for William Anthony White), "Criminals At Large," *New York Times Book Review*, Section 7 (August 10, 1952), p. 14.

[34]William F. Nolan, *Hammett: A Life At the Edge*, NY: Congdon & Weed (1983), pp. 8-31. The first chapter details the complex record of Hammett's service with Pinkerton and is dense with factual and anecdotal material.

[35]Harold Knott, "Some Important Detective Fiction First Editions in Paperback Books," *The Mystery Reader's Newsletter*, Vol. III, No. 1 (October 1969), pp. 2-3. All nine Hammett collections were issued by various sub-units of the Mercury Press as 5-1/2 x 7-1/2" paperbacks. Titles and associated data are provided under *Bibliography*. Of these paperbacks, the first seven were immediately reprinted by Dell as 4 x 6-1/2" paperbacks, usually in the same year as the Mercury Press edition. In addition, the World Publishing Company issued inexpensive hardback editions of the first two collections: *Blood Money* and *The Adventures of Sam Spade*; these were released in 1945.

[36]Ellery Queen, "Thou Art the Man" (Introduction to "Who Killed Bob Teal?"), *Dead Yellow Woman*, NY: Dell (1947), p. 141.

[37]Dashiell Hammett, "The Gutting of Couffignal," *The Return of the Continental Op*, NY: Dell (1945), p. 112.

[38]Dashiell Hammett, "Arson Plus," *Woman in the Dark*, NY: Jonathan Press J 59 (1952). The two quotations given are, respectively, from pp. 14-15 and 22.

[39]Hammett, "Slippery Fingers," *Woman in the Dark*, pp. 30-31.

[40]Hammett, "House Dick," (retitling of "Bodies Piled Up"), *Dead Yellow Women*, NY: Dell (1947), p. 126.

[41]Hammett, "One Hour," *The Return of the Continental Op*, NY: Dell (1945), p. 133.

[42]Hammett, "Zigzags of Treachery," *The Continental Op*, NY: Dell (1945), p. 102.

[43]Hammett, "Arson Plus," pp. 10-11.

[44]Hammett, "Zigzags of Treachery," p. 112.

[45]Hammett, *Blood Money*, NY: Dell (undated), p. 19.

[46] *Ibid*, p. 189.

[47]Hammett, "Fly Paper," *The Big Knockover*, NY: Random House (1966), p. 33.

[48]Joe Gores, "Hammett the Writer," *Xenophile*, Number 38 (March-April 1978), p. 7.

Chapter VII—Cops

[1]George N. Dove, *The Police Procedural*, Bowling Green, Ohio: Popular Press (1982), p. 36.

[2]Victor Maxwell, "The Work of an Artist," *Flynn's*, Vol. IX, No. 3 (September 5, 1925), p. 477.

[3] *Ibid*, p. 476.

[4]Maxwell, "A Darned Good Tailor," *Flynn's Weekly*, Vol. XIX, No. 6 (November 20, 1926), p. 856.

[5]Maxwell, "Halloran Makes a Case," *Detective Fiction Weekly*, Vol. LXI, No. 5 (September 12, 1931), p. 621.

[6]Maxwell, "What the Cipher Told," *Flynn's*, Vol. X, No. 4 (October 24, 1925), p. 485.

[7]E. R. Hagemann, "Cap Shaw and His 'Great and Regular Fellows': The Making of *The Hard-Boiled Omnibus*, 1945-1946," *Clues* 2:2, Fall/Winter 1981, p. 147.

[8]Ellery Queen, introduction to "You Can Take So Much," *Ellery Queen's Mystery Magazine*, Vol. 28, No. 4, Whole No. 156 (October 1956), p. 75.

[9]Frederick Nebel, "Wise Guy," *Black Mask* Vol. XIII, No. 2 (April 1930), p. 27.

[10] *Ibid*, p. 19.

[11]Frederick Nebel, "Be Your Age," *Black Mask*, Vol. XVII, No. 6 (August 1934), p. 79.

[12]Nebel, "Winter Kill," *The Hardboiled Dicks*," edited by Ron Goulart, NY: Pocket Books (1967), p. 91.

[13]Nebel, "Rough Reform," *Black Mask*, Vol. XVI, No. 1 (March 1933), p. 62.

[14]Nebel, "Too Young To Die," *Ellery Queen's Mystery Magazine*, Vol. 3, No. 5, Whole No. 7 (November 1942), p. 30.

[15]The hardboiled reporter was already a recognized fictional character in 1928. *The Front Page* opened in New York, August 14, 1928. The first appearance of Kennedy was in "Raw Law," *Black Mask*, September 1928, and issued in August of that year. The story had been written at least two months before.

[16]Nebel, "Rough Reform," *Black Mask*, Vol. XVI, No. 1 (March 1933), p. 64.

[17]Nebel, "Wise Guy," *Black Mask*, Vol. XIII, No. 2 (April 1930), p. 29.

[18]Nebel, "Rough Reform," p. 66.

[19]Nebel, "Farewell To Crime," *Black Mask*, Vol. XVI, No. 1 (April 1933), p. 67.

[20]Nebel, "Lay Down the Law," *Black Mask*, Vol. XVI, No. 9 (November 1933), p. 59.

[21]Nebel, "Farewell To Crime," p. 58-59.

[22]Nebel, "Bad News," *Black Mask*, Vol. XVII, No. 1 (March 1934), p. 36.

[23]Nebel, "Fan Dance," Black Mask, Vol. XVIII, No. 11 (January 1936), p. 44.

[24]"Bad News," p. 49.

Bibliography

Anonymous, Editorial, *Flynn's*, Vol. IV, No. 3, February 7, 1925.

—— "The Fiction of Hulbert Footner," *Argosy-All Story Weekly*, Vol. CL, No. 3, March 31, 1923.

—— "George Allan England," *Famous Fantastic Mysteries*, Vol. 2, No. 3, August 1940.

—— "Heart to Heart Talks," *All-Story Weekly*, Vol. CI, No. 1, August 30, 1919.

—— Introduction to "The Ghost Detective," *Detective Story Magazine*, Vol. L, No. 4, July 15, 1922.

—— Introduction to "The Mysterious Goddess," *All-Story Cavalier Weekly*, Vol. XLIV, No. 1, April 17, 1915.

—— "The Manuscript Market," *The Writer*, Vol. 39, No. 10, December 1927.

—— "The Men Who Make The Argosy: Hulbert Footner," *Argosy-All Story Weekly*, Vol. 223, No. 5, September 5, 1931.

Adrian, Jack (ed.), "Introduction", *Sexton Blake Wins*. London: Dent, 1986.

Ashdown, Clifford (pseudonym for R. Austin Freeman and John J. Pitcarin).*From a Surgeon's Diary*. London: Ferret Fantasy, 1975.

Ball, John, ed., *The Mystery Story*. NY: Penguin Books, 1978.

Bargainnier, Earl F. "Agatha Christie's Other Detectives," *The Armchair Detective*, Vol. II, No. 2, April 1978.

Barson, Michael S. "'There's No Sex In Crime': The Two-Fisted Homilies of Race Williams," *Clues*, 2:2, Fall/Winter 1981.

Billman, Carol. *The Secret of the Stratemeyer Syndicate*. NY: Unger, 1986.

Bode, Carl, *Mencken*. Southern Illinois University Press, 1969.

Boucher, Anthony (pseudonym for William Anthony Parker White). "Criminals At Large," *New York Times*, Book Review, Section 7, August 10, 1952.

Brenn, George J. *Voices*. NY: The Century Co, 1923.

Carr, John Dickson. *The Life of Sir Arthur Conan Doyle*. NY: Harper, 1949.

Christie, Agatha. *An Autobiography*. NY: Dodd, Mead & Co., 1977.

—— *The Big Four*. NY: Dell, 1965.

—— *The Mysterious Mr. Quin*. NY: Dell, 1964.

—— *Poirot Investigates*. NY: Bantam, 1961.

—— *13 Clues for Miss Marple*. NY: Dell, 1967.

—— *The Tuesday Club Murders*. NY: Dodd, Mead & Co., 1933.

Cook, Michael L. *Mystery, Detective and Espionage Magazines*. Westport, Conn: Greenwood Press, 1983.

Cousse, P. R. "The Argosy and a Dissertation, *Edgar Wallace Newsletter* No. 26, June 1975.

Cox, J. Randolph. "More Mystery for a Dime: Street & Smith and the First Pulp Detective Magazine," *Clues*, 2:2, Fall/Winter 1981.

Crofts, Freeman Wills. *Enemy Unseen*. NY: Dodd, Mead & Co, 1945.

Daly, Carroll John. *Murder From the East.* NY: International Polygonics, 1978.
_____ *The Tag Murders.* NY: Clode, 1930.
Derleth, August *A Praed Street Dossier.* Sauk City, Wis.: Mycroft & Moran, 1968.
Dolmetsch, Carl R., ed. *The Smart Set: A History and Anthology.* NY: Dial, 1966.
Dove, George N. *The Police Procedural.* Bowling Green, Ohio: Popular Press, 1982.
Durham, Philip. "The Black Mask School," *Tough Guy Writers of the Thirties.* Southern Illinois University Press, 1968.
Flynn, William J. Introduction to "Red Eye." *Flynn's,* Vol. VII, No. 4, June 20, 1925.
Footner, Hulbert. *The Almost Perfect Murder.* NY: Caxton House, 1939.
_____ *The Doctor Who Held Hands* (retitling of "The Black Ace"). NY: Crime Club, Doubleday, Doran & Co., 1929.
_____ *Easy To Kill.* NY: Harper & Brothers, 1931.
_____ *Madame Storey.* NY: Doran, 1926.
_____ *The Under Dogs.* NY: Doran, 1925
_____ *The Velvet Hand.* London: W. Collins and Co. Ltd, 7th Impression, 1933.
_____ *The Viper.* London: W. Collins & Co. Ltd, undated.
Forge, Guy J., ed. *Letters of H. L. Mencken.* NY: Knopf, 1961.
Fox, David (pseudonym for Isabel Ostrander). *The Doom Dealer.* NY: McBride, 1923.
_____ Ethel Opens the Door (retitling of "The Super Swing"). NY: McBride, 1922.
_____ The Handwriting on the Wall. NY: McBride, 1924.
_____ The Man Who Convicted Himself. NY: McBride, 1920.
Fredricks, Arnold (pseudonym for Frederic Arnold Kummer). *The Blue Lights* (retitling of "The Changing Lights".) NY: Watt, 1915.
_____ *The Film of Fear.* NY: Watt, 1917.
_____ *The Ivory Snuff Box.* NY: Watt, 1912.
_____ *The Little Fortune.* NY: Watt, 1915.
_____ *One Million Francs* (retitling of "The Honeymoon Detectives.") NY: Watt, 1912.
Gores, Joe. "Hammett The Writer," *Xenophile* No. 38, March-April 1978.
Greene, Hugh. *Cosmopolitan Crimes.* NY: Pantheon Books, 1971.
_____ *The Further Rivals of Sherlock Holmes.* Baltimore: Penguin, 1974.
Hagemann, E. R. *A Comprehensive Index to Black Mask, 1920-1951. Bowling Green, Ohio: Popular Press, 1982.*
Hammett, Dashiell. *The Big Knockover.* NY: Random House, 1966. (Edited and with Introduction by Lillian Hellman.)
_____ *Blood Money.* NY: Dell #53, undated.
_____ *The Continental Op.* NY: Dell #129, 1945.
_____ *Dead Yellow Women.* NY: Dell #308, 1947.
_____ *Hammett Homicides.* NY: Dell #223, 1946.
_____ *A Man Named Thin.* NY: Mercury Mystery #233, 1962.
_____ *The Return of the Continental Op.* NY: Dell #154, 1945.
_____ *Woman In the Dark.* NY: Jonathan Press #J59, 1951.
Hammett, Dashiell and Alex Raymond. *Secret Agent X-9.* NY: Nostalgia Press, 1976.
Haycraft, Howard. *The Art of the Mystery Story.* NY: Grosset & Dunlap, 1946.
Hogan, John A. "The Mission That Succeeded," *Edgar Wallace Newletter* No. 48, November 1980.
_____ "Seek and You Will Find," *EWN* No. 26, June 1975.

Hubin, Allen J. "Patterns in Mystery Fiction: The Durable Series Characters," *The Mystery Story*. NY: Penguin, 1978.

Kittredge, William, and Steven M. Krauzer. *The Great American Detective*. NY: New American Library, 1978.

Knott, Harold. "Some Important Detective Fiction First Editions in Paperback Books," *The Mystery Readers' Newsletter*, Vol. III, No. 1, October 1969.

Leithead, Edward J. "Nick Carter in Another Man's Shoes," *Dime Novel Round-up* #350, Vol. 29, No. 11, November 15, 1961.

Lewis, Dave. "The Backbone of *Black Mask*," *Clues*, 2:2, Fall/Winter 1981.

Lowndes, Robert A. "The Editor's Page," *Startling Mystery Stories* #16, Summer 1970.

MacGowan, Kenneth, ed. *Sleuths*. NY: Harcourt, Brace & Co., 1931.

McIntyre, John Thomas. *Ashton-Kirk Criminologist*. Phila: Penn Pubs., 1918.

——— *Ashton-Kirk Investigator*. Phila: Penn Pubs., 1910.

——— *Ashton-Kirk Special Detective*. NY: Burt, 1914.

Madden, David, ed. *Tough Guy Writers of the Thirties*. Southern Illinois University Press, 1968.

Manchester, William, *H. L. Mencken: Disturber of the Peace*. NY: Collier Books, 1962.

Most, Glenn W. and William W. Stowe, *The Poetics of Murder*. NY: Harcourt, Brace Jovanovich. 1983.

Mott, Frank Luther. *A History of American Magazines*. Cambridge, Mass.: Belknap Press of Harvard University Press, 1957.

Mundell, E. H. *A List of the Original Appearances of Dashiell Hammett's Magazine Work*. Ohio: Kent State, 1968.

Murphy, Michael, "Vincent Starrett on the Hard-Boiled School," *Xenophile* No. 21, Vol. 2, No. 8, February 1976.

Nolan, William F. "Hammett in Hollywood," *Xenophile* No. 21, Vol. 2, No. 8, February 1976.

——— *Hammett, A Life At the Edge*. NY: Congdon & Weed, 1983.

——— *The Black Mask Boys*. NY: Morrow, 1985.

Orczy, Baroness. *Lady Molly of Scotland Yard*. London: Cassell, 1926.

Penzler, Otto. "Collecting Mystery Fiction: Father Brown," *The Armchair Detective*, Vol. 16, No. 3, Summer 1983.

Queen, Ellery (pseudonym for Fred Dannay and Manfred B. Lee). *The Great Woman Detectives and Criminals* (retitling of *The Female of the Species*). NY: Blue Ribbon Books, 1946.

——— Introduction, *A Man Named Thin*, Mercury Mystery No. 233, 1962

——— *101 Years' Entertainment*. Boston: Little, Brown & Co., 1942.

——— *Twentieth Century Detective Stories*. NY: Popular Library, 1964.

Rasco, Burton. "Smart Set History," *The Smart Set Anthology*, NY: Reynal & Hitchcock, 1934.

Reeve, Arthur B. *Constance Dunlap, Woman Detective*. NY: Hearst's International Library, 1916.

Ruhm, Herbert. *The Hard-Boiled Detective, Stories from Black Mask Magazine 1920-1951*. NY: Vintage Books, 1977.

Russell, Alan K. *Rivals of Sherlock Holmes*. NJ: Castle Books, 1978.

——— *Rivals of Sherlock Holmes 2*. NJ: Castle Books, 1979.

Sampson, Robert *Yesterday's Faces: Strange Days, Volume 2*, Bowling Green, Ohio: Popular Press, 1984.

Sarjeant, William Anthony S. "In Defense of Mr. Fortune," *The Armchair Detective*, Vol. 14, No. 4, 1981.

Sayers, Dorothy. *The Omnibus of Crime*. NY: Payson & Clarke, 1929.

Schisgall, Oscar. Barron Ixell: Crime Breaker. NY: Longmans, Green & Co., 1929.

Shiel, M. P. *Prince Zaleski & Cummings King Monk*. Sauk City, Wis.: Arkham House, 1977.

Slung, Michele B. *Crime On Her Mind*. NY: Pantheon Books, 1975.

Sparafucile, Tony. "Introduction," *Murder From the East*. NY: International Polygonics, 1978.

Starrett, Vincent. *The Casebook of Jimmie Lavender*. NY: Bookfinger, 1973.

Steinbrunner, Chris, and Otto Penzler. *Encyclopedia of Mystery and Detection* NY: McGraw Hill, 1976.

Stribling, T. S. *Best Dr. Poggioli Detective Stories*. NY: Dover, 1975.

———— *Clues of the Caribbees*. NY: Doubleday, Doran, 1929.

Symons, Julian. *Bloody Murder*. NY: Viking, 1985.

Thorwald, Jurgen. *The Century of the Detective*. NY: Harcourt, Brace & World, 1965.

Thwing, Eugene, ed. *The World's Best One Hundred Detective Stories* (in ten volumes). NY: Funk & Wagnalls, 1929.

Wallace, Edgar. *The Big Four*. Readers Library, 1929.

———— *The Mind of J. G. Reeder*. London: Pan Books, 1962.

———— *Mr. Reeder Returns*. NY: Doubleday, Doran, 1932.

———— *Red Aces*. London: Hodder & Stoughton, 1953.

———— *Room 13*. London: John Long, 1935.

———— *Terror Keep*, London: Pan Books, 1964.

Westlake, Donald. "The Hardboiled Dicks," *The Armchair Detective*, Vol. 17, No. 1, Winter 1984.

Wolcott, James. "Hammett's Long Goodbye," *Harper's, Vol. 267, No. 1601, September 1983*.

Wolfe, Peter. *Beams Falling: The Art of Dashiell Hammett*. Bowling Green, Ohio: Popular Press, 1980.

Wynne, Nancy Blue. *An Agatha Christie Chronology*. NY: Ace Books, 1976.

Checklists of
Magazine Appearances

The following checklists record magazine appearances of certain series characters discussed in this book. Not all listings are complete, since few collections are comprehensive enough, or accessible enough, to allow bibliographic rigor. That information can be provided at all is because a great many magazine collectors dug into the past with a complete indifference to the time and effort required. I can hardly overstate my debt to Dave Arends, Randy Cox, Diggs LaTouche, Steve Miller, and John F. Suter. They searched and advised and recorded, and without their assistance, these listings would be lean indeed. I particularly want to thank Walker Martin for his detailed, almost day-to-day support; his patience was never exhausted by interminable questions and his contributions stiffen virtually every entry.

T. Ashley by George Allan England

in All-Story:

1918	Sept 28	Ping Pong

in Detective Story Magazine

1922	Aug 19	A Worthwhile Crime
	Sept 2	On the Turn of a Test Tube
	Sept 23	Without Publicity
1923	March 17	When Sleep Spelled Death
1929	April 13	Perfume of Death
1930	Oct 4	The Severed Head

in *Detective Fiction Weekly:*

1931	Oct 31	The Moving Finger Writes
1933	Jan 14	The Finger of Evidence
	Jan 28	Too Clever By Half
	July 15	The Sole of Evidence
	July 22	The Kiss of Death
	July 29	Extra Dry
	Sept 16	Pipes of Death

	Dec 23	Almost 100%
1934	Jan 29	The Samurai Sword
	Feb 3	Pieces of the Puzzle
	Mar 10	Poison Spurs
	Apr 28	The Plot of Dr. X
	June 2	Lead Pipe Cinch
	July 28	Crystal Clues
	Sept 8	Fatal Afterthought
	Nov 3	Murder Plus
1935	June 8	Five Minutes
	Aug 31	The Silent Witness
	Oct 5	Stones of Para-Hotep

Note: DFW checklist material derived from Bernard A. Drew's article, "Hoh-Hoh to Satan", *Clues* 2:2 (Fall/Winter 1981), p. 100.

in Best Detective Magazine:

1933	June	Without Publicity
1936	March	When Sleep Spelled Death

Balbane, Conjurer Detective by Lewen Hewitt

in Detective Story

1921	Jan 22	Balbane, Conjurer Detective
	Jan 29	Balbane Traps a Trickster
	Feb 5	With Ouija's Aid
	Feb 12	The Twisted Bullet
	Sept 3	Beneath the Brand
	Sept 10	Curtain—Quick
	Oct 1	You Never Can Tell
1922	Mar 11	Trapped By Trumpets
	Apr 1	The Very Curious Canvas
	May 20	The Crooked Roulette Wheel
	May 27	Balbane Bows To the Real Thing

in Best Detective

1930	Oct	Balbane, Conjurer Detective
	Dec	With Ouija's Aid
1931	Jan	Beneath the Brand
	May	The Crooked Roulette Wheel
	Aug	Curtain—Quick
	Sept	Trapped By Trumpets
1932	June	The Twisted Bullet

Brady and Riordan by Victor Maxwell
in Flynn's:

1925	Sept 5	The Work of an Artist
	Sept 19	Threads of Evidence
	Oct 24	What the Cipher Told

in Flynn's Weekly

1926	Sept 4	For a Point of Honor
	Sept 11	Quick Work
	Oct 2	Something New in Vanities
	Nov 20	A Darned Good Tailor
	Dec 18	Died From Other Causes
1927	Mar 5	The Staples Case
	Mar 12	The Bomb
	Apr 7	The Stolen Street Car
	Apr 23	Framed

in Flynn's Weekly Detective Fiction:

	Oct 15	All Crossed Up
1928	Feb 18	One Thing After Another
	Feb 25	
	through	
	March 10	The Truth About the Prince (3-part serial)
	May 5	A Young Man In Trouble

in Detective Fiction Weekly

| | Sept 1 | The Other Side of the Story |
| | Dec 15 | Mostly Head Work |

1929	Oct 12	The Bullet Hole in the Ceiling
1930	Apr 19	Hit-and-Run
	Oct 18	The Hazardous Path
1931	Feb 28	A Fine Night for Murders
	May 2	The May Who Left No Trace
	Sept 12	Halloran Makes a Case
1932	June 11	The Corpus Delicti
1934	Mar 31	The Death in the Binoculars
1936	Aug 1	Dangerous Millions
1939	Jul 1	The Devil Wears Diamonds

Robert Brewer, The Policy Sleuth by Edgar Wallace

NOTE: The following stories were published as the book, *The Big Four*. The chapters were slightly rearranged from the published sequence of the stories, as shown.

| *in Argosy All-Story Weekly* | | | *Big Four,Chapter* |
| *1920* | Dec 25 | Reddy At Monte Carlo | 1 |

1921	Jan 1	The Burglary at Greenwood	2
	Jan 8	Baccarat at Cowes	3
	Jan 15	A Race at Ostend	4
	Jan 22	The Heppleworth Pearls	5
	Jan 29	The Star of the World	7
	Feb 5	The Big Four and the Bank	6
	Feb 12	The Lucky Dip	8

The Big Four (Chapter Titles):

Chapter
1. The Big Four Syndicate and the Man Who Smashed It
2. The Burglary At Greenwood
3. Baccarat at Cowes
4. A Race at Ostend
5. The Heppleworth Pearls
6. "Pinky" and the Bank Manager
7. The Star of the World
8. Bob Brewer's Biggest Coup

Hon. Stanley Brooke by E. Phillips Oppenheim
in Munsey's Magazine

1913	Dec	The Deliberate Detective (series title; not used after the first story): Tale the First: The Rescue of Warren Tyrrwell
1914	Jan	The Princess Pays
	NOTE: The second and subsequent stories are identified only by title, with "Tale the—" and "The Deliberate Detective" heading omitted.	
	Feb	The Other Side of the Wall
	Mar	The Murder of William Blessing
	Apr	The Disappearance of Monsieur Dupoy
	May	The Spider's Parlor
	June	The Silent People
	July	The Glen Terrace Tragedy

Jack Calhoun by Edward Parrish Ware

in Flynn's Weekly:

1926	Sept 18	One Good Man
	Oct 30	The Swamp Angel
	Nov 20	The Negative Clue

in Flynn's Weekly Detective Fiction

1927	June 18	Calhoun Sets a Trap
	July 9	The Panther
	Sept 10	Calhoun's Ally
	Sept 17	The Splitting Edge

in Detective Fiction Weekly

1928	Sept 1	Common Sense
1929	Aug 10	The Grave on Number 10
	Sept 14	The Red Record
1930	Jan 18	Calhoun's Way
1933	July 29	Calhoun Obeys Orders
1934	Aug 25	Satan's Sink Hole
1935	Jan 19	Killers in the Cave

The Continental Op by Dashiell Hammett (* designated stories signed Peter Collinson)
in Black Mask

1923	Oct 1	*Arson Plus
	Oct 15	*Slippery Fingers
		Crooked Souls (reprinted as "The Gatewood Caper")
	Nov 1	It (reprinted as "The Black Hat That Wasn't There.")
	Dec	Bodies Piled Up (reprinted as "The House Dick")
1924	Jan 1	The Tenth Clue
	Feb 1	Night Shots
	Mar 1	Zigzags of Treachery
	Apr 1	One Hour
	Apr 15	The House on Turk Street
	Jun	The Girl with the Silver Eyes
	Sept	Women, Politics and Murder (reprinted as "Death on Pine Street")
	Nov	The Golden Horseshoe
1925	Jan	Mike or Alec or Rufus
	Mar	The Whosis Kid
	May	The Scorched Face
	Sept	Corkscrew
	Nov	Dead Yellow Women
	Dec	The Gutting of Couffignal
1926	Mar	The Creeping Siamese
1927	Feb	The Big Knock-Over
	May	$106,000 Blood Money
	Jun	The Main Death
	Nov	The Cleansing of Poisonville (#1 of Red Harvest)
	Dec	Crime Wanted—Male or Female (#2 of Red Harvest)

1928	Jan	Dynamite (#3 of Red Harvest)
	Feb	The 19th Murder (#4 of Red Harvest)
	Nov	Black Lives (#1 of The Dain Curse)
	Dec	The Hollow Temple (#2 of The Dain Curse)
1929	Jan	Black Honeymoon (#3 of The Dain Curse)
	Feb	Black Riddle (#4 of The Dain Curse)
	Aug	Fly Paper
1930	Feb	The Farewell Murder
	Nov	Death and Company
1974	Aug	Women, Politics and murder (reprinted as "Death on Pine Street")

in True Detective:

| *1924* | Nov | Who Killed Bob Teal? |

in Mystery Stories:

| *1928* | Jan | This King Business |

X. *Crook* by J. Jefferson Farjeon

in Flynn's:

1925	June 20	Red Eye (1st of series)
	June 27	The Bilton Safe
	Jul 11	Thomas Doubts No Longer
	Jul 18	Fisherman's Luck
	Aug 22	Nine Hours To Live
	Aug 29	Elsie Cuts Both Ways
1926	Apr 10	Crook Goes Back To Prison
	Apr 17	Who Killed James Fyne
	Apr 24	Caleb Comes Back
	May 1	The Vanished Gift
	May 15	The Death That Beckoned

in Flynn's Weekly:

	Sept 18	The Kleptomanic
	Nov 20	The Hotel Hold-up
	Nov 27	The Silent Client
	Dec 18	It Pays To Be Honest
1927	Jan 8	Whose Hand?
	Mar 5	LQ 585
	Mar 26	Prescription 93b
	May 28	In the Diamond Line
	Jun 4	The New Baronet

in Flynn's Weekly Detective Fiction:

| | Jul 9 | The Fourth Attempt |
| | Sept 3 | The Man Who Forgot |

in Detective Fiction Weekly:

| 1928 | Sept 8 | August 13th |

Charlie Fenwick by George J. Brenn

in All-Story Weekly:

1919	June 7	No Publicity
	Sept 6	A Morsel of Scandal
	Nov 1	Lady Tsai Disappears

in Argosy All-Story Weekly:

1920	June 5	No Guess Work
1921	May 7	Making a Martyr
	Aug 5	Clear as Crystal
1922	Jan 7	Fenwick Shoots Trouble
	Feb 11	The Man Who Looked Upward
	Nov 25 through Dec 23	Voices (5-part serial)
1923	Apr 28	"We Have With Us Tonight—"
1924	Dec 13 through Jan 3, 1925	Babble (4-part serial)
1925	Feb 14	You Can't Get Away From It

Reginald Fortune by H. C. Bailey

in Flynn's:

1925	Jan 24	The Young God (Beginning First Series)
	Feb 7	The Profiteers
	Feb 21	The Hermit Crab
	Mar 7	The Only Son
	Mar 21	The Furnished Cottage
	Apr 4	The Long Barrow

in Flynn's Weekly:

1926	Sept 18	The Missing Husband (Beginning Second Series)
	Oct 2	The Lion Party
	Oct 9	The Little House

	Oct 16	The Quiet Lady
	Nov 6	The Cat Burglar
1927	Jan 22	The Violet Farm

in Flynn's Weekly Detective Fiction:

	Nov 12	The Lion Fish (Beginning Third Series)
	Nov 19	Zodiacs
	Nov 26	Painted Pebbles
	Dec 10	The Hazel Ice
1928	Feb 4	The Pink Macaw
	Mar 17	The Woman In the Wood

Douglas Greer by Peter Perry

in Flynn's:

| 1925 | Oct 24 | Trapping "Mousie" |

1926	Mar 6	No. 1331 Quinn Street
	Apr 17	The Talking Piano
	May 15	The Scrambled Egg Thief
	May 29	Like a Broken Butterfly
	June 5 & 12	The Mad March Hares (2-part serial)
	Sept 4	The Queer Ambulance
	Oct 9	Hell's Secret
	Nov 13	The Radio Fiend
	Dec 4	The Liquid Bullet
1927	Apr 7	Guns of Gangland
	May 28	
	through	
	June 18	The Forty Thieves (4-part serial)

in Flynn's Weekly Detective Fiction:

1927	Sept 10	The Suicide Clause
	Oct 8	Twice Dead
1928	Jan 21	Blodgett's Return

in Detective Fiction Weekly:

| 1928 | June 2 | Murder Will Out |
| | Dec 22 | The Nicked Blade |

Digby Gresham by Florence M. Pettee

in Detective Tales:

| 1923 | June | Ashes |

in Argosy All-Story Weekly:

1923	June 9	Cleopatra's Eye
1924	Jan 19	The Gray Friar
	Mar 1	Dead Men May Tell Tales

in Flynn's:

1925	Jan 10	Touch of the Dead
	May 9	Prey of the Lagoon

Dr. Eustace Hailey by Anthony Wynne (pseudonym of Robert McNair Wilson)

in Flynn's:

1924	Nov 29 through Jan 3, 1925	The Sign of Evil (6-part serial)
1925	Feb 7	The Moveable Hands
	Mar 14	The House of Death
	Mar 21	Monte Carlo Madness
	Mar 28	The Lonely Skipper
	Apr 25	The Death Moth
	May 9	The Mark of the Chain
	Sept 5 through Sept 26	The Double Thirteen (4-part serial)
	Oct 10	The Revolving Death
	Oct 24	The Lost Ancestor
	Oct 31	The Heel of Achilles
1926	Mar 6	The Wizard's Race

in Flynn's Weekly:

	Nov 20 through Dec 11	The Tiger's Spring (4-part serial)

in Flynn's Weekly Detective Fiction:

1927	July 9	The Telephone Man
	Sept 17 through Oct 15	The Horseman of Death (5-part serial)

in Illustrated Detective Magazine:

| *1930* | May | The Face of the Assassin (published as *The Yellow Crystal*) |

The Honeymoon Detectives by Arnold Fredericks (pseudonym of Frederic Arnold Kummer)

in The Cavalier:

1912	Mar 23 through Apr 20	The Honeymoon Detectives (5-part serial)
	May 11	The Ivory Snuffbox
1913	Jan 11 through Feb 1	The Changing Lights (4-part serial)
	Aug 9 through Aug 30	The Little Fortune (4-part serial)

in All-Story Cavalier Weekly:

| *1915* | Apr 17
through
May 8 | The Mysterious Goddess (4-part serial) |

In All-Story Weekly:

| *1917* | Mar 17
through
Apr 14 | The Film of Fear (5-part serial) |

Ex-Inspector John F. Hopper by Betrand Royal

in Flynn's:

1924	Nov 8	The Handcuffed Ghost
	Nov 22	Through To a Showdown
	Dec 27	Across the Border
1925	Feb 21	White Bubbles
	May 30	Clews in Ambush
	June 20	When Time Stood Still
	Sept 26	When Clews Converged

in Flynn's Weekly:

| *1926* | May 22 & 29 | The Super-Speed Master (2-part serial) |

	Sept 11	Clews Concealed

Judith Lee by Richard Marsh

in All-Story Weekly:

1915	July 10	The Clarke Case
	July 24	The Finchley Case
	Aug 7	The Tango Tangle
	Aug 21	The Hand Invisible

Captain MacBride and Kennedy by Frederick Nebel
in Black Mask:

1928	Sept	The Crimes of Richmond City: Raw Law
		NOTE: The following four stories continue "The Crimes of Richmond City" as related cases, not serial parts
	Oct	Dog Eat Dog
	Nov	The Law Laughs Last
1929	Apr	Law Without Law
	May	Graft
	Sept	New Guns for Old
	Nov	Hell-Smoke
1930	Jan	Tough Treatment
	Feb	Alley Rat
	Apr	Wise Guy
	Aug	Ten Men from Chicago
	Sept	Shake-Down
1931	Mar	Junk
	May	Beat the Rap
	Jul	Death for a Dago
	Dec	Some Die Young
1932	Mar	The Quick or the Dead
	May	Backwash
1933	Feb	Doors in the Dark
	Mar	Rough Reform
	Apr	Farewell to Crime
	Sept	Guns Down
	Nov	Lay Down the Law
1934	Feb	Too Young to Die
	Mar	Bad News
	June	Take It and Like It
	Aug	Be Your Age
1935	Jan	He Was a Swell Guy
	Feb	It's a Gag
	May	That's Kennedy
	Aug	Die-Hard
	Nov	Winter Kill

1936	Jan	Fan Dance
	Feb	No Hard Feelings
	Apr	Crack Down
	June	Hard to Take
	Aug	Deep Red

Miss Marple by Agatha Christie
in Detective Story Magazine:

1928	June 2	The Solving Six (published as The Tuesday Night Club)
	June 9	The Solving Six and the Evil Hour (published as The Idol House of Astarte)
	June 16	The Solving Six and the Golden Grave (published as Ingots of Gold)
	June 23	Drip, Drip (published as The Blood-Stained Pavement)
	June 30	Where's the Catch (published as Motive vs Opportunity)
	July 7	The Thumb Mark of Saint Peter

in Great Detective: (Under the series title, "The Tuesday Club Murders")

1933	Nov	Ingots of Gold

NOTE: The listing for *Great Detective* is incomplete. Miss Marple short stories appeared in at least the September and October 1933 issues of this magazine.

Initiating Noggins by Harrington Strong (pseudonym for Johnston McCulley)

in Detective Story Magazine:

1920	Apr 6	Initiating Noggins
	Apr 20	Noggins Shows His Nerve
	Jun 8	Noggin's Souvenir
	Jun 29	Noggins Uses His Brains
	Aug 24	Noggins See It Through
	Oct 19	Noggins Gets His Man

Dr. Poggioli by T. S. Stribling
in Adventure:

1925	Oct 10	The Refugees
	Nov 10	The Governor of Cap Haitien
	Dec 10	Cricket
1926	Jan 20	The Prints of Hantoun
	Feb 20	A Passage to Benares
1929	June 1	A Pearl at Pampatar
1930	Oct 15	Shadowed

1932	Apr 15	The Resurrection of Chin Lee
	May 1	Bullets
	Nov 1	The Cablegram
1933	Feb 1	The Pink Colonnade

in Blue Book:

1933	Aug	Private Jungle

in Ellery Queen's Mystery Magazine:

1945	Jul	The Mystery of the Chief of Police
1946	Jan	The Mystery of the Sock and the Clock
	Jul	The Mystery of the Paper Wad
	Sept	Count Jalacki Goes Fishing
	Oct	A Note to Count Jalacki
1947	Jul	The Mystery of the 81st Kilometer Stone
1948	Apr	The Mystery of the Seven Suicides
1950	Mar	A Daylight Adventure
	May	The Mystery of the Personal Ad
1951	Jan	The Mystery of the Choir Boy
	Sept	The Mystery of the Andorus Enterprises
1952	Apr	The Mystery of the Half-Painted House
1953	Mar	The Warning on the Lawn
1954	Mar	The Mystery of the Five Money Orders
1955	Jan	The Telephone Fisherman

in Famous Detective Stories:

1952	Nov	Death Deals Diamonds
1953	Feb	Figures Don't Die

in Redbook:

1934	?	The Shadow

in The Saint Mystery Magazine

1953	June-July	Poggioli and the Refugees
1954	Dec	Poggioli and the Fugitive
1955	Mar	Murder At Flowtide
	Sept	The Case of the Button
1956	Feb	Murder in the Hills
1957	Apr	The Man in the Shade

in Smashing Detective Stories:

1953	Mar	Dead Wrong

Poirot, Hercule by Agatha Christie
in Blue Book

1923	Sept	The Affair at the Victory Ball (first of the series) (3)
	Oct	Mrs. Opalsen's Pearls (1 as "The Jewel Robbery At the Grand Metropolitan")
	Nov	The King of Clubs (3)
	Dec	Mr. Davenby Disappears (1 as "The Disappearance of Mr. Daverheim")
1924	Jan	The Plymouth Express Affair (3 as "The Plymouth Express")
	Feb	The Western Star (1 as "The Adventures of the Western Star")
	Mar	The Marsdon Manor Tragedy (1 as "The Tragedy At Marsdon Manor")
	Apr	The Great Bond Robbery (1 as "The Million Dollar Bond Robbery")
	May	The Adventure of the Cheap Flat (1)
	June	The Hunter's Lodge Case (1 as "The Mystery of Hunter's Lodge")
	July	The Kidnapped Premier (1 as "The Kidnapped Prime Minister")
	Aug	The Egyptian Adventure (1 as "The Adventure of the Egyptian Tomb")

Second Series: "New Exploits of Hercule Poirot"

	Dec	The Italian Nobleman (1 as "The Adventure of the Italian Nobleman")
1925	Jan	The Missing Will (1 as "The Case of the Missing Will")
	Feb	The Chocolate Box (1)
	Mar	The Veiled Lady (1)
	Apr	The Lost Mine (1)
	May	The Market Basing Mystery (3)
	June	The Adventure of Johnny Waverly (2)
	July	The Submarine Plans (3)
1925		
	Aug	The Double Clue (4)
	Sept	The Clapham Cook (3 as "The Adventure of the Clapham Cook")
	Oct	The Cornish Mystery (3)
	Nov	The Lemesurier Inheritance (3)
1927		The Big Four (presented as sequential short stories rather than a serial):
	Mar	The Unexpected Guest (first of series) (Chapter 1)

Apr		The Dartmoor Adventure
May		The Lady On the Stairs (5, Chapter 6)
June		The Radium Thieves (Chapter 7)
July		In The House of the Enemy (5, Chapter 8)
Aug		The Yellow Jasmine Mystery (5, Chapter 9)
Sept		The Chess Problem (5, Chapter 11)
Oct		The Baited Trap
Nov		The Peroxide Blonde (5, Chapter 14)
Dec		The Enemy Strikes

in Detective Story Magazine:

1929	March 30	Double Sin (4)

1. *Poirot Investigates*
2. *Three Blind Mice*
3. *The Under Dog*
4. *Double Sin*
5. *The Big Four*

Quicksilver, Beau by Florence Pettee
in Argosy All-Story Weekly: "Exploits of Beau Quicksilver"

1923	Feb 24	A Tooth for a Tooth
	Mar 3	An Eye for An Eye
	Mar 10	The Claws of the Weasel
	Mar 17	The Hand of the Hyena
	Mar 24	The Green Rajah
	Mar 31	Blistering Tongues
	Apr 7	Murder Incognito

J. G. Reeder by Edgar Wallace
in Flynn's

1924	Nov 8	The Poetical Policeman
	Nov 22	The Treasure Hunt
	Dec 6	The Troupe
	Dec 20	The Stealer of Marble
1925	Jan 3	Sheer Melodrama
	Mar 14	The Green Mamba
	May 23	Trapped by a Word
	June 6	The Investors

in Detective Story Magazine:

1926	Nov 6	
	through	
	Dec 4	Terror Keep (5-part serial)
1931	June 27	The Man From Sing Sing

in Clues:

| 1929 | Nov 2 | Kennedy the Con Man |

in Star Novels Magazine:

| 1932 | Fall | Kennedy on the Con Man |
| 1933 | Summer | The Treasure House |

in Dime Mystery Book:

1932	Dec	The Poetical Policeman
1933	Jan	The Treasure Hunt
	Feb	The Troupe
	Mar	The Stealer of Marble
	Apr	Sheer Melodrama
	May	The Green Mamba
	June	The Strange Case
	July	The Investors

Nan Russell by Raymond Lester
in Argosy All-Story

1920	March 13	Beneath the Make-up
	March 20	In the Light
	March 27	None So Dumb
	April 3	An Affair of Diplomacy
	April 17	The Better Day

Malcolm Steele by Mansfield Scott
in Flynn's:

1924	Nov 29	Horror of the Crags
1925	Jan 3	*Footprints of Guilt
	Mar 14	Shadow of a Shade
	Mar 21	Solved From Afar
	June 6	
	through	
	June 20	The Town Without a Law (3-part serial)
	July 11	Dissolved with Death

in Flynn's Weekly:

| 1926 | May 29 | In the Murder Moon |

in Flynn's Weekly Detective Fiction:

| 1927 | Apr 16 | At the Eleventh Hour |

| | Aug 27 through
Sept 24 | Defenders of the Law (5-part serial) |
| 1928 | Jan 21 | Death Dealers |

*Signed Melville Hume for this issue only.

Madame Storey by Hulbert Footner

in Argosy All-Story Weekly:

1922	Mar 11	Madame Storey's Way
1923	May 26	Miss Deely's Diamond
	Aug 4	The Scrap of Lace
1924	Mar 1	In the Round Room
	Apr 12	The Viper
	June 28	The Smoke Bandit
	Aug 2	The Steerers
1925	Jan 3 through Feb 7	The Under Dogs (6-part serial)
	Aug 29	Madame Storey in the Toils
	Nov 7	The Three Thirty-Twos
1926	Jan 9	The Handsome Young Men
	Sept 18	The Legacy Hounds
	Nov 20	Putting Crime Over
1927	Jan 22	The Blind Front
	Apr 30	The Pot of Pansies
1928	Mar 24 & 31	It Never Got into the Papers (2-part serial)
	Jul 28	The Perfect Blackguard
	Nov 24	The Murder at Fernhurst
1929	Jan 12 through Feb 16	The Black Ace (6-part serial)
	Dec 14	Taken for a Ride

in Argosy:

1930	June 28	The Butler's Ball
	Dec 27	The Death Notice
1931	Aug 8 through Sept 12	Easy To Kill (6-part serial)
1933	Aug 5	Wolves of Monte Carlo
	Dec 2	The Kidnapping of Madame Storey
1934	Mar 3	Pink Eye
	Jul 14 through Aug 18	The Hated Man (6-part serial)
	Nov 17	The Murders in the Hotel Cathey
1935	Jan 12	The Cold Trail

| | Aug 31 | The Richest Widow |

in Mystery:

1933	Jul	The Sealed House
	Nov	Murder in the Spotlight
	Dec	Which Man's Eyes
1934	Mar	The Girl Who Dropped from Earth
	May	The Last Adventure with Madame Storey

Terry Trimble by Johnston McCulley

in Detective Story Magazine:

1917	Mar 5	Trimble, Trouble Maker
	Apr 5	Germs of Bedlam
	May 5	Seven Circles
	June 5	The Perfect Crime
	July 5	Four Squares
	Aug 5	The Lost Disk
	Dec 18	Terry Trimble and the Imposter
1919	June 3	Murderer's Mail
	August 5	Tragedy Trail
	September 2	Terry Trimble's Fox Hunt
	December 9	Terry Trimble and the Hidden Tube

Race Williams by Carroll John Daly

in The Black Mask

1923	June 1	Knights of the Open Palm
	July 15	Three Thousand to the Good
1924	June	The Red Peril
	Aug	Them That Lives By Their Guns
	Nov	Devil Cat
1925	Feb	The Face Behind the Mask
	Apr	Conceited, Maybe
	June	Say It with Lead
	Aug	I'll Tell the World
	Oct	Alias Buttercup
	Dec	
	through	
	Jan	Under Cover (2-part serial)
1926	May	South Sea Steel
	July	The False Clara Burkhart
	Aug	The Super Devil
	Nov	Half-Breed
1927	Apr	Blind Alleys

	June through Sept	The Snarl of the Beast (4-part serial)[1]
1928	Mar	The Egyptian Lure
	June	The Hidden Hand (serial, part 1 of of 5)[2]
	Jul	Wanted for Murder (2 of 5)
	Aug	Rough Stuff (3 of 5)
	Sept	The Last Chance (4 of 5)
	Oct	The Last Shot (5 of 5)
1929	Mar	Tags of Death (serial, Part 1 of 4)[3]
	Apr	A Pretty Bit of Shooting (2 of 4)
	May	Get Race Williams (3 of 4)
	June	Race Williams Never Bluffs (4 of 4)
	Oct-Nov	The Silver Eagle (2-part serial; never completed)
1930	June	Tainted Power (serial: Part 1 of 3)[4]
	Jul	Framed (2 of 3)
	Aug	The Final Shot (3 of 3)
	Oct	Shooting Out of Turn
1931	Mar	Murder by Mail
	June through Aug	The Flame and Race Williams (3-part serial)[5]
	Sept	Death for Two
1932	Apr through Jul	The Amateur Murderer (4-part serial)[6]
	Dec	Merger with Death
1933	May	The Death Drop
	July	If Death Is Respectable
	Oct	Murder in the Open
1934	May	Six Have Died (Serial: Part 1 of 3)[7]
	June	Flaming Death (2 of 3)
	Aug	Murder Book (3 of 3)
	Nov	The Eyes Have It

in Dime Detective:

1935	Sept	Some Die Hard
	Nov	Dead Hands Reaching
1936	Feb	Corpse & Co.
	Apr	Just Another Stiff
	Oct	City of Blood
	Dec	The Morgue's Our Home
1937	Feb	Monogram in Lead
	Aug	Dead Men Don't Kill
	Oct	Anyone's Corpse
	Dec	The $1,000,000 Corpse
1938	Jan	The Book of the Dead

	Mar	A Corpse on the House
	Jul	A Corpse for a Corpse
	Oct	Men in Black
	Dec	The Quick and the Dead
1939	Mar	Hell with the Lid Lifted
	June	A Corpse in the Hand
	Aug	Gangman's Gallows
	Nov	The White-Headed Corpse
1940	Feb	Cash for a Killer
1948	Aug	Race Williams' Double Date
1949	May	Half A Corpse
	Oct	Race Williams Cooks a Goose

in Clues:

1940	Sept	Victim for Vengence
1911	Mar	Too Dead To Pay

in Detective Story Magazine:

1944	Oct	Body, Body, Who's Got the Body?
1945	Mar	A Corpse Loses Its Head
1947	Mar	Unremembered Murder

in Detective Story Annual:

1942		Too Dead To Pay
1946		Body, Body, Who's Got the Body?

in Popular Detective:

1950	Mar	The $100,000 Corpse

in Smashing Detective:

1952	June	Little Miss Murder
	Sept	This Corpse Is Free
1953	June	Gas
1955	May	Head Over Homicide

in Thrilling Detective:

1947	June	This Corpse On Me
	Dec	I'll Feel Better When You're Dead
1948	June	Not My Corpse
1949	Feb	The Wrong Corpse
1950	Apr	The Strange Case of Alta May

[1]Published as *The Snarl of the Beast* (1927)

[2]Published as *The Hidden Hand* (1929)
[3]Published as *The Tag Murders* (1930)
[4]Published as *Tainted Power* (1931)
[5]Published as *The Third Murderer* (1931)
[6]Published as *The Amateur Murderer* (1933)
[7]Published as *Murder From the East* (1935)

Index